Buenos Aires is Argentina's national capital and largest city. Throughout the twentieth century the capital and its surrounding suburbs have contained between one-quarter and one-third of the nation's population. It has served as Argentina's main economic and political center, and has dominated the rest of the country as few other capital cities have. This book traces the history of the city from 1910 to the early 1940s, a period of continued growth and expansion. It focuses in particular on the role of politics and municipal government in directing the city's growth, highlighting elections, party competition, and debates over important issues of public works, public transportation, and public utilities.

The political story, in turn, takes place within the larger context of urban development over the course of these decades. Not only is it the first comprehensive treatment of this period in Buenos Aires' history; it is also one of the few works to deal with the role of local government in the general literature on Latin American urbanization. In preparing the book, Walter worked extensively with the minutes of city council meetings, the national congressional record, the observations of foreign officials and visitors, popular magazines and newspapers, and a wide variety of other materials.

CAMBRIDGE LATIN AMERICAN STUDIES

GENERAL EDITOR
SIMON COLLIER

ADVISORY COMMITTEE
MALCOM DEAS, STUART SCHWARTZ, ARTURO VALENZUELA

74

POLITICS AND URBAN GROWTH IN BUENOS AIRES
1910–1942

For a list of other books in the Cambridge Latin American Studies series, please see page 279.

POLITICS AND
URBAN GROWTH
IN BUENOS AIRES
1910–1942

RICHARD J. WALTER

CAMBRIDGE
UNIVERSITY PRESS

Published by the Press Syndicate of the University of Cambridge
The Pitt Building, Trumpington Street, Cambridge CB2 1RP
40 West 20th Street, New York, NY 10011-4211, USA
10 Stamford Road, Oakleigh, Melbourne 3166, Australia

First published 1993

Printed in the United States of America

Library of Congress Cataloging-in-Publication Data
Walter, Richard J.
Politics and urban growth in Buenos Aires, 1910–1942 / Richard J.
Walter.
p.   cm. – (Cambridge Latin American studies ; 74)
Includes bibliographical references and index.
ISBN 0-521-44165-X (hardback)
1. Buenos Aires (Argentina) – Politics and government.
2. Argentina – Politics and government – 1910–1943.   3. Cities and
towns – Argentina – Buenos Aires – Growth.   4. Urban policy – Argentina –
Buenos Aires – History.   5. Urbanization – Argentina – Buenos Aires –
History.   I. Title.   II. Series.
F3001.3.W35   1993   93–2918
982'.11–dc20   CIP

A catalog record for this book is available from the British Library.

ISBN 0-521-44165-X hardback

For Susana

Contents

Tables and illustrations

Tables

Maps

Photographs

Acknowledgments

This book could not have been completed without the generous advice and support of various individuals and institutions. As always, I am indebted to the administration of Washington University, which provided me with the financial assistance to travel to Buenos Aires for field research on this project in 1987 and granted me leave time for writing up my results in 1990. A grant from the Fulbright Commission in 1989 allowed me to stay for six months in Buenos Aires and was invaluable in supplying needed research assistance. Once again, I owe a continuing and special debt of gratitude to the executive director of the commission in Argentina, Dr. Rolando Costa Picazo, and to the administrative director, Dr. Oscar "Paco" Risso, both of whom have aided me and countless other "Fulbrighters" in ways too numerous to mention.

In Buenos Aires, I was also aided by the staffs of the following libraries, archives, and research institutions: the Archivo General de la Nación (Sección Gráfica), the Biblioteca Nacional, the Biblioteca Obrera "Juan B. Justo," the Biblioteca de la Municipalidad de Buenos Aires, and the Instituto Torcuato Di Tella. In addition to allowing me to use its resources, the Instituto Histórico de la Ciudad de Buenos Aires provided me with the opportunity to discuss the preliminary stages of my work in a series of lectures.

In St. Louis, the personnel of the Olin Library at Washington University were consistently helpful in allowing me liberal use of their collection and in acquiring needed material from other libraries. Bette Marbs and Sheryl Peltz of the Department of History at Washington University went above and beyond the call of duty in helping me to prepare this manuscript.

Particular thanks go to Simon Collier, who read this manuscript with great care and offered extremely useful editorial comments as well as badly needed encouragement. I also would like to acknowledge the helpful comments of Roberto Cortés Conde, Raúl García Heras, Leandro H. Gutiérrez, Luis Alberto Romero, and Juan Carlos Torre, who listened to the preliminary results of my work. Thanks go also to Charles Fleener for helping with movie titles.

Finally, my wife, Susana, was a consistently understanding and supportive partner during the often difficult process of researching and writing this book. I hope the result justifies the many sacrifices she made on behalf of its completion.

All photographs are courtesy of the Archivo General de la Nación.

The responsibility for any errors in fact or interpretation is entirely mine.

Introduction

Flying over Buenos Aires, Argentina's capital and largest city, the North American traveler might be reminded of Chicago. Arriving from the east one sees modern skyscrapers close to the edge of a large body of water, in this case the muddy brown of the broad estuary of the Río de la Plata rather than the gray–blue of Lake Michigan. The city itself is laid out in a grid pattern, interlaced with broader boulevards and a handful of superhighways. To the north stretch affluent suburbs and to the south, blue-collar, industrial concentrations. Beyond the city and its sprawling suburbs, today containing eleven million inhabitants, or one-third of the national population, is a seemingly endless prairie of rich, dark soil and abundant grasses, the immensely fertile and productive Argentine *pampa*. A network of railroads and highways crossing the pampa converges from the north, west, and south and terminates in Buenos Aires like the ribs of a fan.

Once on the ground, there are some additional reminders of the midwestern metropolis. The terrain of the city is essentially flat, but with several gentle rises here and there and a pronounced embankment along the eastern and northeastern edge leading down to the Río de la Plata estuary. Another river, the Riachuelo, provides the southern boundary of the federal capital itself. Slaughterhouses and meat-packing plants can be found in the western and southern parts of the city. However, the image also begins to change. Buenos Aires is a multiethnic city, but one that is overwhelmingly southern European in composition instead of the mix of largely Irish, Polish, and African Americans found in Chicago. The richness of culture, the pace of life, and the general cosmopolitanism of the city's inhabitants, the *porteños* (residents of the port city), are reminiscent of New York. The broad avenues, sidewalk cafés, fine restaurants, and elegantly dressed men and women produce echoes of Paris. The language and the late hours for dining and entertaining are reminiscent of Madrid or Barcelona; the exaggerated gestures, the rhythm and intonation of daily conversation, and the driving habits belong to Rome and Milan.

Although one is tempted to compare Buenos Aires with many other large cities, a closer examination reveals special features. As the national capital, the city is dominated by government and the people who work for it. The additional characteristic of being the nation's major port and its commercial and industrial center gives it a national predominance of which few cities can boast. Its particular ethnic mix, predominantly Spanish and Italian, but containing as well a substantial Jewish community, also makes it unique.

Whereas to many it is the most European of Latin America's cities, it is also clearly a new world metropolis, whose greatest growth has occurred over the past century. Like the larger nation that it dominates, it seems to be part European, part American, producing something of an identity crisis that continues to bedevil many of its inhabitants. Adding to the sense of uncertainty has been the decline of the capital and the nation from a clear position of continental preeminence before World War II to a yet-to-be defined lesser rank when compared with, for example, Brazil and the dynamic metropolis of São Paulo.

Whatever its relative position, since the beginning of the twentieth century Buenos Aires has continued to be one of the world's foremost cities. As such, it attracts the casual visitor as well as the scholar. Foreigners and Argentines alike have produced an abundance of literature about the city, ranging from impressionistic essays to studies of local neighborhoods to one- or two-volume tomes filled with photographs and maps that seek to cover the history of the city from its initial founding in 1536 to the present.

Despite the outpouring of works on the city, there are relatively few overviews of particularly important periods in its growth. A significant exception is James R. Scobie's pioneering social history of the formative years (1870–1910) of the modern city, *Buenos Aires: Plaza to Suburb*, published in 1974. In this work, Scobie analyzed the demographic growth and characteristics of the city, the locational forces of ports and railroads, the composition and lives of various social groups, cultural aspects, the role of public transportation, and what he called the "commercial–bureaucratic" nature of the federal capital.

The purpose of my book is to continue along the trail that Scobie blazed. I shall focus on the subsequent thirty years or so, from 1910 to the early 1940s, a period in the city's history that has not yet been studied in its totality. Like the preceding four decades examined by Scobie, these were years of dynamic expansion and growth. They were characterized by many significant continuities with the past, but were also marked by equally significant changes; both patterns will be explored in the pages that follow.

Attempting to write the history of a city as large and complex as

Buenos Aires, even for what appears a relatively limited period, is a formidable task. The number of subjects that might be covered and the approaches that could be adopted seem almost endless. With this in mind, I have chosen to focus on local politics and government, particularly on the role of the city's executive branch, led by the *intentende*, or mayor, and the *Concejo Deliberante*, or city council, in the process of Buenos Aires' growth. The focus seems justified for three reasons: First, the local administration, although not the sole decision-making authority to affect the capital, was nonetheless the main actor in this process. To a large extent, the city that emerged at the end of the period I am writing about was guided and shaped by local officials. Second, whether or not it affected certain aspects of city growth, local government, especially through the activities of the legislative branch, served as a reflection of larger developments in the metropolis. The debates of the city council over numerous issues reveal a great deal about the nature of urban growth and its associated problems. Third, despite their importance, there has been no comprehensive study of local politics and administration in Buenos Aires or, for that matter, in other major Latin American cities. This oversight is particularly striking when compared, for example, with the many studies of U.S. city politics that scrutinize mayors, city councils, and other mechanisms of municipal administration.

As this is essentially its first telling, the story will be related in a chronological, narrative fashion. It will describe in particular the struggle to make local government more democratic, notably through a major reform in the manner of electing the city council implemented in 1918. The story will also describe the background and subsequent impact of that reform during the years 1918 to late 1941 when the council was dissolved and the experiment in local democracy temporarily halted. The periodic elections held in Buenos Aires to select the city council (the intendente was appointed by the national government), the composition of the council that resulted from these contests, and the issues that came before it will also receive attention. Drawing upon the minutes of the council debates as a principal source, I shall review how various parties and participants acted within that institution and the relation of these actions to larger developments.

During the period under consideration, the council dealt with myriad concerns related to the city's growth. These ranged from questions of public health and the management of municipal hospitals to the naming of streets and plazas to the granting of licenses for commercial purposes to the operation of places of amusement and culture. Although I will touch on many of these, a full treatment of every one would be impractical. Therefore, I have determined to focus on debates involving major public works projects, public transportation, and the provision of services like

gas and electric power to the city. These issues were consistently prominent in the council's deliberations and in the public's concerns with
municipal affairs. The results of the debates on these fundamental matters
had a wide and lasting impact on the city's inhabitants. Public works,
often constructed with the aim of improving the movement of vehicles
and pedestrians, enhancing the "monumental" appearance of the capital,
and providing access to popular areas of recreation, dramatically changed
the physical aspect of Buenos Aires in these years. Public transportation,
which played a key role in opening up outlying areas of the city to settlement, was used by just about everyone every day, and its operations and
costs were constant concerns for the public. Electricity and gas powered
the development of the city, and the operation of the enterprises that
controlled and provided these services and the rates they charged for them
also affected nearly every porteño consumer.

In addition to considering the role of the city council, I shall also
describe the part played by the various intendentes who headed the
municipality in these years. In their role as highly important officials in
the Argentine republic, several intendentes during this period made an
indelible mark on the capital's progress, mainly through their sponsor-
ship and implementation of major construction projects and public works.
The intendentes worked closely and well with the council on the many
occasions when both branches of government agreed on the course of
municipal management and growth. There were numerous other occasions,
however, when they disagreed fundamentally with the council, producing
conflict and deadlock.

The story of the local government's actions will be interlaced with
general material on the city's development. Summary chapters, using
census data, information on popular culture, the observations of foreign
visitors, and other sources, will describe the overall growth of the city.
These chapters will serve as the basic framework in which to locate the
functions of the local government and the part it played in the history of
Buenos Aires between 1910 and the early 1940s.

Although the principal emphasis will be on local government, I shall
also consider the role of the other main participant in the city's growth:
the national government of the Argentine republic. To achieve this, I
shall review the elections in the capital to select national executives as
well as representatives to the national Congress. The results of these
contests, like those at the local level, often had a direct bearing on decisions affecting the capital, not the least of which involved appointment
and approval of the city's intendente. Other aspects of the federal government's role will be discussed where pertinent. Like the often discordant
nature of the relations between the intendente and the council, relations
between the local and federal authorities were frequently uneasy and

confrontational, although productive periods of cooperation occurred as well.

This book evolves from my previous studies of Argentina's Socialist party, whose main base of support was in the federal capital, and of politics in the province of Buenos Aires for roughly the same period. It also stems from a long-standing interest both generally in urban politics and particularly in the city of Buenos Aires, which I first visited in 1964 for a year of dissertation research. Since then, I have returned on several occasions for periods ranging from two months to a year. Throughout those visits, the city and its history have never ceased to intrigue me. Like most relatively privileged foreign visitors, I probably harbor a more favorable image of Buenos Aires than do its inhabitants, who over the years have had to deal with it and the nation's many frustrations. Nonetheless, in this study I have attempted to provide a balanced and comprehensive account, noting both the failures and successes of local administrations in their management of municipal affairs as well as the flaws and positive aspects of the metropolis they have created. I have also tried to give an inkling of the flavor of city life and the concerns and character of the bulk of the population. Some matters of undoubted importance, such as the role of immigrant communities, the state of the working classes, and the status of women in the city, have probably received less attention than they deserve. Others have dealt with these subjects more satisfactorily and in greater depth. Some might also find that I have provided either too much or too little detail on certain crucial issues and events, while omitting altogether others of significance. To this potential complaint I can only respond that I hope my efforts stimulate others to look more deeply into and to expand on matters that I have raised. Although there is much we do know of the history of the city of Buenos Aires, there is clearly a good deal yet to be learned.

1

Buenos Aires after the centenario

In May 1910 Argentina celebrated the hundredth anniversary of its first steps toward independence with a spectacular exposition called the *centenario* in the city of Buenos Aires. Parades and processions through the downtown area and exhibitions in a park in the center of the city attracted thousands of visitors. Representatives from other American nations and from Europe marveled at the tremendous progress achieved in what was then Latin America's wealthiest and most advanced nation. Spanish writer Vicente Blasco Ibáñez, an enthusiastic admirer of the South American republic, attended the celebration and produced a costly and well-illustrated volume, *Argentina y sus grandezas*, intended to attract even more of his fellow countrymen to the booming new nation.[1] Of Argentina's *"grandezas,"* none was more notable than the capital city of Buenos Aires. For the French statesman Georges Clemenceau, another centennial-year guest, Buenos Aires was like "a great city of Europe, giving the sensation of premature growth, but, by its prodigious advancement, the capital of a continent."[2]

Indeed, the growth had been both "prodigious" and spectacular. From a riverside town of almost 180,000 persons in 1870, Buenos Aires had become a modern metropolis of 1.2 million by 1910. The growth of the city, like that of the country, had been fueled by the development of a soaring agricultural export economy, heavy foreign investment, especially from Great Britain, and massive foreign immigration, mostly from Italy and Spain. Symbols of the city's expansion and modernity included the magnificent Colón opera house, which opened in 1908 and rivaled any such hall in the world, and the beautiful Avenida de Mayo, the "Champs d'Elysées" of Buenos Aires inspired by Baron Georges Eugène Haussmann's Parisian design.

The *avenida*, a broad tree-lined boulevard completed in the late

---

1 Vicente Blasco Ibáñez, *Argentina y sus grandezas* (Madrid, 1910).
2 Susana Pereira, *Viajeros del siglo xx y la realidad nacional* (Buenos Aires, 1984), p. 22. For a description of the centennial celebration, see Thomas F. McGann, *Argentina, The United States and the Inter-American System, 1880–1914* (Cambridge, Mass., 1957), pp. 274–5.

nineteenth century, ran east to west and connected the presidential mansion, the Casa Rosada, with the newly finished Palacio del Congreso, or national Congress building. The plaza in front of the Congress, inaugurated in 1910, remained unfinished, but was destined to be one of the city's most important open spaces, not least because of its strategic location as the site of numerous political demonstrations.[3]

From the time of the centennial to the outbreak of World War I, the growth of the city continued along much the same lines as before. Between 1910 and 1913, almost 1.4 million foreigners entered Argentina. Although almost half as many of them also left the country in these years, about 670,000 stayed, the majority settling in the capital city. As a result, Buenos Aires had an overall population of close to 1.6 million by 1914, making it one of the fastest growing and populous cities in the world at the time.[4] By 1914, too, one of every five Argentines resided in the capital and one of every four lived in the metropolitan area, reinforcing a primacy that continued and grew throughout the twentieth century (see Table 1.1).

Few cities in the world so dominated the rest of the nation as did Buenos Aires and few, in turn, were so ruled by the foreign component. The municipal census of 1909 had counted 46 percent of the city's population as foreign-born. By 1914 and the third national census the foreign proportion was almost half the total (see Table 1.1), with a sizable percentage of the Argentine component undoubtedly represented by the offspring of the waves of foreigners who had been arriving constantly since the 1880s. Immigrants came from all corners of the globe. The leading groups, however, were from Italy (312,267) and Spain (306,850); by 1914 they composed almost 80 percent (619,117) of the 777,845 immigrant total. Other significant foreign communities were Russian Jews (28,846), Uruguayans (28,436), French (27,923), immigrants from the Ottoman empire, generically called *"turcos"* (15,847), Germans (10,942), and Englishmen (9,195).[5] The typical immigrant was an unattached adult male looking to strike it rich in Argentina and return to his homeland. Accordingly, foreign males outnumbered foreign females by a margin of three to two, leading to a citywide preponderance of males (54 percent of the population in 1914) over females. Despite the lack of foreign females, most foreigners appeared to prefer to marry within

3 Ricardo Luis Molinari, *Buenos Aires, 4 siglos* (Buenos Aires, 1980), pp. 400–1. For an overview of the growth of the city before the centennial, see James R. Scobie, *Buenos Aires: Plaza to Suburb, 1870–1910* (New York, 1974).
4 Municipalidad de la Ciudad de Buenos Aires (hereafter as MCBA), *General Census of the Population, Buildings, Trades, and Industries of the City of Buenos Aires* (taken on October 16 to 24, 1909).
5 República Argentina, *Tercer censo nacional, levantado el 1° de junio de 1914* (Buenos Aires, 1916), vol. 2, pp. 129–48.

Table 1.1. *Population of Argentina, the city of Buenos Aires, and the metropolitan area, by sex and nationality, 1914 and 1947*

Sex and nationality	Argentina		City of Buenos Aires			Metropolitan area[a]		
	Totals (N)	%	Absolute (N)	%	% of nation	Absolute (N)	%	% of nation
1914								
Argentine males	2,753,214	34.9	394,463	25.0	14.3	527,666	25.9	19.2
Argentine females	2,774,071	35.2	403,506	25.6	14.5	536,547	26.4	19.3
Foreign males	1,473,809	18.7	455,507	28.9	30.9	568,031	27.9	38.5
Foreign females	884,143	11.2	323,338	20.5	36.6	402,787	19.8	45.6
Total males	4,227,023	53.6	849,970	53.9	20.1	1,095,697	53.8	25.9
Total females	3,658,314	46.4	726,844	46.1	19.9	939,334	46.2	25.7
Total Argentines	5,527,285	70.1	797,969	50.6	14.4	1,064,213	52.3	19.3
Total foreigners	2,357,952	29.9	778,845	49.4	33.0	970,818	47.7	41.2
Total	7,885,237		1,576,814		20.0	2,035,031		25.8
1947								
Argentine males	6,730,739	42.3	1,005,206	33.7	14.9	1,701,238	35.5	25.3
Argentine females	6,727,161	42.3	1,156,756	38.8	17.2	1,845,967	38.5	27.4
Foreign males	1,414,436	8.9	444,200	14.9	31.4	687,477	14.3	48.6
Foreign females	1,021,491	6.4	376,418	12.6	36.8	564,078	11.8	55.2
Total males	8,145,175	51.2	1,449,406	48.6	17.8	2,388,715	49.8	29.3
Total females	7,748,652	48.8	1,533,174	51.4	19.8	2,410,045	50.2	31.1
Total Argentines	13,457,900	84.7	2,161,962	72.5	16.1	3,547,205	73.9	26.4
Total foreigners	2,435,927	15.3	820,618	27.5	33.7	1,251,555	26.1	51.4
Total	15,892,827		2,982,580		18.8	4,798,760		30.2

[a] Includes surrounding counties of greater Buenos Aires.

Sources: República Argentina, *Tercer censo nacional*, vol. 2, pp. 3 (city), 3–37 (metropolitan area), and 109 (national), and República Argentina, *Cuarto censo general de la nación, 1947* (Buenos Aires, 1947), pp. 12 (city and national) and 99–102 (metropolitan area).

their own ethnic group rather than to seek mates in the Argentine community.[6]

In Buenos Aires, foreigners dominated the ownership of real estate, industry, and commerce. In 1909 they owned 60 percent of the landed property in the city of Buenos Aires, with one group, the Italians, owning almost as many parcels as the Argentines.[7] Foreign owners of industries outnumbered Argentines by three to one, proportions that remained pretty much the same five years later.[8]

Foreigners at first clustered in the downtown area near the river, moving into old colonial homes converted into tenements or *"conventillos."* Gradually, however, they and many Argentines began to move outward from the city's center to what were then distant suburban districts.[9] The trend was noted in the five years between the 1904 and 1909 municipal censuses, which recorded a marked increase in the districts to the south, west, and north of the central city and stagnation or decline in the central districts. The trend continued over the next five years with outlying census districts 1 and 15 through 17 almost doubling in population and accounting for better than 50 percent of the city's growth overall (see Map 1 and Appendix, Table A.1). With the rush to districts such as Flores, Vélez Sársfield, Palermo, and Saavedra, municipal services were slow to follow. Many new areas of settlement lacked running water, sewers, lighting, and paved streets and the city government often took many years to provide these services.[10] Nonetheless, the move continued.

Foreigners came to be associated with particular parts of the city. Spaniards tended to settle in the central districts, particularly on or near the Avenida de Mayo. The best-known Italian district was the waterfront area of La Boca, at the mouth of the Riachuelo River, home to an important community originally from Genoa.[11] The district around the Plaza Once de Septiembre, the main terminus of the western railroad, was the

6 Samuel L. Baily, "Marriage Patterns and Immigrant Assimilation in Buenos Aires, 1881–1923," *Hispanic American Historical Review* (hereafter as *HAHR*), 60, 1 (1980), pp. 32–48.

7 *General Census of the Population*, vol. 1, p. 103. See also Carl Solberg, *Immigration and Nationalism: Argentina and Chile: 1890–1914* (Austin, Tex., 1970), pp. 56–8.

8 *General Census of the Population*, vol. 1, pp. 134 and 152 and República Argentina, *Tercer censo nacional*, vol. 7, p. 120 and vol. 8, p. 145.

9 Scobie, *Buenos Aires*, pp. 178–200 and Charles S. Sargent, *The Spatial Evolution of Greater Buenos Aires, Argentina, 1870–1930* (Tempe, Ariz., 1974).

10 According to one report, in 1910 only 46,530 houses in Buenos Aires had sewer services whereas 64,605 were without them and only about half of the city's homes had running water. F.R. Cibilis, "La descentralización urbana de la ciudad de Buenos Aires," *Boletín del Departamento Nacional del Trabajo*, no. 15 (Buenos Aires: December 31, 1909), pp. 87–97.

11 For more on the Italian immigrant community, see Samuel L. Baily, "The Adjustment of Italian Immigrants into the United States and Argentina: A Comparative Analysis," *The American Historical Review*, 88, 2 (April 1983), pp. 281–305.

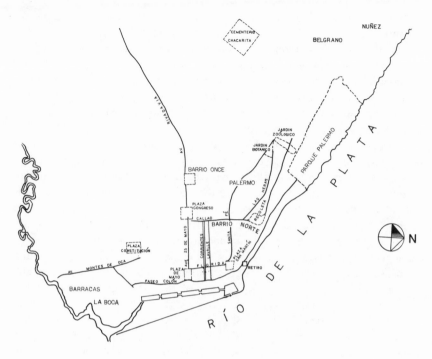

Map 1. Buenos Aires downtown, 1913 (drawn by Fredy Merico).

center of the Jewish community. A 1912 article in the popular weekly *Caras y Caretas* described suburban Belgrano as an "English square," the areas of downtown Calle Suipacha as French as Montmartre, and the blocks close to Plaza Retiro, dominated by immigrants from the Middle East, as a "suburb of old Istanbul."[12]

Despite these clusters, Buenos Aires in general had fewer of the well-defined ethnic neighborhoods that characterized North American cities. Representatives of all sizable immigrant communities, especially the Spanish and Italian, could be found scattered throughout the city. It was true that, by 1914, foreigners came to make up larger proportions of downtown districts than did Argentines, whereas the native-born came to predominate in the suburbs. Nevertheless, in no census district, either in 1909 or in 1914, did foreigners comprise less than 35 percent or more than 66 percent of the total population. This general diffusion and lack of clear ethnic clustering may have resulted from the fact that so many of the foreign-born were from Italy and Spain, thereby sharing the Catholic religion, the same general cultural values, and, if not the identical

12 Coyo Cuello, "Buenos Aires Cosmopolita," *Caras y Caretas*, 15, 716 (Buenos Aires: June 22, 1912).

language, at least a linguistic base, which made communication possible. Missing were the strong religious, racial, and language barriers that produced greater separation in the United States.[13]

No matter where they lived, foreigners contributed significantly to profound changes in the city's occupational and social structure. Foreigners made up three-quarters of the city's working classes, which had grown substantially since the late nineteenth century and continued to expand between 1909 and 1914. Immigrants also moved into the emerging middle classes, which, by the time of the third national census, represented almost 30 percent of the city's total population. Argentines, however, dominated the influential and prestigious professional classes, especially law and medicine.[14]

A closer look at the figures from the 1914 census, which lists the city's inhabitants over fourteen years of age by occupation, sex, and nationality, throws more light on the balance between foreigners and native-born in certain occupations. Table 1.2 groups these occupations into larger categories suggested by the work of Mark D. Szuchman and Eugene F. Sofer. As the table shows, in addition to dominating skilled industrial and artisan activities (category 4), foreigners also far outnumbered Argentines among menial (category 1) and semiskilled service workers (category 2). For example, 51,411 of 58,083 day laborers (part of category 1) were foreign-born, as were about 76 percent of those engaged in transportation (part of category 2). Higher up the scale, there were almost as many foreigners as Argentines who were financiers (*rentistas*) and more than twice as many foreign-born as native-born engaged in commerce (both in category 7). In most other middle and higher categories (5–10), however, the situation was reversed. In public administration, jurisprudence, public education, health (excepting nurses), and among the wealthy landowning elite who resided in and dominated the city (*hacendados* and *estancieros*), Argentines had the advantage over foreigners by margins of at least four to one. Foreigners were well represented, however, in the areas of fine arts, including architecture, and letters and sciences, where many well-known European-born individuals made their mark.[15]

In addition to describing the significant occupational and class differences between native-born and foreign-born, the 1914 census also shows important distinctions between men and women. Women made up 40 percent of the unskilled menial (category 1) and 50 percent of the

---

13 This may not have been true, however, for the city's Jewish population. See Eugene F. Sofer, *Invisible Walls: Jewish Residential Patterns in Gran Buenos Aires: 1880–1947* (New York, 1977). The numbers of foreigners by nationality for each district can be found in *General Census of the Population*, pp. 3–18 and *Tercer censo nacional*, vol. 2, pp. 129–48.

14 In 1914 there were only 201 foreign lawyers in a total of 1,992 in the city and only 354 foreign-born doctors of the total 1,765. *Tercer censo nacional*, vol. 4, pp. 209–10.

15 República Argentina, *Tercer censo nacional*, vol. 4, pp. 201–12.

Table 1.2. *Social structure of the city of Buenos Aires by occupational category, sex, and nationality, 1914*[a]

Occupational category[b]	Argentine			Foreign			Total			Occupational category (%)
	Male	Female	Total	Male	Female	Total	Male	Female	Total	01–10
01	7,792	17,046	24,838	80,062	41,809	121,871	87,854	58,855	146,709	19
02	18,312	37,573	55,885	58,565	39,418	97,983	76,877	76,991	153,868	20
03	106	—	106	77	—	77	183	—	183	
04	50,615	6,863	57,478	133,059	9,174	142,233	183,674	16,037	199,711	25
05	1,391	4	1,395	4,810	62	4,872	6,201	66	6,267	1
06	68,873	12,291	81,164	63,204	4,971	68,175	132,077	17,262	149,339	19
07	18,219	5,308	23,527	48,582	4,858	53,440	66,801	10,166	76,967	10
08	6,451	616	7,067	9,316	1,651	10,967	15,767	2,267	18,034	2
09	8,628	7,906	16,534	5,009	3,198	8,207	13,637	11,104	24,741	3
10	5,693	56	5,749	1,966	64	2,030	7,659	120	7,779	1
11	11,910	121,386	133,296	24,221	191,240	215,461	36,131	312,626	348,757	
Total	197,990	209,049	407,039	428,871	296,445	725,316	626,861	505,494	1,132,355	

[a] For persons over the age of fourteen.
[b] Key: 01, unskilled and menial; 02, semiskilled service; 03, rural semiskilled; 04, skilled; 05, rural skilled; 06, low nonmanual; 07, middle unspecified nonmanual; 08, high nonmanual; 09, low professional; 10, high professional; 11, miscellaneous; 01–04, working class; 05–07, middle class; 08–10, upper class.

Source: República Argentina, *Tercer censo nacional*, vol. 4, pp. 201–12. Organized according to the categories suggested in Mark D. Szuchman and Eugene F. Sofer, "The State of Occupational Stratification Studies in Argentina," *Latin American Research Review*, 11:1 (1976), 159–72.

semiskilled service (category 2) categories. In the first-named category, better than 90 percent of the total were women employed as domestic servants, 72 percent of whom were foreigners.[16] In the second category, 96 percent were seamstresses, dressmakers, washers and ironers, and cooks, almost evenly divided between Argentine and foreign-born females. There were almost no women involved in transportation, and relatively few (less than 10 percent) who were skilled workers (category 4), engaged in commercial activity (category 7), or employed in public administration (mostly category 5). Women were a significant proportion of the low professional category (mostly schoolteachers), but were almost nonexistent among the high professionals. There were no female architects; of the 1,992 listed lawyers, only three were women; of 1,765 physicians, twenty-seven were women. There were somewhat more women among the estancieros and hacendados (102 of 2,276), but still a small number overall.

The situation of the Buenos Aires working classes, native- and foreign-born, male and female, has been abundantly documented and described.[17] Generally, workers were forced to live in crowded tenements and other substandard housing in the central and southern parts of the city. Working conditions were usually oppressive, with excessively long work days and work weeks. Although wages may have gone up during these years, the cost of living rose with them, especially as the world war approached, bringing with it higher prices and rising unemployment. In addition to working as domestic servants or as seamstresses doing piecework at home, women composed much of the work force in food processing and textiles. Like the many children who were also employed in these areas, they were subjected to the same exploitative conditions as their male counterparts while generally receiving only half of the salary paid to men.[18] A

16 For information on the life of domestic servants, see Isabel Laura Cárdenas, *Ramona y el robot:El servicio doméstico en barrios prestigiosos de Buenos Aires (1895–1985)* (Buenos Aires, 1986).
17 See, for example, Leandro H. Gutiérrez, "Los trabajadores y sus luchas," in José Luis and Luis Alberto Romero, eds., *Buenos Aires: Historia de cuatro siglos* (Buenos Aires, 1983), vol. 2, pp. 67– 83; José Panettieri, *Los trabajadores* (Buenos Aires, 1967); and Hobart Spalding, *La clase trabajadora argentina (Documentos para su historia 1890–1912)* (Buenos Aires, 1970).
18 Donna Guy, "Women, Peonage, and Industrialization: Argentina 1810–1914," *Latin American Research Review* (hereafter *LARR*), 16, 3 (1981), pp. 65–89; Nancy Caro Hollander, "Women: The Forgotten Half of Argentine History," in Ann Pescatello, ed., *Female and Male in Latin America: Essays* (Pittsburgh, 1973), pp. 141–58; Asunción Lavrin, "Women, Labor and the Left: Argentina and Chile, 1890–1925," *Journal of Women's History*, 1, 2 (Fall, 1989), pp. 88–116; and Marysa Navarro, "Hidden, Silent, and Anonymous: Women Workers in The Argentine Trade Union Movement," in Norbert C. Solden, ed., *The World of Women's Trade Unionism:Comparative Historical Essays* (Westport, Conn., 1985), pp. 165–98. The overwhelming presence of women in the garment and textile industries is discussed in Roberto P. Korzeniewicz, "Labor Unrest in Argentina, 1887–1907," *LARR*, 24, 3 (1989), pp. 74–98.

relatively small, but growing number of women engaged in prostitution, a situation that, because it involved the forced subjugation of foreign females into "white slavery," made Buenos Aires notorious throughout the world.[19] Opportunities for women to advance socially and economically were generally fewer than for men, although the gradual opening up of the university system, especially the University of Buenos Aires, promised more professional careers for women who were fortunate enough to attend.

Exploitation of the working class led to protests. From the turn of the century, anarchists, socialists, and syndicalists had helped to organize the capital's laboring groups to seek improvements in their conditions, either through direct action or by participation in the political process. The route of direct action predominated in the years before the centenario, highlighted by an increasing number of mostly anarchist-inspired strikes (almost 300 in 1910), the assassination of the city's police chief in 1909, and a bomb explosion in the Teatro Colón during the centennial celebration.[20] Most strikes revolved around wages, hours, and the right to organize, with salary issues usually at the forefront. Women also participated in these activities, although relations with their male colleagues often produced as many difficulties for them as employer confrontations. After 1910 and until 1917, the number of strikes in the capital city generally declined and the ones that did occur usually did not produce favorable results for the strikers.[21] Those who, like the leaders of Argentina's Socialist party, hoped that foreign-born workers would become naturalized citizens and hence eligible to vote and to choose the peaceful path to change, were disappointed by the slow rate of this process. Although better than ten thousand foreigners did become Argentine citizens between 1909 and 1914, the total of 18,450 represented only a small percentage of the capital's overall foreign population.[22]

For the middle class, these were years of continued growth and oppor-

19 An excellent recent study of this issue, with useful information on the city's history, is Donna J. Guy, *Sex and Danger in Buenos Aires: Prostitution, Family and Nation in Argentina* (Lincoln, Neb., 1991).

20 A recent overview of the history of the Argentine labor movement is Ronald Munck et al., *Argentina: From Anarchism to Peronism; Workers, Unions and Politics, 1855–1985* (London, 1987), especially pp. 34–69. See also, Julio Godio, *Historia del movimiento obrero argentino: Inmigrantes asalariados y lucha de clases, 1880–1919* (Buenos Aires, 1973) and Jacinto Oddone, *Gremialismo proletario argentino* (Buenos Aires, 1949), especially pp. 223–35.

21 Information on strikes can be found in the works cited in the previous footnote. A compilation of strike statistics for the city of Buenos Aires, gathered by the National Department of Labor for the years 1907–27, is "Información social," *Revista de Ciencias Económicas*, año 17, serie 2, no. 20 (Buenos Aires, January 1919), pp. 75–82.

22 *Tercer censo nacional*, vol. 2, p. 403.

tunity.[23] The expansion of the public sector, at both the national and municipal level, offered reasonably secure white-collar employment. The move to outlying districts, particularly to neighborhoods like Palermo and Flores, was a sign not only of spatial, but also of socioeconomic, mobility. Crucial to mobility for the middle class and for working-class parents who hoped to see their Argentine-born offspring better themselves, was public education, which, beginning in the latter part of the nineteenth century, had received special attention from the national government as a vital ingredient in the modernization of the country. The federal capital, which by the turn of the century had an extensive and comprehensive system of primary, secondary, and university education, was a principal beneficiary of this emphasis. By 1914 the literacy rate in the capital for males and females over seven years of age was calculated at almost 80 percent, compared with 62 percent for the nation as a whole.[24]

For the city's small but powerful upper class, the period after 1910 represented years of significant challenge. A small, interlocking group of wealthy landowners, financiers, and professionals, closely tied to foreign investors, the Buenos Aires oligarchy had dominated the nation and the city since the 1880s. The centennial celebration had been their show, a prideful example of the great strides forward the country had made under their direction. Beginning in the late nineteenth century, however, they had been buffeted by the winds of change and by the ever-expanding working and middle classes demands for both a greater voice in the nation's government and increased attention to their economic needs.

Under reform-minded President Roque Sáenz Peña, elected in 1910, the oligarchs agreed to electoral reforms as a means to stave off more radical changes. The results of the reform spelled the end of the elite's monopoly over the political process. In the first elections following the reform, for national senators and congressmen in the federal capital in 1912, representatives of the Radical party (Unión Cívica Radical, or UCR), with a strong middle-class element, and the Socialist party, representing the interests of the working classes, won one of the two senatorial posts being contested and ten of the twelve deputy positions. In 1913 the Socialists and the Radicals captured one of the two Senate positions and all three (two to the Socialists and one to the Radicals) congressional seats. In 1914 the Socialists took seven and the Radicals three of the national deputy slots. For the next three decades, these two parties shared control of the capital's electorate and elections, relegating the conservative

23 The classic study of social mobility in Argentina, showing the growth of the middle classes over the course of the late nineteenth and early twentieth centuries, is Gino Germani, *Estructura social de la Argentina: Análisis estadístico* (Buenos Aires, 1955).

24 *Tercer censo nacional*, vol. 3, pp. 321 and 329.

parties, which represented upper-class interests, to a frequently insignificant minority status.[25]

Despite the diminution of their political status, the oligarchy still enjoyed social and economic predominance in Buenos Aires. Clustered in the center of the city and the near north side, they sought, with considerable success, to transform their exclusive neighborhood, known as the Barrio Norte, into a replica of the most fashionable districts of Paris. Influenced by French architectural styles, they continued to construct sumptuous mansions, which adorned the Plaza San Martín and the Avenida Alvear and the area surrounding "their" cemetery, the Recoleta.

Gradually, as the downtown and the Barrio Norte became more crowded, elite families moved in a northwesterly direction toward Palermo and Belgrano (see Map 1). To the northwest, another exclusive district, that of Palermo Chico, had its beginnings in these years. Breaking from the rigid Spanish-colonial grid pattern that characterized most of Buenos Aires, the planners of Palermo Chico designed curved streets to accommodate their exclusive cul-de-sac neighborhood, the site today of several foreign embassies. A few blocks further on was the city's most famous park, that of Palermo, compared by porteños to the Bois de Boulogne. On weekends, Palermo was crowded with the horse-drawn carriages of the elite as they promenaded past its well-cultivated gardens and stopped for coffee or tea at one of its fashionable cafés or restaurants.

The power of this elite rested on their ownership of vast expanses of the infinitely valuable agricultural land of Argentina and their control of the export-oriented agricultural economy. Within and around the city of Buenos Aires, however, a turn-of-the-century development offered yet another challenge to oligarchical dominance. Between 1910 and 1914 the number of industries in the city grew from 8,119 to 10,275 and the number of personnel they employed increased from 93,163 to 149,289.[26] By 1914, the city contained 21 percent of all the nation's industries and 36 percent of all persons employed in industrial activity, establishing a concentration in and around the capital that has persisted throughout the twentieth century.[27] In Buenos Aires, industries, first by choice and then by municipal ordinance, were located primarily in the southern and

25 For more on these developments, see Natalio R. Botana, "Conservadores, Radicales y Socialistas," in Romero and Romero, *Buenos Aires*, vol. 2, pp. 107–20; Miguel Angel Cárcano, *Sáenz Peña:La revolución por los comicios* (Buenos Aires, 1963); and, Richard J. Walter, *The Socialist Party of Argentina, 1890–1930* (Austin, Tex., 1977), pp. 93–114.

26 *General Census of the Population*, vol. 1, pp. 149 and 157 and *Tercer censo nacional*, vol. 7, p. 320.

27 Richard J. Walter, "The Socioeconomic Growth of Buenos Aires in the Twentieth Century," in Stanley R. Ross and Thomas F. McGann, eds., *Buenos Aires: 400 Years* (Austin, Tex., 1982), p. 95.

Palermo Park at the turn of the century

far-western districts of the city, although small-scale establishments could be found scattered throughout the city.[28] Most were involved in the manufacture of clothing and furniture, food processing, metal working, and construction. Most, too, were small, often family-run artisan enterprises, employing only a handful of people. A small but significant number, however, were large-scale ventures that employed over 100 persons and were increasingly mechanized.[29]

Foreigners made up the majority of the owners and employees of these industries. Among the owners were individual entrepreneurs who had arrived with scant resources in the nineteenth century, but who had managed to achieve considerable economic success by the twentieth century, realizing the immigrant dream of social ascent through hard work and good fortune. Other enterprises, notably the large meat-packing plants along the Riachuelo River, were owned by powerful, foreign-based companies. Domestic manufacturers, whether native- or foreign-born, often had less political influence than their foreign counterparts. Although the influence of industrialists was slow to develop, once established, it provided

---

28 Scobie, *Buenos Aires*, p. 199 and Jorge Schvarzer, "La implantación industrial," in Romero and Romero, *Buenos Aires*, vol. 2, pp. 223–40.
29 Korzeniewicz, "Labor Unrest," pp. 78–9.

a new challenge for the traditional upper class and yet another ingredient in the social mix of the city.[30]

Another important element in this blend was the growing marginal population. Found mostly in the southern and western slum districts, the marginals – beggars, drifters, petty criminals, confidence men – emerged as distinctive urban types at the turn of the century. They included the *compadrito*, an urban version of the Argentine gaucho, and the *cafishio*, or pimp.[31] The rich variety of these characters and their seemingly romantic characteristics made them prominent figures in the popular plays and *sainetes* (musical comedies) of the period.[32]

Less romantic and romanticized were the *atorrantes*, or vagrants, mainly immigrants, who either failed to find or disdained regular employment.[33] For *Caras y Caretas*, the atorrantes were a plague, which fortunately had been confined to the outskirts of the city, although a sizable number could still be found in the port area. There, they offered a sad spectacle of a "muddy, dirty, and smelly group . . . with absolutely no desire to live by working as do other men," and who would ultimately, according to this article, succumb to a life of crime.[34] Other marginal types, however, were viewed more sympathetically. In an article published a few months later, the same magazine featured a sidewalk vendor near the Plaza de Mayo, who, through his verbal skills and clever presentations, was able to sell products of dubious quality with considerable success. An immigrant from Spain, he was known as *"El Charlatán Miro,"* one of many foreigners who had learned to adopt *"la viveza criolla,"* or the ability to pull a fast one, which was an increasingly admired characteristic in Buenos Aires. He was also one of a growing number of downtown characters who added spice to the daily life of the city.[35]

Public transportation was a basic factor in the growth of the city. With an area of 18,854 hectares, Buenos Aires was one of the largest capitals, in terms of size, in the world. An extensive transportation network was a vital means to spread the population from the crowded center to the more spacious suburbs and to link the various parts of the city together. Streetcars, at first horse-drawn and then electric, along with railroads,

30 Oscar Cornbilt, "European Immigrants in Argentine Industry and Politics," in Claudio Véliz, ed., *The Politics of Conformity in Latin America* (London, 1967), pp. 221–48.

31 E.M.S. Danero, *El cafishio* (Buenos Aires, 1971) and Scobie, *Buenos Aires*, pp. 228–31.

32 A good treatment of this subject is Domingo F. Casadevall, *El tema de la mala vida en el teatro nacional* (Buenos Aires, 1957).

33 Leandro H. Gutiérrez, "La mala vida," in Romero and Romero, *Buenos Aires*, vol. 2, pp. 87–8.

34 "Los atorrantes del puerto," *Caras y Caretas*, 17, 750 (February 15, 1913).

35 Emilio Dupuy de Lome, "El Charlatán Miro," *Caras y Caretas*, 16, 773 (July 26, 1913). For a brief description of some other notable downtown characters, see Molinari, *Buenos Aires*, pp. 410–11.

contributed significantly to the development of outlying districts and provided porteños with some of the best and cheapest transportation found anywhere in the world.[36] By 1910 there were over 400 miles of streetcar track carrying over 300 million passengers per year at a uniform price of ten centavos. The national railroad system, which was the most extensive in Latin America, terminated in Buenos Aires at the Constitución, Once, and Retiro stations, providing almost 100 miles of track within the federal capital. These lines served outlying communities within the city limits as well as the growing towns just beyond the capital's borders.[37]

A new method of transportation was added in late 1913 with the inauguration of Latin America's first subway. This project was constructed by the same company that controlled most of the city's streetcars, the British-owned Anglo–Argentine Tramway Company, which had received its concession to build the subway from the city in 1909 and had begun construction in 1911. The first part of the line ran from the Plaza de Mayo to the Once station, where it combined with the underground portion of the Western Railway. The second part, opened in 1914, terminated at the edge of the Flores district at the Primera Junta station. Following its gala opening, attended by the president of the republic and other dignitaries, the subway attracted numerous curious passengers. After the novelty wore off, it became a favored means of transport for people who lived along or close to its route. Although it provided rapid transit and helped to ease somewhat the problem of downtown congestion, as a single line its utility was relatively limited. The Anglo, however, also had concessions to construct two additional subways, one linking the main north and south railroad terminals, Retiro and Constitución, and the other connecting the Plaza de Mayo with the growing Palermo district.[38]

More traditional means of transportation, such as horse-drawn carriages and carts, persisted, but their numbers declined steadily in these years. A new conveyance, the automobile began to make its mark. Whereas there

36 This was the opinion, for example, of the consul general of the United States, who in 1912 reported back to Washington "that the tramway service of Buenos Aires is unexcelled in the number of enterprises in this direction, the territory served, the cheapness of the passages and the regularity and speed in which the greatest distances are covered. It is claimed that in proportion to the urban radius and the population there is no other city in the world better served in these respects than this capital." United States National Archives, *Department of State Records Related to the Internal Affairs of Argentina, 1910–1919*, Record Group 59, Microcopy 514, roll 30, 835.78/6 (March 24, 1912). Hereafter as *State Records* with date and file number.

37 Sargent, *The Spatial Evolution*, pp. 66–74 and Scobie, *Buenos Aires*, pp. 160–78. See also Miguel Angel Scenna, "El tranvía porteño," *Todo es Historia*, 2, 20 (Buenos Aires: December 1968), pp. 64–86.

38 "Inauguration of Buenos Aires Subway," *Bulletin of the Pan American Union* (hereafter as *BPAU*), 38, 1 (Washington, D.C.: January 1914), pp. 1–8 and "Pequeño calendario contemporáneo," *Todo es Historia*, 2, 20 (December 1968), pp. 92–5.

had been only a hanful of such vehicles in the city at the turn of the century, there were almost six thousand in Buenos Aires by 1914.[39] As in so many cities, the automobile would have profound consequences for the course of urban development in Buenos Aires. In the short run, its most immediate impact was to add to the downtown traffic congestion that the subway was intended to alleviate and to allow for the emergence of a new and potentially potent competitor to the streetcar and railroad: the car for hire or taxi. As the number of taxis grew, pressure increased, both from the streetcar companies and the general public, to regulate the operation of these often reckless and independent drivers. The ensuing confrontation between the municipality and the city's taxi drivers produced a constant struggle between the would-be regulators and this new group of individualistic entrepreneurs.[40]

A salient feature of the city's transportation system was the fact that, aside from taxis and carriages, it was almost totally dominated by foreign enterprises. The Anglo–Argentine enjoyed a virtual monopoly over streetcar service and it owned and operated the new subway. The railroads also were mainly British-owned. Few voices of protest or concern were raised over the possible consequences of such one-sided control at a time when the system was expanding, modernizing, and providing reliable and reasonably priced service. After World War I, however, as will be seen, foreign ownership of just about everything that moved by rail in the city would emerge as a major political issue.

Although a visit to the suburbs required the use of public transportation, much of the dynamism and growth of Buenos Aires could be determined by a stroll through the heart of the city centered on the Plaza de Mayo. Following the suggestions of the 1913 *Baedeker*, a tourist might start out first with a walk along the Avenida de Mayo from the plaza of the same name to the newly opened Plaza del Congreso. Beginning with the Casa Rosada at the eastern edge of the square and proceeding past the national cathedral on its northern side, he or she, moving westward, would pass the city hall, or intendente's office, and the headquarters of *La Prensa*, one of the city's most important dailies. Further along, the visitor might stop for refreshment at the by-then venerable Café Tortoni, established in 1858 and a favorite gathering place of the city's literati. Flanking the avenue were many other cafés, many of them open to the sidewalk in mild weather, and some of the city's finest hotels, including the recently opened Majestic, "a magnificent building . . . provided with

39 Statistics on horse-drawn vehicles and automobiles are from Intendencia Municipal de la Ciudad de Buenos Aires, Comisión de Estética Edilicia, *Proyecto orgánico para la urbanización del municipio: El plan regulador y de reforma de la capital federal* (Buenos Aires, 1925), p. 200.

40 A detailed treatment of this struggle is Alberto Parapugna, *Historia de los coches de alquiler en Buenos Aires* (Buenos Aires, 1980).

every comfort."[41] Buildings along the avenida were, for the most part, of a uniform height of five stories more or less, and of a generally uniform architectural design.

Turning north at the intersection of the Avenida de Mayo and Calle Callao at the Plaza del Congreso led one past the recently opened Savoy Hotel. A few blocks further, Callao intersected with what already had become the "Broadway of Buenos Aires": Calle Corrientes, or the "street that never sleeps." Eastward along Corrientes, or along its immediate parallel to the north, Calle Lavalle, could be found most of the city's many theaters, restaurants, cafés, cabarets, and beer halls. The better than two dozen theaters concentrated in this area offered a wide variety of performances, from serious dramas by foreign- and native-born playwrights to light musicals, comedies, and vaudeville-style reviews. The Spanish sainete, often with an Argentine twist, was especially popular. Also popular, and growing more so all the time, was the moving picture, with cinema houses drawing about one in four of all theatergoers by 1909.[42] Among the recommended restaurants in this area was the famous Royal Keller at Esmeralda and Corrientes. There, as elsewhere in the entertainment district, one could listen to or dance the tango, a popular art form that developed in the disreputable suburbs, but garnered increasing acceptance and respectability downtown.[43]

A second recommended tour was along Calle Florida, rivaling the Avenida de Mayo as one of Buenos Aires' most famous thoroughfares. Although only ten blocks in length, Florida was renowned for its luxurious shops and elegant mansions. Beginning one block west of the Plaza de Mayo, a traveler passed the first of two British-owned department stores, Gath and Chaves, which had been opened in the latter part of the nineteenth century and was greatly expanded in the years just prior to the first world war. In these years, too, Calle Florida was home to some of the best-known residences of the oligarchs as well as being the site of two of their principal organizations, the Sociedad Rural Argentina, or cattlemen's association, and the exclusive and magnificently appointed Jockey Club.[44] Also along Florida, construction was begun in 1913 on the Galería Güemes, a commercial complex that, upon its completion two years later, reached 80 meters in height, making it the tallest building in the city. Another gallery at the corner of Córdoba and Florida, originally the site of the Bon Marché department store, was the property of the Pacific Railroad and

41 Albert B. Martínez, *Baedeker of the Argentine Republic, 1913*, 4th edition (Barcelona, 1914), p. 88.
42 *Second General Census*, vol. 2, p. 356.
43 Eduardo Stilman, "El nacimiento del tango," in Romero and Romero, *Buenos Aires*, vol. 2, pp. 165–72.
44 For information on the Jockey Club and its members, see Francis Korn, "La gente distinguida," in Romero and Romero, *Buenos Aires*, vol. 2, pp. 45–55.

came to be known as the Galería Pacífico. In 1914 the other famous British store on Florida – Harrods – opened for business and soon became an established landmark.[45]

Florida terminated at the Plaza San Martín. This plaza was dominated by two magnificent oligarchical palaces: one on the south side belonged to the Paz family; the other, on the north, was the property of the Anchorena family. Today they house, respectively, the Círculo Militar, or officers' club, and the Argentine Ministry of Foreign Affairs. On the east side was the Plaza Hotel, a fourteen-story building opened in 1909 and from that date the city's most elegant hotel.

Although Florida was essentially a commercial street, it served other functions as well. For those porteños who sought to compare their city with the great capitals of Europe, the stores and shops along Florida were symbols of the nation's advancement, wealth, and "civilization." The most common comparison was with Paris's Rue de la Paix. Moreover, its central location, combined with its commercial attractiveness, made Florida an important social center, a place where the well-dressed ladies and gentlemen of the capital's high society, and those who aspired to that status, congregated. The men, if they were members, met at the Jockey Club, then had tea with their wives at the Richmond Café, or dined, until it was destroyed in 1914, at the Sportsman Grill. The street was the favored promenade for the city's most beautiful women, who attracted admiring glances and gallant and sometimes not so gallant comments from the males who lined the sidewalks to observe them.[46]

A third tour, from the Plaza de Mayo to the Palermo district by way of the Paseo de Julio, required public transportation for all but the most hardy or adventurous. Leaving the plaza and heading in a northwesterly direction, the traveler passed first through the Nueve de Julio Park, graced by well-designed gardens and attractive statuary, including a monument donated by the city's Syrian community to commemorate the centennial. At the intersection of Corrientes and the Paseo, construction was beginning on the imposing new main post office building. The Paseo de Julio itself, today including the avenidas Alem and Libertador, was both a thoroughfare and the center of a particular neighborhood, a barrio that *Caras y Caretas* called the "most exotic of our metropolis." Located at the edge of a sloping embankment, the paseo was characterized by a street level of successive covered archways, which sheltered a wide variety of commercial establishments. The first major city neighborhood to be

---

45 For more on the establishment of Gath and Chaves and Harrods, see Roger Gravil, *The Anglo–Argentine Connection, 1900–1939* (Boulder, Colo., 1985), pp. 93–5.

46 An evocative portrait of life along Florida, which by a 1922 municipal ordinance was closed to vehicular traffic for part of the day, can be found in Juan Manuel Pintos, *Así fué Buenos Aires: Tipos y costumbres de una época, 1900–1950* (Buenos Aires, 1954), pp. 15–25.

encountered by curious newcomers emerging from the new immigrant hotel in the port district, or by visiting seamen from the same area, the barrio had a particularly cosmopolitan flavor. *Caras y Caretas* went on to point out that there could be found "Italian trattorias, French buvettes, German beer halls, Swedish, Danish, Russian, Syrian, Turkish, and Greek cantinas" as well as many employment agencies offering job opportunities for the newly arrived. The Paseo de Julio barrio also had a shady reputation, both as a neighborhood of bars and brothels and as a place where police vigilance was required to prevent the unwary immigrant from being deceived by the many sharpies and confidence men who frequented the area.[47]

As the paseo made its turn to the southwest in 1913, the traveler saw the ongoing construction of the great Retiro Railway Station. Finally completed in 1915, after ten years of labor, it was at the time the largest and most modern terminal in Latin America and one of the largest in the world. Built on land reclaimed from the Río de la Plata, the Retiro was the main terminus for the Central and Pacific railways. In front of the station stood an imposing clock tower, completed in 1916 as the gift of the British community to mark the centennial. To the northeast of Retiro, work proceeded on the construction of the new port facilities to complement those that had been planned and completed further south in the latter part of the nineteenth century.[48] Farther up the paseo, at its intersection with Callao, was the city's first major amusement park, the Parque Japonés, opened in 1911, and beyond that the Ice Palace, "where, during the winter numerous young people belonging to the high society of Buenos Aires go to skate . . . ."[49]

At the Recoleta cemetery and adjacent park, the route to Palermo changed from the Paseo de Julio to the Avenida Alvear. At this transition point could be found yet another monument by a foreign community to the centennial, in this case the French. Palermo Park, the ultimate destination of this tour, contained the racetrack and stands of the Jockey Club, whose contests occupied the sports pages of the city's newspapers and attracted thousands of spectators annually. Just southwest of and adjacent to the park were the city's zoo, which also drew large crowds, and exposition grounds of the Sociedad Rural, whose annual midyear exhibition of livestock and agricultural products was a regular and important highlight of the city's life. Opposite the zoo at the intersection of avenidas Santa Fe and Las Heras were the city's well-regarded botanical gardens, which had been opened in 1898. The gardens were the creation

47 "Barrios Pintorescos: El Paseo de Julio," *Caras y Caretas*, 17, 813 (May 2, 1914).
48 For more on the port, see Scobie, *Buenos Aires*, pp. 70–91.
49 Martínez, *Baedeker*, p. 242.

of Carlos Thays, a French landscape architect who in the 1890s had been named Director General de Paseos de la Municipalidad (city parks director). In that position, Thays was largely responsible for expanding and beautifying the city's parks and plazas and for planting the hundreds of thousands of trees – especially jacarandas, tupias, and acacias – that so enhanced the overall appearance of the city.[50]

A fourth and final recommended tour offered a sharp contrast to the first three. As the 1913 *Baedeker* and numerous other commentators observed, "The most animated, modern, elegant and richest part of Buenos Aires is that part north of Rivadavia street [site of the first three tours]; this part of the town forms a strange contrast to that which extends south of Rivadavia street, to such an extent that one could say they are two quite different towns."[51]

Beginning again at the Plaza de Mayo, the fourth tour proceeded southward along the Paseo Colón. It skirted the eastern edge of the San Telmo district, formerly the preferred residential area of the nineteenth-century elite, but now largely abandoned to working-class immigrants and conventillos. The tour also included a visit to the colorful waterfront district of La Boca, known for its strong Italian flavor, its brightly painted houses, and a sense of isolation and independence from the rest of the city, leading its citizens to declare their neighborhood a "republic." In this instance, isolation and independence also were a function of general neglect by the city fathers.[52] Just to the southwest of La Boca was a similarly poor and neglected neighborhood, that of Barracas, home to numerous industries and a large working-class population.

These tours to particular areas attested to the dynamism and diversity of the city. The taller buildings going up along Florida and the Paseo de Julio, for example, suggested the beginnings of a vertical as well as a horizontal growth. By 1914, some 20 percent of the city's buildings were two stories or more in height, compared with 18 percent in 1909 and 13 percent in 1904.[53] Nonetheless, the most common dwelling was still a simple one-story, narrow residence, popularly known as a "*casa chorizo*," or "sausage house."[54] Prominent buildings such as the new Congress or the Plaza Hotel clearly dominated what was still a low-lying city skyline.

50 Molinari, *Buenos Aires*, pp. 392–3.
51 Martínez, *Baedeker*, p. 242.
52 The census district in which La Boca was located contained the greatest number of conventillos (613, of a citywide total of 2,697 in 1919) and the greatest number of buildings made of wood in contrast to the more substantial materials of most city buildings. Sargent, *The Spatial Evolution*, p. 65 and Walter, *The Socialist Party*, p. 77.
53 Sargent, *The Spatial Evolution*, p. 64.
54 Blas Matamoro, *La casa porteña* (Buenos Aires, 1971), pp. 32–45.

During these years, the city government imposed a building code that sought to control the quality of materials used, the height of the structures in relation to the width of the street upon which they were constructed, and the overall appearance.[55] To encourage the development of aesthetically pleasing constructions, the municipality also offered an annual prize to the most notable work of architecture designed and completed in a given year. The results were mixed. Building heights were subject to frequent exceptions and many blocks were an odd mixture of one-story and multistory buildings. Many beautifully designed structures appeared in these years, but so did numerous others that did little to enhance the city's appearance.

Throughout its history, Buenos Aires was subject to the influence of many architectural styles, which appeared in dominant waves and then faded away. During the years before the war, the "academic architecture" of the French Ecole des Beaux Arts had a major influence. So, too, at this time and into the 1920s did art nouveau, with its emphasis on elaborate and graceful ornamentation. Rather than any particular style, however, what came to characterize Buenos Aires was the eclectic nature of its architecture, which, combined with its heterogeneous population, reminded visitors and residents alike not of any single European or North American capital, but rather of a not unpleasing mixture of many.[56]

Following the centenario, a steady stream of distinguished foreigners continued to visit this new metropolis and comment on its growth. These included the great Cuban chess master José Raúl Capablanca, who arrived in May 1911 to encourage the development of a game that continues to enjoy great popularity in Buenos Aires, and, in the same year, noted French socialist leader Jean Jaurès. Another visitor, England's Lord Bryce, was effusive in his praise of Buenos Aires, complimenting the city on the appearance of the Avenida de Mayo, Palermo Park, the Congress, the Teatro Colón, the streetcar service, the Jockey Club, and observing that "Buenos Aires is something between Paris and New York. It has the business rush and the luxury of the one, the gaiety and pleasure-loving aspect of the other. Everybody seems to have money, and to like spending it, and to like letting everybody else know that it is being spent."[57] Like others, however, he noted the contrasts between wealth and poverty in the city, particularly commenting on the shacks and shanties of the western

55 MCBA, *Reglamento de construcciones: Noviembre 1910* (Buenos Aires, 1911).

56 For more on the architecture of Buenos Aires at this time, see Matamoro, *La casa porteña*, pp. 40–85 as well as Francisco J. Bullrich, "La arquitectura: El eclecticismo," in Romero and Romero, *Buenos Aires*, vol. 2, pp. 201–12; Ramón Gutiérrez, *Arquitectura y urbanismo en iberoamérica* (Madrid, 1983), pp. 533–47; and, José Xavier Martini and José María Peña, *La ornamentación en la arquitectura de Buenos Aires, 1900–1940* (Buenos Aires, 1967).

57 James Bryce, *South America: Observations and Impressions* (New York, 1913), p. 318.

and southern suburbs, "dirty and squalid, with corrugated iron roofs, their wooden boards gaping like rents in tattered clothes."[58]

Three well-known North Americans also visited the city in these years. Hiram Bingham, the discoverer of Macchu Pichu, was impressed by the city, but somewhat restrained in his praise. He found the materialism and the behavior of the newly rich distasteful and thought the public manners of the porteños by far the worst in South America.[59] Typically less restrained was former U.S. President Theodore Roosevelt, who was well received by the Argentines in late 1913. He ranked Buenos Aires on a par with the leading European and North American cities and proclaimed its "great future."[60] Finally, world heavyweight boxing champion Jack Johnson, who visited Buenos Aires in early 1915, sought to promote the development of his sport in Argentina. Although boxing was prohibited within the confines of the city, Johnson was able to hold several exhibitions during his visits in 1915 and 1916 and to provide impetus to yet another diversion that captured the interest and imagination of many porteños.[61]

If any one individual symbolized and incarnated the vitality and spirit of Buenos Aires in these years it was Jorge Newbery. The son of a dentist from the United States who had settled and prospered in Buenos Aires in the latter part of the nineteenth century and an Argentine mother, Newbery grew up in comfortable surroundings at Florida 251. The wealth of his parents allowed him to study electric engineering at Cornell University and the Drexel Institute. In 1900 he was named director general of lighting for the Municipality of Buenos Aires, a post he held until his death. As director, he published various articles on the lighting and electric power needs of the city and emerged as an advocate for the eventual municipalization of this service.[62]

It was, however, as a sportsman and as an aviator that Newbery was best known. A versatile athlete, he excelled at wrestling, boxing, fencing, and rowing, the latter a sport that on the weekends regularly drew numerous participants and spectators to the river delta town of Tigre some twenty miles northeast of the city. As owner of an automobile, he enjoyed racing and touring Palermo Park. Beginning in 1907, he became an

58 Ibid., p. 320.
59 Hiram Bingham, *Across South America* (Boston, 1911), pp. 31–41.
60 "Buenos Aires: A fine modern capital," *BPAU*, 38, 5 (May 1914), pp. 706–9. Another favorable and informative view of the city is provided in Harry Weston Van Dyke, *Through South America* (New York, 1912), pp. 201–13.
61 Molinari, *Buenos Aires*, pp. 413–14.
62 For example, Jorge Newbery, "The Lighting of Buenos Aires," *General Census*, vol. 3, pp. 181–91.

Jorge Newbery in his monoplane (ca. 1910)

enthusiastic balloonist, setting the existing South American record in 1909 for duration and distance in a balloon called El Huracán. The fame attached to that feat led one of the newly formed clubs for soccer, or *fútbol* – fast becoming *the* number one sport in the country – to adopt Huracán as their name. In that same year, Newbery was named president of the Aero Club Argentino, which he had helped to found, and in 1910, after setting the South American altitude record in a balloon, he began to fly the monoplanes that had just been introduced into the country; four years later he set the world altitude record for an airplane at more than six thousand meters.

Newbery enjoyed life to the fullest. Handsome, athletic, bold, and with a ready smile (in contrast to the general somber and melancholy aspect traditionally associated with porten˜os), Newbery was closely associated with the younger members of the wealthy elite who made the Barrio Norte their home (Newbery's own residence was on the Avenida Las Heras) and the rest of the city their playground. Newbery personified the unbounded optimism, pride, and sheer enjoyment that many porteños associated with their city and Argentines with their country.

On March 1, 1914, Newbery took off by plane from a field in the western city of Mendoza with the intention of crossing the Andes. After only a few seconds in the air, however, his craft crashed in flames, killing Argentina's most renowned aviator and first great popular hero of the twentieth century. The subsequent funeral and burial in Buenos Aires' Chacarita cemetery produced an unprecedented outpouring of public grief. Soon, a street in the city was named for Newbery and several decades later so, too, was the municipal airport. The date of his death was regularly commemorated with gravesite ceremonies and homages and, in later years, as often happens, he became even more of a legend in death than he had been in life.[63]

The tragic death of Jorge Newbery at the age of thirty-nine coincided with the end of an era. The onset of World War I temporarily halted the frenetic pace of growth, expansion, and modernization that had characterized the city of Buenos Aires and the Argentine republic for the past quarter of a century. After the war, however, the pace would resume and new popular heroes would emerge – aviators, sports figures, and entertainers – to occupy the affections and attentions of the porteño public. In the meantime, changes would occur in the way local city government was chosen and managed that affected not only how the capital was governed, but also how it grew.

63 Raúl Larra, *Jorge Newbery: El conquistador del espacio* (Buenos Aires, 1960) and Molinari, *Buenos Aires*, pp. 414–15.

2

Prelude to reform

City government had much to do with Buenos Aires' growth before, during, and after the centennial celebration. The form of that government had been established by the national Congress in 1882, shortly after the city had become the nation's capital, through national law number 1260. The basic features of that law remained in effect, with some modifications, well into the twentieth century.

According to law 1260, municipal government was divided between a legislative and executive branch. The legislature, called the Concejo Deliberante (Deliberative Council), was elected by the city's taxpayers, with both native-born and foreign-born eligible to vote and to run for office under certain conditions. Candidates for the council had to be literate and at least twenty-five years of age, to have lived in the city for at least six months (five years for foreigners), and either to have paid some local taxes (at least 100 pesos a year for foreigners) or practiced a liberal profession. Voting and candidacy were restricted to males. Elected councilmen served four-year terms and elections to fill half the council were held every two years. The council assembled on the first of the year to select its presiding officers: a president and two vice-presidents. There were two regular sessions, which began in April and usually ran, with a recess, until the end of the year. After 1882 the council was suspended several times and elected officials were replaced by a special governing commission named by the national Senate. In 1907, however, elections were resumed for twenty-two councilmen elected on a citywide basis.

The executive was the intendente, or, as he came to be known popularly – underscoring the country's English influence – the "Lord Mayor." Unlike the councilmen, the intendente was named by the president of the nation and confirmed by the Senate, at first for a term lasting two years and later for three years, with the possibility of renewal. The intendente had to be an Argentine citizen and meet the same eligibility requirements as council members. The intendente named two secretaries to assist him: one for public works, security, and hygiene and the other for finance and administration. Having many of the same powers as provincial governors, the intendente called the concejo into regular sessions and, if desired, special sessions, issued decrees, proposed ordinances, prepared the annual budget, and named all municipal employees. It was the responsibility of the intendente to implement measures enacted by the council, although he could also veto those of which he disapproved.

The division of executive and legislative authority was intended to provide a balance of powers. The intendente had considerable appointive and initiative authority, often backed up by the federal government. The council could override the executive's vetoes with a two-thirds vote taken within five days of executive action, could call the executive's secretaries to account through interpellation, and had the power to impeach the intendente. Although the council and the intendente worked closely and well on many matters, in numerous other instances, they sharply disagreed. The divisions became increasingly obvious as city politics and government became more democratic and complex. Exacerbating the tension was the built-in distinction between the federally appointed executive and the elected council.

The responsibilities of the local government were broad and varied. The city provided such services as street paving, electrification, garbage disposal, and maintenance of an extensive hospital system. Regulation was a crucial area of local responsibility, ranging from setting the heights and general construction of buildings, to establishing standards in markets, restaurants, theaters, and other places of business, to controlling public transportation. The widening of existing streets and the construction of broad boulevards like the Avenida de Mayo to increase traffic flow continued to be pressing matters of attention and concern. To pay for these various activities and functions, the city government had the authority to levy a number of different taxes. These ranged from a tax on theater admissions to fees charged for construction to a tax on private companies that contracted to provide municipal services. The single most important tax, supplying about one-third of all revenue, came from the charge on street lighting, cleaning, and trash removal.

The office of the intendente was located on the Avenida de Mayo at the edge of the Plaza de Mayo. From 1882 until 1931, the city council met a few blocks away at Perú 272 in the cramped former *sala de representantes* of the legislature of the province of Buenos Aires in a collection of colonial-period buildings known as the *"manzana de las luces."* Two other poles of governmental power, which exerted perhaps greater influence on the city, could be found at the opposite ends of the Avenida de Mayo: the Casa Rosada and the national Congress. In addition to naming the intendente, the president of the republic, according to section 3, article

86 of the Argentine Constitution, was "the immediate and local head of the Capital of the Nation."[1] According to the same constitution, the national Congress had the authority to exercise "an exclusive legislation in all the territory of the Capital of the Nation." Indeed, in practice, much of the most important legislation affecting the capital, including changes in the form of municipal government and how it was elected, originated more often in the national than in the local legislature.

The powers of the federal government in the city of Buenos Aires were considerable. It controlled the port, public education, the water supply and sewer services, the collection and distribution of property taxes, and fire and police protection. The rapid expansion of the national government at the turn of the century also had clear consequences for the city's growth, most visibly in the construction of new and imposing government offices, especially around the plazas de Mayo and del Congreso. Because the city was the headquarters of the national government, it was much affected by decisions in which the local authorities often had little say and limited control. On the other hand, their circumstance did not put the city's officials in the same situation as existed in Washington, D.C., for example. For one thing, about 20 percent of the republic's national congressional deputies were elected from the city of Buenos Aires, as were two of the country's thirty senators. This gave the city substantial representation of its interests in the Congress. For another, it was clearly the intention of the federal government, from the late nineteenth century on, to make the capital city the showplace of the nation, the principal symbol of Argentina's growth and modernity. As a result, Buenos Aires often benefited disproportionately in the dispensation of federal largess, adding to the growing historical resentment of the city by the rest of the country, which often felt both neglected and overwhelmed by the capital's dominance.[2]

Late in the centennial year of 1910, recently inaugurated president Roque Sáenz Peña named Joaquín Samuel de Anchorena to serve as intendente of the city of Buenos Aires. In so doing, he continued a presidential practice of selecting capital executives from close friends and political allies, mostly from the upper classes, a pattern that was to be repeated for the next three decades.

Assuming office at the relatively tender age of thirty-four, Anchorena was a prominent member of one of Argentina's wealthiest and best-known

---

1 República Argentina, *Constitución de la Nación Argentina* (Buenos Aires, 1961).
2 For more on the structure and mechanics of city government, see Ismael Bucich Escobar, *Buenos Aires, Ciudad* (Buenos Aires, 1936), pp. 136–42 and Austin F. Macdonald, *Government of the Argentine Republic* (New York, 1942), pp. 415–25.

Municipal Intendente Joaquín Samuel de Anchorena (1914)

families.[3] He was raised in the family home at Maipú 262, which was only a block away from that of Jorge Newbery; Anchorena's cousin, Aaron, had accompanied Newbery on his first balloon ascent in 1907. After receiving his law degree from the University of Buenos Aires in 1898, he spent some time managing one of his family's large estates in the territory of La Pampa before embarking on a career of public service. Following two years in the post of president of the section of the Department of Agriculture charged with combating locust plagues, he was elected in 1908 to the position of national congressional deputy from the city of Buenos Aires. During his service as a deputy, Sáeñz Peña named him intendente. After four years in that office, Anchorena continued to lead

3 An entertaining, informative, and less than flattering view of the family is provided in Juan José Sebrelli, *Apogeo y ocaso de los Anchorena* (Buenos Aires, 1972). For information on how the family fortune was made, see Jonathan C. Brown, *A Socioeconomic History of Argentina, 1776–1860* (Cambridge, 1979), pp. 174–200.

such important oligarchical institutions as the Jockey Club, the Sociedad Rural, and, in 1918, the Asociación Nacional del Trabajo, an organization of elite interests mobilized to counter the spread of supposedly Bolshevist-inspired labor activity.[4]

During Anchorena's administration, the Concejo Deliberante underwent two elections to renovate the council. Both contests, in late November of 1911 and 1913, partly reflected the larger political currents at the national level. The most notable feature of the 1911 contest was the appearance of a new party, the Unión Comunal, to compete with the two existing parties for eleven council seats: the official government party, the Unión Nacional, and a conservative splinter from the Radical party, the Unión Cívica. According to its preelection manifesto, the Unión Comunal was in tune with the new democratic sentiments unleashed by the proposed electoral reforms of President Sáenz Peña. It was, the statement averred, a party of principles rather than of personalities, its main focus would be on municipal affairs and it would promote the most "progressive ideas" for the city's construction and growth; all citizens, "from the proletariat to the powerful," would enjoy the benefits of these developments.[5] Engaging in an aggressive and enthusiastic campaign, the new party won eight seats to the Unión Nacional's three, gaining almost half its votes from the southern districts of the city.[6]

The elections of November 1913 took place after the national electoral reforms had been enacted. Although the full impact of these changes were yet to be felt at the local level, the national government determined to apply at least some features of the new procedures to the November contest. This meant that rights were expanded for representatives of all participating parties to observe and monitor the voting process and vote count and to question the credentials of individual voters. Although it objected to these new procedures as a violation of municipal autonomy, the Unión Comunal nevertheless again captured the majority of seats contested, this time winning six places to five for the newly formed Unión Vecinal de la Capital.[7]

Although these elections showed some signs of being affected by larger changes, they were still far from meeting even minimal democratic

4 Biographical information from *Quien es quien en la Argentina: Biografías contemporáneas, año 1939* (Buenos Aires: Guillermo Kraft, Ltda., 1939), p. 22 and Enrique Mario Mayochi, "Joaquín Samuel de Anchorena (1910–1914)," in *Tres intendentes de Buenos Aires: Joaquín Samuel de Anchorena; José Luis Cantilo; Mariano de Vedia y Mitre* (Buenos Aires, 1985), pp. 7–38.

5 *La Prensa* (Buenos Aires: November 11, 1911), p. 14.

6 "Las elecciones del domingo," *Caras y Caretas*, 14, 687 (December 2, 1911) and MCBA, *Versiones taquigráficas de las sesiones del Concejo Deliberante de la Ciudad de Buenos Aires* (hereafter as *VTCD*) (November 28, 1911), p. 544.

7 *VTCD* (December 2, 1913), p. 276.

standards. According to the 1909 municipal census, 70,000 potential voters were enrolled in the capital, but in 1911 fewer than 15,000 cast their ballots in the municipal elections.[8] In the April 1912 national deputy elections in the capital, the first held under the Sáenz Peña laws, more than 106,000 voters participated.[9] In the November 1913 municipal contest, fewer than 10,000 did so, prompting one publication to observe: "As far as the general public are concerned these elections elicited no interest, and if it had not been for the plastering of the city with electioneering placards we doubt if eighty per cent of the public would have known that anything out of the ordinary was taking place."[10] A lack of interest, along with irregularities and restrictions, combined to keep turnout low. Of even greater significance was the decision of the two new major parties on the scene, the Radicals and the Socialists, who by 1914 would capture between them almost 70 percent of the capital's national electorate, not to take part in the city council elections until they had undergone a thorough reform.

On many issues, Anchorena and the council collaborated. In April 1911, for example, the council approved a proposal from the executive to provide 100,000 pesos (the peso was about two and a-half to the dollar at this time) to aid the victims of recent flooding in the city.[11] This was the first of several such subsidies that the Anchorena administration directed to assist affected residents in the low-lying southern and working-class districts of La Boca, Barracas, and Nueva Pompeya, which were particularly susceptible to the effects of heavy rains. These floods caused considerable damage and produced many complaints and protests from the affected neighborhoods, which requested a permanent remedy for this periodic catastrophe. The city government, however, was hampered in its response to these complaints by the limited authority it exerted over sewer construction and large-scale projects needed to channel properly the Matanza and Riachuelo rivers. The overflows from these rivers, which formed the southern border of the city, were mainly responsible for the floods. In this instance, the national government would have to take the lead if any major improvements were to be made.[12] Although the Matanza and

8   *General Census*, 1909, vol. 2, p. 378 and República Argentina, *Memoria del Ministerio del Interior, 1911* (hereafter as *Memoria*) (Buenos Aires, 1911–12), pp. 148–50.
9   Darío Cantón, *Materiales para el estudio de la sociología política en la Argentina* (Buenos Aires, 1968), vol. 1, p. 81.
10 *The Review of the River Plate* (hereafter as *RRP*), 15, 1149 (Buenos Aires: December 5, 1913), p. 1431.
11 *VTCD* (April 25, 1911), pp. 15–21.
12 The general problem of flooding in the southern part of the city was discussed in the national Congress on September 15, 1913. Resulting legislation provided for aid to the victims and funds to straighten the winding course of the Riachuelo. During the discussion, speakers reiterated that this matter by necessity had to fall under the jurisdiction of the national government because flooding affected not only the federal capital, but also the bordering cities of the province of

Riachuelo were eventually channeled, the problem of flooding continued to be a constant preoccupation throughout ensuing decades.

Another area of concern in these years was the increased cost of living, especially ever-higher prices for foodstuffs. Anchorena responded by encouraging the development of *"ferias francas,"* or free markets, an initiative endorsed by the council in March 1911. These markets were composed of informal stalls set up along city sidewalks, benefiting from tax breaks and from the fact that the owners and operators could sell their goods directly and without intermediaries, so as to reduce the prices they charged. Although early efforts met with only mixed success, by 1913 some two thousand popular and thriving markets operated throughout the city.[13]

There were other achievements of the Anchorena administration in which the council either collaborated or acquiesced: the development of the exclusive Palermo Chico neighborhood, the continued beautification of Palermo Park, the opening of new parks and plazas in the southern and western parts of the city (Lezama, Olivera – later Avellaneda – and Chacabuco), and the beginnings of the expansion of major downtown streets and avenues – Santa Fe, Córdoba, Corrientes, and Belgrano. In September 1912, the council, in a move that was little discussed at the time, agreed to grant a fifty-year concession to the Compañía Italo Argentino de Electricidad (CIAE) to provide electric service to the city. With this concession, the Italo prepared to compete with the German-owned Compañía Alemana Transatlántica de Electricidad (CATE), which had come to dominate the expanding and profitable Buenos Aires market after making a similar arrangement with the city in 1907.[14] In October 1913, the council unanimously endorsed an Anchorena scheme to build 10,000 new houses for workers and employees over a five-year span, a scheme, like several others, whose intention was to meet the urgent need for cheap and affordable housing in the city, but whose results were meager.[15]

Buenos Aires. This argument would reappear frequently in various other contexts as the area of Greater Buenos Aires continued to expand and as its links with the city, especially transportation links, continued to grow. República Argentina, Cámara de Diputados de la Nación, *Diario de Sesiones, año 1913* (Buenos Aires: September 15, 1913), pp. 228–45 (hereafter as *Diputados*).

13 Emilio Dupuy de Lome, "Las ferias francas," *Caras y Caretas*, 16, 788 (November 8, 1913) and Mayochi, "Joaquin Samuel de Anchorena," p. 33.

14 VTCD (September 20, 1912), pp. 739–59 and MCBA, *1880–1930 Cincuentenario de federalización de Buenos Aires: Comprende el proceso de su evolución histórica, política, económica y social* (Buenos Aires, 1932), p. 57. For more on electrification of the city, see Molinari, *Buenos Aires*, pp. 368–70.

15 VTCD (October 17, 1913), pp. 153–63. For a discussion of the general ineffectiveness of this and other public housing projects between 1910 and 1940, see Leandro Gutiérrez and Juan Suriano, "Vivienda, política y condiciones de vida de los sectores populares, Buenos Aires 1880–1930," in Municipalidad de la Ciudad de Buenos Aires, Secretaría de Cultura, Instituto Histórico de la Ciudad de Buenos Aires, *Primeras jornadas de historia de la ciudad de Buenos Aires: La vivienda en Buenos Aires* (Buenos Aires, 1985), pp. 15–28 and Scobie, p. 190.

Customarily, the council itself initiated a number of resolutions and ordinances on a wide range of relatively noncontroversial matters. Although these were not major items in the larger scheme of things, they showed how the city government both affected and reflected the ever-changing nature of urban life. One measure lowered the age for a chauffeur's license from twenty-two to eighteen whereas another approved the replacement of kerosene street lamps with electric lights. A few months later, the council passed an ordinance that prohibited persons under eighteen from attending public racetracks. In mid-1911 the council passed a proposal to restrict the activities of sidewalk vendors on Florida, in the words of its proponent, "our most chic street," and to discourage the crowds that gathered to hear the playing of phonograph records at the entrance to various commercial establishments. In May 1914 the council voted to change the name Calle Ushuaia to Jorge Newbery.

Various measures had to do with public health and welfare. These included proposals to establish special schools for handicapped children, set up municipally sponsored soup kitchens, provide subsidies for local neighborhood libraries, form special municipal brigades to kill the large number of rats unearthed in the destruction of downtown property, subsidize the distribution of sewing machines that had been placed as collateral at the municipal loan bank, and call for the sanitary inspection of fish that were sold commercially at the point of disembarkation. In May 1913 the council also voted a special subsidy of 20,000 pesos to aid the survivors and the families of victims of a gas explosion in La Boca.[16]

The new building code for the city, written in 1910, set conditions for the quality of construction materials, general appearance, and height. During the Anchorena administration and thereafter, the council considered numerous exceptions to these rules. In discussing one of these, a proposal to erect a building at Paseo de Julio and Tucumán, the councilmen in favor of the proposal argued that its rejection would slow the development of the city. The increasingly popular use of skyscrapers in North American cities like New York and in various European capitals was clearly the wave of the future, they claimed, and one that Buenos Aires should ride with rather than swim against. In one of that period's relatively few roll call votes, these arguments prevailed seven to six, although with a restriction of 80 meters in height for the proposed building.[17] This was but one of many exceptions that encouraged the appearance of taller buildings and a significant change in the Buenos Aires landscape.

It was also customary for the council and the intendente to disagree about numerous items, some minor and some major. The council, for

16 From a review of the *VTCD* for the years 1911–14.
17 *VTCD* (November 18, 1913), pp. 242–57.

example, overrode the intendente's vetoes of an ordinance to require meters to be installed in taxis and carriages for hire and another that stipulated payment of fees to persons who were formulating a new tax registry.[18] Anchorena did prevail, however, in his veto on December 1911 of an ordinance that would have forgiven fines on persons who had missed the deadline for paying certain municipal taxes.[19] This particular issue often produced disagreements between the executive and the legislative branches of city government, with the appointed intendente standing firm on the collection of fines to bolster his often imbalanced budget and the elected council seeking to curry favor among its constituents by advocating forgiveness. In addition to matters that involved the intendente and the council directly, there were also council criticisms of the entire executive branch, which continued even after Anchorena's administration to be expressed through various interpellations of the secretaries of finance and public works.

The major bone of contention between Anchorena and the council centered on the construction of two new avenues, or "avenidas." These boulevards, the "Diagonal Sur" and the "Diagonal Norte," significantly altered the structure of downtown Buenos Aires. Their construction, however, entailed many years, considerable cost, and bitter political disputes.

The idea for the avenues stemmed from the work of a commission named by Intendente Manuel J. Güiraldes in 1908 and headed by French architect André Bouvard. This commission recommended the creation of two broad diagonal avenues extending out from the intersection of the Plaza de Mayo and the Avenida de Mayo, one running northward to the Plaza Lavalle and the other southward to the intersection of México and Bernardo de Irigoyen. Eventually, the two diagonals would also intersect with a proposed north–south boulevard running along the lines of Lima–Cerrito and Bernardo de Irigoyen–Carlos Pellegrini streets and would connect the Retiro and Constitución rail terminals. The purpose of these constructions, combined with the development of the Plaza de Mayo, was to supply more open space in the cramped and congested central core and to improve the flow of both vehicular and pedestrian traffic. It was hoped, too, that the new boulevards, like the Avenida de Mayo, would be monumental in style and improve the overall physical aspect of the capital.

Anchorena was a strong and enthusiastic proponent of the avenidas. He clearly saw the new boulevards as lasting monuments to his administration and he lobbied hard on their behalf. These efforts bore fruit in January 1912 when the national Congress passed legislation allowing the

18 *VTCD* (September 26, 1911), pp. 377–8 and (November 19, 1912), pp. 943–8.
19 *VTCD* (December 22, 1912), p. 657.

municipality to proceed with the construction of the Diagonal Norte and the north–south avenue. The enabling legislation gave the city government the authority to expropriate the property in the path of the proposed avenues and then resell the property along the reconstituted line, using the profits gained to help pay for the project. To initiate construction, the city was permitted to float a loan, either on the internal or external market, of 15 million pesos to be used to pay for expropriated property. The city also was to regulate the form of the avenues in terms of their "architecture, hygienic conditions, light, decoration, and height."[20]

The plan was ambitious, bold – and very expensive. The estimated total cost of the projected Diagonal Norte alone, which involved the expropriation of a sizable chunk of the city's most highly prized and valuable real estate, was set at 500 million pesos. In addition, because it cut diagonally across several streets, the new avenue required the expropriation of entire square plots, of which only triangular sections might be used.

The initial reaction of the city council to the proposal was generally favorable. In March 1912, after some minor disagreement, the council voted to authorize the intendente to float the 15-million peso loan for the needed expropriations.[21] By May, however, divisions within the council began to appear. Councilman José Guerrico of the Unión Comunal, for example, was quoted as believing that "the most fundamental and interesting matter at the moment is to carry out the construction of the avenues" while the Unión Nacional's Juan A. Boeri argued that "before thinking in avenues it is necessary to supply the capital with adequate water and sewer services."[22]

Doubts and divisions increased shortly thereafter. In June the council's committee on public works recommended approval of various ad referendum (subject to council approval) contracts signed between the city executive and property owners in the first block scheduled to be cleared for the Diagonal Norte. Four councilmen signed the report, but three members registered their dissent. Speaking for the majority, Councilman Enrique Palacio argued that the avenues would not only enhance the beauty of the city and ease traffic flow, but also, as in the United States, where similar avenues had been constructed, improve public health by providing more space for the free circulation of light and air.

Although most councilmen agreed on the general desirability and future benefits of the avenidas, many were concerned by what appeared to them

20 *Diputados*, 1911 (1912), p. 229. The complete texts of the enabling laws, numbers 8854 and 8855, are on pages 228–33.

21 *VTCD* (March 5, 1912), pp. 90–1.

22 "Buenos Aires: Cáculo de recursos y gastos ordinarios y extraordinarios para 1912," *Caras y Caretas*, 15, 709 (May 4, 1912).

to be the excessive costs involved and the lack of a coherent and well-conceived plan of development. The intendente's initial agreements with the property owners of the first block to be cleared included homes and businesses owned by some of the city's wealthiest families and led to payments sometimes exceeding five times the assessed value. Critics pointed out that arrangements for the first block alone would consume the fifteen million pesos slated for all expropriations. These expenditures, as the leading spokesman for the dissenters, the Unión Comunal's Sylla Monsegur noted, would add to the growing deficit in the city budget. This financial burden, in turn, would divert attention and resources from such important matters as extending street cleaning and waste collection services to suburban areas and filling in flood-prone lands in La Boca and Barracas.

Anchorena's secretary of finance, Ernesto Vergara Biedma, sought to counter these criticisms by observing that the avenidas, whatever the expense, represented a sound investment in the future of the city. He also trotted out an argument that was to be reiterated whenever such costly projects were considered, namely, that they were necessary to give Buenos Aires "the aspect of any of the great capitals of Europe." When the avenues were finished, he continued, porteños would be able to move more rapidly from one point to another in the downtown area and businessmen, who would benefit the most from their construction, would see the removal of many "insuperable obstacles" to free transit. He further observed that the poor would benefit as well because they not only would be able to use the avenues, largely paid for by the rich, but also would find employment in their construction. He concluded that no matter what the council decided, the intendente was determined to continue the project. These arguments, however, did not convince the skeptics. In a roll call vote, the committee report was defeated ten to eight. The vote crossed party lines, with representatives of the Unión Comunal and the Unión Nacional on both sides, for and against.[23]

The distance between the intendente and the council on this matter widened two weeks later when the executive repeated his request that the contracts be approved. Vergara Biedma, again appearing on behalf of the executive, argued that the mayor had signed these contracts in good faith, in the belief that the majority of the council would agree to them and that this procedure was both more efficient and, ultimately, less lengthy, conflictive, and expensive than the alternative of submitting each expropriation to adjudication through the courts. Opposing councilmen, however, blamed Anchorena first for exceeding his authority in this matter

---

23 *VTCD* (June 5, 1912), pp. 307–52. A story on the vote, along with photographs of the councilmen and some of the properties involved, can be found in "El asunto de las avenidas," *Caras y Caretas*, 15, 715 (June 15, 1912).

and then for trying to place the onus for the problem on them. As one put it: "The council studied all the contracts in question and opposed all of them, because it considered the prices set as too high, and it rejected them . . . The intendente, perhaps, has not considered adequately the consequences of his actions." The council then unanimously supported the committee report, which reaffirmed the earlier rejection.[24]

The debate continued in somewhat different form when Vergara Biedma appeared in September to discuss the state of municipal finances. Although admitting that there was room for improvement, he contended that the overall fiscal situation of the city was sound and that prospects for a balanced budget for the coming year were good. The Unión Comunal's Monsegur, emerging as the council's leading critic of the executive, took issue with the secretary's assessment.[25] The state of municipal services was, in his words, "deficient and incomplete": public welfare did not meet the needs of the population, public works like street paving absorbed large sums of money but did not extend to outlying neighborhoods, plazas and gardens were too often neglected and abandoned, street cleaning was haphazard at best, and municipal employees did not satisfy community requirements. The local government, too, was ignoring such pressing matters as the increased cost of living, the demand for more workers' housing, and the municipalization of certain basic city services. The major culprit in this state of affairs, Monsegur alleged, was the mayor's seemingly one concern: the construction of the avenidas. He calculated that building them would absorb 35 percent of the city's ordinary resources and would, Vergara's assurances notwithstanding, produce a large deficit in the following year.[26] Monsegur's assertions led to no immediate action. Nonetheless, they reflected the increasing polarization between the intendente and the council and they forecast similar conflicts over major public works projects in the future.

Despite its disagreements with the intendente, the council did approve specific expropriations for the avenidas. Moreover, in December 1912 the council grudgingly agreed to expand the original expropriation loan from fifteen million to thirty million pesos while continuing to criticize the intendente for his behavior and his apparent lack of respect for the position and the opinions of the council.[27]

By this time, it was clear that the construction of the avenidas had

24 *VTCD* (June 18, 1912), pp. 400–10.
25 Monsegur, like so many Argentine politicians, was a graduate of the law school of the University of Buenos Aires, where he had written his thesis, "The Condition of the Working Class." He was also a member of the Jockey Club. Before being elected to the city council, he had served in the Chamber of Deputies of the legislature of the province of Buenos Aires. *Quien es Quien, 1939*, p. 292.
26 *VTCD* (September 13, 1912), pp. 701–28.
27 *VTCD* (December 3, 1912), pp. 996–1011.

developed a momentum and a life of its own, which would be hard to resist. Buildings, including the central market, had already been leveled (leading to the rat-elimination resolution previously mentioned) and other work was proceeding. Whereas the council might object to Anchorena's procedures and the excessive costs involved, the project had apparently reached an early point of no return. Once such leveling occurred, especially in the downtown area, construction had to follow or the city would be left with strewn rubble and vacant lots at the location of its most valuable property. Irate citizens would ignore the legal and financial niceties and blame the city government as a whole for the delays. The council, then, was placed in a trap from which it could not easily extricate itself. If it resisted the intendente's efforts too strenuously, it would take the bulk of the blame for the failure to complete the project. This, too, was a dynamic of the relation between the council and the intendente that would often be repeated.

The dispute over the avenidas continued for the next two years. Generally, the council gave its approval to the various individual expropriations submitted by the executive and, in May 1913, agreed to an additional fifteen million peso loan to meet the obligations of the avenidas' construction.[28] On July 9, 1913, as part of the celebration of Argentina's independence day, Anchorena presided over the inauguration of the first block of the Diagonal Norte, showing off the initial concrete results of the city's efforts and expenses. Nonetheless, financing continued to be a problem. In early 1914, the council agreed to a contract signed between Anchorena and the British banking house of Baring Brothers for a 2.5 million pound loan to meet avenida expenses.[29] Half of the loan, however, was subcontracted by Baring to three German banking houses. With the outbreak of the war a few months later, payment from Europe was suspended, further deepening the financial morass into which avenida expenditures were sinking the city of Buenos Aires.

Soon after approving the Baring loan, the council also agreed, by a vote of eight to four, to an Anchorena-inspired measure to authorize a series of further expropriations along the projected diagonals. In the session following this approval, Juan Maglione of the Unión Comunal accused Anchorena of playing a double game with the council: on the one hand requesting the measure on expropriation while, on the other, urging his allies in the press to attack the city legislature as obstructionist. Moreover, in Maglione's opinion, the avenidas would never be completed unless new funding sources were found, an unlikely prospect as the world war unfolded. He proposed, therefore, a temporary halt in construction until these matters could be resolved.[30]

28 *VTCD* (May 23, 1913), pp. 175–95. 29 *VTCD* (February 6, 1914), pp. 220–4.
30 *VTCD* (June 9, 1914), pp. 220–4.

These matters, however, became even more complicated in the follow-ing months. On June 23, 1914, Anchorena vetoed the very expropriation ordinance that he himself had advocated earlier in the month, arguing that the matter of more solid financing had to be considered before al-lowing any further property acquisitions.[31] One week later, the council considered two projects from the finance committee on this issue: one calling for a suspension of work on the avenidas and another recommend-ing the resale of fractions of land already purchased to help pay for construction expenses. After debate, the council voted eight to six instead to approach the national government to help bail the city out of this dilemma.[32] Anchorena, however, rejected this course, arguing that given the deepening war-induced economic crisis, the national government would be neither inclined nor able to aid the city. He also rejected the idea of suspending construction of the avenidas and instead backed the idea of selling off leftover properties as an alternative source of funding.[33]

The avenidas were only one of several problems confronting Anchorena at this time. The council was also critical of the contract that the intendente had signed for the 1914 opera season in the municipally controlled Teatro Colón, arguing that once again the mayor had exceeded his authority by not properly consulting the legislative branch before proceeding.[34] Ag-gravating the council's displeasure was the fact that the concessionaire for the season had died unexpectedly, which, added to declining attendance because of the general economic situation, left the city with a sizable bill to pay.[35] Buffeted on the one side by the council, Anchorena also found himself at odds with the national government, which in midyear had ceded city land across from the Palermo racetrack to the army. Consid-ering this action an affront to his authority and the rights of the munic-ipality, Anchorena threatened to resign in protest, which led finally to a compromise on the issue.[36]

The intendente was not the only member of city government under fire. In July 1914, Socialist national deputy Mario Bravo, who was leading his party's campaign for reform of the federal capital's municipal elections and government, charged in a general criticism of the November 1913 elections that councilman Juan A. Boeri of the Unión Nacional was holding his position on the council illegally and improperly. The root of the accusation lay in the city government's decision in 1912 to expropriate certain lands along the Arroyo Maldonado, one of several major creeks

31 *VTCD* (June 23, 1914), p. 259.   32 *VTCD* (June 30–July 1, 1914), pp. 296–343.

33 *VTCD* (July 17, 1914), pp. 393–4.

34 The report from the committee investigating this matter and censuring the executive's actions came after Anchorena had resigned his post. *VTCD* (December 30, 1914), p. 245.

35 *RRP*, 42, 1189 (September 11, 1914), p. 621.

36 "El conflicto entre la Intendencia y el ministro de guerra," *Caras y Caretas*, 17, 821 (June 27, 1914) and Mayochi, "Joaquin Samuel de Anchorena," p. 34.

running through the city and a main contributor to periodic flooding in the northern and western parts of Buenos Aires. The charge against Boeri was that he and his sons, who held property along the arroyo, had benefited financially from the expropriation while Boeri was a member of the city council that voted on the measure. In these circumstances, Bravo and others argued, Boeri should have stepped down from the council. The council committee investigating the matter, however, countered that, according to the ordinance regulating such practices, Boeri had not acted improperly. They added that many councilmen, by the fact of being property owners and taxpayers, could be affected by the frequent decisions on expropriation and could not be expected to resign each time a case arose that involved their own interests.[37]

Two days after the council voted to approve the committee's report, the newspaper *La Nación* broadened the attack. In a series of articles and editorials, *La Nación* questioned the council's very legitimacy given the small number of voters that had selected it, and implied that the Boeri case was only one of many suspected instances of impropriety, reinforcing a general popular impression that venality was an ingrained feature of its operation.[38] Stung by this charge, the council named a special committee to look into the allegations. After little more than a month of deliberation, the committee reported that there was no substance to them and the matter was dropped.[39] Nonetheless, in both the Boeri incident and the confrontation with *La Nación*, the council had investigated itself. For anyone concerned with the honesty, efficiency, and democratic openness of local government, this was not a reassuring procedure. The public discrediting of the council associated with these events reinforced a growing movement within the national Congress to reform both the way the capital's government was chosen and the manner in which it functioned.

While the council investigated *La Nación*'s charges, President Roque Sáenz Peña died in office. He was succeeded by his vice-president, Victorino de la Plaza. For the increasingly beleaguered Anchorena, who had named the new Diagonal Norte for his patron Sáenz Peña (the Diagonal Sur was named for oligarchical kingpin and former president Julio A. Roca, who also died in 1914), this was the final blow. Although reaffirmed in 1913 for a second term, he submitted his resignation in late October 1914. In so doing, he cited his growing difficulties with the city council, whose legitimacy was coming under growing scrutiny. Congressional critics argued that eight councilmen chosen in 1913 were not eligible for their seats because they had failed to pay the requisite amount of taxes to meet eligibility requirements.[40]

---

37 *La Prensa* (July 22, 1914), p. 6 and *VTCD* (July 21, 1914).
38 *La Nación* (Buenos Aires: July 23, 1914), p. 10.
39 *VTCD* (September 4, 1914).   40 *La Prensa* (October 24, 1914), p. 8.

In the opinion of the editors of *La Nación*, Anchorena's resignation was further evidence of the disrepute of the city council, whose continued existence made "any intelligent and useful action of communal government impossible."[41] Not all publications, however, placed the full burden of blame for the resignation on the council. As early as September, *The Review of the River Plate*, reflecting the interests of the British community, had judged Anchorena to be an able promoter of grandiose projects, but lacking the practical business sense needed for the kind of economic conditions that prevailed in late 1914; the *Review* demanded more careful and efficient financial management. Calling him "utterly unsuitable" for continuing in office, the *Review* claimed that "the resignation of the Mayor would be cordially received by the inhabitants [of the city]."[42] When the intendente did resign, the *Review* commended his projects for the development in the northern part of the city, but criticized his "excessive" expenditures on the avenidas, which by the end of the year had help to produce a deficit of thirty-seven million pesos.[43]

Following the resignation, the president of the council, Enrique Palacio, assumed the executive post until the national government could name a successor. In the sessions of October 30, José Guerrico of the Unión Comunal responded to Anchorena's charges against the council. Guerrico, who would be a prominent councilman over the next two decades and himself intendente in 1930–31, pointed to the many times the council had cooperated with the executive on such matters as free markets and the development of Palermo Chico. He admitted that there were disagreements on spending for the avenidas wherein the council had tried to control the very expenditures that now were producing debts and deficits. Despite the "systematic" opposition of the intendente, often seconded by the press and the leadership of the Socialist and Radical parties, the council, he summarized, had "always fulfilled its duty, and one should not forget its uncompensated labor [at this time council members did not receive any salary], its fortunate initiatives, or its efficacious control of the administration which has just concluded."[44]

Both branches of government, then, had their supporters and detractors. Both sides, too, had valid arguments for their respective positions. The council and the intendente had cooperated on certain matters that had led to major improvements for the city and had disagreed on others, reflecting the natural tension between an executive and legislative branch. This particular confrontation, however, carried certain significant implications for the future. First, if this much tension developed between an

41 As cited in Mayochi, "Joaquín Samuel de Anchorena," p. 37.
42 *RRP*, 42, 1189 (September 11, 1914), p. 621.
43 Ibid., 42, 1196 (October 30, 1914), p. 1103 and 42, 1201 (December 4, 1914), p. 1291.
44 *VTCD* (October 30, 1914), pp. 151–2.

intendente and a city council who shared the same social background and represented basically the same interests, even greater disagreements and difficulties could be expected between a more democratically elected council that represented a broader range of interests and an intendente who came from the upper classes and was named by the national government. Second, a certain level of discord between the two branches of government could be tolerated so long as the municipality progressed in terms of extending public works and services. When the squabbling reached a level that slowed development, public patience often grew short and the overall reputation of local administration suffered. Usually on such occasions it was the deliberative body, composed of conflicting political interests and open to public examination, that suffered the greatest loss of public confidence and esteem.

Anchorena's successor as intendente, Arturo Gramajo, inherited a debt-ridden city government that faced continuing financial difficulties. In addition, the city council was on the verge of total disintegration. Early in 1914, a number of councilmen had resigned for ostensibly personal reasons, leaving the council short-handed for the rest of the year. The growing drumbeat of criticism, especially the implications of malfeasance in office and questions about the legitimacy of the 1913 elections, led most of the remaining councilmen to submit their resignations in March 1915. With only four councilmen retaining their posts, Gramajo had no option but to request President de la Plaza to dissolve the council and to replace it with an appointed commission of twenty-two men. Such was the discredit into which the council had fallen that when the commission was officially confirmed later in the year, one publication observed of the elected council's demise, "The mourners are few, very few."[45]

The commission held its first official meeting on March 24, 1915. As Socialist party leader Juan B. Justo observed when confirmation of the commission was discussed in the national Congress, the new legislative body was a homogeneous group of men from some of the most important families of the Argentine oligarchy (Bosch, Herrera Vegas, Casares, Martínez de Hoz, Achával, Guerrero, Lanusse, Paz, Unzué), many of whom

45 From the *Buenos Aires Herald* of August 13, 1915, as cited in *State Records* (August 18, 1915), 835.101/4. Although *La Prensa*, which like *La Nación* ran many articles on "municipal deficiencies," did not exactly mourn the loss of the council, it did oppose the named commission and called for rapid reorganization of the city government overall and a new council elected by reformed procedures. "La disolución del Concejo Deliberante," *La Prensa* (March 17, 1915), p. 10. For more on these events as debated in the national Congress, see *Diputados* (May 21, 1915), pp. 83–7 and (August 6–11, 1915), pp. 521–631 and República Argentina, Congreso Nacional, *Diario de Sesiones de la Cámara de Senadores, año 1915* (Buenos Aires: September 2–7, 1915), pp. 481–99. Hereafter as *Senadores*.

were members of the Sociedad Rural and the Jockey Club and most if not all of whom lived in the Barrio Norte. Their overall knowledge of the city, Justo observed, was probably limited. He caustically commented: "It is possible that of the twenty-two persons named, there is not one that has traveled [in the city] farther south than the Plaza Constitución, where they take the train to [the fashionable seaside resort of] Mar del Plata. I doubt that there is a single one that has dedicated a quarter of an hour to study of the price of meat and bread or to problems of garbage disposal."[46]

Whatever their limitations, the commission had the advantage for Gramajo of being a relatively congenial and cooperative group with which to work. Together, they agreed to severe budgetary constraints and cutbacks, matters that dominated most of their deliberations and actions over the next two years. Salary reductions for municipal employees, approved as part of the city budgets for 1915 and 1916, produced the greatest crisis of the Gramajo administration. In January 1916, a union of municipal workers and employees (Unión Obreros Municipales) was formed in reaction to the rising cost of living and the city government's belt-tightening measures, which led, in the words of the union's most important leader and founder, to "salaries and wages which did not succeed in covering the most basic necessities . . . ."[47] As a result, the union engaged in three strike actions in 1916, the most serious being a two-week work stoppage by the city's sanitation workers in midyear. As garbage began to pile up and the danger to public health grew, the municipal government found itself under increasing pressure to meet the workers' demands. In July and August, the council and the executive agreed to rescind the salary cuts included in the 1916 budget and to remove the sanitation director, a person seen by the union as having "despotic authority," from his post and to initiate a reorganization of that department.[48] From this victory, the municipal workers' union went on to be one of the best-organized and most successful labor organizations in the country.[49]

For the Gramajo government, resolution of the sanitation workers' strike was its final major piece of business. In April 1916 Radical party leader Hipólito Yrigoyen had been elected president of Argentina, ending the half-century rule of the conservative oligarchy. Scheduled for

46 *Diputados* (August 11, 1915), p. 612.
47 From an interview with union leader Francisco Pérez Leirós in Julio N. Arroyo, "Lo que puede una buena organización sindical," *Aquí Está*, 1, 29 (Buenos Aires: August 27, 1936).
48 *VTCD* (August 8, 1916), p. 261.
49 For more on this union, which became closely associated with the Socialist party, see Joel Horowitz, *Argentine Unions, the State and the Rise of Perón, 1930–1945* (Berkeley, 1990), pp. 63–4.

inauguration in October, he would name a new intendente and a new commission. The Gramajo administration, therefore, increasingly took on a caretaker quality, with few new initiatives and only a bare majority present at many commission sessions. A municipal election reform two years later would relegate the appointed commission system to historical obscurity for the next quarter of a century. Nonetheless, it would reappear in 1941 with many of the same characteristics and under circumstances remarkably similar to those that had led to its reemergence in 1915.

3

Reform and its consequences

The outbreak of World War I in Europe signaled the beginning of a five-year halt in the spectacular expansion of Buenos Aires. Foreign immigration, which had fueled the city's demographic growth, declined to about one-fifth of what it had been prior to the war. During the period between 1914 and 1919 more than 200,000 persons left the republic than entered it, with many foreigners returning to their homelands to fight in the war. Although no censuses were taken in those years, the capital's estimated population grew by only a little over sixty thousand inhabitants, or less in five years than had occurred annually before the war.[1]

The interruption of trade and the flow of foreign investment also had severe consequences. Construction on the new port, the avenidas, and major building schemes in general ground to a halt. The Anglo–Argentine tramway company, which had contracted to build two new subways, was forced to abandon those projects. The general economic slowdown produced growing unemployment in Buenos Aires; one study commissioned for the Congress found a 20 percent drop in the number of persons employed in the capital, with the construction industry particularly hard hit.[2] Unemployment continued to grow until 1918 when an upturn took place, aided by the expansion of domestic industry in the face of the wartime-induced drop in imports and the continued decline in the number of immigrants entering the country.[3] At the same time, the cost of living accelerated, especially between 1916 and 1918.

In these years, which coincided with the transition of executive power from the conservative oligarchy to the Radical party of Hipólito Yrigoyen, Argentina and the city of Buenos Aires experienced one of its most

1 MCBA, *Cincuentenario*, pp. 51–2.
2 República Argentina, Ministerio del Interior, *La desocupación obrera en 1915: Minuta del Honorable Senado (junio 10 de 1915) Mensaje del Poder Ejecutivo (agosto 13 de 1915). Antecedentes nacionales* (Buenos Aires, 1915), pp. 15–21.
3 República Argentina, *Memoria, 1920–1921* (Buenos Aires, 1915), pp. 15–21.

turbulent periods of labor activity. The number of strikes and strikers, which had dropped precipitously after 1910, grew steadily after 1916, peaking in 1919 with 367 work stoppages in the capital city involving more than 300,000 strikers.[4] This year of agitation and protest was initiated by a week-long conflict that paralyzed the city of Buenos Aires, resulted in considerable loss of life and destruction of property, and, for many, seemed to place the country on the edge of revolutionary, class-based civil war.[5] "La semana trágica," or "the tragic week," became indelibly implanted in the minds of many Argentines as the worst experience of urban violence and threat to national order in the nation's twentieth-century history, until the "cordobazo," a similar urban outburst in the interior city of Córdoba, in May 1969.[6]

During this period of turmoil, less spectacular but nevertheless important changes occurred at the level of municipal government in Buenos Aires. In early 1917 President Yrigoyen named for the capital a new intendente and a new municipal commission whose members were to serve until reforms being debated in the national Congress were approved and implemented. The new local executive was Joaquín Llambías, a forty-eight year-old physician who had served as president of the Radical party's central committee in the capital. The twenty-two man commission was also made up of Radical loyalists, generally young lawyers, doctors, and engineers. Eight of the twenty-two would go on to serve as national congressmen from the capital and at least three would assume important posts in future municipal administrations.[7] Overall, the group was less homogeneous and less "aristocratic" than its conservative predecessor.[8]

4 "Información Social," *Revista de Ciencias Económicas*, p. 79.
5 For more on these events and the circumstances that produced them, see Edgardo J. Bilsky, *La semana trágica* (Buenos Aires, 1984); Julio Godio, *La semana trágica de enero de 1919* (Buenos Aires, 1972); Munck et al., *Anarchism to Peronism*, pp. 70–90; and David Rock, *Politics in Argentina, 1890–1930: The Rise and Fall of Radicalism* (Cambridge, Eng., 1975), pp. 95–200.
6 On the long-term effects of the "tragic week," see Carlos H. Waisman, *Reversal of Development in Argentina: Postwar Counterrevolutionary Policies and Their Structural Consequences* (Princeton, N.J., 1987), pp. 211–29.
7 The eight to be elected to Congress from the city of Buenos Aires, with their terms in parentheses, were Francisco Beiró (1918–22), Jacinto Fernández (1918–22), Matías Gil (1920–24), Domingo Guzzo (1928–32), Juan C. Hiriart (1926–30), Pedro López Anaut (1920–24), and Eduardo Tomasewsky (1920–24). Commissioner Juan B. Barnetche later served briefly as intendente. Carlos A. Varangot was secretary of public works in a subsequent Radical administration where fellow commissioner Victor Spota served with him. *VTCD* (January 1, 1917) and República Argentina, Cámara de Diputados, de la Nación, *El parlamento argentino: 1854–1957* (Buenos Aires, 1948).
8 Five of the eight commissioners who went on to become national deputies were considered by Peter H. Smith, in his study of the Argentine Congress noted below, to be "nonaristocrats," most probably of the middle class. As determined from the information compiled by Smith and provided by the University of Wisconsin Data Service Center.

Like the party's national leadership, the Radical appointees represented a new generation of basically middle-class men with considerable political background, but relatively little administrative experience.[9]

Differences over social class composition aside, the Radical commission operated in much the same way and faced many of the same issues as its predecessor. Its overriding concern continued to be the precarious financial situation of the municipality, a situation that led to tight budgets and salary reductions. The intendente submitted draconian budgets for 1917 and 1918; the council restored some cuts, but ultimately went along with a proposal to reduce all municipal salaries, from 5 percent for the lowest paid to 10 percent for the highest paid.[10] There were also suggestions to extend the tax on street lighting, cleaning, and waste disposal to unimproved properties, which were generally either exempt or taxed at a low rate. Llambías argued, however, that although desirable, such an extension could not be made, according to the law of 1882, without the permission of the national government.[11] The issue would be raised again a few years later. Unable to raise taxes and faced with scarce revenues to meet its various obligations, especially on loan payments, the Radical commission reluctantly agreed to sell off municipally owned property to raise the necessary funds.[12] Like its predecessor, this commission confronted another strike by municipal employees who protested budget reductions and the failure of the administration to fulfill certain of the commitments made during the previous strike. This confrontation led to the dismissal of several thousand employees and a dispute that dragged on for two years until its final resolution in 1919.[13]

The financial crisis left little room for grandiose public works or bold initiatives to respond to social and economic concerns. There was, however a change in the ordinance regulating the maximum number of passengers in a streetcar (the *"completo"*) to allow special seating privileges for women and children and it was under Llambías that the Balneario Municipal, or public swimming beach, basically a pier that jutted out some hundred meters into the Río de la Plata east of the main docks, was opened in 1918.

For the most part, the intendente and the commission seemed to work well together. There was disagreement over a proposal from Llambías to provide a concession to establish an automatic telephone system in the capital, a proposal that the commission eventually rejected on the grounds

9 For the class backgrounds of Radical deputies in the national Congress, see Peter H. Smith, *Argentina and the Failure of Democracy: Conflict among Political Elites, 1904–1955* (Madison, 1974), pp. 29–33.
10 *VTCD* (March 30, 1917), p. 135.   11 *VTCD* (September 14, 1917), p. 133.
12 *VTCD* (September 30, 1917), pp. 343–54.
13 Arroya, "Lo que puede una buena organizacion sindical."

that more than one bid for the project should be considered.[14] On the other hand, although they made amendments to the executive's budget proposals and expressed reservations about his proposal to sell off municipal property, they passed these measures nearly unanimously.

While Llambías shared Gramajo's fortune in working well with an appointed commission, he also shared Anchorena's fate of leaving office under a cloud. When rumors of Llambías's resignation in the face of allegations of scandal involving the misappropriation of funds to build the Balneario Municipal surfaced in mid-1919, the U.S. embassy observed: "His successor cannot avoid being more efficient than Dr. Llambías since the administration of the municipality during his two and a half years of incumbency has been unparalleled in inefficiency and maladministration."[15] Subsequent commentators were somewhat more generous, noting the serious economic difficulties and constraints under which Llambías had been forced to operate.[16]

During the years between the end of the Anchorena administration to the Radical commission under Llambías, the major decisions concerning municipal government were being made not at the eastern end of the Avenida de Mayo, but rather at the western end in the national Congress. The changes that emanated from the Congress affected significantly the way the city council was chosen as well as the composition, tenor, and role of that body.

The push for reform flowed directly from the changes initiated by Sáenz Peña. Those changes, beginning in 1912, had led to the election of Socialist and Radical congressmen and senators from the federal capital in 1912 and 1913 and of Radicals, after 1914, from other provinces as well. In 1916, in addition to winning the presidency, the Radicals captured eight congressional seats in the federal capital, which, combined with victories elsewhere, gave them a total of 44 seats, or a little better than one-third of the 120 in the lower house. Joining them, in addition to nine Socialists, were eight members of the newly formed Progressive Democratic party, based primarily in the provinces of Santa Fe and Córdoba. Combined, the representatives of those three new parties by 1916 could command a majority in the lower house. Although they disagreed on numerous issues, they were in general accord, as were a number of conservatives, on the need to reform the way the city of Buenos Aires elected its local administration.

The main proponent of reform was Socialist Deputy Mario Bravo, elected to Congress in 1913. In September of that year he introduced the

14 *VTCD* (September 27, 1917), p. 226.   15 *State Records* (May 16, 1919), no file number.
16 Bucich Escobar, *Buenos Aires*, p. 203 and MCBA, *Cincuentenario*, p. 175.

The Avenida de Mayo, with the national Congress building in the background
(November 1926)

first of several initiatives aimed to extend the spirit and the letter of the Sáenz Peña law to the local level. Bravo called for the election of a forty-man city council chosen at large and under the same procedures as the national law. Requirements for voters in city elections were also to be the same as for national contests, with tax-paying and property-owning restrictions removed. Foreigners were to be allowed to vote, also under reduced restrictions, but with some minimal residency (two years) and tax-paying (50 pesos a year) requirements. Drawing on North American and European examples, Bravo noted that universal suffrage had begun to transform the nature of municipal government in other countries and even in interior cities of the Argentine republic. In some cases, he noted, the right to vote in local contests had even been extended to women, although he was not including them in this particular proposal.[17]

One of the worst effects of the existing system, Bravo observed, was that it had encouraged the division of the city into the wealthy north and the poverty-stricken south. As he argued in a later presentation, contemporary Buenos Aires offered the "spectacle . . . of the north and that of the south, one with clean neighborhoods and the other with dirty neighborhoods, the city that has complete municipal services and the city where the street cleaners never visit; the city that has great avenues, with areas of recreation for the benefit and pleasure of the class that can pass by in carriages with rubber tires, and the city that has none of these improvements and where not even the municipal orchestra plays; in sum, the city with neighborhoods that never flood and that of neighborhoods which suffer flooding every year." The solution to these inequities was a municipal election system that broadened the electorate and the parties for which they voted to include the entire city and all the groups within it. "It is undoubtable," he argued, "that a municipality constituted by all its inhabitants is not going to support the metropolitan divisions that we presently see; the city of today is the result of past administrations . . . ."[18]

By 1916, despite Socialist efforts for prompt consideration, the Bravo initiative still remained in committee. In July of that year Víctor M. Molina, a newly elected Radical deputy from the capital, proposed his own more sweeping reform. Not only did he seek to expand the city council to sixty persons, but he also included provisions for the direct election of the intendente. This measure, he claimed, emanated from a long-standing Radical commitment to greater municipal autonomy.[19] Two months later, several Progressive Democratic deputies introduced a similar measure.[20] By this time, therefore, all three of the new major parties on the Argentine political scene, or at least some of their representatives,

17 *Diputados* (September 15, 1913), pp. 256–66.   18 *Diputados* (August 6, 1915), p. 535.
19 *Diputados* (July 17, 1916), pp. 832–9.   20 *Diputados* (August 14, 1916), pp. 1279–90.

had come out squarely in favor of a significant reform in the governance of the nation's leading city.

Finally, late in September 1916 the municipal legislation committee of the Chamber of Deputies presented its version of municipal electoral reform. Like many such proposals, it was something of a compromise. Many of the provisions of the Bravo bill were retained, although the size of the city council was reduced from forty to thirty. Provisions to allow foreigners to vote were spelled out in detail, but Molina's idea of an elected intendente was rejected. The new law was approved in general by a large margin, indicating a general consensus in favor of some change. But the voting on particular items produced some legislative fireworks. An amendment by a Progressive Democratic deputy to extend the vote to certain categories of women led to some lively exchanges and was ultimately defeated. An amendment by Molina to require that foreigners be literate in order to be eligible to vote, something not required of Argentine citizens, was approved.

The major discussion, however, revolved around the selection of the intendente. Bravo, a member of the drafting committee, who had dissented from the majority report on this issue, offered an amendment to restore the Molina proposal of direct election of the local executive. In arguing for the amendment, he noted the prevalence of popularly elected mayors in the United States and the generally positive results of this practice. Molina, also referring to North American examples, argued that only through an elected intendente could the city of Buenos Aires enjoy real autonomy and fulfill all the functions of a modern city. Conservative Mariano de Vedia, however, based his objections on potential difficulties in Buenos Aires arising from having an intendente of one party and a president of the republic of another. By September 1916, the Radicals had captured the presidency and were gaining the upper hand over the Socialists in the capital, making that an unlikely eventuality. Nonetheless, it appeared to be a risk some Radicals were unwilling to take. When it came time to vote on the Bravo amendment, eleven Radicals, including Molina, eight Socialists, four Progressive Democrats, and a scattering of others voted in favor whereas fifteen Radicals, nine conservatives, and others voted against. The amendment passed by a single vote. Among those voting against was José Luis Cantilo, Radical deputy from the city of Buenos Aires who was named intendente of the capital in 1919 by President Yrigoyen.[21]

The Senate considered the Chamber's version almost one year later. The Senate measure accepted most of the lower house's recommendations, but rejected the elected intendente. The resulting legislation (law number

21 *Diputados* (September 28–29, 1916), pp. 2481–578.

10,240:Reform of the Organic Municipal Law of the Federal Capital), although retaining the appointed executive, significantly changed the way the city council was chosen. Extending the national eligibility provision to the local level, all Argentine males over the age of eighteen, without restrictions, had both the right and the obligation to vote in elections for the council. Foreign adult males, as in the past, also had the right but not the obligation to vote under certain conditions. Although the limits on these conditions had been lifted somewhat, they did include a literacy requirement and at least two years' residency in the capital.[22] Foreigners over the age of twenty-five with at least four years of residence in the capital could also present themselves as candidates for the council.

The first election under the new procedures called for the selection of a full thirty-man council, an increase of eight in the size of the local legislature. Thereafter, elections would be held every two years to renovate half of the council, with councilmen normally elected to serve four-year terms. For Argentines, the conditions for candidacy included an age limit of twenty-five and, like foreigners, they were required to have at least four years of residence in the capital. Candidates ran citywide rather than from the twenty voting and census districts (circunscripciones) into which Buenos Aires was divided (see Map 2). Voters could cast their ballots for as many candidates as there were vacancies on the council; the total sum received by each participating party would then be divided by this number, which produced a quotient for apportioning seats. Perhaps the most important changes involved procedures and regulations. As at the national level, provisions were made to assure the proper and regular formation of the voter registry and careful and fair scrutiny of the vote count. These were two areas where major abuses had occurred in the past.[23]

As a result of this reform, city government, at least at the council level, would never be the same. The main beneficiaries of the reform were the two parties that had promoted it: the Socialists and the Radicals. Together, they dominated the municipal contests in the capital as they did national elections, regularly controlling at least two-thirds of the seats on the council. The proportionate system of voting, however, also encouraged a large number of minor and not so minor parties to participate, including the Progressive Democrats, various conservative parties, and the fledgling Communist party, all of which had some occasional representation on the council after 1918. Moreover, organizations representing particular local interests began to enter the fray. One of these was the Gente del Teatro, formed to speak for the interests of workers in municipally regulated

22 Foreigners married to Argentine women or fathers of one or more Argentine children were also eligible, as were those who exercised a liberal profession or paid at least fifty pesos a year in taxes. Their eligibility requirements had to be proved at the time of registering for enrollment.
23 *Senadores* (June 19–26, 1917), pp. 102–93 and Bucich Escobar, *Buenos Aires*, pp. 138–40.

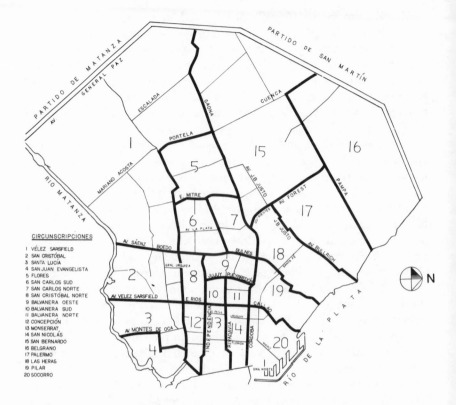

Map 2. Buenos Aires, 1934, by voting district (circunscripción) (drawn by Fredy Merico).

theaters. In 1926 they elected well-known Argentine comedian and actor Florencio Parravicini to the council.

After 1918 the council became clearly more diverse. Although maintaining the citywide selection of councilmen did not necessarily mean a broader geographic distribution of represented interests, many more members from middle-sector and some from working-class backgrounds had seats than before. There were more councilmen, as well, who resided in the poorer southern and newer western districts of the city and others who, either because of genuine personal interest, party commitments, or the need to attract voters from all parts of the city, showed newly emerging concern for the well-being and development of these areas.[24]

24 The nonaristocratic backgrounds of five of the eight Radical commission members who went on to become national deputies already has been noted. Of the twenty-six men who went from council service in the 1918–30 period to serve in the national Chamber of Deputies, twenty, according to Peter Smith's calculations (see note 9, above), were nonaristocrats.

The democratization of the city government was a particular boon to the various neighborhood development societies that sprouted up in these years. Mostly spontaneous cooperative organizations of barrio residents who joined together to push for improvements in their respective localities, these societies numbered in the hundreds by the 1920s. In addition to their own efforts at neighborhood betterment, they constantly besieged the city government, both the intendente and the council, for municipal attention to their particular needs, whether it be a subsidy for a local library or the extension of basic services of street lighting, paving, or cleaning to their respective districts.[25] They represented an increasingly powerful and active lobbying force, which elected officials ignored at their peril.

The increasing democratization, diversity, and debate within the city council helped to hone the political skills of its members. Paralleling the structure and procedures of the national Congress, the council served as a proving and training ground for aspiring politicians to move up the career ladder. Service in the council allowed them to earn their party's recognition for advancement to higher status. In addition to the eight members of the Radical commission who later were elected to the national Chamber of Deputies, sixteen Socialists who served as councilmen between 1919 and 1930 also served in the national Congress as did nine more Radicals (including future president Roberto M. Ortiz) and one conservative.[26]

The first election under the new reform procedures was held on October 6, 1918. Twelve parties participated, including several representing business interests (the Comité Comunal del Comercio, the Confederación Gremial, the Confederación Comercial Popular) and splinter groups of the Socialists (Partido Socialista International, Partido Socialista Argentino) and the Radicals (Juventud Radical Intransigente). The two principal competitors, however, as had been the case in national elections in the capital since 1912, were the mainline Socialists and Radicals.

The Socialists had been taking part in Buenos Aires elections since the 1890s. Over time they had developed effective and practiced campaign techniques and an efficient and hard-working organization to spread the

25 For more on these neighborhood development societies, see Leandro H. Gutiérrez and Luis Alberto Romero, "Sociedades barriales, bibliotecas populares y cultura de los sectores populares: Buenos Aires, 1920–1945," *Desarrollo Económico*, 29, 113 (Buenos Aires: April–June 1989), pp. 33–62. For the actions of one such society and an intimate portrait of the development of an outlying western neighborhood during the interwar period, see Manuel Enrique Pereda, *Nuestra querida Villa Pueyrredón: Narraciones de nuestro barrio y la ciudad* (Buenos Aires, 1985).

26 For a listing of these men, see Richard J. Walter, "Municipal Politics and Government in Buenos Aires, 1918–1930," *Journal of Interamerican Studies and World Affairs*, 16, 2 (May 1974), p. 182.

party message and get out the Socialist vote. This organization was based on neighborhood committees in each of the city's twenty electoral districts, committees that organized lectures, rallies, and cultural and social events. Candidates for office were selected democratically in open party assemblies well in advance of the election dates.[27] In 1918 their candidate list included some who already had served in the national Chamber of Deputies (Francisco Cúneo, Antonio Zaccagnini, and Angel M. Giménez), but it was predominantly composed of younger professionals and skilled workers who were poised to move up the party ladder by using membership on the council as a stepping-stone to elections to the national Congress.[28]

Since the 1890s, the Socialists had issued a specific and comprehensive program for each election and this contest was no exception. The party's platform led off with a call for higher wages, improved working conditions, and recognition of the right to organize for municipal workers and employees. The second and third items advocated tax exemptions for the construction of low-cost housing and gradual municipalization of all markets with price controls set on foodstuffs. The next three articles promised improved health-care services, the end to subsidies for religious entities in municipally run hospitals, encouragement of sports and open-air recreational activities, restrictions on the sale of alcoholic beverages, and the installation of public baths in all barrios. The program also called for opening the Teatro Colón to a wider, popular audience and, significantly, in the light of later developments, "strict control of the companies which provide public services and the private concessions to new companies on the basis of an immediate and direct intervention of the municipality in the administration of such services and participation in the benefits derived." A final article championed the suppression of favoritism and unnecessary expenses in the administration of municipal government and the establishment of a progressive tax on unimproved land within the capital.[29]

The Radicals had only begun to participate in capital elections in 1912. Like the Socialists, the Radicals were governed by an elected central committee in the capital, a committee that oversaw the mechanics of candidate selection and campaigning. They had developed by 1918 a formidable electoral machine based on local neighborhood bosses, or *"caudillos del barrio,"* who provided services and dispensed patronage to

27 For more on Socialist party organization and campaigning, see Walter, *The Socialist Party of Argentina*, pp. 3–157.
28 "Elecciones municipales: El acto ayer en el teatro neuvo; los candidatos del Partido Socialista," *La Vanguardia* (Buenos Aires: September 2, 1918), p. 1.
29 "Partido Socialista: Elecciones municipales de la capital federal, plataforma electoral municipal," *La Vanguardia* (August 29, 1918), p. 1.

party loyalists and potential supporters. Managing local neighborhood committees, the Radical caudillos shared certain characteristics with city bosses of the United States. They did not, however, try to mobilize the potential immigrant voters to support their party, perhaps because naturalization was generally more difficult in Argentina than in the United States. Perhaps, too, the Radicals were reluctant to enfranchise a group, largely working class in composition, that might well have sided with their opponents in the city of Buenos Aires.[30]

After suffering unexpected setbacks in 1913 and 1914, the Radicals began to take the measure of the Socialists. In the 1916 national elections in the federal capital they bested their principal rivals in the congressional contests by more than 17,000 votes and in the March 1918 election to the Chamber of Deputies they won by almost 25,000 votes. In early 1918 the Radicals limited the Socialists to victory in only one of the capital's twenty districts – number 4, which contained the Socialist stronghold of La Boca – and showed signs of capturing a substantial share of the city's working-class vote.[31] These trends, along with the UCR's control of the national government and, through that control, dominance of the local administration, seemed to forecast an easy if not overwhelming win for the Radicals in the October election.

A serious internal dispute, however, undercut these apparent advantages. The dispute involved a division between the more conservative upper-class, office-holding group in the party, which began to object to many of President Yrigoyen's methods and policies – the so-called *Azul*, or Blue, faction – and those persons, mostly middle-class and holding secondary leadership positions, who supported and identified with the president. The division delayed the Radicals' selection of candidates until the end of September; as late as October 3 there were reports that the party would abstain from the election altogether.[32]

Responding in part to Azul faction criticism that the party lacked a coherent program, the Radical candidates to the council ran on a nine-point

---

30 For an analysis of the UCR's organization in the city of Buenos Aires, see David Rock, "Machine Politics in Buenos Aires and the Argentine Radical Party," *Journal of Latin American Studies*, 4, 2 (November 1972), pp. 233–56. Roberto F. Giusti, who was a Socialist party candidate for the council in 1918, in a 1971 interview claimed that the Socialists did not have local caudillos, although there were elements that dominated in some centers, especially before elections and in the party meetings to select candidates. These, however, seemed to have been certain men who played a particular role within the confines of party affairs rather than fulfill the broader functions of the Radical caudillos. Instituto Torcuato Di Tella Oral Interview with Roberto F. Giusti (Buenos Aires: March 17 and 24, 1971), pp. 4–5.

31 Those elections and their results are examined in more detail in Richard J. Walter, "Elections in the city of Buenos Aires during the First Yrigoyen Administration: Social Class and Political Preferences," *HAHR*, 58, 4 (November 1978), pp. 595–624.

32 *La Prensa* (October 3, 1918), p. 11.

platform of municipal improvements. Although it was neither as clear nor comprehensive as the Socialist program, it echoed many of the same main points, including measures to encourage the construction of inexpensive housing, the lowering of costs on basic necessities, more city services and benefits for the working classes, and a tax reform to decrease the burden on the bulk of the population and increase the share provided by wealthier property owners. In their few days of campaigning, Radical candidates emphasized their commitment to improve public health and overall conditions in the city's poorer districts and to reduce the cost of living.[33]

These efforts notwithstanding, the internal dispute took its toll. When the votes were counted, the Socialists had eked out a narrow victory over the Radicals by a margin of 838 votes: 47,977 tallies to 47,139. In the municipal contest the Socialists, at least momentarily, regained their advantage in working-class districts and among the working-class groups among whom they had lost ground earlier in the year. For the Radicals, the results represented a 27,061 vote decline from their performance earlier in March, a decline primarily attributable to both their intramural disagreements and, perhaps, their taking the contest too lightly.[34]

A total of 141,897 votes was cast in this first postreform municipal election, ten times as many as in the last previous council election of November 1913. The total number of registered voters came to 220,980, including 13,625 foreigners. Turnout was 65 percent, again an enormous increase over 1913. Although interest and participation in the council's municipal elections would never be as high as for national contests, from 1918 on they too became important ingredients in the increasingly active, open, and democratic political life of the capital city. As an immediate result of this election, ten Socialists and ten Radicals were chosen to the council. The ten remaining positions went to seven other parties, including one each to the Partido Socialista Argentino and the Partido Socialista Internacional. Thanks to the system of proportional representation, several parties won places on the council with less than 4,000 total votes.[35] (See Appendix, Table A.2.)

A profile of the electorate to which the parties appealed can be constructed from material in the third national census of 1914 and a survey of the voter registry of the capital for 1918. The voter registry, listing all voters by name, date of birth, address, and occupation, is a particularly

---

33 Walter, "Elections," p. 617.   34 Ibid., pp. 600 and 617–18.

35 The other parties represented were the Comité Comunal del Comercio (three seats), the Partido Constitucional (two seats), the Comité del Progreso Comunal (one seat), the Confederación Gremial (one seat), and the Partido Unitario (one seat). *VTCD* (January 1, 1919). Election results from *La Vanguardia* (Buenos Aires: November 1, 1918), p. 1.

valuable source. It not only provides basic information for determining the social class composition of the city's electorate, but, in grouping voters by district, it also allows for judgments about the social ecology of the city. Only adult Argentine males were listed in the registry; in 1918 they represented slightly more then 13 percent of the total population of Buenos Aires. Nonetheless, as one of the few available sources of this kind of information (given the absence of manuscripts from the 1914 census), it still can be used profitably and with some precision to determine the specific zones of the city in which particular occupational groups lived, bolstering more impressionistic evidence on this point.[36]

First, as the census pointed out, the capital electorate was an extraordinarily literate one. In 1916, over 96 percent of the capital's voters were deemed able to read and write, compared with a national average of 50 percent.[37] Residing in Latin America's main publishing center, porteño voters had access to an enormous amount and range of written materials on a wide array of issues. In addition to the extensive political coverage provided by the mainstream press like *La Nación* and *La Prensa*, the major parties also had their own organs – for the Radicals *La Época* and for the Socialists *La Vanguardia* – each with a substantial distribution. Magazines, reviews, pamphlets, and small neighborhood periodicals were also abundant and easily accessible.

Second, the electorate was clearly more middle- and upper-class in composition than was the city as a whole. Using the same categories and classifications that were employed previously to determine the social structure of the city in 1914 (Table 1.2), an analysis of the occupations listed by the capital's voters in 1918 shows that 53 percent had white-collar, middle-class positions, 8 percent were of the upper class, and 38 percent of the working class (see Table 3.1). This contrasted markedly with the pattern for the city overall, in which two out of every three residents were considered to be working class. Moreover, skilled workers predominated within the working-class electorate (72 percent of all enrolled) to a significantly greater degree than for the city as a whole (40 percent of all listed). In the citywide population, almost 27 percent of the

36 República Argentina, *Registro cívico de la nacion: Padrón definitivo de electores, Distrito electoral de la Capital, 1917–1918*, 4 vols. (Buenos Aires, 1918). Some of the difficulties involved in using this source are discussed in Walter, "Elections," 604, n. 22. The following analysis differs somewhat from the material in that article. Although the categories suggested by Mark D. Szuchman and Eugene F. Sofer ("The State of Occupational Stratification Studies in Argentina," *LARR*, 11:1 [1976], pp. 159–72) have still provided the basic framework for organizing the occupations listed in the registry, two main groups, students and financiers, have been moved from separate categories (Szuchman and Sofer place them under "miscellaneous") to middle nonmanual or middle class. I have also placed the "high nonmanual" group, containing estancieros and hacendados, in the general upper-class rather than in the middle-class category.

37 *Tercer censo nacional*, vol. 4, pp. 480–94.

Table 3.1. Social class composition of the electorate of the city of Buenos Aires, by voting district, 1918[a]

District	Occupational category										Class (%)		
	01 (%)	02 (%)	04 (%)	06 (%)	07 (%)	08 (%)	09 (%)	10 (%)	11 (%)	Total	01–04	06–07	08–11
1	454 (6)	794 (10)	2,504 (32)	2,736 (35)	843 (11)	79 (1)	157 (2)	69 (1)	151 (1)	7,787	48	46	4
2	292 (4)	873 (13)	2,457 (38)	1,933 (30)	622 (10)	69 (1)	146 (2)	37 (1)	80 (1)	6,509	55	40	4
3	451 (4)	991 (9)	3,359 (30)	4,688 (42)	1,106 (10)	135 (1)	173 (2)	166 (1)	126 (1)	11,195	43	52	4
4	263 (3)	2,030 (22)	3,276 (35)	2,742 (29)	741 (8)	47 (1)	80 (1)	57 (1)	103 (1)	9,339	60	37	3
5	111 (1)	426 (5)	1,912 (23)	4,112 (49)	996 (12)	167 (2)	289 (3)	181 (2)	188 (2)	8,382	29	61	7
6	137 (2)	504 (6)	2,783 (35)	3,074 (39)	864 (11)	100 (1)	182 (2)	102 (1)	121 (1)	7,867	43	50	4
7	91 (1)	508 (7)	2,252 (32)	2,828 (40)	809 (12)	103 (1)	192 (3)	140 (2)	103 (1)	7,026	40	52	6
8	146 (2)	589 (7)	2,759 (31)	3,592 (41)	952 (11)	185 (2)	307 (4)	136 (2)	104 (1)	8,770	40	52	8
9	130 (1)	428 (5)	1,989 (25)	3,398 (46)	1,159 (14)	174 (2)	262 (3)	247 (3)	98 (1)	7,885	31	60	8
10	78 (2)	180 (4)	965 (23)	1,934 (46)	616 (15)	107 (3)	130 (3)	154 (4)	49 (1)	4,213	29	61	10
11	59 (1)	161 (3)	798 (17)	2,334 (49)	667 (14)	153 (3)	184 (4)	296 (6)	88 (1)	4,740	21	63	13
12	313 (4)	467 (6)	1,663 (20)	4,158 (50)	954 (12)	208 (3)	186 (2)	239 (3)	90 (1)	8,278	30	62	8
13	244 (3)	317 (4)	1,097 (13)	4,442 (53)	1,155 (14)	276 (3)	261 (3)	467 (6)	77 (1)	8,336	20	67	12
14	90 (1)	207 (3)	872 (11)	3,825 (50)	1,264 (17)	394 (5)	265 (3)	650 (9)	62 (1)	7,629	15	67	17
15	252 (4)	662 (10)	2,783 (41)	2,054 (30)	547 (8)	78 (1)	154 (2)	57 (1)	176 (3)	6,763	55	38	4
16	261 (3)	602 (7)	2,234 (26)	3,114 (36)	1,691 (20)	142 (2)	280 (3)	187 (2)	151 (2)	8,662	36	56	7
17	226 (3)	604 (8)	2,437 (34)	2,658 (37)	603 (8)	144 (2)	368 (4)	153 (2)	108 (2)	7,301	45	48	8
18	284 (1)	1,010 (9)	3,689 (32)	4,420 (38)	1,101 (10)	247 (2)	397 (3)	263 (2)	154 (1)	11,565	43	48	7
19	184 (2)	696 (7)	2,433 (24)	4,669 (45)	1,126 (11)	371 (4)	332 (3)	396 (4)	137 (1)	10,344	33	56	11
20	80 (1)	290 (5)	832 (15)	2,581 (46)	683 (12)	357 (6)	129 (2)	587 (11)	48 (1)	5,587	21	58	19
Total	4,146 (3)	12,339 (8)	43,094 (27)	65,292 (41)	18,499 (12)	3,536 (2)	4,474 (3)	4,584 (3)	2,214 (1)	158,168	38	53	8

[a] Key: See Table 1.2.

Source: República Argentina, Registro cívico de la nación; Padrón definitivo de electores, Distrito electoral de la Capital, 1917–1918, 4 vols. (Buenos Aires, 1918). Categories 03 and 05 (rural semiskilled and rural skilled) listed in Table 1.2 have been included in category 11 in this table.

total were menial and semiskilled service workers, whereas within the electorate only 11 percent were so categorized.

Third, like the total population, certain occupations predominated within the various categories. Day laborers and peons made up the menials, whereas butchers, barbers, and drivers made up much of the semiskilled service category. Among the skilled workers, bakers, bricklayers, carpenters, electricians, ironworkers, machinists, mechanics, painters, tailors, and telegraph operators were most numerous. The single largest group of any category were white-collar *empleados* or employees, representing 31 percent of the electorate.[38] The second and third most numerous, also within the white-collar category, were merchants (*comerciantes*) and students, making up, respectively, 11 and 10 percent of the total. Lawyers, doctors, and estancieros and hacendados were most prominent within the upper-class group.

Fourth, representatives of every social group in the electorate could be found spread throughout the city and in each of the twenty voting and census districts. Socially, and ethnically, most areas of the city seemed to be marked more by heterogeneity than homogeneity. Nonetheless, the distribution of those groups, as Tables 3.1 and 3.2 indicate, reflected certain patterns of residential differentiation based on class. As other accounts imply, the greatest concentration of working-class voters, and by implication the working-class population, could be found in the southern (districts 2–4), western (1, 15–18), and certain central (6–8) areas of the city. The district with the single largest concentration of working-class voters (60 percent of the total) was number 4, encompassing the Socialist party stronghold of La Boca. In contrast, section 5, the Flores district and a bastion of strength of the Radical party, had one of the highest proportions of middle-class voters (61 percent of the total) of any district in the city. This was also the case for central and northern districts 11 through 14 and 19 and 20. Districts 14 and 20, including much of

38 The designation *empleado*, or employee, is a troublesome one that may obscure some major class differences. An employee at a certain level in a large business, for example, could enjoy a much higher status than a clerk in a small store or government office. Nonetheless, as the classification itself is the only existing information, it seems reasonably safe to assume that these were mostly of the middle-class, white-collar category. Another problem lies in determining how many employees actually worked for the government. In the registry, 44,166 citizens identified themselves as unspecified employees, 3,199 as commercial employees, only 1,237 as national employees, and 222 as municipal employees, for a total of 48,824. The 1914 census, however, counting Argentine males over the age of fourteen (rather than age eighteen, as cited in the registry), listed 7,043 commercial employees (including 842 railroad employees and 188 streetcar employees), 14,313 unspecified employees, and 33,775 governmental or administrative employees for a total of 55,131 (*Tercer censo nacional*, vol. 4, pp. 201–12). Using the census information, it would seem, then, that about two-thirds of the total employees in the registry were probably public employees, even though they did not specifically identify themselves as such.

Table 3.2. Selected occupations of voters enrolled in the 1918 registry of the city of Buenos Aires, by voting district

District	Employees	Students	Merchants	Lawyers	Estancieros/ Hacendados	Seamen	Physicians	Financiers	Day Laborers	Others
1	2,320	380	703	14	23	7	9	39	35	4,257
2	1,646	256	514	1	9	11	8	34	53	3,977
3	3,797	823	1,037	19	64	55	51	61	114	5,174
4	2,342	357	722	5	4	1,101	13	14	52	4,729
5	3,211	871	861	27	71	9	31	111	19	3,171
6	2,421	619	760	10	18	2	22	76	21	3,918
7	2,161	625	743	20	34	2	38	49	27	3,327
8	2,846	711	875	11	42	6	34	54	34	4,157
9	2,607	944	1,081	35	80	8	59	67	64	3,140
10	1,401	510	569	24	48	1	37	43	28	1,552
11	1,360	960	607	72	74	2	89	57	34	1,485
12	3,203	915	875	42	121	36	67	71	63	2,885
13	3,125	1,277	1,063	143	182	18	112	88	65	2,263
14	2,641	1,115	1,115	193	241	9	205	145	46	1,882
15	1,686	311	508	3	15	4	10	29	125	4,072
16	2,373	670	1,616	36	58	6	31	69	121	3,682
17	2,034	562	541	36	40	7	19	57	118	3,787
18	3,279	1,064	977	68	88	11	41	109	147	5,781
19	2,832	1,769	976	185	222	6	118	138	94	3,994
20	1,539	1,023	561	261	282	6	157	117	37	1,604
Total	48,824	15,762	16,704	1,205	1,716	1,307	1,151	1,428	1,297	68,837

Source: See Table 3.1.

the downtown and Barrio Norte, also had the highest proportion of upper-class voters – 17 and 19 percent, respectively – in the city.

A look at the location of some specific occupational groups throws further light on those concentrations. Fifty-seven percent of the electorate's slaughterhouse workers (*matarifes*), for example, were located in the Mataderos section of district 1, close to several meat-packing plants. As Table 3.2 shows, 84 percent of the merchant seamen (*marineros*) could be found in the fourth district of La Boca. Although skilled and semiskilled workers were found throughout the city, these concentrations suggest that at least certain groups of laborers lived close to their particular places of employment.

There were relatively few students in working-class districts. Over 50 percent could be found in central and northern sections 11 through 14 and 18 through 20. This concentration reinforced the impression that, in the year of the university reform movement, most university students in Buenos Aires – who presumably were over eighteen years of age – were from the middle and upper classes.[39] Middle-class employees and merchants, two of the three largest groups, could be found in substantial numbers in all districts. So, too, could financiers, although better than 40 percent of these were located in sections 5, 14, and 18 through 20.

The city electorate's upper-class landowners and professionals clearly preferred to reside in the downtown center and northern areas. Of the 1,205 lawyers on the voter list, two out of three lived in districts 13 and 14 and 19 and 20. Fifty-four percent of the estancieros and hacendados and 51 percent of the physicians could be found in the same districts.[40] It is striking to observe, as Table 3.2 illustrates, that downtown district 14 was home to 193 lawyers whereas the then sparsely populated but rapidly growing western district 15 had only three lawyers. The same stark discrepancy could be seen with regard to landowners (241 to 15) and physicians (205 to 10).

Political party leaders by 1918 had developed a clear and sophisticated understanding of the social composition and distribution of the Buenos Aires electorate and often tailored their appeals accordingly. Both Radicals and Socialists, as well as minor parties, tried to develop programs and policies to encourage coalitions of middle- and working-class voters. At both the national and local levels, elected and appointed officials responded to specific requests from particular districts of the city with their

39 For more on the university reform movement, see Richard J. Walter, *Student Politics in Argentina: The University Reform and Its Effects, 1918–1964* (New York, 1968).
40 For more information on the residences of the city's elite landowning families, especially along Calle Florida and in the Barrio Norte at this time, see Walter, "Socioeconomic Growth," pp. 108–11.

social composition firmly in mind. During the years between 1918 and 1930 the Radicals had some clear advantages in these matters. Most important, they controlled the national administration and with it the power to dispense favors, particularly in the form of government jobs, and to make and influence decisions that would directly aid their constituents. Control of the national government also meant control of the policies and action of the municipal executive through appointment of the intendente, thereby broadening and deepening the influence of the party throughout the city. Finally, the predominantly middle-class nature of the capital's electorate promised continued support for a party that from its origins had a prominent sector of middle-class representatives among its leadership, a sector that became even more prominent with the election of Yrigoyen and with the passing of time. The Radicals' appeal to the Argentine-born sons of first-generation immigrants, increasingly entering the electorate in these years, was another potent factor in the party's favor.

Despite these Radical advantages, the Socialists managed to provide persistent and often formidable competition in the struggle for support from the city's electorate. Maintaining their backing in working-class districts, the Socialists also managed to attract some middle-class adherents of their own. Taking advantage of Radical divisions in the mid-1920s, they scored a few surprising election victories at both the national and local levels. Although the Radicals won most contests rather handily during the decade, the Socialists continued to maintain a substantial presence in the national Congress and an even stronger one in the city council. At the municipal level, they often combined with minor parties, especially Progressive Democrats, to challenge successfully both the Radicals on the council and the Radical intendente. On their own, or working with others, they helped to make the council and city government something quite different from what it had been before 1918.

4

A new council

The first meeting of the new democratically elected city council was held on January 1, 1919, just a few days before the outbreak of the "semana trágica." The first order of business was to elect presiding officers; Radical Saturnino J. García Anido won the post of council president when the Socialist candidate, following party procedure, refused to vote for himself. The election of a Socialist might have proved interesting in light of the fact that the president of the council assumed the chief executive office if the intendente resigned before his term expired. A Socialist, Angel Giménez, and a conservative, Alejandro Mohr, were selected as the two vice-presidents of the council, with Giménez slated to become president if García Anido should become intendente.[1]

Radical and Socialist dominance of the city council irrevocably changed its nature, its tone, and its activity. The role of the Socialists was particularly important. Although representing only one-third of the council, they easily took up two-thirds of its time and introduced most of the initiatives for consideration. Debates on matters like annual approval of the budget, which in the past often had only been pro forma, became extended marathon sessions, thanks to Socialist scrutiny of virtually every item. The transcripts of council meetings, usually a slim one or two volumes before 1918, grew to massive multivolume sets, largely to transcribe Socialist speeches and intervention.

The Socialist bloc of concejales performed in much the same fashion as the party's deputies in the national Congress. Although no one was assigned to an explicit division of responsibility, each Socialist concentrated on matters that particularly interested him. A chosen leader of the bloc usually arranged caucuses and discussed strategy for tackling matters before the council. Like the party's deputies, concejales had to possess energy, dedication, and stamina. Most worked full time at the job, without an office or secretary, and, during the early 1920s, without compensation. The Socialist councilmen were required to make weekly tours

1 VTCD (January 1, 1919), pp. 1–2.

of particular barrios in the city in order to observe and listen to the problems and complaints of their constituents. The Socialists were also expected to give regular lectures, which, if held on the outskirts of Buenos Aires, entailed a long and tiring trip, sometimes by public transportation, other times on foot through dusty or muddy unpaved streets. Finally, the councilmen often had to study esoteric subjects that became part of council debate and were far removed from their training in law, medicine, or journalism.[2]

Socialist initiatives in the council were based primarily on the party's municipal electoral platform of 1918. In the early months of 1919 Socialist councilmen introduced measures intended to regulate prostitution in the city and to establish free public dispensaries for the treatment of venereal diseases, to set an eight-hour day and a minimum wage for all municipal employees, to designate May 1 as an official paid holiday, and to prohibit the sale of lead-based paints and night work in bakeries. The Socialists introduced into the Buenos Aires city legislature the same agenda of social issues that they had presented to the national Congress beginning in 1912. The Radicals often echoed these initiatives with their own proposals that similarly reflected their national program.

Although in most of their initiatives the Socialists dealt with the capital at large, they took pains to consider the needs of particular constituents and specific areas of the city. A typical example was an April 28, 1919 resolution from Socialist Councilman Antonio Zaccagnini, who lived in La Boca, to improve the pavement and water drainage in the barrio of Nueva Pompeya. Located at the southeastern edge of the city, the district was one of those most susceptible to flooding from the nearby Riachuelo River. Following a personal tour of the area that was prompted by a request from the local neighborhood association for assistance, Zaccagnini charged city officials had long ignored the predominantly working-class area. The lack of paved streets and proper sewers, he claimed, led not only to inconveniences for pedestrians, but also to the creation of stagnant pools, which bred diseases that could affect both Nueva Pompeya and other parts of the city. Those were matters, he concluded, which demanded immediate municipal attention and action.[3]

This was but the first of many Socialist responses to petitions from local neighborhood groups. Often, as in this case, members of a barrio association would request that a councilman visit their area to view conditions firsthand and transmit their complaints to the council and the

---

2 From a personal interview with Américo Ghioldi (Buenos Aires: March 17, 1971), conducted as part of my research on the Socialist party. Ghioldi served on both the council and in the national Congress from the 1920s to the 1940s and was a major figure in the Socialist party until his death in 1980.

3 *VTCD* (April 28, 1919), p. 748.

intendente. Petitions and written statements calling for improvements and signed by the interested citizens of the locale usually accompanied these requests. Although Socialist councilmen were the most frequent transmitters of barrio petitions, especially from working-class districts, Radical councilmen and others also served this function as the council opened up and became more responsive to an ever-broader constituency.

During the first term of the new council, the representatives of the two Socialist factions, the "Argentines" and the "Internationalists," supported most of the main party's initiatives. Occasionally, too, the Radicals and the Socialists would collaborate on a projected ordinance. Generally, however, the ten Socialists and their two allies found themselves in the minority, outvoted by the ten Radicals and eight conservatives. As a result, few Socialist projects became law. At the end of the first term only two significant Socialist-sponsored measures were enacted: one, a Zaccagnini resolution to establish vacation camps for underprivileged city children; another, a Socialist proposal to compensate garbage workers for half of their salary lost in a recent strike.[4]

The major political rivalry within the council was between Socialists and Radicals, and in these sessions the most bitter differences between them arose during debate over streetcar fares. This debate was the major issue of the council's first term and became the principal and most publicized concern of the council throughout the 1920s. I will present it here in some detail because it occupied much of the Concejo's attention during the 1920s, provided the framework within which much of the Radical–Socialist interaction occurred, and was the major municipal issue eventually to stimulate a broader national concern over the role and control of foreign capital investment in the country.

The issue first arose in April 1919. In that month, both the Anglo–Argentine Tramway company and the Lacroze company, which dominated the all-important streetcar service in Buenos Aires, requested of the city government, as was required by their concessions, to increase their fares from ten centavos to twelve centavos a ride. The ten-centavo fare had been in effect since 1904, but the companies claimed that the increase was necessitated by the demands of a new national law, approved in March of that year, calling on the owners of "private companies of tramways, telephones, gas and electricity" to contribute to a pension fund for their employees. The tramway concerns argued that such contributions represented a new demand unforeseen in the original concession agreement. Later arguments cited higher costs for electricity, higher prices for rolling stock, losses of revenue during labor disturbances after 1917, and destruction of trams – a favorite target for urban rioters – as additional

4 The ordinances for 1919, as for every year, are listed in the appendix to *VTCD* (January 1920).

factors making continued operation and expansion impossible without a higher price for each ride.[5]

Shortly after the submission of this request, the employees of Lacroze and the Anglo went on strike for increased wages and company recognition of their union. At this point, both the strike and the twelve-centavo request became a matter of discussion in the council. Under Socialist prompting, Intendente Llambías appointed a five-man commission to investigate, and, if possible, arbitrate the strike. At the same time, Llambías recommended that the council act favorably on the fare-increase request. After three weeks the strike was settled, with the company agreeing to a salary increase, but refusing to recognize the union or to rehire men laid off during the walkout. The fare proposal, meanwhile, was discussed in committee and presented to the full council on January 7, 1920 in extraordinary session.

The Radical–conservative majority on the committee approved the increase under certain conditions: the setting of an eight-hour day and minimum wage for company employees; the submission of labor disputes to the intendente for arbitration; an employer contribution of an amount representing 8 percent of each worker's salary to the pension fund; and submission to the municipality of a complete financial statement within two years of the increase taking effect. The higher rate was to last for three years, at the end of which it would be renegotiated.

The Socialist councilmen determined to make the increase a political issue. On January 5, the party held a public meeting to protest the proposed twelve-centavo ticket. The Socialist representative on the council committee, Alejandro Comolli, on January 7 stated his dissent with the majority report. The increase should not be granted, he argued, because the wartime emergency that had caused higher prices was now over, because an ever-increasing number of passengers would cancel previous debts, and because the true financial status of the companies was inadequately documented. Considering the alleged unfair labor practices and deteriorating services of the companies, Comolli concluded, eventual municipalization of the privately owned lines seemed advisable.

Radical Pedro I. Imaz responded to the Socialist arguments in defense of the majority position. The favorable decision, he claimed, was based on a careful review of the companies' profits and losses by municipal accountants and a basic agreement that new salary and pension demands justified the increase if service were to continue and expand to meet the growing needs of the city. Moreover, few signs pointed to lower prices for fuel and electricity after the war, nor was there necessarily any correlation

---

5 The Anglo also claimed that in the past few years its profit margin had been too small to allow dividend payments to stockholders. *RRP*, 1440 (July 11, 1919), p. 89.

between a higher number of passengers and the size of profit margins. Municipalization of urban public transport, he concluded, had not worked well in other cities and any attempt to do so presently in Buenos Aires would send the municipality deep into debt.[6]

The debate went on for three full days. Sessions lasted late into nights made oppressive by the summer of Buenos Aires. Tempers flared and bitter words flew through the muggy air. Imaz, with frequent assistance from fellow Radical Roberto M. Ortiz, was the principal defender of the increase. All Socialists joined Comolli in attacking the decision. They charged the tramway companies with exploiting the Argentine public for the benefit of British stockholders. Whereas the increase meant a higher dividend abroad, they claimed, it meant for the working family of six in Buenos Aires an extra eighty-six pesos per year for transportation (assuming all six took one round trip per day). Encouraging the remittance of greater profits abroad, the Socialists pointed out, was a strange position for the supposedly nationalist Radicals to support. It was a "very special kind of nationalism," they asserted, to ask "the porteño public to contribute two extra centavos every trip to please the British." They implied that President Yrigoyen favored the companies' position and that the Radical councilmen were simply following the president's orders, a charge the Radical delegation hotly denied.[7] Finally, the Socialists observed that municipalization of transport under Radical auspices would indeed not be much of an improvement. However, with the creation of an elected intendente, who would undoubtedly be Socialist, public control of urban transport would be feasible. As Comolli put it, "I am convinced that after the first mistakes, which could persist for two or three years, the municipalization of the service will proceed perfectly, especially under a popular council, composed of genuine representatives of the people, which will manage affairs efficiently and adopt the most appropriate means of administration."[8]

Voting on the majority report took place as dawn broke over the city on January 10. Eight conservatives and seven Radicals voted in its favor, eleven Socialists against.[9] The Socialists lost the immediate struggle, but adopted a stance that could lead to future political benefits. "The tramway,"

---

6 VTCD (January 7, 1920), pp. 149–57.

7 Adding some substance to the Socialists' charge was a statement by the chairman of the Anglo's board at the annual general meeting of the company's stockholders, held in London on June 29, 1920. On that occasion, the chairman observed that in a message from Yrigoyen to the company, relayed by prominent banker Ernesto Tornquist, "the President of the Republic stated, in most friendly and unqualified terms, that he welcomed British capital in the Argentine, and would afford it the greatest possible protection." RRP, 1496 (August 6, 1920), p. 367. Although this may not have been an outright presidential endorsement of the fare increase, it was certainly, from the company's point of view, the next best thing to it.

8 VTCD (January 9, 1920), pp. 199–223.   9 Ibid., p. 227.

as Comolli noted in his report, was "the essentially popular means of locomotion." Almost everyone in the city used the streetcars and the fare increase touched many consumers. A Radical executive, with the sanction of a majority of Radicals on the council, had approved this increase. The 1920s were a decade when public attention in Argentina was gradually turning to the role of companies that were owned and operated by foreign interests. Discontent, articulated by political leaders, increasingly focused on the financial arrangements of these companies, their alleged neglect of public welfare for private interests, and the deterioration of service. The Radicals had captured the antiforeign banner at the national level with a strong position on Argentinian control of the republic's petroleum reserves. The activities of urban transport companies, which had more immediate impact on the general public, afforded the Socialists an opportunity to adopt the nationalist stance at the local level, an opportunity they were quick to take.

About one month prior to the vote on the fare increase, Yrigoyen had named his close political ally, José Luis Cantilo, as his new intendente. Cantilo, unlike his predecessor, Llambías, was by 1919 an experienced and highly regarded politician and administrator. A Radical loyalist from his youth, he had served in the legislature of the province of Buenos Aires, as chairman of the party's central committee in the city of Buenos Aires, and as an elected national deputy from the capital for two four-year terms, beginning in 1912. In 1917, Yrigoyen had appointed Cantilo to one of the most important positions in his administration, that of federal intervenor in the province of Buenos Aires, where he would return as elected governor in 1922.[10] During the turbulent labor agitation of this period, Cantilo also often served as Yrigoyen's main agent for resolving various disputes.

Like many distinguished porteño politicians, Cantilo had studied at the prestigious Colegio Nacional de Buenos Aires, located in the same block as the Concejo Deliberante. Unlike many of his colleagues, however, Cantilo failed to complete the common second step up the political career ladder, abandoning the study of law at the local university to concentrate on journalism and history. Associated with several Radical-influenced publications, in 1915 he became the editor of the party's principal newspaper, *La Epoca.* Like most intendentes, Cantilo was, in

10 Yrigoyen sought to change the balance in the national Senate to the Radicals' favor by using the federal power of intervention to replace local governors and legislatures with his own loyalists. The province of Buenos Aires, the largest in the country, was an early and primary target of this policy. For more on Cantilo as intervenor and governor, see Richard J. Walter, *The Province of Buenos Aires and Argentine Politics, 1912–1943* (Cambridge, 1985), pp. 47–9 and 65–74.

Peter Smith's terms, a "definite aristocrat": he had married into the Achával family, was a member of the Jockey Club, and owned a productive estancia. When named intendente, he was residing in a large downtown home at Paraguay 920 where he and his wife raised eight children.[11]

An able and experienced administrator, enjoying the full support of the president of the nation, Cantilo proved to be a strong and effective city executive. Like many intendentes, Cantilo sought to keep in close touch with the city's problems and his constituents by regular tours of various neighborhoods and on-site inspections of locations such as markets, movie houses, and garbage dumps to determine how the city should best operate and regulate them. Tall and heavy set, he cut an imposing figure in his superbly tailored topcoat, walking stick and gloves, a cigarette jutting out of a mouth framed by a neatly trimmed moustache. He also proved to be a good listener to the opinions and complaints of the many porteños he interviewed on these tours, often transforming their requests into initiatives and resolutions for either direct executive action or council consideration.

The major problems Cantilo faced had to do with another increase in the cost of living, especially for foodstuffs. Working with the council to bring these costs down, he initiated a number of measures, including a scheme to import meat directly into the city from regions of the country where cattle raising was cheaper. He also sought to regulate the sale of foodstuffs by cracking down on illegal and unfair pricing practices; having food prices in free markets openly posted; initiating, in concert with the national Congress, a campaign to confiscate the huge quantity of adulterated food that had found its way into Buenos Aires during the cost crisis; and implementing, among other measures, the imposition of heavy fines in order to assure an end to this practice.[12]

While Cantilo and the council fought to control the cost of food in the capital, the national Congress addressed the other major culprit in the escalating cost of living – rents charged for residential and commercial property; these had sometimes doubled or tripled over the past few years. With Radical and Socialist congressmen from the capital leading the way, the Congress eventually approved in 1921 a law that froze rents throughout the republic for the next two years at the level they had been on January 1, 1920. To mollify owners, separate legislation allowed them a wider latitude in forcing the eviction of renters who failed to meet their obligations. To encourage continual building in the postwar era, and to meet the problem of scarce housing, which was seen as a principal factor

11 Félix Luna, "José Luis Cantilo," in *Tres Intendentes*, pp. 47–52 and *Quien es Quien*, 1939, p. 89.
12 Luna, "José Luis Cantilo," pp. 52–8 and *State Records* (May 15, 1920), 835.00/203.

in the increase of rent in the capital, new buildings in Buenos Aires were exempt from construction taxes for the next five years and customs duties on building material were eliminated for the same period.[13]

The second set of postreform municipal elections was held in Buenos Aires on November 21, 1920. Fresh from a comfortable triumph in the capital's national deputy election earlier in the year, the Radicals' approach to this local contest was more cohesive and they were better prepared than they had been two years earlier. The Radicals turned attacks on the Socialists into the centerpiece of their campaign, accusing them, in a familiar refrain, of being "obstructionists" on the council and seeking to exploit the Socialist party's intense debate at the time over adherence to the Third International by linking it to the "Bolshevist threat," which had emerged as a major issue during the "semana trágica." President Yrigoyen sought to lend a helping hand to his party by touring flood-stricken Nueva Pompeya one week before the election and ordering Cantilo to do all he could to aid the victims and prevent future disasters. The Radicals also stressed their efforts to control prices over the previous months.

The Socialists continued to depend on their superb organization and their clearly articulated municipal program. Countering the doubts the Radicals had cast on their nationalist credentials, the Socialists hit hard on the governing party's vote in favor of higher streetcar fares. Indeed, throughout the year the Socialists had highlighted this issue, giving it prominent coverage in *La Vanguardia*, and accusing the Radicals not only of favoring the Anglo, which they argued was reaping unprecedented profits as a result of the council's decision, but also of contributing significantly to the rising cost of living in the city.[14]

These arguments apparently swayed few voters. This time the Radicals defeated the Socialists by a total of 56,848 votes to 52,082, bettering their 1918 performance by almost 10,000 votes. The Socialists held on to their strength among the working class, carrying districts 1 through 4, 7, 8, and 15, but failing to cut into the Radical hold on the mainly middle-class

13 This was an issue, like municipal electoral reform, on which most Radicals, Socialists, and Progressive Democrats in the Chamber of Deputies collaborated. In the various votes on these initiatives, the majority of the representation of these parties (and in the case of the Socialists, all of their deputies) stood firm in their advocacy of the legislation and successfully resisted the efforts of the Senate to dilute their proposals. *Diputados* (July 29, 1920), pp. 668–91; (August 3, 1920), pp. 718–48; (August 4, 1920), pp. 760–800; (August 5, 1920), pp. 835–79; (August 19, 1920), pp. 334–408; (April 29, 1921), pp. 855–8; and (June 9, 1921), pp. 472–87.

14 For example, "El aumento de las tarifas tranviarias en el Concejo Deliberante," *La Vanguardia* (April 10, 1920), p. 1 and "Las ganancias del Anglo Argentino: nunca fueron mayores que en 1919," *La Vanguardia* (September 4, 1920), p. 1.

districts of the city.[15] The Progressive Democrats, participating in the city election for the first time, gained about 20,000 votes, which gave them three seats on the council. Capturing two seats, with a little less than 6,000 votes, were Juan Ferlini and José F. Penelón of the Partido Socialista Internacional, soon to be the Argentine Communist party. Other elected councilmen of note were Pedro Bidegain, the Radical caudillo of the party's stronghold of Flores (district 5) and, chosen for the second time, British businessman Henry C. Thompson for the Unión Nacional del Comercio.[16] The fact that the council now contained a well-known Radical caudillo del barrio, two communists, a British businessman, numerous Socialist party representatives from humble backgrounds, as well as several young professionals, attested dramatically to both the diversity of the city's legislative branch and the notable changes in its composition since 1918.

Because of resignation and the redistribution of seats following the election, the Socialists actually gained more places on the council (their share grew from ten to eleven seats), whereas the Radicals maintained ten positions. In addition to being able usually to count on the support of the "Internationalists," the Socialists increasingly allied with the Progressive Democrats to gain a slight majority of the council votes on certain issues. This balance sometimes forced the Radicals to depend heavily on their conservative allies to block Socialist initiatives or to follow the practice common to all legislative parties that find themselves at a disadvantage and simply not appear for scheduled sessions, thereby preventing the formation of a quorum and stymieing any action at all.

The Socialist advantage was seen first when one of the party, physician Alfredo L. Spinetto, was elected president of the council. The Socialists voted as a solid bloc on all issues that came up for a roll call (and presumably for those that did not as well). In almost all cases they were on the opposite side of the fence from the Radicals, who also usually voted as a bloc. The swing votes, then, were provided by the conservatives and the Progressive Democrats, who more often split their votes and

15 For more on the campaign and its result, see Walter, "Elections," pp. 621–2. This election was also one of several in the capital during these years where women associated with the Socialist party pushed for women's suffrage by promoting their own candidates and holding parallel contests of their own in which several thousand women took part. Víctor O. García Costa, "Los primeros diez años del movimiento feminista y la primera sufragista sudamericana," *Boletín del Instituto Histórico de la Ciudad de Buenos Aires*, 4, 6 (1982), pp. 65–75, and Katherine S. Dreier, *Five Months in the Argentine From a Woman's Point of View: 1918 to 1919* (New York, 1920), pp. 235–58.

16 Results from *La Vanguardia* (November 25–December 4, 1920). When he was first elected in 1918, the *Review of the River Plate* saw the victory of Thompson, with "his well known business capacity and high integrity," as a compliment "to the entire British community here." *RRP*, 1407 (November 15, 1918), pp. 1235, 1239.

sided with either the Radicals or the Socialists, depending on the issue. The Progressive Democrats, for example, voted with the Socialists to override Cantilo's veto of a measure to increase the salaries of municipal workers, but they failed to get the necessary two-thirds.[17] In other instances, the Progressive Democrats allied with the Radicals and conservatives to approve municipal participation in a patriotic celebration to commemorate the birth of Argentine statesman Bartolomé Mitre and to approve a subsidy to a local religious organization, two measures of a kind that the Socialists consistently and vehemently opposed.[18] Increasingly, however, on most votes the Progressive Democrats joined with the Socialists, in the process sometimes posing serious difficulties for the Radical council members and the Radical executive.

Whatever the ebb and flow of party preference, on most issues the intendente and the Radicals managed to prevail. As a result, the Cantilo administration was a generally productive one. In addition to taking measures to reduce the cost of basic items, the intendente also enhanced the life of the city by having the municipality show free films outdoors in the summer months and allowing youth soccer clubs the free use of city land for their practices and games. Together, by the end of 1921, the council and the executive had produced 640 ordinances and resolutions. Although many of these involved relatively minor matters like opening, paving, widening, and naming streets, granting subsidies to individuals and neighborhood associations, permitting exceptions to the building code, and giving tax breaks to vendors who sold flowers on the city's streets, it also included passing ordinances to assure the healthful quality of food products sold in the capital, granting land in Palermo Park to the Club de Gimnasia y Esgrima (Gymnastics and Fencing Club) for the formation of a popular athletic facility, constructing public baths in Nueva Pompeya, reorganizing the municipal office of chemical analysis, and regulating the hours of theaters and movie houses. The council and the executive also approved, over certain Socialist objections, the transfer of the major electric company providing service to the city from German to Spanish ownership.[19] As a result, what had formerly been the Compañía Alemana Transatlántica de Electricidad (German Transatlantic Electric Company) became the Compañía Hispano–Americana de Electricidad (Spanish–American Electricity Company), or CHADE.

Inevitably, as a counterbalance to the positive aspect of their relations, there were moments of bitterness between the intendente and the council,

17 In this vote, the three Progressive Democrats voted with nine Socialists to override the veto, the two representatives of the Unión Nacional joining nine Radicals in opposition. *VTCD* (June 9, 1921), pp. 1034–54.
18 *VTCD* (May 16, 1921), pp. 699–711 and (December 30, 1921), pp. 3151–2.
19 *VTCD* (June 30, 1921), pp. 1597–600.

or at least between the executive and the Socialist members of the council. When Cantilo resigned his post in late October 1921 to become his party's nominee for governor of the province of Buenos Aires, the Socialists used the occasion to blast him for alleged violations of his office. According to council president Spinetto, who led the charge, Cantilo had allowed his office to be open to bribery, a common complaint against city government, and had failed adequately to enforce various ordinances and resolutions. He also accused the intendente of ignoring the requests of numerous neighborhood development societies to attend to their particular needs, reading some twenty of these petitions into the record. The Radicals responded with a predictable defense of Cantilo's actions and counterattacked against Spinetto with allegations of improprieties. Committees were appointed to look into both sets of charges, which eventually proved exaggerated and basically groundless.[20] The dispute was rooted in the legitimate differences between Socialists and Radicals and their competition for the allegiance of the capital's voters. Nonetheless, such clashes did little to improve the public image of the council, obscuring its positive accomplishments with the appearance of partisan wrangling and serving to bring to public attention the taint of corruption and scandal too often associated with local government.

During the council sessions of 1921, the main confrontation between the Radicals and the opposition continued to revolve around the streetcar fare increase. Although the Socialists were the most prominent and persistent critics of the increase and of streetcar service overall, the Progressive Democrats, whose party favored municipalization of public transport in their main stronghold, the city of Rosario in Santa Fe province, also became increasingly vocal in the discussion of this issue. In March, for example, the party's three representatives addressed an appeal to the intendente to improve the quality of Anglo service on line 47, which connected Nueva Pompeya and other working-class areas with the Plaza de Mayo. They reported that during their own travels on this route they heard "the complaints of the passengers about lengthy waits they had to endure because of . . . the lack of rolling stock," making it faster to walk some blocks than to ride and often causing riders to be late for work.[21]

Socialist Esteban Jiménez, that party's leading spokesman on public transportation issues, echoed these complaints. He called on the executive to inform the council about what action the company had taken, in light of the fare increase, to improve overall service, particularly in the cars earmarked for workers. "For the enormous working-class population in this city," he stated, "the streetcar service is a real problem since it is a

20 *VTCD* (November 10, 1921), pp. 2206–311.   21 *VTCD* (March 18, 1921), p. 123.

vital part of daily life which must be expanded, improved, and maintained in the best condition possible . . . . The council, since it approved the fare increase, producing an extra profit [for the companies] of 10 million pesos a year, has a right and a duty to assure that this service be improved." The company's claims to improvement notwithstanding, he concluded, fare increases had resulted in a deterioration of service.[22]

Throughout the year, the Socialists and Progressive Democrats continued to hammer home these and other points. They called for the extension of existing lines, new routes to suburban districts, and improved service overall. On June 30, the Socialists introduced several more resolutions with regard to streetcars, urging the installation of automatic counting devices to determine the exact number of passengers, a thorough modernization by the Anglo of all its cars, the imposition of stiff fines for company violations of safety requirements, and the strict enforcement of a city ordinance that prohibited passengers from spitting on the floors of the trams. Jiménez also read into the record various complaints from neighborhood associations about the deficiencies in the streetcar lines intended to serve their districts, especially suburban areas such as Liniers and Vélez Sársfield. He bemoaned the apparent lack of executive concern evidenced by the continued failure of the secretary of public works to appear before the council to address these matters. As a result, he concluded, "We are under the dictatorship of companies which lack the control of municipal regulation and enjoy the favor of all the [public] authorities and the press of the wealthy [*la prensa rica*]."[23]

Although Jiménez's conclusion was perhaps exaggerated and partisan, some substance to it was provided by the clear reluctance of the executive and his Radical allies on the council to address the issues raised by the opposition. In October, the Socialists and Progressive Democrats prevailed over Radical opposition to set a specific date for questioning Secretary of Public Works Carlos A. Varangot on the quality of existing streetcar and subway service. The Radicals, in response, failed to show up for the next few sessions.

Finally, on December 14, Varangot appeared to face the fire of the opposition. Admitting that the streetcar system suffered from some problems, he saw these as basically minor and susceptible to remedy through stricter enforcement of existing regulations. The quality of rolling stock, he agreed, had deteriorated somewhat, a fact that he traced to the European war, which had interrupted the construction of new vehicles. Now that the war was over, improvements could be expected soon. He discounted claims that the cars for workers were not operating normally, saying that he personally had not received any complaints about them. Whatever its

22 Ibid., pp. 124–6.   23 *VTCD* (June 30, 1921), pp. 1579–618.

faults, Varangot concluded, the Buenos Aires streetcar–subway system was still a good one, comparing favorably with systems in other countries.

Jiménez, of course, disagreed. In a lengthy and detailed presentation, which stretched over several days, he argued that comparisons with other systems were immaterial and only obscured a public transportation situation in Buenos Aires that was worsening every day. The picture he described, buttressed with statistics, photographs, and more complaints from neighborhood associations, was not pretty. Whereas the number of passengers, fares, and company profits had gone up, the number of cars available and in good order had gone down. Workers' requests for new lines had generally been ignored. Schedules were rarely adhered to and, once anxious passengers were able to board a car, they often found themselves jammed into a crowded conveyance whose aged windows refused to open, making a trip in the humid Buenos Aires summer an experience in a rolling inferno. "It is a disgrace," he said, "that cars in this condition are still in use; and the executive should not allow this to happen." Passengers desperate to reach work or home often clung to the outside of overloaded cars like barnacles on a rusting hull, endangering life and limb in the process. Conditions in the one subway line were not much better.

The Radical administration, Jiménez argued, had too often backed the companies to the detriment of the public. Claiming that there was a close relationship between the company and the Radical leadership, Jiménez questioned the nationalist stance of the incumbents and the sincerity of their professed commitments to economic sovereignty. He observed sarcastically that most Radical administrators and councilmen owned automobiles, suggesting that, if they had to depend on public transportation, they might be more attentive to the growing chorus of popular complaint. Finally, he accused the companies of deliberately obstructing the councilmen's search to obtain information about their operations, citing an instance when he and a colleague were denied access to one of the company's workshops. Despite all the deficiencies, he concluded, the company probably would seek to increase its fares even more, from twelve to fifteen centavos per ride.

Jiménez's remarks were aimed primarily at the Radical government and its relations with the Anglo. The Progressive Democrats, on the other hand, focused on the smaller Lacroze company, painting a picture of that line's operation very similar to Jiménez's portrait of the Anglo. Drawing on the same kind of information that their Socialist colleagues had used, they depicted a transport company that failed to adhere to established schedules, arbitrarily suppressed lines to working-class areas, and used rolling stock in such poor condition that it represented a danger to public health and safety. They concluded their presentation with a resolution requiring the Lacroze to remedy these problems or face stiff penalties and fines.

During these discussions the Radical councilmen said and did little other than occasionally to express their irritation at the time being consumed on these matters. They left it to Varangot to respond to the various accusations. Refusing to comment on the implication of collusion with the company, the secretary claimed that the local government was deeply concerned with the quality of public transportation in the city. Referring to reports from his own technical office in charge of overseeing the streetcars and subway, he argued that these showed the system operating normally and city inspectors working diligently to correct any problems. He agreed with the critics that crowded conditions existed, because of a failure fully to enforce the completo, but that to do so would only cause more delays and disruptions. New rolling stock, he reported, had been ordered and would soon be in service, thereby relieving some of the crowding. Although he did not say so outright, he implied that the faults of the system, at least so far as the Anglo was concerned, had been blown out of proportion and concluded on a note of caution that "the executive is going to consider those ideas to improve streetcar service which he believes to be sound and appropriate . . . . [A]t the same time, he is going to consider carefully all circumstances so as not to take an action that will make matters worse."[24]

Typically in such debates it was difficult to separate the substantive wheat from the polemical and political chaff. It did seem clear that the Radicals were sympathetic to the company position, having voted, after all, for the fare increase. The motives behind that decision, however, are more obscure. It may have been, as the Socialists charged, that there were strong connections between Radical officials and company representatives. It seems more likely, however, that the Anglo, monopolizing the most important and widespread means of transportation in the city, had the government over the proverbial barrel. Either the company got its increase or service would worsen even more, and the incumbent government would assume the blame. By backing the unpopular fare increase, the Radicals could hope that service would improve and that they could share some of the credit. Their reluctance to face the Socialists in the council on the issue might well have been based more on a calculation to avoid political embarrassment and to limit political losses than on any desire to defend the company.

24 The interpellation of Varangot is in *VTCD* (December 14, 1921), pp. 2710–20; (December 19, 1921), pp. 2753–64; (December 21, 1921), pp. 2788–96; (December 22, 1921), pp. 2798–811; (December 27, 1921), pp. 2842–55; (December 29, 1921), pp. 2948–63; and (December 30, 1921), pp. 3070–86.

It also seems clear, however, that by the end of 1921 the desired effects of the fare increase, namely improved service, had not been achieved. Although there may have been some partisan exaggeration in the presentations of the Socialists and others, these were also based on rather extensive evidence and buttressed by well-documented specific cases and individual accounts. A system that had been almost universally praised before the war was now coming in for harsher criticism. The city council, which before 1918 had said little if anything about the quality of services provided to the city by foreign private enterprises, was, thanks to the more democratic procedures by which it was chosen and operated, becoming a more common and open forum for the expression of public discontent with how those enterprises operated. Because few services more directly touched the daily lives of most porteños than public transportation, the quality and cost of that service was an issue with potentially explosive political implications. So long as Socialists, Progressive Democrats, and other critics continued to be elected to the council, the various Radical administrations could be assured that this issue would not disappear from public view.

5

Buenos Aires in the 1920s

The democratic flowering of the Buenos Aires city council came into full bloom in the 1920s. Following the end of World War I, both the city of Buenos Aires and the Argentine Republic resumed the rapid growth of the prewar era. A period of relative domestic peace and restored prosperity, the decade of the 1920s was another "golden age" of physical and demographic development for the city.

Exports, foreign investment, and foreign immigration again provided the main stimuli for growth. After a downturn at the beginning of the decade, the production of grains and meats recovered to previous levels and, with some fluctuations, continued to expand.[1] The flow of foreign investments and credits, halted by the European conflict, also resumed, although not at prewar levels. Increasingly, investments, imports, and loans came from the United States, which emerged as the principal competitor to Great Britain's preeminent role in Argentina. Most notably, North American automobile manufacturers began to market their products aggressively in Argentina. The Ford Motor Company had established an assembly plant in Argentina in 1917, followed by General Motors in 1925. By the middle of the decade, Ford was publicizing the assembly of its one hundred thousandth motor car in Argentina and by the end of the decade U.S. companies dominated the Argentine market.[2] Between 1920 and 1930, the number of automobiles in the country increased almost ten times – from 48,007 to 435,822 – and by 1936 almost 63,000 of these were located in the federal capital.[3]

Between 1914 and 1919, more foreigners left Argentina than entered it. Beginning in 1920, however, immigrants again poured into the

1 Guido Di Tella and Manuel Zymelman, *Las etapas del desarrollo económico argentino* (Buenos Aires, 1967), pp. 356–420.
2 Raúl García Heras, *Automotores norteamericanos, caminos y modernización urbana en la Argentina, 1918–1939* (Buenos Aires, 1985), pp. 9–20.
3 Héctor J. Iñigo Carrera, "El transporte automotor entre la Ciudad de Buenos Aires y los partidos vecinos (1936–1941). Aproximación a su influencia metropolitana," *Boletín del Instituto Histórico de la Ciudad de Buenos Aires*, 4, (1982), p. 40.

country at rates ranging from 87,000 to 195,000 a year. In contrast to the pattern of prewar immigration, the retention rate was perceptibly higher, with better than three of every four foreigners who entered the country remaining, in contrast to two of every three before 1914. As was the case before the war, most immigrants came from Spain and Italy and Italians outnumbered Spaniards by a three to two margin.[4] Italian immigration was most marked at the beginning of the decade, but fell off sharply by 1928. Also significant in these years, although their numbers were in the tens of thousands as opposed to the hundreds of thousands, were Polish immigrants, who assumed their place in the flow behind the Italians and the Spaniards.[5] A 1929 article in *Caras y Caretas* observed that Poles, Czechs, and Yugoslavs were taking over the Avenida Alem in the Paseo de Julio neighborhood near the port. Photographs displayed stores that advertised products in the languages of these nationalities and catered to a neighboring clientele.[6]

During the 1920s, the Radical government and others made some attempts to convince immigrants to settle in the countryside. These efforts, however, were sporadic at best, and usually remained as proposals that were either not ratified or, if approved, not implemented.[7] Although the lack of a national census in these years (and indeed not until the mid-1940s) makes precise calculations impossible, it seems likely that most immigrants preferred to reside in urban areas. Undoubtedly, the city of Buenos Aires absorbed a large portion of them. Although the very rapid pace of the prewar period was not duplicated, the city's population, now that large immigrant flows had resumed, was estimated to have grown from a little less than 1,700,000 in 1920 to 2,153,200 in 1930.[8]

Within the city, the movement to the outlying southern and western districts continued. All districts registered growth in these years, but expansion in numbers 1, 15, and 16 was particularly striking. Between 1914 and 1936, these three areas grew from a combined population of almost 300,000 (20 percent of the total city) to almost one million (40 percent of the total) (see Appendix, Table A.1). In 1924, the magazine *El Hogar* observed that the effective outskirts of the capital's downtown, which were more or less at the Calle Callao (about sixteen blocks west of the Plaza de Mayo) at the turn of the century, had now pushed well

4 Mariano González-Rothos y Gil, "La emigración española a Iberoamérica," *Revista Internacional de Sociología*, 7, 26/27 (Madrid: April/September 1949), p. 190.
5 María Silvia Ospital, *Estado e inmigración en la década del 20: La política inmigratoria de los gobiernos radicales* (Buenos Aires, 1988), p. 28.
6 "Notas populares: Los polacos, los checoeslovacos y los yugoeslavos se van posesionando de la avenida Alem," *Caras y Caretas* (July 13, 1929).
7 Ospital, *Estado e inmigración.*   8 MCBA, *Cincuentenario*, p. 52.

beyond the Calle Medrano (about forty blocks west of the Plaza de Mayo) and into the Flores district.[9] A few years later, another article in the same publication described with astonishment the seemingly overnight appearance of new neighborhoods that were rapidly eliminating the large and open rural spaces still to be found within the capital's confines and relegating any neighborhood more than fifteen years old to the status of a *"barrio viejo."*[10]

Those who settled in far-western neighborhoods, such as Villa Luro, Villa Pueyrredón, or Saavedra, were true urban pioneers. At the edge of the capital the boundary between city and rural countryside was still blurred. Workers and employees bought small lots of subdivided land, paying in monthly installments while they constructed their homes on property in areas that still lacked municipal services in the 1920s. The electrification of the Western Railway in the 1920s helped stimulate their development by connecting these distant suburbs to the center of the city. Like other districts, people in these suburbs formed neighborhood associations and development societies, organized social events like picnics and dances, promoted sporting clubs and libraries, and pushed for municipal attention to their particular needs.[11]

Another sign of growth on the periphery of the city was the increase in housing and commercial construction. The number of permits for new buildings in the city overall between 1914 and 1919 had declined to about a third of what it had been before the war. Beginning in 1920 and continuing to the end of the decade, however, with some variations, the number of permits equaled and often exceeded prewar levels. Not surprisingly, the greatest increases occurred again in census districts 1, 15, and 16, with relatively little expansion taking place in the center of the capital. In 1914 these outlying districts had contained 30 percent of all the city's buildings; by 1930 they held a little over 50 percent.[12] Most of these constructions were single-family residences in contrast to the

9 "Las antiguas espaldas de Buenos Aires," *El Hogar* (Buenos Aires: November 28, 1924).
10 Mario Luis Mendy, "Mi barrio tiene quince años y ya es viejo: Como crece otro más lindo a su orilla," *El Hogar* (January 13, 1928).
11 There is a considerable and growing literature on the forty-six recognized neighborhoods of Buenos Aires. A useful collection is *Buenos Aires Nos Cuenta*, directed by Elisa Casella de Calderón. The city of Buenos Aires also published a series entitled *Cuadernos de Buenos Aires* in the 1960s and 1970s. A brief description of two of the three western neighborhoods referred to are Juan José Bianchi, "Villa Luro," and Raul H. Roque, "Versalles, ese desconocido," in *Lyra*, 26, 213/15 (1969), a special edition devoted to the history of Buenos Aires. A more detailed study of Villa Pueyrredón is the previously cited work by Enrique Peseda, *Nuestra Querida Villa Pueyrredón*.
12 These figures are from a presentation in the city council by José Rouco Oliva, a councilman particularly concerned with the physical growth of the city and urban problems in general. He collected his information from the national census and the city's statistical office. *VTCD* (November 10, 1932), pp. 4010–12.

growing number of multistory and multifamily apartment buildings in the downtown area.

In the postwar era, work also resumed on major public projects. By the end of the decade the new port was completed and a new municipally owned and operated *frigorífico* (meat-packing plant) was inaugurated. The Arroyo Maldonado, which had caused flooding problems in its traverse over the western and northern sections of the city, was channeled and covered. The resultant broad avenue over what had once been a muddy creek was later named for Socialist party founder Juan B. Justo. Progress on the suspended north and south *diagonales* was somewhat slower, but did proceed throughout the decade.

Construction in general was marked by vertical as well as horizontal growth. The eighteen-story Palacio Barolo office building on the Avenida de Mayo near the Plaza del Congreso, completed in 1923, was the most dramatic early example of this trend. Designed by Italian architect Mario Palanti, it combined monumental classical features with art nouveau characteristics to form a distinctive landmark. Billed at the time as the tallest building both in Buenos Aires and in all of South America, it was serviced by eleven elevators and topped by a powerful spotlight that could be seen on clear nights across the estuary in Uruguay. It dominated the Buenos Aires skyline until 1929. That year saw the inauguration of the Mihanovich Building at Arroyo and Esmeralda, a twenty-story building strongly influenced by the Chicago architectural style and generally considered the city's first "modern" skyscraper.[13]

Eclecticism was still the watchword of Buenos Aires architecture. Many apartment and office buildings of the 1920s showed the continuing influence of art nouveau. Near the end of the decade, another European current, art deco, began to make its mark on residences and businesses. Itself the product of diverse currents and influences, art deco implied simpler lines and more geometric design than did art nouveau. Its best-known practitioner in the Buenos Aires of the 1920s was architect Alejandro Virasoro, whose best-known work was the Casa del Teatro on Avenida Santa Fe, opened with much fanfare in 1927. Reacting against these influences, some architects sought to restore Spanish colonial features to Buenos Aires public and private buildings of the 1920s. One of the best examples of this trend was the beautiful, municipally managed Teatro Cervantes at Córdoba and Libertad, opened in 1921. Its facade copied that of the Spanish University of Alcalá de Henares and it was built largely with materials imported from Spain. Also showing some of the Spanish-style influence was the new building of the Banco de Boston at the corner of Florida and the Diagonal Norte, inaugurated in

13 Molinari, *Buenos Aires*, p. 391.

The Palacio Barolo, finished in 1923

The Banco de Boston at the corner of Florida and the Diagonal Norte in the
late 1920s

the mid-1920s. Across the Diagonal another design by Virasoro, the
Equitativa del Plata, completed in 1929, contributed to the distinguished
row of office buildings going up along the new avenue. Another distinctive
building of these years was the Law School of the University of Buenos
Aires on Las Heras near its intersection with Pueyrredón. A monumental
red-brick edifice in gothic style, it resembled a cathedral more than a
school, and represented yet one more example of the diverse architectural
mixture that characterized the city.[14]

The resurgence of economic growth in the 1920s did much to defuse the
aggressive labor activism that had characterized Buenos Aires between
1917 and 1920. Except for widespread protests against a pension law in
1924, the number of strikes and strikers in the federal capital declined
to the relatively low levels attained between 1911 and 1916. The leadership of the labor movement passed from the militant anarchists to the
more moderate syndicalists and socialists. The movement attracted relatively few workers and continued to be afflicted by ideological struggles

14 Gutiérrez, *Arquitectura y urbanismo*, pp. 533–72; Martini and Peña, *La ornamentación*, pp. 29–50;
and Federico Ortiz, "La arquitectura de Buenos Aires, 1870–1970," *Lyra*, 26, 210/12 (1969).

and divisions.[15] Official figures showed a steady rise both in employment and in real wages in the city during this decade.[16] Significant national legislation limited the hours and regulated the working conditions for female workers, and in 1929 the eight-hour workday, already the standard practice in most establishments, became law. Whereas in 1919 10 percent of the population, presumably mostly of the lower classes, lived in conventillos, by 1927 only 5 percent did.[17]

In general, then, while labor militancy declined, life seemed to improve for porteño workers in the 1920s. Wages climbed, employment grew, more proletarians moved out of crowded downtown conventillos to single-family homes in suburban districts, and the opportunities for mobility and an even better life for their children seemed brighter than before the war. There may have been, however, some shadows in this generally bright picture. After carefully examining official figures, Robert Shipley argued that unemployment was higher and opportunities for mobility less in this period than generally was assumed.[18] The growth in wages, as even government surveys showed, was absorbed by the ever-rising costs of food, clothing, and housing, with very little left over for saving. Official figures also stated that throughout this period women made up 19 percent of the work force and minor children 5 percent; the latter figure probably represented an undercount because of the more "informal" means by which children were employed.[19] According to one source, the differential in wages between men and women grew rather than lessened in the 1920s.[20] Furthermore, whereas protective legislation, improvements in their legal status, and the eight-hour day aided many female workers, many more who worked at home or as domestic servants did not receive these benefits.

Although the number both of conventillos and of their inhabitants declined in the 1920s, tenements remained a prominent feature of some districts. District 4 of La Boca still contained the greatest number, with districts 1 and 5 maintaining the fewest.[21] A 1927 government survey of

15 "Información Social," *Revista de Ciencias Económicas*, 79–80, and Munck et al., *From Anarchism to Peronism*, pp. 99–105.

16 Charles Bergquist, *Labor in Latin America: Comparative Essays on Chile, Argentina, Venezuela, and Colombia* (Stanford, Calif., 1986), pp. 112–14, and Di Tella and Zymelman, *Las etapas*, pp. 356–420.

17 Gutiérrez-Suriano, "Vivienda," p. 18.

18 Robert E. Shipley, "On the Outside Looking In: A Social History of the 'Porteño' Worker During the 'Golden Age' of Argentine Development, 1914–1930" (Ph.D. Diss.: Rutgers University, 1977) and as cited in Bergquist, *Labor in Latin America*, p. 114.

19 From a review of *Memoria* for 1921–29. For 1929, of the 476,932 workers employed in the city, 364,853 were men, 89,186 were women, and 22,893 were minors. *Memoria*, 1929–1930, p. 302.

20 Caro Hollander, "Women: The Forgotten Half of Argentine History," p. 143.

21 Francis Korn et al., *Buenos Aires: Los huespedes del 20*, 2nd ed. (Buenos Aires, 1989), p. 136.

five thousand rental housing units for workers in the city found the largest concentration of substandard residences in districts 3 and 4.[22] Other central and downtown areas, even areas of upper-class residences like districts 14 and 20, had substantial numbers of conventillos intermixed with palatial houses, modern apartments, and new public and commercial buildings. The popular press highlighted these contrasts. The newspaper *Crítica*, for example, often gave detailed descriptions of conditions in particular conventillos, some of which were located in the heart of the Barrio Norte. For this muckraking publication, the continued prevalence of the conventillo was a stain on the modern and progressive image the city sought to project to the rest of the world.[23] An editorial in a March 1929 edition of *El Hogar* speculated that whereas an official count had determined that the number of conventillos in the capital had declined to 1,673 from 2,470 in 1924, many more had sprung up just outside the boundaries of the city and remained an integral part of the larger metropolitan scene. Moreover, "any neighborhood doctor can certify that many private homes have been converted into small conventillos [with all the attendant public health problems], and that many cheap hotels and boarding houses are no more than conventillos. The classic conventillo is disappearing, but the general impression is that Buenos Aires is more 'conventillo' than ever."[24]

At the other end of the scale, the Buenos Aires elite found the 1920s a reassuring return to normalcy. The specter of continued labor turmoil exploding into class-based civil war, which had arisen with the "semana trágica," had dissipated by the early years of the decade. Moreover, in late 1922 the smiling and sociable Marcelo T. de Alvear replaced the silent and secretive Hipólito Yrigoyen as president of the republic. Although Yrigoyen had not proved as "radical" as some had feared, conservatives found little good to say about him. They distrusted his continuing popularity and blamed him for failing to control more forcefully the labor violence that had erupted during his term in office. Despite the fact that he was also a Radical and Yrigoyen's personal choice as successor, Alvear was a "definite aristocrat" from one of the nation's best-known elite families.[25] As such, the porteño upper class was much more comfortable

22 "Valor locativo de la vivienda en la capital federal," *Memoria, 1927–1928*, pp. 307–8. Not surprisingly, the study also found that rents downtown were considerably higher than in southern or western working-class districts. The average monthly rental for a three-room property in district 14, for example, was 158.64 pesos, whereas in district 15 it was 90.00 pesos.

23 For example, "Mientras no se suprima el conventillo, tendrán razón todos los que en el extranjero denigran a Buenos Aires," *Crítica* (Buenos Aires: October 29, 1926), p. 9.

24 "Desaparecen los conventillos," *El Hogar*, 1014 (March 22, 1929).

25 For more on Alvear and his family, see Pedro Fernández Lalanne, *Los Alvear* (Buenos Aires, 1980) and Félix Luna, *Alvear* (Buenos Aires, 1958).

with him than they had been with his predecessor. Alvear, for example, thoroughly enjoyed going to the many glittering functions of the Teatro Colón, events that Yrigoyen had attended only grudgingly.[26] The Teatro Colón's symphony concerts and opera season, graced by music's greatest international stars, remained one of the main meeting places of the city's elite.

The upper classes continued to live in the high style to which they were accustomed. Benefiting again from the resumption of the nation's export-oriented trade to Europe, they returned to the old continent and again spent so lavishly in Paris, Rome, London, and Madrid that the phrase "as rich as an Argentine" became the standard by which all extravagant and wealthy foreigners were measured. At home, they continued to frequent the Jockey Club on Florida and the even more exclusive Círculo de Armas on Corrientes, to defend their interests through the Sociedad Rural, and to partake fully of the ever-expanding social, cultural, and sporting events the city had to offer. They still promenaded in Palermo Park on the weekends, in the 1920s more frequently in an automobile then in a horse-drawn carriage. During a time when aspiring members of the middle class sought to achieve higher status by moving into aristocratic neighborhoods and many aristocrats moved northward, the Barrio Norte remained an upper-class bastion.[27] The Avenida Santa Fe, which cut through the heart of the Barrio Norte, began to house the kind of exclusive stores and shops that allowed it to compete with Calle Florida as the city's most "chic street" and sprouted theaters, movie houses, and cafés that made it a more aristocratic version of Corrientes.[28]

The city's middle classes continued to expand in these years. A study of the Once district found that the number of commercial establishments likely to be owned by and to employee many persons of the middle classes almost doubled during the decade.[29] Gino Germani, using unpublished reports from the 1936 municipal census, counted a continued and marked increase in the city's middle classes, from 38 percent of the Buenos Aires population in 1914 to almost 46 percent by the mid-1930s.[30] Although specific information is not available, it is well known that the Radical governments of the period, especially those of Yrigoyen, significantly

---

26 Horacio Sanguinetti, "Breve historia política del Teatro Colon," *Todo es Historia*, 1, 5 (September 1967), p. 73.

27 María Angelica, "El barrio norte," *Lyra*, 26, 213/15 (1969).

28 Enrique Horacio Puccia, *Avenida Santa Fe: Ayer y hoy* (Buenos Aires, 1989).

29 Korn et al., *Buenos Aires*, pp. 164–80.

30 Among particular groups, Germani calculated that for these years the number of financiers (*rentistas*) grew from 13,732 to 34,446, the number of professionals from 44,766 to 89,644, and the number of employees from 129,190 to 201,414. Gino Germani, "La clase media en la Ciudad de Buenos Aires," *Desarrollo Económico*, 21, 81 (April–June 1981), p. 125.

Palermo Park in the 1920s

expanded the federal bureaucracy, opening up many white-collar public jobs to persons who were either members of the middle classes or aspired to that status.[31] Public employees, in turn, undoubtedly made up the single largest component of the capital's middle classes.

"After 1916," according to one writer, "few were the porteños who did not aspire to occupy positions in public administration."[32] Even free-spirited bohemians, wrote another, were increasingly inclined to enroll in bureaucratic ranks.[33] The attractions were clear. After gaining the requisite letter of recommendation from a well-placed politician, the newly appointed employee found himself or, less commonly, herself, in a reasonably secure and decently paid position that usually demanded little in the way of energy and ambition. Usually, too, the position provided some small power over others, especially persons who had need of approval for the many official documents and papers required of all porteños. Opportunities to augment official salaries by accepting extra, "unofficial"

31 See Rock, *Politics in Argentina*, pp. 107–11.
32 Domingo F. Casadevall, *El carácter porteño* (Buenos Aires, 1970), p. 27.
33 José Antonio Saldias, *La inolvidable bohemia porteña: Radiografía ciudadana del primer cuarto de siglo* (Buenos Aires, 1968), p. 89.

compensation for services rendered also existed. The drawbacks to the relative stability, security, and undemanding nature of public employment were the stifling of creativity and individuality and the deadening monotony and uniformity common to all bureaucracies. As one observer put it, after a certain time "the public employee becomes part of the office, like the invariable serving of café con leche. He can never be a free man, until after six in the afternoon, the hour when the timeclock tells him:enjoy your happiness while you can, because your life begins exactly the same in the morning."[34]

Colorful marginal characters still populated the urban scene in Buenos Aires in the 1920s. Many who performed services on the capital's sidewalks became established and well-known as figures associated with their particular corners of the city. Cigarette dealers set up their small stands to accommodate the incessant porteño demand for their product. Peanut vendors and food wagons providing quick lunches and snacks at low prices became common features of plazas in front of the railroad terminals and the downtown banking district. The men who painted the benches in the city's botanical gardens, collected tickets at the racetrack, took photographs at the entrance to the zoo, delivered milk, and directed streetcar traffic downtown were familiar figures to most porteños.[35]

As increasing numbers of multistory apartment buildings made their appearance in the city, their caretakers, or *porteros*, emerged into prominence. A combination doorman and building supervisor, the portero was responsible for apartment security and maintenance. In return, he usually received a rent-free room on the street floor or the roof and gained a small income from the monthly tips of the building residents. Tens of thousands of porteños had daily contact with their porteros, who delivered their mail, stoked their furnaces, cleaned their hallways, and generally became indispensable figures in their day-to-day lives.[36]

For many porteño middle- and upper-class women, the 1920s were years of significant change. Reflecting the greater social freedom for women in postwar Europe and the United States, porteñas appeared more often alone or in unchaperoned groups in cafés and restaurants, frequently smoking, drinking, or engaging in other "scandalous" behavior that would have been unthinkable before 1920. Women's fashions in Buenos Aires imitated those of their foreign sisters, with skirts slowly rising to just above the knee and bare shoulders, necks, and arms exposed for all to see. Women began to participate actively in the various sports that so fascinated porteños in the 1920s, especially golf, tennis, and swimming.[37]

34 Pintos, *Así fué Buenos Aires*, p. 124.
35 From a review of *Caras y Caretas*, 1925–30.   36 Pintos, *Así fué Buenos Aires*, pp. 113–14.
37 Héctor Iñigo Carrera, *Los años 20* (Buenos Aires, 1971), pp. 35–43.

Certain women became prominent in entertainment and the arts. At the beginning of the decade, all-female orchestras appeared in several downtown night clubs and cafés. Paquita Bernardo, who appeared at the Bar Domínguez at Corrientes 1537, was known as one, of the few female players of the bandoneón (the accordionlike instrument associated with the tango) in the city.[38] Other females, like Azucena Maizani, Rosita Quiroga, Mercedes Simone, and Libertad Lamarque, became famous as tango singers.[39] In the field of literature, writers like Norah Lange and Alfonsina Storni began to reflect in their work the frustration of women exposed to new ideas and experiences but constrained by the limitations still imposed on them by a male-dominated and conservative society. By their efforts, they, like Victoria Ocampo, novelist, essayist, poetess, and founder of the important literary journal *Sur*, gave women a newfound prominence and presence in the field of letters, a field previously dominated almost exclusively by men.[40]

Although the lack of a census for this period again makes precise estimates impossible, various accounts indicate that women were increasingly moving into white-collar occupations and the liberal professions. This meant that more women were becoming consumers in their own right, a fact reflected in the increasing number of advertisements in publications geared to women – *El Hogar, Caras y Caretas, Mundo Argentino, Plus Ultra* – urging them to purchase, as "new women," articles of clothing, makeup, electric appliances for the home, and other items claiming to make them "modern" and fashionable. In 1926, the national Congress passed legislation giving women equal legal footing with men and further enhancing their movement toward greater individuality and independence.[41]

The automobile was perhaps the most potent symbol of this evolution toward greater independence for women. Carmakers directed a surprising amount of their efforts toward the female market in the 1920s. Advertisements often featured drawings of young, attractive, and smiling women at the wheel of their automobiles, their hair blowing in the breeze and their golf clubs or tennis rackets prominently displayed in the back seat. Some advertisements had women driving alone, or in the company of other women, and a few featured women behind the wheel with male passengers. An article in *El Hogar* in 1929 estimated that by that year there were about five thousand female drivers in Buenos Aires, devotees of "the means of modern locomotion *par excellence*" and, popular opinion

38 Jeanette López, "Buenos Aires emergó así," *Lyra*, 26, 213/215 (1969).
39 Horacio Salas, *El tango* (Buenos Aires, 1986), pp. 212–26.
40 Beatriz Sarlo, *Una modernidad periférica: Buenos Aires, 1920 y 1930* (Buenos Aires, 1988), pp. 69–93.
41 Caro Hollander, "Women: The Forgotten Half," pp. 145–6.

to the contrary, *not* involved in a disproportionate number of traffic accidents.[42]

Two years later, *El Hogar* published another article, this time seeking to portray the daily schedule of the typical urban woman and to indicate thereby the changes in women's lives over the past decade. Estimating that 80 percent of "las chicas porteñas" were *empleadas* (employees), *El Hogar* traced their weekend leisure hours outside of the home. Beginning with an early morning tennis match, or a brisk walk ("footing") in Plaza Francia, or a round of golf ("the most chic activity of the porteño day"), the porteña, after lunch, got into her small automobile (*voiturette*) and made the mandatory tour through Palermo Park. There she received "the devouring glances of the young men," but only stopped to give her female friends a ride to downtown. Parking on the newly completed Diagonal Norte, she joined the fashion parade on Florida and stopped for tea at Harrods. After greeting friends and perhaps enjoying a cigarette, she completed her day by attending the cinema, presumably on her own or with other female companions.[43]

This picture was undoubtedly far from "typical." At best, by *El Hogar's* own reckoning, only five thousand women out of a total female population of about a million had licenses to drive. Although some women were moving into white-collar occupations and the professions, the majority were still employed in industries, did piecework at home, or were domestic servants. Several thousand young women continued to practice prostitution in establishments that could be found scattered throughout the city, but that were mostly concentrated in downtown districts. The 1926 legislation on the legal rights of women contained provisions that still reinforced male dominance in marriage. The right to divorce, which, among the major political groups in the country, only the Socialist party strongly advocated, would not become fully effective until the 1980s. Although in a few provinces elections gave women the right to vote during these years, women were still denied suffrage in the federal capital.

The Buenos Aires world of entertainment, sports, and culture continued to expand in these years and to become more accessible to ever-wider audiences. Restaurants and cafés grew in number and variety to meet the insatiable porteño need to socialize over food and drink. Reflecting not only the influence of foreign examples, but also the faster pace of city life, automats with prepared foods enjoyed a brief popularity in the 1920s. More lasting were the city's cafés, which could be found in profusion both

---

42 Patricia Dorn, "Más de cinco mil porteñas manejan automovil," *El Hogar*, 1049 (November 22, 1929).

43 "En que emplea su tiempo una niña porteña de ahora," *El Hogar*, 1138 (August 7, 1931).

downtown and in each barrio. Many became associated with the development and diffusion of the tango. One, the Confitería Molino at the corner of Rivadavia and Callao, across from the national Congress, became the most important political café. Others, such as La Brasileña on Maipú, La Helvetica at the corner of San Martín and Corrientes, and Los Inmortales in the 900 block of Corrientes joined the Royal Keller, the Richmond, and the Tortoni as renowned gathering places for the city's growing literary and artistic set.[44]

The 1920s also saw the introduction of popular French-style cabarets. Elaborately decorated, often with a Middle Eastern motif, they proliferated downtown, especially along Corrientes, Esmeralda, Maipú, and Florida, although one of the most popular, the Palais de Glace, was located in the Barrio Norte at Posadas 1725. Bearing names like El Chanteclair, Ta-Ba-Ris, Montmartre, Royal Pigall, the Abdullah Club, and featuring drinks and music, they provided opportunities for instrumentalists and singers, primarily of the tango, to make names for themselves. The audience, which often spent the night doing the tango or the fox-trot on the dance floor, was usually an elegantly and formally dressed collection of the distinguished and wealthy: "A member of the Jockey club, a journalist, a famous teacher of billiards, a young national congressman accompanied by his French girlfriend (the most fashionable of companions), an *hacendado*, a jockey who had run a memorable race, or a 'play-boy'; in other words, anybody who was anybody in nocturnal Buenos Aires."[45]

The city's theaters also grew in number and variety. Again, as before the war, the porteño theatergoer could select from performances that ranged from serious drama to light musical comedies and vaudeville reviews. Domestic companies and performers competed with foreign groups, mostly from Europe, who made Buenos Aires a regular stop on their off-season tour. Theaters with tango orchestras and singers, as well as occasional performances featuring jazz and other forms of popular music from the United States, accommodated larger and more varied groups than would fit into a cabaret.

There were, according to one report, 137 motion picture houses in Buenos Aires in 1923; approximately 85 percent of the movies screened were made in the United States.[46] Hollywood films and stars of the silent era – Chaplin, Fairbanks, Garbo, and Valentino – predominated. In addition, a national cinema also began to make its mark; many films of the 1920s were set in and used the city itself as their subject. These included,

44 A more detailed picture is provided in Miguel Angel Scenna, "Las cafés: Una institución porteña," *Todo es Historia*, 2, 21 (January 1969), pp. 68–90. See also, Saldias, *La inolvidable bohemia porteña*, pp. 143–54.
45 Enrique Cadicamo, "Cabaret," *Lyra*, 26, 213/15 (1969).
46 "The Movie Business in Buenos Aires," *BPAU*, 58 (March 1927), 285–6.

for example, stories of young men and women struggling to overcome their humble origins in slums and tenements (*La muchacha del arrabal, El Guapo del arrabal, Sombras de Buenos Aires*, and *Tu cuna fue un conventillo*) and attempts to depict the evils of urban prostitution (*La casa del placer*).[47] During the 1920s, new movie houses like the Astral, the Broadway, and the Cataluna opened along Corrientes and the Grand Splendid, on the 1800 block of Santa Fe, inaugurated in 1919, became the "preferred cinema of the porteño elite."[48]

A notable feature of almost all these activities was the late hour at which many of them commenced. Much of the city's social life revolved around the hours when restaurants opened for meals, and these generally followed the Spanish pattern of late and long lunches and equally late and long dinners. Theaters, cinemas, and cabarets adjusted accordingly, scheduling performances that ran well into the early morning hours and contributing, along with the many cafés that also maintained long hours, to Buenos Aires' vibrant night life.[49] When the local government tried, without much success, to enforce an earlier end to theatrical productions and cinema showings, *El Hogar* noted that these measures would have little effect until dining hours were changed. Such a change, *El Hogar* argued, would be all to the good, improving public health and overall efficiency by cutting down on nighttime traffic noises and encouraging more rest.[50] This suggestion, however, fell on deaf ears.

An important addition to the diffusion of music and entertainment, as well as information on national and international affairs, was the introduction of the radio in the 1920s. The first broadcast, on August 27, 1920, was of Wagner's opera *Parsifal* from the Teatro Coliseo. Seven years later, the first performance from the Teatro Colón, Verdi's *Rigoletto*, was transmitted.[51] Although radio broadcasting was not as widespread as it would become later, by the end of the decade there were three stations in Buenos Aires, paving the way for an even wider dispersion of entertainment and culture in future years.[52]

The decade was also was a golden age for the development of professional sports. Attendance at the racetrack, which had remained high through the war years, continued to climb in this decade, averaging about one million spectators a year until the economic depression of the early 1930s caused it to fall off sharply. All newspapers, even party organs like

47 Jorge Miguel Couselo et al., *Historia del cine argentino* (Buenos Aires, 1984), pp. 30–1.
48 Puccia, *Avenida Santa Fe*, p. 24.
49 A fine description of Buenos Aires' night life is in Ulyses Petit de Murat, *La noche de mi ciudad* (Buenos Aires, 1979).
50 "El horario de Buenos Aires," *El Hogar*, 21, 816 (June 5, 1925).
51 Sanguinetti, "Breve historia política del Teatro Colón," p. 74.
52 Iñigo Carrera, *Los años 20*, pp. 77–8.

the Socialist *La Vanguardia*, gave increasing coverage to sporting activities. The weekly sports magazine *El Gráfico* provided photographs and detailed coverage of Argentine participation in practically every sport imaginable, from archery to yachting. Horse racing, boxing, and soccer were the most popular sports of the period. The dominant Argentine sports hero of the decade was Luis Angel Firpo, who won the South American heavyweight championship in 1920 and entered the "fight of the century" with Jack Dempsey for the world title in 1923. Although he lost the bout – despite knocking Dempsey out of the ring – Firpo nonetheless became the best-known Argentine outside the confines of the republic and the first of a long line of Argentine fighters who would make their mark in international competition. Following the same path, Argentine soccer clubs contributed players to a national team that won the South American championship in 1921 and 1925. Also in 1925, the porteño club of Boca Juniors toured Europe for a series of exhibition matches and in 1930 the national team reached the finals of the first World Cup before losing to neighboring Uruguay.

Gradually, soccer, like boxing, moved from amateur to professional status. From their origins as local neighborhood teams in the southern working-class districts, six major teams emerged during the 1920s. Within the city, the two best-known were Boca Juniors and River Plate. In 1923, River moved from the south side to a forty-thousand-seat stadium on the edge of the Barrio Norte at Avenida Alvear and what is today Libertador. One year later Boca Juniors, which remained in La Boca, moved into a new stadium of their own. The separate locations signified an identification of the working class with Boca and the middle and upper classes with River, akin in some respects, perhaps, to the rivalry between the New York Yankees and the Brooklyn Dodgers. Although this distinction might be overdrawn, there was no mistaking the growing and passionate popular identification, at least among porteño males, with one of these two teams, an identification that perhaps rivaled, or even exceeded, loyalties to political parties.[53]

The 1920s ushered in something of a golden age of literature as well. A new generation of young playwrights, essayists, novelists, and poets made Buenos Aires home to some of the most innovative and exciting creative writing talents in the hemisphere. For the most part middle class, they tended to be porteño-born, although there were several from the provinces who were attracted to the cultural mecca that was Buenos Aires. Well read and well traveled, they absorbed the fashionable philosophical and literary influences of postwar Europe and incorporated them

53 Ibid., pp. 78–82; Molinari, *Buenos Aires*, pp. 411–12; and J. Puente, *El fútbol* (Buenos Aires, 1971), pp. 9–43.

into their own works set within the Argentine context. An active and expanding publishing world, of which Buenos Aires was *the* Latin American center, provided them with ample opportunities to display their wares. Several literary journals, such as *Nosotros*, had been founded before the war. In the 1920s, others, such as *Prisma*, *Proa*, and *Martín Fierro*, appeared as vehicles for young talents aiming to revolutionize Argentine literature. During the decade, two main groups struggled for dominance of the porteño literary scene. One clustered around Calle Boedo, a street that ran through the working-class district of the same name and on into Nueva Pompeya. The Boedo group claimed to favor content over form, were preoccupied with the less fortunate of society, and were committed to radical political change. The other band of writers was associated with the cafés and salóns of Calle Florida and their emphasis was stylistic and thematic innovation and a focus on aesthetic rather than social change.[54]

Whatever their affiliation, the writers of this generation increasingly turned to the city of Buenos Aires and the characters who populated it both for inspiration and for the settings and themes of their work.[55] In so doing, many aspired both to reflect and to comment on the dramatic changes that were brought on by the rapidly ongoing growth and modernization of the city. Boedo's Raúl González Tuñon, for example, crafted poems that described neighborhoods on the fringe of society and explored the marginal characters of the city, highlighting "an exciting and Beaudelarian world of schemers, drug traffickers [cocaine use among certain porteños was increasingly common as the decade progressed], Jewish prostitutes and Arab morphine addicts, informers and hustlers."[56] Florida's Jorge Luis Borges, freshly returned from a lengthy stay in Europe, renewed his ties with the city through a collection of beautifully constructed poems that hauntingly depicted various aspects of the urban landscape in "Fervor de Buenos Aires," published in 1923.[57] In 1929 his "The Mythic Founding of Buenos Aires" brilliantly recapitulated his version of the eternal nature of the city.[58] The popular poet, essayist, and critic Carlos de la Púa skillfully used the rich Buenos Aires slang as the

54 Jorge Lafforgue, "La Literatura: El naturalismo y los vanguardistas," in Romero and Romero, eds., *Buenos Aires*, 2, pp. 155–63 and Christopher Towne Leland, *The Last Happy Men: The Generation of 1922, Fiction and the Argentine Reality* (Syracuse University Press, 1986), pp. 23–44. See also, Leonidas Barletta, *Boedo y Florida: Una versión distinta* (Buenos Aires, 1967).

55 A good view of the city through the eyes of various Argentine writers is provided in Delfin Leocadio Garada, *La otra Buenos Aires: Paseos literarios por barrios y calles de la ciudad* (Buenos Aires, 1987).

56 Sarlo, *Una modernidad periférica*, p. 159.

57 Jorge Luis Borges, *Selected Poems, 1923–1967* (edited with Introduction and Notes by Norman Thomas Giovanni) (New York, 1972), pp. 2–29.

58 Merlin Foster, "Buenos Aires: Culture and Poetry in the Modern City," in Ross and McGann, eds., *Buenos Aires: 400 Years*, pp. 130–3.

linguistic framework for his writings. This slang, or *lunfardo*, like the tango and soccer, originated in working-class immigrant neighborhoods, was gradually enriched by the mixture of races and languages in the city, and eventually came to be incorporated into the everyday usage of most porteños.[59]

Two important and representative novelists of this period, many of whose writings were set in Buenos Aires, were Manuel Gálvez and Roberto Arlt. Both described a hostile or indifferent urban milieu, wherein profoundly unhappy characters, caught up by forces they could not control, sought to destroy others and often themselves. For many of Arlt's characters, in particular, their main antagonist was the urban context itself, a context against which they constantly struggled. Their depiction of Buenos Aires was far from flattering and diverged sharply from the often romantic and enthusiastic descriptions of others.[60]

A substantial number of novelists, poets, essayists, and literary commentators found employment with *Crítica*, in accordance with its subtitle, "The Buenos Aires Daily for the Entire Republic." Founded by Uruguayan-born Natalio Botana just before the war, *Crítica* reached the height of its popularity and influence in the 1920s and 1930s when it became Argentina's most widely distributed and read newspaper. Offering a sharp contrast to the traditionalist pillars of the journalistic establishment, *La Nación* and *La Prensa*, Botana's creation produced a small revolution within the Argentine press. Although the crime in Buenos Aires, for example, evidenced some growth in mid-decade, it did not greatly exceed the prewar rate.[61] One would never have known that, however, from scanning the pages of *Crítica*, which splashed its front pages with photographs, diagrams, and detailed accounts of almost every robbery, homicide, and assault that occurred in Buenos Aires. The newspaper seemed to take perverse pride in the "Chicago-style" bank and armored-car assaults and shootouts between rival gangs that became part of the city's lore in the 1920s. Certain criminals became public celebrities as

59 Luis C. Villamayor and Enrique Ricardo del Valle, *El lenguaje del bajo fondo: Vocabulario lunfardo* (Buenos Aires, 1969).

60 For more on Gálvez, see Myron I. Lichtblau, *Manuel Gálvez* (New York, 1972) and Jefferson Rea Spell, "City Life in the Argentine as seen by Manuel Gálvez," in *Contemporary Spanish-American Fiction* (Chapel Hill, N.C., 1944), pp. 15–63. An excellent analysis of Arlt's work is Stasys Gostautas, "Roberto Arlt: Novelista de la Ciudad" (Ph.D. Diss.: New York University, 1972). See also Leland, *The Last Happy Men*, pp. 95–117.

61 According to official figures, 11,238 crimes were committed in Buenos Aires in 1920 and 14,405 in 1930. This compares with 13,462 in 1914. *Revista de Estadística Municipal*, 1940, p. 359. For more on this subject, see Lyman L. Johnson, "Changing Arrest Patterns in Three Argentine Cities: Buenos Aires, Santa Fe, and Tucumán, 1900–1930," in Lyman L. Johnson, ed., *The Problem of Order in Changing Societies: Essays on Crime and Policing in Argentina and Uruguay* (Albuquerque, N. Mex. 1991).

their every activity was seized upon as grist for the paper's sensationalist mill.

In addition to highlighting crime, *Crítica* also placed great emphasis on sports and entertainment. Photographs, cartoons, and regular columns of criticism and commentary accompanied lengthy stories on soccer and boxing matches, horse races, and the latest plays and movies. *Crítica* also claimed to champion the cause of the common citizen, often featuring spectacular exposés of alleged injustices perpetrated on the weak by the strong. Stories on the lives of individuals in conventillos, in labor protests, or in the midst of hardship and disease served to personalize the larger social problems that prevailed through the economic renewal of what some called *"los años locos"* ("the crazy years"). Politically, the daily adopted a populist stance, which often took sarcastic aim at officeholders and governing institutions. Municipal government was frequently attacked for either ignoring or inadequately addressing local problems or for its insensitivity and unrealistic manner of implementing ordinances and resolutions, which often made conditions worse than before.

These complaints and criticisms were often exaggerated in *Crítica*'s typically unrestrained style, but frequently they were on target. Even when succumbing to hyperbole, *Crítica* served as an important conduit of popular dissatisfaction with urban life and municipal affairs, providing readers and neighborhood groups with yet another forum through which to make their demands known to higher authorities. For a time in the mid-1920s, for example, *Crítica* featured a column entitled "What I Would Do If I Were the Intendente," in which man-on-the-street interviews solicited individual suggestions for municipal improvements. On the national scene, *Crítica* seemed generally well disposed toward the Alvear government, but its unrelenting hostility toward the Yrigoyen administration in the late 1920s contributed significantly to the atmosphere surrounding the overthrow of the Radical president by the Argentine military in September 1930.[62]

Another prominent feature of Buenos Aires life in the 1920s was the tango. Indeed, the city and the tango became almost synonymous in these years. Having already moved into the downtown area before the war, the tango predominated in the city's cafés, cabarets, music halls, and theaters in the 1920s and 1930s. Phonograph records and the radio transmitted the tango's strains throughout the city. After the war the tango's popularity and acceptability continued to spread to the rest of the continent and to Europe.

62 Raúl González Tuñon, " 'Critica' y los años 20," *Todo es Historia*, 3, 32 (December 1969), pp. 54–67; Petit de Murat, *La noche de mi ciudad*, pp. 161–83; and Saldias, *La inolvidable bohemia porteña*, pp. 131–41.

Thousands of tangos were written in the 1920s. Like some of the literature of the period, they often dealt with unrequited love, betrayal, disappointment, and frustration. They were also characterized by nostalgia and a longing for the old and the familiar in the face of rapid change, which gave many tangos the plaintive and melancholy air that many took to be an authentic reflection of the Argentine – and, specifically, the porteño – temperament. Many tangos were set in specific locations within the city of Buenos Aires: "An Alley of Pompeya" (*"Sobre El Pucho"*); "The Love Nest on Calle Ayacucho" (*"El Bulin de la Calle Ayacucho"*); "A Street in Barracas al Sud" (*"Silbando"*). Others dealt with the city as a whole, such as *"Mi Buenos Aires Querido"* ("My Beloved Buenos Aires") or the 1923 tango simply labeled *"Buenos Aires,"* which began:

> Buenos Aires, queen of the Río de la Plata,
> Buenos Aires, my cherished home,
> Listen to my song – for with it goes my life.[63]

In some tangos, as with the writings of novelists like Arlt, the city, or places in the city, were personalized as virtually living entities. The seductive – and corrupting – qualities of the night life along Corrientes were captured in the last stages of the tango of the same name:

> Corrientes . . . Street of vice,
> One night you intoxicated me with your wickedness
> And the venom you gave to me was so strong
> > That nobody could resist
> > Your fatal brilliance.
> Corrientes . . . Damned Street,
> I shall never exchange you for my suburban slum,
> Even though there are times when I want to abandon you
> I cannot leave you,
> > Street of my wickedness.[64]

The most renowned interpreter of the tango was the legendary Carlos Gardel. Born in France and raised by his mother in Buenos Aires, Gardel spent much of his youth along Corrientes and the area near the city's central market. Singing informally in cafés and political gatherings, Gardel gradually moved on to music halls, theaters, phonograph records, and tours of the interior. By the latter part of the 1920s he had emerged as one of the nation's and the continent's most popular and beloved

63 José Gobello and Eduardo Stilman, *Las letras del tango de Villoldo a Borges* (Buenos Aires, 1966), p. 37.
64 "'Corrientes' Tango," *Crítica* (October 17, 1926), p. 9.

entertainers, and his voice was heard throughout Latin America. European tours to Spain and France made him an international celebrity. By the late 1920s he had clearly replaced Luis Firpo as the world's most renowned Argentine.

Like Jorge Newbery before the war, Gardel personified the Buenos Aires of the 1920s. A charming, talented, and handsome man, with a ready smile, he became a hero and, to use the current jargon, "role model," for generations of Argentines. Enjoying the success that his talent brought him, he attended nightlong parties, cavorted with beautiful and glamorous women, caroused with porteño playboys, and traveled with the elite on luxurious ocean voyages to Europe. Unlike Newbery, however, he was not born to wealth and privilege, but instead to poverty and marginality, which made his accomplishments all the more remarkable. For many, he symbolized the fullest expression of the immigrant dream of an ascent from humble origins to fame, fortune, and adoring admiration. Thanks to his talent, he seemed to have achieved this almost effortlessly. His life encapsulated the image of Argentina, like the United States, as a land of unlimited opportunity.[65]

Among the notable foreign visitors who resumed their pilgrimages to Buenos Aires following the wartime interruption were the young Peruvian political leader Víctor Raúl Haya de la Torre; the ex-president of Chile Arturo Alessandri; the 1921 winner of the Nobel Prize for physics, Albert Einstein; World War I hero General John Pershing; and Italian playwright Luigi Pirandello. Elaborate receptions were given two royal visitors from countries with close ties to Argentina, Italy's Prince Humberto I of Savoy and England's Prince of Wales. A lavish welcome was extended to the crew of the Spanish seaplane *Plus Ultra*, which terminated its ten thousand kilometer trans-Atlantic flight from Spain in Buenos Aires in early 1926. The copilot was Ramón Franco, younger brother of the future Spanish dictator who, with his mates, was treated to a weeks-long celebration during which the streets of Buenos Aires were jammed with enthusiastic well-wishers. The flight of the *Plus Ultra* was a particular source of pride to Argentina's Spanish community and reaffirmed the nation's long-standing love affair with heroic aviators.[66]

Most visitors continued to be impressed by Buenos Aires, still comparing it favorably with other world capitals. Despite the renewal of urban growth and beautification in the era of the *"vacas gordas"* (fat cows), however, one also heard an increasing number of critical remarks

65 An excellent and evocative biography of Gardel is Simon Collier's, *The Life, Music, and Times of Carlos Gardel* (Pittsburgh, 1986).

66 The details of the flight and the warm reception in Buenos Aires are chronicled in Ramón Franco, *De Palos al Plata* (Madrid, 1926).

and observations from both the famous and the not so famous. Katherine S. Dreir, a rare female observer who spent five months in the country in 1919, not only severely criticized the treatment of women and children in Buenos Aires, but also described the city as monotonous, provincial, and out of touch with the rest of the world. To compare Buenos Aires with Paris, she claimed, was "a mockery" because, even in Palermo Park, the Argentine capital lacked the spontaneity and gaiety so characteristic of Paris. Like many observers, she saw the porteño as somber and serious: "If people would only laugh," she complained; "there is so little laughter, no matter where one goes. The [porteños] seem to be too self-conscious to have humor, or to see the humor in others."[67] Even more critical than Dreir was Colombian poet José María Vargas Vila, who visited Buenos Aires in 1923. To Vargas Vila, Buenos Aires was a "second-rank" city whose greatest aim was to copy every other city, with "everything imported, everything transported, everything imitated"; the end result was that it had nothing unique or original to call its own.[68]

These observations, then as now, might have started some heads nodding in agreement. Because they were not widely disseminated, however, they produced little reaction. Of greater consequence for many porteños were the observations of two well-known European writers and philosophers, Spain's José Ortega y Gasset and Germany's Count Hermann Keyserling. Although they directed their remarks to all Argentines, not just to porteños, they were addressing issues of national character in a country that was clearly dominated by the capital city and its inhabitants.

Ortega lectured in Argentina on several occasions, beginning in 1916. For him, essential characteristics of the Argentines were a defensiveness and superficiality based on insecurity and a lack of identity. "The typical Argentinean," he wrote, "has only one vocation, that of forthwith believing what he imagines he is. He therefore lives devoted not to a reality but to an image."[69] Ortega traced these features to the immigrant experience and the "newness" of the Argentine nation. Keyserling, who visited Argentina in the late 1920s as part of a tour of South America, emphasized the melancholy nature of the Argentines, which he compared to that of the Russians. "Argentine *tristeza* [sadness]," he claimed, ". . . is of so elementary, nay massive a powerfulness, that it at once conquers any sensitive newcomer; I know of many who at first harbored thoughts of suicide for a whole week."[70] So much for the economic expansion, the

67 Dreir, *Five Months in the Argentine*, p. 268.   68 Pereira, *Viajeros del siglo 20*, p. 36.

69 José Ortega y Gasset, *Toward a Philosophy of History* (New York, 1941), p. 266.

70 Count Hermann Keyserling, *South American Meditations: On Hell and Heaven in the Soul of Man* (translated from the German, in collaboration with the author, by Theresa Duerr) (New York, 1932), p. 303.

cultural vitality, and the golden opportunities for social mobility during the "años locos" of the "Paris of the Pampa"!

The comments of all these foreign observers, of course, were broad generalizations based on individual experiences and impressions, with all of the methodological and conceptual weaknesses that mode of analysis implies. Nonetheless, it is striking to observe the greater frequency of critical observations from foreigners in the postwar as opposed to the pre-war period. More to the point, many of these remarks coincided with an increased internal debate over the benefits of urban growth and the role of Buenos Aires in the nation's development.

From the mid-nineteenth century, the prevailing opinion in Argentina held that the growth and modernization of Buenos Aires was a positive factor for the whole country. The great Argentine statesman and thinker, Domingo F. Sarmiento, had argued that enlightenment and progress prevailed in the capital city, in contrast to the backwardness and tradi-tionalism of the largely rural interior. As Buenos Aires grew, those sharing Sarmiento's views saw urban "civilization" triumphing over rural "bar-barism."[71] Furthermore, with the celebration of the centennial in the capital, Buenos Aires clearly was the symbol and reality of all that had been accomplished, and there was every indication that the city would continue to play its "progressive" role into the foreseeable future.

This view continued to predominate in the 1920s. Any review of the newspapers and magazines of the period reveals the generally positive assessment most Argentines, or at least most porteños, had of the renewed postwar growth of their city. Typifying this attitude, for example, was a statement in Caras y Caretas about the progress of the Diagonal Roque Sáenz Peña:"a beautiful aesthetic reality, with its buildings and its thou-sands of windows, showing to the eyes of strangers the tenacity and the enthusiasm of a people that will make of Buenos Aires a new capital of the Latin world and, for its beauty and its culture, one of the world's most formidable metropolises."[72] A pamphlet published in 1923, which promoted the establishment of more frigoríficos in the capital, claimed that Buenos Aires was already the leading capital of the Americas and through its rapid growth bid fair to be at "the head of world progress."[73] In 1924, a group of distinguished citizens organized "Los Amigos de la Ciudad" to stimulate further the beautification and modernization of the city.[74] Throughout the decade local and national governments remained

---

71 The classic statement of this proposition is Domingo F. Sarmiento, *Life in the Argentine Republic in the Days of the Tyrants, or, Civilization and Barbarism* (New York, 1961), first published in 1845.
72 *Caras y Caretas*, 30, 1524 (December 17, 1927).
73 *La ciudad de Buenos Aires a la cabeza del progreso mundial*, 1923 (Buenos Aires, 1923).
74 Amigos de la Ciudad, *Cinco lustros al servicio de la ciudad: MCMXXIV–MCMLXIX* (Buenos Aires, 1951).

committed to improving the city's services, appearance, and role as show-case of the nation.

Along with the pride and boosterism, however, grew doubts and crit-icism. Politicians, especially Socialists, increasingly brought to light what they considered flaws and inequities in how the city was developed and governed. They highlighted especially the people in groups and neighborhoods who had been left out of the process of expansion and who suffered from the crowded and unhealthy living and working conditions that seemed inescapably associated with urban growth. For every poet, novelist, essayist, or songwriter who extolled the virtues of the city, there were others who criticized its materialism, corruption, and impersonality. Manuel Gálvez, among others, suggested a reform of urban ills inspired by the traditional values found in the provinces, thereby turning Sarmiento on his head. Civilization, he implied, now resided in the countryside, barbarism in the city. For the literary anarchist Roberto Arlt, the aliena-tion he perceived in urban life could only be resolved through apocalyptic destruction and a new beginning out of the ashes. Few, of course, were ready to go that far, but it was a vision that reflected a deeper disquiet with "modern" Buenos Aires than appeared on the surface.

As Andrew Lees has shown in examining images of urban life in Europe and the United States, conflicting views of the consequences of urbanization accompanied the growth of all major cities. In the final analysis, he concluded, "the majority of those who wrote about urban phenomena can be classified neither as city haters nor as city lovers. They saw the urban world as a complex mixture of both good and evil, a realm marked by sharp contrasts that suggested a superabundance of both changes and opportunities."[75] For the most part, the critics of Buenos Aires were engaged in this same process of evaluation and writing within this same context of "changes and opportunities." The analysis began in earnest in the 1920s and would continue and intensify in the following decade.

75 Andrew Lees, *Cities Perceived: Urban Society in European and American Thought, 1820–1940* (New York, 1985), p. 307.

6

Noel and the council

The presidential election victory of Marcelo Alvear in April 1922 reaffirmed the Radicals' dominance of the nation and its capital. Nationwide, Alvear received almost half of all votes cast, the rest scattered among Socialist, Progressive Democratic, and conservative opponents as well as representatives of various Radical dissident groups in the provinces. In the city of Buenos Aires, Alvear defeated the second-place Socialist presidential ticket by fourteen thousand votes.[1] The national deputy election, held concurrently, was closer, with the Radicals prevailing by about five thousand votes over the Socialists. The pattern of most elections of the period continued, with the Socialists carrying six working-class districts (2–4, 7–9) and the Radicals winning the rest.[2]

Alvear assumed the presidency on October 12, 1922. Two days later, *Crítica* noted with obvious satisfaction:"For the first time, after six years, the President of the Republic attended the races at the Argentine Hippodrome."[3] Equally reassuring to many was his decision to appoint Carlos M. Noel as his new intendente for the capital. Born in Buenos Aires in 1886, Noel had studied and received degrees in literature in Paris, where he had known Alvear and other Radicals of the porteño upper class. Returning to Buenos Aires in 1912, he became involved in Radical politics and the running of the family chocolate business. In 1916 he was chosen president of the Unión Industrial Argentina, an association of the country's leading industrialists, and was named to his first public position as director of the municipal loan bank. When labor agitation broke out during the war years, he also became a member of the right-wing Liga

---

1 Cantón, *Materiales*, vol. 1, p. 91.
2 Walter, *The Socialist Party*, pp. 182–3.
3 The rest of the headline on this story read: "Dr. Alvear is acclaimed – Rico wins the Grand National Prize in two minutes, 37 seconds," *Crítica* (October 14, 1922), p. 1. When the Congress in 1920 approved legislation to allow the Jockey Club to hold races on Thursday as well as Saturday and Sunday, Yrigoyen had vetoed the measure on the grounds that it would distract citizens from leading "moral, healthy, and positive lives." Félix Luna, *Yrigoyen* (Buenos Aires, 1964), p. 262.

Intendente Carlos M. Noel in his office (1923)

Patriótica Argentina and the misnamed National Labor Association, organized by his predecessor as intendente, Joaquín de Anchorena, to protect the rights and position of employers in the face of social protest. Added to his already impressive curriculum vitae was an appointment as special ambassador to Chile from 1920 to 1922.

There were few doubts as to Noel's aristocratic credentials. He was a member of the Círculo de Armas, the Jockey Club, the Buenos Aires Rowing Club, and the Argentine Yacht Club.[4] The 1918 voter registry listed him as residing with his brother Martín at Avenida Quintana 230 in the Barrio Norte. His brother was a well-known architect, who led the movement toward a nationalist neocolonial style in the 1920s. Later, Carlos Noel credited many of his achievements to Martin's aid and advice, recalling the times they returned from a party to sit, still in their tuxedos, and talk well into the early morning hours of their plans for the city.[5] Slim and debonair (*Crítica* almost automatically added the adjective *"elegante"* to any reference to the intendente), albeit with an oversized nose

4 *Quien es Quien*, 1939, pp. 306–7.
5 Pedro Alcázar Civil, "Las grandes figuras nacionales: Carlos M. Noel," *El Hogar*, 27, 1,136 (July 24, 1931), pp. 14, 57–8.

that fixed him as an unmistakable figure in cartoons and caricatures, Noel was the perfect complement to Alvear as a man well tailored to the mood and needs of the times. He also had the good fortune to lead the city during a period of relative social peace and renewed prosperity. As a result, and thanks to his own abilities and vision, he proved to be one of the most successful of the city's intendentes.

The composition of the council with which Noel would work was determined in elections held on November 26, 1922. Of the parties competing, the Socialists campaigned with the most vigor and optimism, confident they could build on their plurality. A new campaign organization, the Federación Socialista de la Capital, directed the party's effort, which emphasized reform of local government that would establish women's suffrage and an elected intendente. Looking ahead to the following year, when the agreement with the Anglo was due to expire, the Socialists also pledged a return to the ten-centavo fare.[6]

Part of the Socialists' optimism lay in the perceived and real vulnerabilities of the Radicals. Despite their sweeping presidential and congressional victory early in the year, the party was already showing the early signs of division between *Alvearistas* and *Yrigoyenistas*, which would lead to a decisive split two years later. Accordingly, there were disputes and delays over candidate selection and the initiation of the party's campaign. Moreover, the press was beginning to report on investigations into alleged irregularities and scandals during the Yrigoyen administration, which did little good for the overall image of the party as the date for the local election approached.

A generalized attack on Yrigoyenismo was a main feature of the campaign of the Concentración Nacional, a conservative coalition formed for the presidential election and also participating in the municipal contest. Meeting in the Teatro Coliseo on November 21, a meeting attended by "numerous ladies of our high society in the front-row boxes," the supporters of the Concentración heard party spokesman Adolfo Mugica blast the "disastrous administrations of the city during the period of *irigoyenismo.*"[7] The Progressive Democrats joined the chorus of criticisms of Yrigoyen's legacy and also joined the Socialists in pledging a return to the ten-centavo streetcar fare. The party's strong support for allowing professional boxing matches, moreover, won it the backing of sports-minded *Crítica*, which found the Concentración too conservative, the Radicals too corrupt, and the Socialists too doctrinaire.[8]

6 "Partido Socialista: Elección municipal; 26 de Noviembre, 1922," *La Vanguardia* (October 26, 1922), p. 1.
7 "Fué importantísimo el mitin organizado por los concentracionistas en el Coliseo," *Crítica* (November 21, 1922), p. 2.
8 "Mañana se realizarán las elecciones municipales," *Crítica* (November 25, 1922), p. 6.

The Radicals, who took some time to get their campaign moving, fiercely defended the party's record at both the national and local levels. At a closing rally, council candidates praised the work of recent intendentes and promised continued attention to the general urban problems of health, housing, and the overall poor condition of the southern neighborhoods. Various speakers also advocated more public housing for the working classes, reform of the municipal government law to assure greater autonomy, measures to lower the cost of fuel and electricity, improvement of bathing areas along the Río de la Plata, and the greater diffusion of city-sponsored popular sporting activities.[9] These points all had considerable popular appeal.

Contrary to the predictions of some, the Radicals easily bested the Socialists, winning by a margin of twelve thousand votes and doubling their advantage in the previous municipal election. In the process, the Radicals swept all districts except 2 and 8 and defeated the Socialists in their stronghold of La Boca by several hundred votes. Whatever their internal problems, the Radical political machine still had enough strength and cohesiveness to maintain the hold on the capital's electorate that the party had enjoyed since 1916. The conservatives and Progressive Democrats came in a distant third and fifth, respectively, the latter even bested by a dissident Radical faction, the Unión Cívica Radical Principista. Overall, public interest in this election was slight, with only a little better than half of the city's eligible voters bothering to cast their ballots.[10]

For Noel, the results were good news. When the new council met on January 1, the mainline Radicals had twelve seats plus one for the "*Principistas*," outnumbering the Socialists, who had ten, and the Communists, who had one. Again, the conservatives and Progressive Democrats, with three seats each, held the swing votes on the council.

During the preelection period, Noel had maintained a high profile by continuing the practice of his predecessor and making frequent tours of city neighborhoods at the behest of local development associations. To begin to realize his plans for the growth of the city, Noel made one of his first items of business with the new council a request for its approval of a $175 million peso loan (with the peso still at about two and one-half to the dollar at the time), which he intended to use for paying off past debts and for continuing, completing, and initiating certain municipal improvements. These included the following: fifteen million pesos apiece

9 *La Prensa* (November 25, 1922), p. 11.
10 The final results gave the Radicals 61,786 votes, the Socialists 49,581, the *Concentración* 11,905, the "Principista" Radicals 9,888, and the Progressive Democrats 8,394. Turnout was about 57 percent, with 159,020 voters of 280,026 registered. "Escrutinio de las elecciones municipales de la Capital," República Argentina, *Memoria, 1922–1923*, p. 585. See also, Appendix, Table A.2.

for city hospitals, amplification of the Balneario Municipal, and the construction of a riverside highway; twelve million for park and plaza enlargements and improvements; and, ten million for a new municipal frigorífico. In addition to these projects, substantial sums were also earmarked for a new city hall, continued work on the diagonales, expansion of Avenida Santa Fe and the Plaza del Congreso, extension of sanitation and other services to suburban districts, construction of low-cost housing, and garbage disposal.[11]

Approval of this loan would be the keystone to Noel's success or failure as intendente. In the meantime, as the council considered this proposal in early 1923, other important matters came up for consideration. One involved the continuing problem of streetcar fares. The concession of a twelve-centavo fare was due to expire in April 1923. Accordingly, on January 15, 1923, the Anglo and the Lacroze companies presented new petitions for a fare increase, this time raising the cost of a simple ride on both subway and tramway to fifteen centavos and the price of combination tickets between surface and underground transportation to twenty centavos. In justifying their new request, the companies pleaded that a continued narrow profit margin prevented the payment of dividends to stockholders, and cited rising costs of power, equipment, and wages. They promised to increase the wages of personnel by 20 percent once the new fares went into effect. In addition, the Anglo pledged to initiate the construction of a second subway line after approval of the increase, projecting a route that would run from the Retiro railway station in the north through the Constitución station in the south and on to the growing suburb of Avellaneda.[12]

Noel appointed a commission to study the matter. Composed of municipal accountants and technical personnel, the committee was to review company books, determine costs and profits, and judge the validity of the petitions' arguments. In the meantime, the Anglo and the Lacroze requested a six-month extension of the twelve-centavo fare. The council met in early April to decide on the extension. During the latter weeks of March numerous messages were sent to the councilmen urging that the higher fare not be granted. For example, a letter from the Centro de Fomento Juan B. Alberdi, representing the district near the Charcarita cemetery, claimed that the increase to twelve centavos had not produced better service, but, as opponents had argued, just the reverse. "Most trains," the petition claimed, "circulate without bells that work, without glass in the windows, with broken seats and the rails in very bad condition."

11 *State Records* (February 24, 1923), 835.51/B86.

12 "The Anglo–Argentine and Lacroze Tramway Companies' Application to Municipal Authorities for Permission to Increase Tariffs," *RRP*, 1625 (January 26, 1923), pp. 229–31.

Repeating the litany of Socialist and Progressive Democratic complaints, the centro pointed to poor scheduling, the hardship that the previous fare increase had imposed on workers, and the failure of future subway projects to address the needs of the center–west part of the city as additional reasons to reject this new fare proposal.

At the same time, the municipal investigative committee reported that "the present economic situation of the Company is good." It argued that costs, particularly of electricity, had decreased, while passenger traffic had increased, resulting in adequate profits. Moreover, with regard to the subway proposal, the committee urged initiation of the Retiro–Constitución line as soon as possible, but judged an extension to Avellaneda as impractical for the present.

Political considerations and the committee report had their effect on the council. An interested public jammed the limited galleries on April 6, the night of the debate. The Progressive Democrats joined with the Socialists to form the major opposition to the extension. Alejandro Castiñeiras, the principal Socialist spokesman, observed that in the past foreign concerns had operated in the republic without regulation of any kind. He urged the refusal of the extension as the sign of a new attitude on the part of freely elected public officials "to demonstrate that the rule of arbitrariness and abuse is no longer possible and that great capitalist enterprises, which provide public services, have to encounter in this council, at all times, a strong resistance to all which implies excessive exploitation to the detriment of the public."[13] The Radicals, caught in a political crossfire, challenged Socialist assertions of lax regulation of the companies, but in the end went along with the refusal. The major supporter of the extension was conservative José Guerrico, who repeated and reaffirmed the arguments of the original petition. After several hours of debate, the voting began in the early morning hours. By an overwhelming margin of twenty-five to three, with only the members of the Concentración Nacional voting in favor of the companies, the extension request was denied.[14] On April 10, porteños rode their subways and streetcars for the prewar price of ten centavos.

The council decision caught the transport companies by surprise. Because Noel was sympathetic to their cause, they had failed to foresee the adverse reaction. The Anglo, however, soon recovered and initiated a series of measures to gain another increase. Immediately after the April 6 decision, the company halted its contribution to the employees' pension fund and suspended special fares for surface–subway combinations. The council, for

13 *VTCD* (April 6, 1923), p. 245.
14 Ibid., p. 286. The full discussion of the issue is found between pages 236 and 286; an appendix contains the companies' request and petitions in opposition from many neighborhood associations.

its part, resolved to pressure the executive to enforce the ten-centavo rate and to restore the combination fares, some of which later were resumed. The Anglo also presented long and detailed counterarguments to the report of the municipal committee, claimed that Buenos Aires already enjoyed the cheapest and most efficient public transportation of any major city in the world, and warned that politically motivated denials of fare increases discouraged foreign investment, hindered attempts to modernize transportation, and, in the long run, harmed rather than benefitted the public. Company employees signed petitions and demonstrated in favor of the fare increase, arguing that without such action they would continue to be denied higher salaries and retirement benefits.

In November 1923 the intendente proposed a compromise. With the approval of his accountants and in consultation with the companies, Noel submitted to the council for their consideration an "ad-referendum" contract that established a central zone in downtown Buenos Aires: within the zone rides on trams were set at fifteen centavos; outside of it, rides were ten centavos. All subway fares were set at fifteen centavos. In return for the increases, the Anglo promised salary hikes of twenty percent for their employees, not to exceed 250 pesos per month, and the company bound itself to complete within three years of the signing of the contract the Retiro–Constitución line.[15] The intendente sent a similar proposal on behalf of the Lacroze Company to the council in August 1924.

Although the council took its time to consider these proposals, it acted in October of 1923 to regulate a new form of public transportation, which, along with the growing number of taxis, began to offer real competition to the streetcar. In 1922 the city had granted seventy-five licenses to operate new buses in the capital. Often domestically owned and operated, bus lines, unburdened by rails, offered more flexibility and a longer range than did the streetcars. Responding to their appearance, the council approved an ordinance that set up procedures for the municipality to register and regulate them and set a fare schedule of ten centavos for direct trips under five kilometers, fifteen centavos for direct trips over five kilometers, and twenty centavos for combinations between lines.[16] The popularity of the new conveyance was instantaneous and by the end of the decade there were 1,839 buses in operation carrying an average of forty million passengers per month, almost equaling the number carried on streetcars.[17] Although the buses were popular with the porteño public,

15 "The Anglo–Argentine Tramways Company, Limited: Proposed new tariff system and new underground line," *RRP*, 1667 (November 16, 1923), pp. 1155–7.

16 The ordinance regulating bus service was approved unanimously. The fare schedule was approved without a roll call by a vote of fourteen to ten. *VTCD* (October 19, 1923), p. 2213 and (October 26, 1923), pp. 2254–62.

17 MCBA, *Cincuentenario*, p. 95 and *Revista de Estadística Municipal*, 1940, pp. 73–5.

they represented yet another problem for the streetcar companies, already under fire for the deteriorating quality of their service and caught in a seemingly irresolvable conflict with the city council over their demands for a fare increase.

The furor over streetcar fares was only one of several controversies that Noel confronted during his first year in office. For most of the latter half of 1923, the principal dispute stemmed from the executive's proposal, introduced in July of that year, to change the basis upon which the tax on street lighting, sweeping, and cleaning was assessed. The proposal aimed to make the tax more uniform and inclusive, thereby increasing revenue. The Socialists strongly supported the measure, as did most Radicals, and the council ultimately approved the change at the end of the month.[18] The new tax, however, soon produced a firestorm of protest from property owners and their political representatives and Noel was forced to change course and rescind the measure in November.[19]

The rebuff on tax reform was part of a series of setbacks that Noel suffered at the end of his first year. In November, he had to accept the resignation of his head of the office for control of concession contracts and his director of public works, both of whom had publicly protested their exclusion from the deliberations of the technical committee established to consider the Anglo's new concession request. At the same time, Noel found himself caught up in a confrontation with the national government that recalled some of the difficulties Anchorena had experienced. Following up on a request initiated by his immediate predecessor, Juan B. Barnetche (an interim appointment between Cantilo and Noel), Noel had asked that the municipality have the right to review the construction plans of any new federal government buildings in the capital. A decree signed by Alvear, however, said that such a review was not obligatory, touching off a dispute between Noel and Alvear's main representative on the matter, Minister of the Interior Nicolás Matienzo, over the question of municipal autonomy. Tension was dissipated somewhat when Matienzo resigned over an unrelated matter on November 22. In the meantime, rumors circulated that Noel himself would resign, rumors that Noel firmly denied.[20]

Although resignation might not have been in the cards, it was clear that Noel was under fire on several fronts. Articles in *Crítica*, for example, depicted the mayor as too much under the control of, and ill-served by,

18 Voting in favor were ten Socialists, eight Radicals, one conservative, and one Communist. Voting against were three Progressive Democrats, two conservatives, two Radicals, and one Radical "Principista." *VTCD* (July 24, 1923), p. 1605.
19 *VTCD* (November 30, 1923), p. 2606 and *State Records* (November 30, 1923), 835.512/44.
20 "Se va o no se va de la intendencia el Dr. Noel?," *Crítica* (November 17, 1923), p. 1.

his secretaries – Emilio Ravignani in finance and Carlos Varangot in public works. They claimed that Noel had delegated too much responsibility, putting him out of touch with his own administration and public opinion. They criticized his apparent willingness to support higher streetcar fares, his reversal on tax reform, and the apparent instances of his buckling under pressure from the national government.[21]

Despite these difficulties and disappointments, Noel could still look back on his first year in office with some satisfaction. Most importantly, the council in August had overwhelmingly approved his loan request, which would enable him to embark on the capital improvements he envisioned for the city. Late in the year, accompanied by French landscape architect Jean Forestier, who had been contracted by the city as a special advisor on urban planning, and public parks director Carlos Thays, he toured the capital areas for which he planned major embellishments. Furthermore, despite his problems with the city council, the local legislature had agreed to many of his initiatives. In December, too, the council had given a boost to the city's sports aficionados by agreeing to allow previously prohibited professional boxing matches under controlled and regulated circumstances.[22]

Noel's relations with the council did not noticeably ease during the following year. Disagreements over the creation, operation, and costs of a government office designed to control the distribution and price of food in the city (Junta de Abastecimiento) led council opponents to consider impeachment of the executive. In October 1924, a proposal to look into the removal of the intendente failed by only a few votes to get the needed two-thirds to proceed; the executive was saved from this embarrassment only by the continued loyalty of the Radical bloc, which voted solidly against the measure.[23]

Although Noel managed to dodge this particular bullet, he continued to face the persistently nettlesome problem of the convenience and cost of public transportation. Questions of traffic flow, congestion, and safety, especially in the downtown area, continued to preoccupy and irritate many porteños. The introduction of bus service had provided a new alternative for the city's commuters. Moreover, as *El Hogar* pointed out, coming as they did in all sizes and colors – "lake blue, liquid yellow, philosophic black, sky violet, ill-tempered red, cinemagraphic white"

21 "El intendente es un prisionero de sus secretarios, los doctores Ravignani y Varangot," *Crítica* (December 12, 1923), p. 7.
22 Nine Radicals, three Progressive Democrats, two conservatives, and one "Principista" voted to overturn the ordinance prohibiting boxing over the opposition of nine Socialists. *VTCD* (December 10, 1923), pp. 2720–39.
23 *VTCD* (October 17, 1924), pp. 1398–1405 and (October 20, 1924), pp. 1408–38.

– the new vehicles added a picturesque and pleasing note to the cityscape. At the same time, however, as *El Hogar* also explained, pity the poor porteño who had to ride on these new conveyances, which, because of the municipality's failure to enforce the "completo," were invariably crowded, uncomfortable, and dangerous. Adding to the danger were drivers who delighted in stopping abruptly at the last moment, throwing standing passengers rudely against each other or to the floor.[24] Adding insult to injury, a Socialist councilman reported that many bus companies sought to avoid the limits on fares set the previous year by purposely establishing short routes, which required long-distance passengers to purchase more expensive combination and transfer tickets.[25] To relieve these problems, *El Hogar* and others argued, not only did existing ordinances have to be enforced more strictly, but work on new street expansion and subway construction also had to proceed more rapidly.[26]

At the end of the year, the city council addressed the compromise Noel had suggested twelve months earlier to break the stalemate on street-car fares and subway construction. The committee assigned to study the proposed contracts made its report on November 6, 1924. The majority finding was the toughest stance yet against the Anglo and Lacroze tramway companies. It recommended rejecting the ad-referendum contracts, maintaining all fares – surface and underground – at ten centavos, stabilizing all combinations at present fares, and cancelling the second subway concession to the Anglo and opening the contract to new bids. Echoing their role in the refusal to extend the 1920 twelve-centavo increase, Progressive Democrats and Socialists led the charge against the companies. Progressive Democratic councilman Carlos Acevedo accused the Anglo of violating its original 1909 subway contract with the city, in which it promised to maintain a ten-centavo fare for eighty years. He also stated that his personal review of company books revealed that the Anglo had reaped large profits and dividends for 1923, while refusing to contribute to the pension fund. Acevedo suggested that profits were hidden in the transfer of funds from the administrative seat of the firm in London to the headquarters of the majority stockholder, the Sociétè Financiére de Transports et d'Enterprises Industrielles (SOFINA) of Brussels.[27]

After several days of discussion, the council on November 21 voted seventeen to twelve in favor of the majority report. All ten Socialists voted in the affirmative, as did the three Progressive Democrats and one Communist. The Radicals divided, with two members of the UCR and the Radical Principista voting in favor, nine Radicals allying with the

24 Mono Sabio, "Sobre la inconstitucionalidad del omnibus," *El Hogar*, 22, 772 (August 1, 1924).
25 *VTCD* (April 25, 1924), pp. 164–79.
26 "El pobre público de Buenos Aires," *El Hogar*, 22, 791 (December 12, 1924).
27 *VTCD* (November 6, 1924), pp. 1609–14.

three representatives of the Concentración Nacional against.[28] The victory, however, was short lived. In early December, Noel vetoed the council's proposal, arguing that if allowed to stand the cancellations would "endanger the normal march of municipal government in the future."[29] The opposition, unable to muster a two-thirds majority to override the veto, settled on compromise ordinances, which required the Anglo to present definite plans for opening the work on its second subway line and allowing alternative proposals for such construction. These ordinances were approved sixteen to nine, with only the Radical bloc, that had voted against the cancellations, expressing its opposition.[30] In essence, however, the stalemate was little changed. Streetcar fares still stood at ten centavos, and so long as that was the case, it was evident that the Anglo would do little to fulfill its obligation to commence the second subway or do much to improve its deteriorating service.

The year also included its instances of fruitful collaboration between the intendente and the council. In September and October, the local legislators agreed to the mayor's plans to expand the riverine boulevard known as the ˋCostanera, as well as the Balneario Municipal, develop a major park in the Retiro area, and extend public works to suburban areas of the city.[31] In December, the council approved the next year's budget with relatively few objections, even from the Socialists, and gave the city executive authority to go ahead with purchases that would move forward the completion of the Diagonal Norte and the expansion of Santa Fe.

The fourth set of postreform municipal elections was held in the midst of the council debate over the transportation contracts. The Socialists continued to try to take advantage of their position on this issue. A leaflet distributed by the party during the campaign, for example, asked of the voter:"Do you want your streetcar ticket to increase to 15 and 20 centavos? Vote for Radicals and Conservatives or throw away your votes. Do you want the 10 centavo ticket? Vote for the Socialist candidates."[32]

Of greater significance, however, was the division that had occurred among the Radicals between the supporters of Alvear, or the *"antipersonalistas"* opposed to Yrigoyen's excessive personal control of the party,

28 *VTCD* (November 21, 1924), p. 1844.
29 *VTCD* (December 5, 1924), p. 2006.   30 *VTCD* (December 19, 1924), pp. 2232–3.
31 *VTCD* (September 30, 1924), pp. 1214–16 and (October 14, 1924), p. 1374. There were still many indications that southern and western districts of the city were being ignored by the local government. For example, an article in *Crítica* of November 9, 1923 (p. 8), entitled "Es necessario que el Dr. Noel se preocupe de los barrios suburbanos," painted a bleak picture of a landscape dotted by burning garbage, frequent flooding, stagnant pools, and houses infested by flies and mosquitos in the areas of Parque Patricios, Nueva Pompeya, and Puente Alsina.
32 *La Vanguardia* (November 15, 1924), p. 2.

and the *"personalistas"* associated with the ex-president. The beginnings of that split had already helped Socialist Mario Bravo defeat Radical Arturo Goyeneche in the February 4, 1923 election tò fill a national Senate seat from the capital. In that contest, the Yrigoyenistas had refused to support Goyeneche, a political enemy of the former president. One year later, the Socialists defeated the Radicals by about six thousand votes citywide to capture thirteen of nineteen national deputy seats from the capital and party leader Juan B. Justo bested Radical Pablo Torello by about ten thousand tallies to give the Socialists both national Senate seats. Again, the dissension within Radical ranks was a crucial factor in the Socialist triumph.[33]

The Radical dispute did not often manifest itself in the city council. Whatever the disagreements between Alvearistas and Yrigoyenistas, the Radical councilmen generally voted as a bloc on most issues. The Radical split, however, did influence the outcome of the municipal elections held on November 16. The Radicals entered two slates:one the Yrigoyenista-backed UCR de la Avenida de Mayo and the other Alvearista, or perhaps more accurately, anti-Yrigoyenista UCR Tacuari.[34] Combined, the Radicals polled better than eighty-one thousand votes, reaffirming that party's grip on the capital's electorate. However, dividing the vote, with almost fifty-six thousand going to the Yrigoyenistas and almost thirty-six thousand to the Alvearistas, some of which probably came from conservative supporters, allowed the Socialists to finish in first place with a little more than fifty-seven thousand votes. The conservatives, Progressive Democrats, and Communists finished a far distant fourth, fifth, and sixth, respectively. Turnout, at about 58 percent, was only slightly higher than it had been two years earlier.[35]

When the new council met in January 1925, it marked the beginning of the seventh year of popularly elected city government in Buenos Aires. Opinions on the success of the experiment were decidedly mixed. An article in *El Hogar* early in the year, for example, described the council as a hard-working and productive institution. Councilmen, the article noted, labored day and night – often not completing sessions before dawn – with no staff and, at the time, for no pay. Many councilmen devoted long hours to tours of the city, visits with constituents, and inspections of hospitals, workshops, conventillos, and other facilities. Public impression notwithstanding, *El Hogar* argued that councilmen, at least in the mid-1920s, were generally more resistant to the temptation to bribery

33 Walter, *The Socialist Party*, pp. 189–91.
34 These names referred to the respective streets in the city where the competing factions had their headquarters.
35 *La Vanguardia* (November 20–30, 1924) and "Elecciones municipales del 16 de Noviembre de 1924," República Argentina, *Memoria, 1924–1925*, pp. 186–7. See also Appendix, Table A.2.

or undue influence from lobbying organizations than were national congressmen.[36]

The ever-skeptical *Crítica* took a contrary position. Perhaps more accurately reflecting general opinion, the daily claimed that the postreform city council had been a disappointment for those who had hoped popular suffrage would improve its performance. Instead, it argued, the council had succumbed to the "Argentine vice" of excessive politicking and partisanship, engaging in sterile debate and ignoring the basic problems of the city.[37] The council did, however, serve some purpose, according to *Crítica*. Because its sessions were free and open to the public, the porteño with nothing else to do might attend its sessions and be provided with some light entertainment and a few laughs.[38] *Caras y Caretas* reflected the same sentiment with a cartoon showing councilmen trading insults and disagreements on any number of issues, but voting unanimously for a proposal to consider granting themselves a salary.[39] Another cartoon depicted Noel receiving a distinguished foreign visitor and complaining that the council was more of an obstacle than a partner in the business of governing the city.[40]

In reality, although Noel, like all intendentes, had his difficulties with the council, he also had the advantage of a clear Radical majority (seventeen Radical councilmen to ten Socialists, two Conservatives, and one Progressive Democrat) operating on his behalf. Although he suffered some reverses and rebuffs, he continued to see most of his initiatives enacted. Moreover, during the remainder of his term the division within the Radical party did not appear to work to his detriment. Nonetheless, he also continued to have difficulty with the Socialist and Progressive Democratic opposition. In the continuing debate over streetcar and subway issues, for example, little progress was made. The Anglo, for its part, aimed to block the stalemate with the council by proposing a new plan for even more extensive subway construction and applied considerable pressure on both the national and local administrations to lobby on its behalf. Socialist and Progressive Democratic resistance to any plan that implied fare increases, however, prevented consideration of the new scheme.

While the council delayed on streetcars and subways, it again turned its attention to regulating the newly established bus service. In early November, the council approved an ordinance setting the completo for

36 Ernesto B. Carmona, "El concejo deliberante y el negro del cuento: Un balance de actividades," *El Hogar*, 21, 794 (January 2, 1925), p. 6.
37 "No hay mucho interés por los próximos comicios municipales," *Crítica* (October 22, 1924), p. 3.
38 "Si usted está aburrido asista a las sesiones del Honorable Concejo Deliberante," *Crítica* (December 21, 1924), p. 7.
39 "El queso de la concordancia," *Caras y Caretas* (1925).
40 "Meditaciones filosóficas," *Caras y Caretas* (1925).

buses during rush hours.[41] Despite a companion resolution that the executive also enforce more strictly the limits on seated and standing passengers on streetcars, bus owners soon complained that they were being unduly monitored whereas the streetcars continued to evade regulation. More significantly, at the end of December the council passed ordinances that clarified earlier measures regulating bus service overall and reaffirmed, over the objections of some, the fare of ten centavos for a ride under five kilometers.[42] In the same month, the council called for a competition to receive bids for the establishment of electric traffic signals in a city still without them.[43]

Items other than those dealing with public transportation were also considered. All councilmen agreed, as *Caras y Caretas* had noted, to vote themselves a salary of 600 pesos a month. They also authorized the executive to purchase property at the downtown corner of Perú and Victoria (now Hipólito Yrigoyen) to begin the construction of a new building to house the council. There was general agreement, too, on an ordinance to assure the proper physical condition of professional soccer players by taxing the tickets sold to attend these matches in order to cover the cost of the physical examination; the remainder was to go to the development of playing fields and playgrounds for children in the capital.[44]

For Noel, the sessions of 1925 had generally positive results. As the nation's overall prosperity reached full throttle, municipal finances were considered to be in "a flourishing condition" with a budget surplus predicted for the end of the year.[45] Under these circumstances, the intendente was able to earmark increases in spending for hospitals, sanitation facilities, and public works, as well as salary increases for municipal employees, increases that the council approved with little objection. Despite some resistance from the Socialists, the council also approved Noel's efforts to renegotiate the payment due on the Baring Brothers loan contracted by the Anchorena administration before the war. On the negative side, on December 16, three Radicals joined eight Socialists and the Radical Principista to condemn Noel's failure to take action against certain municipal employees charged with abusing their office; additionally, ten Radicals joined with seven Socialists to overturn the mayor's veto of a Socialist-inspired measure to prohibit the manufacture and sale of lead-based paint in the city.[46]

Reviews of Noel's performance at the end of his first three-year term,

41 In buses with a seating capacity for twenty-two passengers, a maximum of six were allowed to stand in the aisle and three on the platforms. *VTCD* (November 6, 1925), pp. 1938–49.
42 *VTCD* (December 16, 1925), p. 2439.   43 *VTCD* (September 22, 1925), pp. 1438–9.
44 *VTCD* (December 30, 1925), p. 3025–92.
45 *State Records* (November 5, 1925), 825.00/370.
46 *VTCD* (December 16, 1925), pp. 2392–935.

as with that of the council, were mixed. *El Hogar*, in a commentary that appeared a few days before Alvear reappointed Noel, accused the executive of spending too many resources and too much attention on high-profile public works and not enough of either to the ever-worsening problems of downtown traffic congestion and the conditions of flood-prone, low-lying suburban districts.[47] Responding to this criticism, Noel promised, on the day he was reappointed, to devote the principal efforts of his second term to improvements in southern and western neighborhoods. *Crítica*, which two years earlier had depicted Noel as the weak "prisoner of his secretaries," now had nothing but praise for the mayor. "Brilliantly" assisted by Ravignani and Varangot, *Crítica* rhapsodized that Noel, "young and hardworking," had been responsible for the continued growth of the downtown area, the spread of paved streets, the ever-greater extension of municipal services, and the initiation of park improvements and street expansion. The future of the city under Noel's enlightened direction, the daily concluded, was bright indeed.[48]

Near the end of his first term, Noel had provided graphic form of his vision for the capital's future. A constant criticism of the city's growth had been the failure to adhere to any overall plan of urban development, producing a helter-skelter approach to the problems of urban design and the efficient use of municipal resources. On September 1, 1925, Noel submitted to the national government a 427-page detailed and clearly illustrated proposal to regulate and to organize more rationally the growth of the city. The result of the work of a commission headed by architect René Karman, it had benefited from the observations of French advisor Jean Forestier and consultation with officials from Brussels and Barcelona. Despite the reliance on European models, the commission recognized that Buenos Aires was distinct from the "traditional cities" of the old world. An "American city" in its basic features, with a "Latin population," it "had an urban development and population growth only comparable to the cities of the North American hemisphere."

The proposal listed as its first objective to respect the "historic face" of the city. This meant retaining colonial buildings, restoring the San Telmo district, and learning to live with the narrow streets in the centro, which would be somewhat alleviated by completion of the diagonales and the projected north–south boulevard linking Retiro with Constitución. Outside of the central city, the report called for the creation of new, planned neighborhoods, workers' districts, and "garden" cities all linked to downtown. To take fuller advantage of the Río de la Plata, the Avenida

---

47 "El progreso edilicio ha quedado en descubierto," *El Hogar*, 21, 834 (October 9, 1925).
48 *Crítica* (October 14, 1925), p. 6 and "La labor municipal del año que hoy termina ha sido proficua para la Comuna de Buenos Aires," *Crítica* (December 31, 1925), p. 4.

Costanera, currently under construction along the southeastern edge of the city, should be extended to the northern limits and include a municipal aquarium, a large restaurant or municipal casino, an outdoor bandstand for the municipal orchestra, and a riverside promenade (*malecón*) with a weather tower. The plan also recommended dividing the city into zones according to the function and purposes of individual districts, multiplying parks and plazas to provide more open recreational space, grouping government buildings to form "monumental centers," and controlling buildings so as to assure the free circulation of light and air. To achieve these goals, the proposal urged the national government to provide municipal authorities with more power to expropriate property through the right of eminent domain and greater flexibility in determining street widths and building heights.

The problems of public transportation also received attention. The major aims of any change in this regard, the plan noted, were to relieve congestion downtown and to improve communication between the center of the city and its periphery. To accomplish this, certain of the most congested streets should be widened, work on the diagonales should proceed, and public plazas and other such spaces should be set aside for automobile parking. Moreover, an overall plan to coordinate traffic in the city, especially railroad and subway traffic, should be prepared.[49]

The 1925 plan, which bore Noel's signature, was not the first of its kind, nor would it be the last. To some extent, it validated works like the Avenida Costanera and the diagonales, which were already in progress. Typically, the city followed through on some of the suggested proposals, modified others, and abandoned or neglected still more. As a document per se, however, it reflected by the mid-1920s city leaders' awareness of the capital's progress and problems and of the need to plan adequately for its future development. It was also clear testimony of Noel's desire to leave his own lasting mark on Argentina's capital.

At the end of 1925, Noel had requested of the national government a leave of absence to attend an international congress on suburban housing problems to be held in Paris. With his reappointment that trip was postponed, but in early 1926 the intendente submitted a similar petition. Despite Socialist objections, Alvear and the council acceded to the somewhat unusual, although not altogether unprecedented, request.[50] As a result, the president of the council, anti-personalista Radical Horacio Casco, was named to serve as acting city executive for several months in mid-1926.

49 Intendencia Municipal, Comision de Estética Edilicia, *Proyecto orgánico para la urbanización del municipio.*
50 *VTCD* (April 16, 1926), p. 143.

The council continued to function under Casco much as it had under Noel. A major item of old business was resolved in May when the council accepted the results of negotiations carried out by city representative Carlos Meyer Pellegrini and officials of the German banks to whom part of the 1914 Baring loan had been subcontracted. Although the city had kept up its payments, the wartime interruption and complications had prevented half of the loan amount being delivered. Thanks to Meyer Pellegrini's intercession, the banks agreed to provide the remaining amount with only a moderate loss overall to the city.[51] At the same time, the Radical majority on the council voted, over Socialist opposition, a measure that forgave penalties imposed on porteños who had failed to pay their municipal taxes on time, repeating a common municipal practice of pardon in this regard.[52]

Under Casco, much of the council's attention was again focused on streetcar fares and subway construction, with several new plans presented for consideration. Again, none of these moved forward because competing proposals did not generate sufficient majority support within a body that was still deeply divided over the best way to resolve the impasse and because political considerations were always present. Generally, the Radicals and conservatives still favored some sort of accommodation with the Anglo so that construction on subways might proceed, whereas Socialists and the Progressive Democratic councilman resolutely objected to any proposal that granted a fare increase.

Noel reassumed his duties on the first of October 1926. In an interview with *Caras y Caretas* upon his return from France, he expressed his concern that Buenos Aires was not progressing at the same rate as European cities he had observed. The Argentine capital, he remarked, was a *"ciudad grande"* (large city) but not yet a *"gran ciudad"* (great city). A main obstacle to greatness remained the problem of traffic congestion, which he hoped to resolve with more rapid progress on boulevard construction and street widening. He showed some irritation with the council for an eight-month delay in acting upon his proposal to install electric traffic signals in the city as a way to control and improve traffic flow.[53]

Noel returned to his usual ups and downs with the council. His budget request for the coming year passed fairly smoothly, as did a bond issue of twenty-six million pesos, more than a third of which was earmarked for the new municipal frigorífico whose construction was also sanctioned. Noel vetoed as too restrictive an ordinance that would have prohibited playing soccer and holding boxing matches indoors during the summer

51 *VTCD* (May 7, 1926), pp. 277–302.   52 *VTCD* (June 24, 1926), pp. 791–808.
53 "El Intendente Municipal Dr. Carlos M. Noel traza la ciudad futura," *Caras y Caretas*, 29, 1482 (October 9, 1926).

months. The council countered with a new ordinance permitting the practice of sports in the summer, but only during the cooler hours of the day and night. The council also voted to override vetoes of ordinances that prohibited the establishment of open markets in and around the Plaza del Congreso and another that sought to regulate the selection of auctioneers for the sale of municipal property. At the end of December, the council, after lengthy debate, also approved a majority report from the finance committee censuring Noel for what they charged were certain irregularities in the management of a large municipal bond issue of 1923; the matter was sent to the committee on interpretation for further review.[54]

In addition to these matters, the council sanctioned a number of other items that would have a lasting impact on the city. These included permission to construct the twenty-story Mihanovich building, the city's first skyscraper; the establishment of the eight-hour day and forty-four-hour week in factories and workshops owned by the municipality; provisions regulating the construction and landscaping both for the proposed southern diagonal and for the highway slated to run along the northern and western edge of the city (Avenida General José María Paz); regulations concerning the acquisition of license plates for automobiles registered in the city; and reduced-price bus fares for the capital's student population.

During the council's deliberations on these and other matters, Noel maintained a high public profile. He presided with Alvear over the laying of the cornerstone of the new city council building and, also in the company of the chief executive, attended the fiftieth anniversary celebration of the Anglo–Argentine Tramway Company's operation in the capital. Probably the mayor's proudest moment, however, had come earlier in the year when he, again with Alvear, inaugurated work on the Costanera Norte, the riverside boulevard proposed in the 1925 city plan. This project would complement and continue the southern Costanera, which was completed earlier in 1926. That avenue, part of which today bears Noel's name, ran along the far eastern edge of the city beyond the old port area. Inspired in part by Forestier's suggestions, it was bordered on one side by spacious, tree-shaded parks, which also housed popular cafés and confiterias and on the other by a majestic promenade, or boardwalk, which at its southern end intersected with the expanded and modernized Balneario Municipal. Built by the firm of Siemens Bauunion, which also had the contract for the northern extension, and under the direction of city engineer Raúl A. Sortini, it had entailed reclaiming land from the river by the sinking of heavy concrete pilings, the construction of a retaining wall,

The Balneario Municipal and the Costanera Sur, with the old port in the
background (January 1936)

and the generous use of landfill. The final result was a prospect that
porteños hoped could compare with similar waterfronts in Nice, Rio de
Janeiro, Coney Island, and Naples and would serve finally to allow them
to take fuller advantage of the river estuary by which so many had arrived
in Buenos Aires and thereafter largely ignored.

Noel was, deservedly, given much of the credit for the Costanera.
Ultimately, it would be the major monumental achievement of his administration.[55] Whether or not this was his intention, there were also
expectations that completion of the southern Costanera and expansion of
the balneario would particularly benefit the previously neglected working-
class districts of the city. The popular daily *La Razón*, a major competitor
to *Crítica*, described this prospect in lyrical tones:

55 Bucich Escobar, *Buenos Aires*, p. 205 and MCBA, *Cincuentenario*, p. 116. In his interview with *El
Hogar* several years later, Noel himself labeled the construction of the Costanera, which in his
words was "one of South America's greatest promenades," as the major achievement of his
administration. *El Hogar* (July 21, 1931).

Today the southern zone of the capital receives, in equal proportion to that of the northern zone, the benefits of municipal action. This new stretch of the balneario, constructed on river banks which just a short while ago were desolate, is a clear demonstration of the new order of things opening up for the neighborhoods of the south. The proud promenade, which profiles its elegant silhouette on the horizon of the Río de la Plata, will see congregated the multitudes of San Telmo, Monserrat, Concepción, La Boca, Barracas, the old porteño neighborhoods . . . . What a grand and beautiful spectacle the promenade of the balneario will provide, with its hundreds of thousands of souls striding along the broad avenue which borders the estuary![56]

Although it is not entirely clear just who used the Costanera and the balneario, there is little doubt as to their popularity. By early 1927, *El Hogar,* which had remarked on the deserted aspect of the area a few months earlier, was now complaining about the inordinate traffic congestion on the Costanera, a congestion that made it almost impossible to move on the weekends.[57] The opening of the bathing season at the balneario became a prominent feature of most popular periodicals, which delighted in publishing pictures of young women of the city displaying the latest styles of swimming costumes as they tested the muddy waters of the estuary. And, from mid-decade through the 1930s, the Costanera Sur and its swimming pier continued to attract large crowds and to serve, at least in the summer months, as a main recreation area for many porteños. Whatever its undoubted benefits, however, as Socialist Antonio Zaccagnini, who represented the city council at the inauguration of the Costanera Norte, observed, it could not overshadow the continuing need to address the problems of the many still neglected and mostly poor areas of the city.[58]

The inequitable distribution of wealth and of public works in the city was a main theme of the November 1926 municipal election. Radical candidates promised to pay more attention to social issues and the needs of the less fortunate in the capital and to shift more attention to the problems of outlying neighborhoods. Radical candidate Francisco Turano argued that the city government should not wait to hear the pleas of neighborhood development associations, but should act to provide necessary public services to neglected areas of the capital before such petitions were raised and indeed even before such associations were formed.[59] As was its custom, *Crítica* continued to publish articles underscoring the contrasts to be found in the city, such as the continuing presence of

56 *La Razón* (Buenos Aires: December 24, 1926), p. 8.
57 *El Hogar,* 23, 901 (January 21, 1927).
58 *VTCD* (April 16, 1926), p. 140. 59 *Crítica* (November 16, 1926), p. 9.

conventillos in the midst of areas of new apartment buildings or the city's failure to respond to the requests of a particular neighborhood for the improvement of a main street that traversed it.[60]

The Socialists, as usual, campaigned on a pledge to defend "the working people . . . against the privileged."[61] They accused the anti-personalista Radicals of seeking only to protect special interests, such as those of the Anglo, and the personalista Radicals of only being concerned with their prospects in the presidential elections two years hence. They also continued to hammer hard on the transport fare question, underscoring their defense of the ten-centavo ticket and the Radicals' apparent sympathy with the companies' request for an increase.

If, as the Socialists charged, the Yrigoyenistas were mainly concerned about the party's position prior to the national election of 1928, then the Radicals must have been greatly encouraged by the results of the municipal contest. Predicting a victory by 10,000 votes, they actually outdistanced their Socialist rivals by almost three times that number (70,548 to 42,897), carried every district of the city, and almost equaled the total of the anti-personalistas (31,165) and Socialists combined.[62] The victory reinforced the pattern of the national congressional election in the capital held earlier in the year, in which the Radicals had bested the Socialists by almost 16,000 votes.

The Socialists may have been hurt by the general lack of interest in the election, which produced a turnout of only 53 percent. They accused the Yrigoyenistas of resorting to their familiar tactics of patronage and the promise of direct benefits as key factors in winning over independent votes, but also admitted that a growing division within their own ranks had contributed to their disastrous showing.[63] Whatever the causes of the Socialist decline, the local contest was one more sign of Radical leader Yrigoyen's continued hold on the loyalties of many voters and his party's successful resistance to challengers from both within and without.

Of immediate benefit to the Yrigoyenistas was the fact that thanks to their victory they now controlled twelve of the seventeen Radical seats on the council. The Socialists had been reduced to eight councilmen, a position that would be further undermined when the party underwent a formal division in 1927. Conservatives José Guerrico and Adolfo Mugica, now representing the Partido Nacionalista, retained their seats on the council. Returning to the council as a Communist party councilman was José F. Penelón. The best-known newcomer was popular comedian and actor

60 "Frente a la belleza de la construcción está el contraste de la calle," *Crítica* (November 1, 1926), p. 9.
61 "El Pueblo debe hacerse presente," *La Vanguardia* (November 20, 1926), p. 1.
62 República Argentina, *Memoria, 1926–1927*, pp. 140–1. See also, Appendix, Table A.2.
63 "A própósito de los resultados del escrutinio," *La Vanguardia* (December 14, 1926), p. 1.

Right to left, Intendente Noel, Socialist Councilman Antonio Zaccagnini, President and Mrs. Alvear at the opening of a public housing project (1925)

Florencio Parravicini, representing the Gente del Teatro, who had garnered 9,450 votes. Referring to his representation of the interests of employees in municipally regulated places of entertainment, *Caras y Caretas* suggested tongue-in-check that Parravicini's main function would be to bring many more laughs to the lips of contentious and somber council members.[64]

Noel did not have much to do with this council. At the end of April

64 "A un paso de las elecciones municipales," *Caras y Caretas*, 29, 1468 (November 20, 1926).

he submitted his resignation as intendente halfway through his second term and withdrew, until 1930, from public and political life in general. "Certain incidents of a political character," were later given as the reasons behind Noel's departure.[65] The precipitating cause was the decision of the anti-personalistas to name as the leader of their ticket for the presidential elections of April 1928, Leopoldo Melo, national senator from the province of Entre Ríos. Because Melo had opposed Noel's reappointment as intendente, the mayor took this as an apparent sign of disapproval from the new leader of his party and hence the resignation. Commenting on these events, *The Review of the River Plate*, a strong sympathizer of the Anglo throughout the debate over the streetcar-fare and subway issue, lamented Noel's decision as it judged he had "done splendid service together with his collaborators at the head of the municipality."[66] Although not everyone, especially the Socialists, might have concurred at the time, and despite the fact that Noel left office before all of his projects were completed, few would argue the fact that Noel's administration had been one of the most productive in the city's twentieth-century history.

Anti-personalista Horacio Casco, who previously had filled in for Noel, was named to complete the former intendente's term. Under Casco, the council approved a variety of diverse measures. On May 24, for example, the Radicals passed a resolution to distribute clothing, sewing machines, and household items to the city's needy as part of the celebration of the May 25th holiday, overcoming Socialist objections that such gestures should be a normal part of city business and not directly linked to patriotic occasions.[67] In June, the council agreed to establish a municipal radio station that, among other things, would broadcast performances of the city orchestra and the deliberations of the council itself.[68] In October, after lengthy discussion, anti-personalistas, Socialists, conservatives, and Penelón joined forces to overcome Yrigoyenista objections – as well as that of Parravicini – to prohibit late-night, or, as the case might be, early-morning theatrical productions. Proponents argued that the ordinance was needed to protect theater employees, whereas opponents countered that it was too restrictive.[69] All agreed, however, to grant a parcel of municipal land on Avenida Santa Fe for the construction of the Casa del

65 Bucich Escobar, *Buenos Aires*, p. 206. A cartoon in *Caras y Caretas* implied that by April Noel was becoming fatigued and annoyed with the problems and complaints associated with managing city affairs and longed to resume his literary career. "Novelista o Intendente," *Caras y Caretas*, 30, 1489 (April 16, 1927).

66 *RRP*, no. 1848 (May 6, 1927), p. 28.

67 Eight personalista Radicals joined with five anti-personalistas to beat back the objections of seven Socialists and Communist Penelón on this issue. *VTCD* (May 24, 1927), pp. 574–86.

68 *VTCD* (June 28, 1927), p. 1140.   69 *VTCD* (October 4, 1927), p. 1844.

Teatro, which would provide lodging for impoverished actors.[70] With somewhat less agreement, but nonetheless by a vote of fifteen to six, the council approved an ordinance to regularize and to regulate the creation and operation of neighborhood development societies.[71]

Party divisions, which had played a relatively minor role in previous sessions, became more prominent in the council proceedings of 1927. The splintering of the Socialist party openly manifested itself on August 19, 1927, when Councilman Manuel Palacín of the mainline party called on Manuel González Maseda and Carlos Manacorda of the newly formed Independent Socialist party to resign their council positions.[72] Palacín argued that Socialist voters supported programs, not personalities. Because the two councilmen had run on the Socialists' 1926 platform and then had abandoned the party, he contended, they served under false pretenses and should surrender their seats. The two "Independents" responded that they still adhered to the Socialist program, regardless of party affiliation, and refused to step down.[73] From the date of this discussion, González Maseda and Manacorda gradually moved apart from the Socialist bloc, introducing legislation on their own and occasionally voting with the opposition against their former colleagues. Most of their proposals, however, were carbon copies of regular Socialist projects and on matters of major importance they usually returned to the fold when it came time to vote.

The pattern for the Radicals was similar. On about half of the items that came up for roll call in 1927, both Radical factions voted as a bloc, but the other half found them on opposite sides. An important issue of apparent disagreement was the controversial and much discussed Junta de Abastecimiento created by Noel to control and distribute food to the city. On December 16 the majority of the committee looking into the operation of the junta – a Socialist and two Yrigoyenista Radicals, with Alvearista Radical Antonio Inchausti in dissent – recommended that it be dissolved. Critics claimed that the junta was a total failure in terms of controlling and lowering prices. Its defenders, although admitting some flaws, claimed that the office and its directors were on the right path toward a realization of its goals. When it came time, on the last session of the year, to vote on the majority report, spokesmen for the personalista Radicals claimed that they and the council were too fatigued to consider the matter. This attitude led Socialist Américo Ghioldi to argue that the Yrigoyenistas were now allied with the Alvearistas in defense of the

70 *VTCD* (December 30, 1927), p. 3503.   71 *VTCD* (November 30, 1927), pp. 2429–35.

72 For more on the Socialist division and the creation of a competing party, see Walter, *The Socialist Party*, pp. 205–10 and Horacio Sanguinetti, *Los Socialistas Independientes* (Buenos Aires, 1981).

73 *VTCD* (August 19, 1927), pp. 1327–35.

junta, a charge the personalista Radicals denied. Finally, the leader of the anti-personalistas led his faction out of the chamber, preventing a quorum and effectively postponing any action on the proposal until well into the following year.[74]

Issues involving public transportation continued to be featured items on the council's agenda. In mid-June, a strike by the capital's taxi drivers against alleged mistreatment by the police prompted the approval of an ordinance that simplified the procedures by which chauffeurs' licenses were granted, increased the personnel in the municipality's traffic control division, and liberalized rules for the circulation and parking of taxis at certain hours of the day.[75] In late July and early August, the chauffeurs' union went on strike to protest restriction on their ability to circulate freely on certain downtown streets between 10:00 AM and 8:00 PM in search of passengers. This protest led to an ordinance that permitted unoccupied taxis to move without restriction throughout the capital so long as they maintained a speed commensurate with the rest of the vehicular traffic in the same area.[76] During approximately the same period, the municipality tried and then abandoned an experiment with electric traffic signals in the downtown area, determining that these produced more delays than they resolved.[77]

The measures involving taxis enjoyed the general support of all factions on the council. More contentious was the continuing matter of streetcar fares and subway construction. In April 1927, England's Lord Ampthill, who, in concert with Argentine interests represented by Celestino and Horacio Marco, headed a syndicate that competed with the Anglo to construct the city's subway system, arrived in Buenos Aires to lobby the local government on behalf of his proposal.[78] Meeting first with Noel, then with Casco and the technical committee reviewing both proposals, Ampthill tried to convince the city's officials that his enterprise had sufficient financial backing to build a system of six new subways at a fare of ten centavos. The Anglo lobbied just as hard for its position, sending communications to the city executive that cast strong doubts on the Ampthill syndicate's ability to raise the necessary funding to support their project.[79]

74 *VTCD* (December 16, 1927), pp. 2658–68 and (December 30, 1927), pp. 3503–6.

75 *VTCD* (June 24, 1927), pp. 1000–24.

76 *VTCD* (August 6, 1927), p. 1324 and Parapugna, *Historia de los coches de alquiler*, pp. 279–80.

77 *State Records* (August 24, 1927), 835.00/406.

78 The Marcos, originally from the province of Entre Ríos, were both lawyers, well connected to banking and business circles. Celestino, a member of the Jockey Club and the Sociedad Rural, had been a national deputy from Entre Ríos (1914–18), governor of that province (1918–22), and the national minister of justice and education (1922–25). *Quien es Quien, 1939*, p. 266.

79 *State Records* (May 4, 1927), 835.00/397 (June 2, 1927), 835.00/398, and (June 29, 1927), 835.00/399.

In September, the technical committee made its report, basically agreeing with the Anglo point of view on the Ampthill–Marco proposal. The committee's major objections were to what they judged to be the syndicate's failure to establish the financial guarantees necessary to carry out their proposal successfully. The committee was also skeptical about the economic feasibility of managing the enterprise with a ten-centavo fare, was concerned about certain technical aspects of the routes to be constructed, and, finally, rejected the syndicate's argument for a complete tax exemption in return for constructing and managing the system. The Marcos responded with a detailed memorandum to the council addressing and seeking to refute each of these points.[80] At the same time, various neighborhood associations submitted petitions in favor of the syndicate's proposal. One such, from the Sociedad de Fomento El Pilar de Nueva Pompeya, argued that the district would be pleased to see the syndicate's projected line reach into their barrio, "not only because of the progress that this construction would bring, but also because the soil extracted could be used to refill the low-lying streets of Nueva Pompeya, today so easily flooded, and because the Municipality, trying to avoid flooding, now uses residential garbage as land fill and thereby endangers the health of thousands of inhabitants."[81]

Political considerations, never far removed from the discussion, became even more paramount as the date for new presidential elections approached. With a decision on the subway proposals due at the end of the month, councilmen from both Radical parties met with their respective leaders to discuss their positions on the issue. President Alvear advised the five anti-personalista councilmen to find a speedy solution to the subway impasse, but was ambiguously noncommittal on the fare increase. Yrigoyen, the Radical candidate for reelection to the presidency in 1928, met with the twelve personalista council members in his apartment and urged them to oppose any fare increase. Sensing naturally enough that party association with the Anglo demand for higher fares would not prove politically popular or prudent, the Radical caudillo advised his allies to delay any final decision on the matter until after the presidential elections.[82]

These determinations doomed whatever chance the Ampthill–Marco proposal might have had for council approval. On December 26, the majority of the council's public works committee, basing their recommendation on the report of the city's technical committee, urged rejection of that alternative. The Socialist minority, arguing that previous

80 *State Records* (October 19, 1927), 835.00/410 and *VTCD* (October 18, 1927), pp. 1978–80.
81 *VTCD* (November 18, 1927), pp. 2223–4.
82 "The Underground Tramways: The Influence of Politics," *RRP*, 1379 (December 9, 1927), 33–4 and *State Records* (December 14, 1927), 835.00/1.

concessions had been granted to the Anglo with even fewer financial guarantees from that company than those offered by the British–Argentine syndicate, argued that the proposal be accepted. Two full days of debates changed few minds. Fifteen Radicals of both factions joined the two conservatives to pass the majority report, thereby rejecting the Ampthill–Marco bid. The two "Independent" Socialists cast the only recorded votes for the minority report. The mainline Socialists, taking a page from the Radical rulebook, walked out of the chamber and abstained from voting as a sign of protest of the entire proceedings.[83]

The decision meant that the Anglo had successfully resisted the entreaties of a major challenger. On the other hand, the new Yrigoyenista opposition to a fare increase, the possibility of future bids from enterprises with more solid financial backing than that of the Ampthill–Marco group, and the delay in consideration of their own proposal indicated the Anglo's growing vulnerability. Although the opposition Socialists had lost the battle on the alternative subway proposal, they were still winning the war of a ten-centavo fare. As the Anglo management woefully pointed out, porteños continued to enjoy some of the cheapest urban transportation in the world, largely due to the efforts of the Socialist councilmen. The other side of that coin, however, was the fact that construction had still not begun on the Retiro–Constitución subway or on any other underground line as the standoff between the council and the company continued. Arguments over who was to blame for this state of affairs would continue to roil the capital's political waters in the months ahead. In the meantime, new competition would enter the fray, further complicating matters for all parties involved.

83 *VTCD* (December 26, 1927), pp. 2950–97 and *VTCD* (December 27, 1927), pp. 3009–15.

7

Cantilo, colectivos, and subways

The April 1928 presidential election gave Hipólito Yrigoyen and his Radical party one of the most sweeping political victories in Argentine history. Carrying every Argentine province, Yrigoyen defeated the anti-personalista-conservative presidential ticket by a two-to-one margin. In the federal capital, he gathered almost 55 percent of the vote, the highest proportion for the Radicals in any contest in the city of Buenos Aires since they had started to participate in elections in 1912. Victories in congressional elections held at the same time gave them 92 of 154 seats in the national Chamber of Deputies. In the capital, the Radical senatorial candidate defeated his nearest rival by almost 96,000 votes and the party won twelve of the eighteen deputy seats contested, their leading vote-getter topping the closest rival by 76,138 votes.

As the Socialists had benefited from the Radical party division in 1924, so did the Yrigoyenistas profit from their opponents' schism four years later. In the congressional election, the "Independent" Socialists captured the six remaining deputy positions: their top vote-getter received 51,273 votes compared with the third-place mainline party's 45,225, and the fourth-place anti-personalistas' 31,140. In the congressional discussion of the April election, the Socialists repeated their common argument that the triumphant Radicals had taken advantage of patronage promises and certain irregularities in the balloting to fashion their victory. Showing their familiarity with the voter registry, they also tried to argue that they had held on to working-class support by receiving the exact number of votes as there were manual laborers inscribed in certain districts. There was no way to prove, however, beyond coincidence that these workers actually had voted for the Socialists and their objections to the electoral process were brushed away by both Radicals and Independent Socialists.[1] In the last analysis, there was no hiding the fact that the Radicals had handily defeated their longtime rivals by margins of three to one in all twenty of the capital's electoral districts and that the Independents had bested them in thirteen of twenty. It was, in sum, the

1 *Diputados* (June 8, 1928), pp. 41–69.

133

worst defeat yet for the Socialists in the city of Buenos Aires since the inception of the Sáenz Peña reforms and represented the apparent nadir of their political fortunes.[2]

During the interval of almost six months between Yrigoyen's election on April 1 and his inauguration on October 12, anti-personalista Horacio Casco continued to serve as the capital's intendente. Despite their "lame-duck" status, Casco and the city council continued to introduce, discuss, and approve matters of lasting importance to the city. In the process, the actions of the city government played an indirect role in precipitating a dramatic change in the nature of public transportation in the city, a change that would add to the debate over how best to organize and rationalize vehicular traffic in the capital.

Early on in the regular sessions, Casco vetoed a previous council decision to prohibit the playing of soccer and "all violent sports" during the months of January and February. Casco repeated Noel's earlier arguments that the measure was too restrictive and the veto was not challenged.[3] The intendente had somewhat less luck, however, with a resolution introduced a few days later to reorganize the still controversial Junta de Abastecimiento. After lengthy discussions, the council eventually rejected the reorganization plan and, at the same time, recommended that the junta be abolished altogether.[4] The intendente, in turn, did not act on this recommendation and the junta continued to operate much as before.

Party differences continued to divide the council, but there was general agreement on two important matters. On June 30, the council unanimously approved a new building code for the city, replacing that of 1910. The new provisions reflected the changing shape of the capital and appeared to incorporate some of the recommendations in Noel's 1925 plan of urban design. Responding to the appearance and rapid growth of multistory office and apartment buildings, many of the new code's articles referred to their height, appearance, and construction materials. With regard to building heights, the code for the first time divided the city into three zones where rules would vary according to the "necessities of various neighborhoods" and whereby taller buildings would diminish in height the further removed they were from the central city. The code also determined that the buildings along the Diagonales "Sáenz Peña" and "Roca" would have a uniform height of thirty-three meters, a provision that, unlike certain others, was closely followed. Drawing upon regulations imposed in New York City, the code also mandated the construction in new buildings of interior courtyards, which were designed to allow for freer circulation of air and light in the interior of taller constructions.[5]

2 Walter, *The Socialist Party*, pp. 213–16.   3 *VTCD* (April 10, 1928), p. 42.
4 *VTCD* (June 26, 1928), pp. 967–94.   5 *VTCD* (June 30, 1928), pp. 1199–248.

The council was also solidly behind reaffirming its right to regulate construction of the city's second subway. In 1912, the federal government had granted a concession to the Lacroze brothers, at the time an Argentine-owned streetcar company, to construct an underground railroad from the Chacarita cemetery to the downtown port area. As with the Anglo's proposed second line, construction had been interminably delayed. By February 1928, however, the Lacroze interests had contracted with a U.S. firm, the Dwight P. Robinson Company, and work on the project was slated to commence. Already embroiled with the Anglo over their subway plans, the city council demanded a say in how the Lacroze line was to be built and the fares it could charge. On May 23, representatives of various parties, including the conservatives, Socialists, and the two Radical groups, urged the intendente to confront the national government regarding the city's rights over these matters.[6] The city's protest led to meetings with Alvear and an extended discussion in the national Chamber of Deputies, where Socialist congressmen sought to champion the cause of municipal autonomy and lambasted both the federal and the local governments for their general ineptitude in dealing with the subway issue.[7] By the end of the year, the Lacroze company had agreed to municipal regulation of such matters as the location of stations, a ten-centavo fare, and service overall, and construction on the new line finally began.[8]

There was more disagreement over yet another attempt to relieve the logjam of downtown traffic congestion. On June 30, the majority of the council's public works committee recommended that, as a thirty-day experiment, the circulation of horse-drawn vehicles and taxis without passengers be prohibited in the downtown center of the city between the hours of eight in the morning and eight in the evening. The Socialists objected, observing that a similar measure tried under Noel had proved unworkable and had aroused the opposition not only of taxi drivers but also of businesses in the zone. Proponents, however, thought it worth another try, and with eight Radicals, three anti-personalistas, and two conservatives in favor, beat back the attempt of five Socialists, one Communist, and one Independent to send the proposal back to committee.[9]

The new rules went into effect on August 15. As the Socialists predicted, they immediately produced an adverse reaction, especially from taxi drivers, who at once engaged in a protest work stoppage. On the same day, the council, with the Socialists and Communist Penelón taking the lead, noted the public uproar over the experiment and urged

6 *VTCD* (May 23, 1928), pp. 408–10.
7 *Diputados* (July 4, 1928), pp. 826–8 and (July 19, 1928), pp. 487–540.
8 *State Records* (July 25, 1928), 835.00/9 and (August 22, 1928) 835.00/10.
9 *VTCD* (June 30, 1928), pp. 1179–97.

revocation of the new ordinance. Radical supporters countered that it should be given some time to work.[10] Only six days later, however, they had come to agree with their critics that the ordinance was a mistake. Ignoring Socialist gibes about their sudden change of heart, the personalista Radicals joined their opponents and voted fifteen to five to overturn the ordinance.[11]

The day after the ordinance was overturned, taxi service resumed in the city. The question of taxi regulation, however, soon again came before the council. In late September, Manuel Pasos, Felipe Quintana, and Aristóbulo Bianquet touched off a revolution in the city's public transportation system. As individual owners of taxicabs, they had grown tired of spending ten to eleven hours a day wandering through the city "fishing" for passengers, frustrated with rules and regulations like the most recent attempt to restrict their activities in the very area where they were most likely to find passengers, and concerned with the growing number of drivers competing for the same clientele. Accordingly, they determined to follow set routes, at first from the Caballito and Flores districts to the Plaza de Mayo, at regular intervals. Instead of depending upon one passenger, as most taxis did, they would "collect" as many as possible, usually four or five, along the way. Instead of charging one passenger four pesos for a trip, they estimated they could carry ten over the same distance and for the same time at forty centavos apiece, thereby making their conveyences more accessible to the middle and working classes.[12]

The experiment was an instant success. Some forty drivers joined the original three and began to establish new routes to connect far-flung districts with each other and with the downtown center of the capital. Drivers formed a spontaneous cooperative to organize lines and their schedules in an attempt to avoid competition with each other. They soon placed signs over their windshields that gave the number of the line and the route traversed. As *El Hogar* noted after the successful inauguration of the new system, "Everybody wanted to try the new collective taxi."[13] Although more expensive than the streetcar or bus, the collective taxi was less crowded, faster – because it did not have to make as many stops as its surface competition – and gave the rider the prestige and sensation of a ride in a hired car at a fraction of the cost. As it had with buses, ridership soon skyrocketed to about twenty million passengers per month.[14]

10 *VTCD* (August 15, 1928), pp. 1277–309.
11 *VTCD* (August 21, 1928), pp. 1318–46. See also, Parapugna, *Historia de los coches de alquiler*, pp. 281–2.
12 Horacio N. Casal, *Historia del colectivo* (Buenos Aires, 1971), pp. 9–17; MCBA, *Cincuentenario*, p. 96; and, "Sufrieron una transformación los automoviles de la zona oeste," *La Razón* (September 25, 1928), p. 4.
13 *El Hogar*, 24, 990 (October 5, 1928).   14 MCBA, *Cincuentenario*, p. 96.

The collective taxi proved, as well, to be more than a passing fad, eventually coming to be the dominant mode of transportation in the capital. Adding to its popularity, aside from the practical conveniences it offered, was the fact that it was an ingenious and indigenous invention, a true product of "*la viveza criolla*," started and sustained by individual entrepreneurs as competitors to a large, foreign-owned company that nearly monopolized the city's public transport and was losing favor with the porteño public.

That company was not long in expressing its disapproval. A few days after its appearance, the Anglo's manager addressed a protest to the intendente, claiming that the colectivos, originally licensed as taxicabs, were now offering unfair competition by operating much as buses but without municipal regulation. In a subsequent document, the company asserted that its allegedly precarious financial position could suffer because the colectivos would drain passengers from its operations and that such losses, coupled with the council's failure to consider proposed fare increases, would cripple its ability to meet subway construction commitments. At least, the company concluded, the colectivos should be submitted to the same regulations with regard to licensing, tax payments, and inspections as other forms of transportation so as to assure fairness and equality of competition.[15]

A different perspective was provided by the Unión Comercial Argentina representing some downtown businesses. Addressing their own petition to the municipality at the same time as the Anglo, the group praised the colectivo as a rapid, inexpensive, sanitary, and safe means of transport, which aided immeasurably in the decongestion of downtown traffic, allowed commercial employees to arrive at work on time, and permitted employees who so desired to have lunch at home. The Anglo's service, on the other hand, so the Unión charged, had continued to decline, with a general failure to adhere to schedules, "abominable" rolling stock, and a total disregard for the completo. The company, which was also secretly buying up many bus lines, rightly feared this new competitor. This did not mean, however, that the city should succumb to the Anglo's blandishments and regulate the colectivos out of business. Whatever regulations were applied, the message concluded, should take into account the fact that "the humble taxi drivers, facing ruin from the competition of streetcars, subways, and buses, have adopted this beneficial public service and do not infringe on any municipal ordinance; they follow regular routes, collect a fare much lower than that authorized, and never exceed the maximum capacity of five or six passengers in their vehicles."[16]

15 *VTCD* (October 5, 1928), pp. 1860–1.   16 Ibid., pp. 1859–60.

The question of colectivo regulation first came to the city council on October 2. On that day, Socialist Miguel Briuolo introduced a message to the intendente, asking what plans the executive had to regulate the new vehicles. In the process, he made clear his and his party's sympathy with this new and popular enterprise. He and Penelón argued that the colectivo drivers had not only exemplified real "patriotism" in devising an alternative to foreign-owned streetcars and subways, but also had confounded critics' predictions that the new drivers would fall into anarchy and competition by their cooperative and efficient manner of organizing the operation. The Radicals supported the initiative, whereas conservative José Guerrico argued that colectivos would only mean more vehicles and more congestion. He added that Socialist opposition to the Anglo fare increase had been the main obstacle to extending streetcar service to distant areas of the city, which now might be served by the colectivo.[17]

Six days later Secretary of Public Works Ricardo A. Moreno appeared before the council to discuss the Briuolo request for information. Reviewing the history of the appearance of the colectivo, which had come as a surprise to the city government, he expressed the executive's reluctance to consider any hard-and-fast rules for this conveyance, given its newness and the fact that he was about to relinquish reins of government to the Yrigoyenistas. He thought it best to allow the new experiment to continue within the general framework of existing ordinances rather than to rush through a set of rules that might soon prove inappropriate. Socialist Américo Ghioldi strongly approved of this "agnostic" position and urged the city to give the colectivo more time to develop before applying any restrictions on its growth.[18] This attitude prevailed and regulation of the colectivos was delayed for several years.

The council's decision to accept the colectivo experiment without special regulation was one more setback for the Anglo. Earlier in the year, the council had required the company to submit detailed plans for the construction of the Retiro–Constitución subway, a request with which the Anglo had complied. While both local and national governments examined these plans, construction was further delayed. The Anglo complained that the council's failure to approve its fare increase remained the principal obstacle to starting work on the subway. The company also estimated that in the previous year it had lost fifty-five million potential passengers to competing bus lines.[19] In an interpellation of the secretary of public works on December 21, 1928, Socialist Ghioldi suggested that the delays, added to a decline in the quality of service, were part of a

17 *VTCD* (October 2, 1928), pp. 1828–45.   18 *VTCD* (October 8, 1928), pp. 1932–41.
19 *RRP*, 1913 (August 3, 1928), pp. 27–31.

planned strategy by the executive and the Anglo to force the council to accede to the company's wishes.[20] Whatever the reason, the standoff continued for yet another year.

Hipólito Yrigoyen assumed the presidency for the second time on October 12, 1928. After a month's delay, he again named José Luis Cantilo to serve as intendente of the capital. Although many of Cantilo's closest friends and colleagues had deserted Yrigoyen to join the anti-personalistas, he had remained steadfastly loyal to the Radical leader. His previous service as head of the capital's government and as governor of the province of Buenos Aires constituted an impressive wealth of experience for the position. Soon after taking office, he presented to the council a host of proposals that were intended to further the embellishments and improvements initiated by Noel and Casco. These included a measure to complete work on an outdoor theater on the Costanera Sur, plans to expand low-cost public housing, and an ordinance to regulate lighted signs advertising products and businesses. He also requested funds to prepare the city for the anticipated visit of U.S. president-elect Herbert Hoover early in the following year.[21]

Shortly after Cantilo was installed in city hall, another set of municipal elections was held to renovate half of the council. The Socialists, trying desperately to recover from their devastating loss in the March congressional election, formulated a new municipal program that stressed a higher minimum wage for city workers and advocated specific projects for particular neighborhoods on the south side of the city. The program also called for the municipalization of all public services and reiterated opposition to any increase in bus, streetcar, or subway fares.[22] Again, the Socialists tried to draw a distinction between their consistent stand on the issue of fare increases and the waffling behavior of the Radicals, which often seemed to benefit the Anglo and the Lacroze.[23]

These efforts proved to be of little avail. The shift by the Yrigoyenistas to opposition to fare increases blunted the effectiveness of the issue for the opposition. Still basking in the glow of their sweeping triumph in the April elections, the Radicals crushed the Socialists in the December election by a two-to-one margin: 88,544 votes to 44,679. The Socialists could find solace in the fact that the margin of their defeat was less than it had been eight months earlier and that they had beaten their Independent rivals, who came in third with 35,233 votes. Nonetheless, although they

---

20 *VTCD* (December 21, 1928), pp. 2880–4.
21 Luna, "José Luis Cantilo," pp. 60–4.   22 *La Vanguardia* (November 16, 1918), p. 1.
23 "La Jornada de hoy," *La Vanguardia* (December 2, 1928), p. 1.

had done better in working-class than in middle-class districts, they had still been severely thrashed by their longtime opponents in each of the capital's twenty wards.[24]

The election gave the personalista Radicals the most councilmen – fourteen – they had ever enjoyed. The remaining seats were divided among Socialists (seven), Independent Socialists (three), anti-personalista Radicals (three), conservatives (one), Communists (one), and the Gente del Teatro (one). Even with this advantage, the Radicals still could not claim an absolute majority on the council. Furthermore, as national politics became increasingly polarized between pro- and anti-Yrigoyenistas over the next two years, the ruling party at the local level commonly found itself blocked by a united coalition, including the council's conservatives and Communists. On many occasions, the vote of Florencio Parravicini, who almost always sided with the Radicals, was indeed no laughing matter and frequently helped them carry the day.

These dynamics did not take long to reveal themselves. Breaking with tradition, the Radicals forced the election of three of their number to the presiding officerships in the council. Then they stacked the council committees in their favor, overcoming objections from the other parties when Parravicini joined thirteen Radicals to force a tie vote on a resolution to close debate on the matter. The president of the council, Radical Pedro Villemur, then cast the deciding vote in favor of ending discussion, thereby sealing his party's advantage on the council committees.[25]

Cantilo, like every intendente, had his differences and difficulties with the council. Early on in the sessions of 1929, he vetoed several measures carried over from the previous year, including one that would have amplified the power of councilmen to investigate more fully the operations of all branches of municipal government.[26] With the solid backing of the fourteen Yrigoyenistas, these and other vetoes were easily sustained. Furthermore, whereas the fourteen Radicals could not always get their way on the council, they could use their numbers to block opposition attempts to question and perhaps embarrass the executive branch. They managed, for example, to frustrate attempts by Independent Socialist Manuel González Maseda to investigate the activities of the city's director of sanitation.[27]

Like most intendentes, Cantilo had moments of significant cooperation with the council. Responding to the need to increase revenue to meet growing budget deficits, the city, lacking its own up-to-date property

---

24 "Elecciones municipales del 2 de diciembre de 1928," República Argentina, *Memoria, 1929–1930*, appendix. See also Appendix, Table A.2.
25 *VTCD* (April 10, 1929), pp. 78–9.   26 *VTCD* (April 23, 1929), pp. 216–27.
27 *VTCD* (June 4, 1929), pp. 643–5 and (June 10, 1929), p. 712.

assessment, had turned to that of the national ministry of sanitary works as a base for determining street-lighting and cleaning rates. The results were so successful that in May the council voted twenty-six to two to lower these tax rates by between 20 and 30 percent, depending on the zone of the city.[28] At the end of the year the council approved the mayor's balanced budget for 1930 by twenty-eight votes and his proposal for a thirty-million peso loan to extend the widening of Calle Corrientes and Avenida Santa Fe by a vote of twenty-five to one.[29]

The issue of subways, however, continued to bedevil both Cantilo and the council. During the sessions of 1929, the Socialists pressed the advantage they saw on this issue. Socialist councilmen, with Communist Penelón, introduced frequent resolutions for information from the executive on the progress, or lack thereof, of work on the Retiro–Constitución line and asked him to investigate a variety of general complaints about streetcar service. In July, Cantilo was forced to veto a resolution calling on him to enforce greater municipal authority over the subway being built by Lacroze. He argued that the work had progressed too far to be halted to meet the concerns of the council, a stance that put him on the side of the line's speedy completion, but served also to cast doubt on his resoluteness in defending the municipality's prerogatives.[30]

In an attempt to move matters forward, Socialist Américo Ghioldi in June introduced a proposal that the municipality itself take charge of future subway construction. Pointing to what was now a fifteen-year hiatus, he suggested that, to break the cycle of promise and delay, the city form a mixed commission with private interests, in which the municipality would control 51 percent of the capital, to promote an inexpensive, electrified system of public transportation. Appealing to civic pride, he envisioned a network similar to that of Paris, noting that the French capital at the time had 110 kilometers of underground lines, compared with Buenos Aires' mere 6 kilometers, 700 meters.[31]

The Ghioldi proposal was sent to committee, never to be heard of again. More serious and lasting in its impact was a bid submitted to the municipality in early August by a Spanish concern to build four new subways in the city, including the long-delayed Retiro–Constitución line. The new proposal, from the Compañía Anónima de Proyectos y Construcciónes de Madrid (CAPYC), apparently backed by Barcelona bankers, promised to build the lines with a fare of ten centavos for direct trips and fifteen centavos for combinations with surface transportation. This promise produced predictable skepticism from *The Review of the River Plate*, which

28 *VTCD* (May 7, 1929), pp. 384–402.
29 *VTCD* (December 28, 1929), p. 2750 and *VTCD* (December 23, 1928), pp. 2486–98.
30 *VTCD* (September 3, 1929), pp. 1294–5.   31 *VTCD* (June 4, 1929), pp. 654–9.

still preferred the Anglo proposal, but earned the Spanish plan the quick endorsement of the Socialists – and eventually of other parties as well.[32] The chances for the Anglo to pursue the Retiro–Constitución line dimmed even further when, on December 30, 1929, the council voted fifteen to twelve to reject the ad-referendum contract the company had signed with Noel in 1925 that would have granted the Anglo its fare increases. The rejection was approved with almost no discussion and, unfortunately, without roll call. The committee report that recommended such action, however, was signed by one Socialist, one Independent Socialist, one anti-personalista, and two Yrigoyenista Radicals.[33]

The years of the second Cantilo administration coincided with either the completion or substantial progress on major public works and other building projects. In mid-1929 the mayor attended the inauguration of the new municipal slaughterhouse and packing plant as well as ceremonies to mark the opening of a new power plant of the Spanish electric company (CHADE) in the new port area northeast of the Retiro rail station. One of the largest and most modern facilities of its kind, it greatly enhanced the company's capacity to supply the capital with electric power. In December, Cantilo, accompanied by other officials, was present as the new building of the Buenos Aires branch of the National City Bank of New York opened its doors to the public. Situated in the heart of the financial district, and judged by the U.S. embassy to be "probably . . . the finest banking office in Buenos Aires," it also housed on its upper floors the headquarters of the American Club.[34]

Work on channeling and covering the Arroyo Maldonado continued in these years, as did construction of the Diagonal Norte and the Costanera. Approval of his thirty-million-peso loan request permitted Cantilo to witness the expansion of Corrientes between calles Uruguay and Paraná and the near completion of the widening of Santa Fe. Construction of the Lacroze subway also went forward in spite of such difficult obstacles as the builder's need to tunnel at a greater depth than was required of the first Anglo line in order to pass under the Arroyo Maldonado. Because of its depth, various stations on the line were provided with electric escalators and underground pedestrian walkways, which helped passengers move safely from one side of a busy street to another without disrupting

32 "More Subway Schemes: Spanish Financiers Seek Sweeping Concessions," *RRP*, 1966 (August 9, 1929), p. 15.
33 *VTCD* (December 30, 1929), p. 2866. *The Review of the River Plate* (no. 1987: January 3, 1930, p. 35) suggested that the intendente had decided not to push for the Anglo's proposal given the entrance of new bids by this time.
34 *State Records* (December 26, 1929), 835.00/26.

street-level traffic. The dirt excavated from the site was used to help push back the Rió de la Plata in the formation of the Costanera Norte, which was undergoing construction twenty-four hours a day.[35]

Although the Lacroze subway represented a significant engineering achievement and promised one more rapid alternative to the traffic flow from the west of the city to downtown, it did little to alleviate the continued problems of congestion in the city center and the widespread complaints about all traffic. *Caras y Caretas* reflected general public frustration with these problems by describing the "invasion" of automobiles parked in downtown streets and using cartoons to depict the confused jumble of pedestrians, buses, colectivos, and private automobiles that characterized the typical intersection.[36] Articles in *El Hogar*, which in the late 1920s began to devote an annual edition to the automobile, objected to the uncontrolled stationing of cars in downtown streets, a practice that threatened to turn the center of the city into a gigantic parking lot. To resolve this problem, the magazine suggested that the municipality imitate the increasingly common practice in North American cities of building either aboveground or subterranean parking garages. A companion piece noted that not only were limited parking facilities adding to downtown congestion, but also a poor road system was providing weekend tourists who hoped to escape the city for the weekends only four exits from the capital. Each of these, especially on Sundays, became crowded and dangerous. *El Hogar* urged the municipality to address this problem, as well as the parking crisis.[37] Although immediate action was not forthcoming, the city fathers would address these matters in the not too distant future.

Cantilo's interaction with the city council in 1930, with a few notable exceptions, retained the pattern of the preceding year. The general context of that relation, however, had changed dramatically. Almost immediately after Yrigoyen's assumption of the presidency, as mentioned, a polarization had developed in the country between pro- and anti-Yrigoyen forces, which grew and deepened as time progressed. One result of these increasingly bitter divisions was an upsurge in politically motivated violence in the capital and elsewhere. In October of 1929, the anti-personalistas had tried to bring one of these incidents, in which one of their own had been killed and another severely injured, to the attention of the council,

35 Félix Lima, "Como se va rellenando con tierra del subterráneo Lacroze la avenida Costanera Norte, de Canning a Pampa," *Caras y Caretas*, 32, 1596 (May 4, 1929).

36 "La invasión de los automoviles," *Caras y Caretas*, 30, 1488 (April 9, 1927) and "Telones porteños: Delicias del Tráfico," *Caras y Caretas*, 31, 1535 (March 3, 1928).

37 Máximo A.F. Armesto, "La calle no debe ser un garage" and Herberto Serra Lima, "Son dificultosas las salidas de Buenos Aires," *El Hogar*, 1049 (November 22, 1929).

but had been rebuffed by the Radical plurality.[38] The consequences of the world economic crisis, which began to be felt at the beginning of 1930, added to the woes of the national administration. As the position of the Yrigoyenistas continued to erode, conservatives – with anti-personalistas and Independent Socialists – began to meet with elements within the Argentine military to plot the removal of the popularly elected president by force.[39]

One of the most dramatic signs of the deteriorating Radical position was provided by the results of the March 2, 1930 congressional election in the capital. In that contest, the governing party suffered a stunning setback when the Independent Socialists captured ten of the fourteen seats up for election, in the process besting the Radicals by twenty-six thousand votes. The mainline Socialists, who had been overwhelmed by the Radicals two to one in the municipal elections fifteen months earlier, earned a virtual tie with their longtime antagonists this time around and regained lost ground in working-class districts. The Radicals carried only district 12, losing badly in what had been their strongest district, number 5 of Flores. The triumphant dissident Socialists did especially well in upper-class areas and appeared to gain substantially from support that ordinarily would have gone to conservatives and anti-personalistas. More significant for the Radicals, however, was the fact that, true to their name, the winners seemed to have won over the "independent" voters who had given the Yrigoyenistas their overwhelming electoral advantage in 1928.[40]

Although no reverse was quite as stunning as the one in the capital, the Radicals also suffered a defeat in the province of Córdoba and saw their strength seriously eroded in several other major districts. Following the elections, a stalemate in the Congress and confusion in the executive branch brought the national administration to a virtual standstill. The local government of the capital, however, continued to function much as it had before and managed to decide on at least one major item of great importance to the city's future development.

The council sessions of 1930 began with the usual mixture of confrontation and collaboration. Opposition councilmen censured Cantilo for certain expenditures while the intendente vetoed several of the council's initiatives concerning the regulation of markets and bus lines. At the

38 The anti-personalistas wanted the council further to investigate the attack, which had occurred on October 24 in the Plaza Once. Thirteen Radicals voted to reject the resolution, with the usual lineup of seven Socialists, three anti-personalistas, two Independents, and one Communist voting to consider. The Yrigoyenista president of the council cast the tie-breaking vote to send the resolution down to defeat. *VTCD* (October 25, 1929), pp. 1852–5.
39 For more on these developments, see Rock, *Politics in Argentina*, pp. 241–64.
40 Walter, *The Socialist Party*, pp. 220–3.

same time, as usual, some significant legislation was approved by both parties, including approval of an ad-referendum contract between the intendente and a North American banking syndicate led by the Chatham Phoenix Corporation to provide a thirty-seven-million peso loan for construction of the long-delayed north–south boulevard to link Retiro and Constitución. An earlier ordinance had agreed to name the proposed north–south avenue the Nueve de Julio in commemoration of Argentina's independence day.[41]

It was in these sessions, too, that the subway question finally came to a head. By early in the year, in addition to the Spanish proposal, projected plans for construction of a subway network in the city had been presented by another British syndicate as well as a German concern.[42] This competition stimulated the Anglo to begin work on its second line, although critics noted that such efforts represented only a few holes in the ground near Plaza Constitución, and to present a new proposal of its own directly to President Yrigoyen. The new Anglo plan called for three lines radiating westward from the Plaza de Mayo, extension of its existing line well past Primera Junta, and a doubling of its planned line from downtown to the Plaza Italia to reach the heart of Belgrano. Yrigoyen apparently reacted favorably to the proposal, but the sticking point remained the Anglo's insistence on a fifteen-centavo fare to underwrite its costs.[43]

In the meantime, the Socialist proponents of the Spanish consortium's bid pushed for its approval. In a May 6 interpellation of Secretary of Finance Rodolfo Arambarri, Américo Ghioldi charged the executive branch with unduly delaying final judgment on the various proposals, hoping that by prolonging matters the backers of the Spanish project would give up their efforts. He accused the local government of negligence and of adopting tactics that would again benefit the Anglo.[44] Whatever the substance behind these allegations, the plans of the Anglo to continue subway construction were greatly dimmed on June 3 when the special committee of the council charged with examining the various proposals recommended unanimously that, whichever bid was accepted, the municipality had to assure guaranteed protection of employees' maximum work hours and days and, most significantly, "the necessity of maintaining the fare of 10

41 *VTCD* (June 27, 1930), p. 1281 and Miguel Iusem, *Diccionario de las calles de Buenos Aires* (Buenos Aires, Letras y Artes, 1971).

42 "The Turning Point in the Subway Issue," *RRP*, 1990 (January 24, 1930), p. 11 and *State Records* (January 2, 1930), 835.00/27.

43 Raúl García Heras, "Los transportes porteños en vísperas de la Revolución del '30: El radicalismo, el socialismo y la embajada británica," *Todo es Historia* (September 1982), 61 and "The New Undergrounds: Anglo Argentine Company's New Proposal," *RRP*, 2006 (May 16, 1930), pp. 27–9.

44 *VTCD* (May 6, 1930), pp. 443–57.

centavos for a direct trip and 15 centavos for a combination." Twenty-four out of twenty-five councilmen approved the resolution, with only conservative José Guerrico, who argued that a subway system simply could not be built based on a ten-centavo fare, in opposition.[45]

Almost two months later, on July 30, the same committee reported favorably on the CAPYC plan to construct four subway lines at a price of ten centavos per ride. Among the four was the Retiro–Constitución route, which meant that the Spanish-backed company would take over this project from the Anglo if the British company did not complete the line. José Guerrico remained the sole dissenter, arguing again that the lines could not be constructed under the proposed fare schedule. Secretary of Finance Arambarri appeared before the council to argue the executive's case that the CAPYC's financial guarantees were not yet sufficient to merit approval and to urge further consideration. Ghioldi, speaking for the committee, stated that the members were satisfied that the phenomenal growth of Buenos Aires would continue to make any means of public transportation, even at ten centavos, profitable. During the debate, Yrigoyenista Eduardo Catan tried to shift the credit for the maintenance of the low subway and streetcar fares from the Socialists to his party. Observing that the decision to keep the present fare came from Yrigoyen himself, Catan concluded that "although all the subway lines of Buenos Aires might go bankrupt, we, the Radicals, are never going to permit the establishment of lines at a price greater than 10 centavos."[46] Finally, the council's twenty-seven members present voted unanimously to grant the subway concession to the CAPYC.[47]

The struggle, however, was not quite over. On August 18, Intendente Cantilo vetoed ordinance number 4070, which had approved the concession, citing again what he considered the company's inadequate financial backing. Both Socialist and Radical councilmen responded with charges that the Anglo was using its influence in European financial circles, especially through its connection with the Brussels-based holding company SOFINA, to discourage bankers from investing in the Spanish proposal and that these maneuvers were unduly influencing the municipal executive's judgment. Reasserting their confidence in their original decision, the council voted twenty-seven to one to override the veto.[48]

During the discussion, Radical councilmen had tried to brush aside the veto of their own party's intendente by calling it "a simple difference of judgement" on the question of financing.[49] They pointed out that the councilmen had followed the lead of President Yrigoyen, not Cantilo, on

45 *VTCD* (June 3, 1930), pp. 878–81.
46 *VTCD* (July 30, 1930), p. 1514.   47 Ibid., pp. 1460–534.
48 *VTCD* (August 22, 1930), pp. 1562–70.
49 This was the explanation given by Yrigoyenista Councilman Ricardo V. Muscio. Ibid., p. 1569.

this issue and, to divert attention from what seemed to be clear executive sympathy for the Anglo, Catan noted that, as the son of Spanish parents, he was especially proud that the council had agreed to the Spanish proposal.[50]

The fact remained, however, that, with his decision, Cantilo seemed to favor the British company. Whether there was more to his veto than his publicly stated concern about the finances of the CAPYC must remain, for the moment, in the realm of speculation. Perhaps the intendente and President Yrigoyen had a real disagreement on this issue or perhaps they were playing an elaborate political game to try to please all sides at once. It must have been clear to Cantilo that by this time the Radical councilmen were bound and determined to support the proposal that included the ten-centavo fare and that his veto would surely be overridden.[51] A fuller explanation of his action awaits further investigation.

Whatever the political maneuvering involved, the council's decision to grant the Spanish concession was significant. For one thing, it meant that serious work would finally begin on the long-delayed Retiro–Constitución subway. That line, when completed, would only cost porteño customers ten centavos a ride. For another, insistence on the ten-centavo fare and its maintenance for both subways and streetcars for most of the 1920s was a substantial political triumph for the Socialist party and its councilmen. Radical claims notwithstanding, the Socialists, from the beginning of the decade, had been the most consistent champions of maintaining low fares for public transportation in the city, and their opponents were latecomers to this point of view. More broadly, however, it was a significant triumph for the council over the intendente and a major vindication of the democratic reform of 1918. Both Noel and Cantilo had favored the Anglo request for higher fares and, consequently, a stranglehold over the main modes of transportation in the capital. In most instances, the intendentes prevailed over the council when there was disagreement on major issues. But on the question of the ten-centavo fare and subway construction, the representatives on the council had successfully channeled what was clearly the prevailing popular sentiment into effective action to overcome the intendentes' opposition.

For the Anglo, the decision was one in a decade-long series of setbacks.

50 Ibid., p. 1568.
51 Examining the complex relationships between the Anglo, the British Foreign Office, and the Yrigoyen administration over these issues, Raúl García Heras suggests that their deteriorating political position led the president and the council to change their minds on the concession to the Spanish company and the maintenance of the ten-centavo fare (García Heras, "Los transportes porteños," pp. 62–3). On the latter point, however, as mentioned, the Yrigoyenistas had come out against any fare increases as early as 1928. The events of 1930 probably only reinforced what was already a firmly held position.

The failure to get a fare increase, and increased competition from buses, colectivos, and other subway companies, meant a steady undermining of the company's once preeminent position. These difficulties, however, provided the context within which the company, aided by the British government, would push for a so-called coordination of public transportation in the capital, a coordination that allowed the Anglo to regain much of the ground it had lost in the previous decade.

During the 1920s, Argentina's experiment with democracy, at both the national and local level, worked reasonably well. Elections were held on a regular basis and, except for occasional complaints, operated fairly. Citizen participation at the ballot box and in party affairs increased noticeably and government institutions, like the national Congress and the city council, despite their many flaws, were more sensitive to the concerns of broader constituencies than they had been in the past. The experiment, however, failed its most important test and suffered a severe interruption on September 6, 1930 when elements within the Argentine military removed Yrigoyen from the presidency and installed a provisional government, which ruled by decree for better than a year. On the day before the coup, Socialist Américo Ghioldi proclaimed in the city council his party's opposition to the prospect of a military dictatorship, which "would only aggravate the situation in which we find ourselves."[52] The Socialists, however, along with the Yrigoyenistas, were among the few to oppose the coup, which initially enjoyed considerable popular support. From the viewpoint of the democratically elected city council, Ghioldi's comments were among the last to be heard from that body until early 1932.

52 *VTCD* (September 5, 1930), p. 1664.

8

Conservative resurgence: Guerrico and Naón

The year 1930 marked a clear watershed in Argentine history. Military interventionism, which began in this year, would continue to mark the political life of the republic in succeeding decades. One of the two main leaders of the coup against Yrigoyen, General José F. Uriburu, ruled the country as provisional president for a year and a half. He was succeeded in office by his co-conspirator, General Agustín P. Justo, who was subsequently elected to the presidency in late 1931. That election, however, like most of those that followed in the decade, was characterized by many of the fraudulent practices that had prevailed before the Sáenz Peña reforms of 1912. These practices, in turn, permitted the traditional conservative forces to regain the grip on national politics and government that they had lost to the Radicals in 1916. Fraudulent elections and the numerous political and financial scandals – some of the most notorious of which involved the city council of Buenos Aires – contributed to the term that was applied to these years – the "infamous decade."[1]

The world depression, whose effects provided the larger context for the move against Yrigoyen, also had significant consequences. The most immediate was a dramatic increase in unemployment in the capital and nationwide. A government study for 1932 counted almost 90,000 persons without work, either permanently or partially, in the city of Buenos Aires, and 334,000 unemployed throughout the county (compared with 15,000 unemployed in 1930).[2] In the city of Buenos Aires, a shantytown for the unemployed sprang up in the Retiro Station–New Port area and similar encampments – the Argentine version of "Hoovervilles" – could

1 Good overviews of the period and these developments can be found in Alberto Ciria, *Partidos y poder en la Argentina moderna* (1930–46) (Buenos Aires, 1964); Mark Falcoff and Ronald H. Dolkart, eds., *Prologue to Perón: Argentina in Depression and War, 1930–1943* (Berkeley, Calif., 1975); and Robert A. Potash, *The Army and Politics in Argentina: 1928–1945; Yrigoyen to Perón* (Stanford, Calif., 1969).
2 República Argentina, Departamento Nacional del Trabajo, *La desocupación en la Argentina, 1932: Informe del Jefe del Censo Nacional de Desocupados, Dr. José Figuerola* (Buenos Aires, 1933).

be found scattered throughout the city.[3] In August of 1931, *Crítica* devoted an entire page to the rapid growth in the number of sidewalk vendors in the city as a result of the employment crisis.[4]

In addition to the lack of jobs, the capital's working classes confronted a general deterioration in their standard of living. A survey of the city in 1930 determined per capita meat consumption at 135 kilos for the year, certainly one of the highest levels in the world.[5] Another study by the National Labor Department, however, found that in 1931 the wages of average working-class families in Buenos Aires had declined whereas the cost of living, especially for food, had grown substantially. According to one economist, these factors made it impossible for workers to feed themselves, "leading to a situation whereby perhaps as much as one-third of the population was undernourished and explaining why the overall health of porteños was so inferior to those of great civilized cities of the world."[6] A similar survey of housing for working families found continued crowded conditions, with almost four persons to a room, rooms that were "unsanitary, of faulty construction, and without proper ventilation."[7] To make matters worse for workers, the conservative governments of the period showed little concern for their plight and were often overtly hostile to the labor movement and its leaders.[8]

There were other indications of the depression's impact. In the early 1930s, new construction in the city declined sharply, repeating the pattern, as with employment, seen during the World War I years.[9] Less serious, but illustrative of the general belt tightening forced on most porteños in these years, was the drop in attendance and betting at the local racetracks. In 1930, a little more than a million persons attended the races and wagered a total of 110 million pesos. By 1933 attendance had fallen to 681,667 persons and betting to 85 million pesos.[10]

---

3 As described by one observer, "In the New Port we had at that time a marginal city, the first Villa Miseria [a term coined to describe Argentine shantytowns in the 1960s and thereafter] in the country. There the unemployed built shacks of wood and tin, no higher than to accommodate a man sitting down, and there they lived in seclusion. It was called Villa Desocupación [Village of the Unemployed]." José Blanco Amor, "Evocación (con ira) de los años 30," *Lyra*, 26 210/12.

4 *Crítica* (August 17, 1931), p. 10.   5 *State Records* (October 20, 1931), 835.00/63.

6 As quoted in *State Records* (September 20, 1933), 835.5017/9.   7 Ibid.

8 For more on the situation of labor in these years, see Joel Horowitz, *Cooperation and Resistance: Argentine Unions, the State and the Rise of Perón*; Hiroshi Matsushita, *Movimiento obrero argentino, 1930–1945: Sus proyecciones en los orígines del Peronismo* (Buenos Aires, 1983); and David Tamarin, *The Argentine Labor Movement, 1930–1945: A Study in the Origins of Peronism* (Albuquerque, N. Mex., 1985).

9 MCBA, Dirección General de Obras Públicas y Urbanismo, Departamento de Urbanización, *Planeamiento de Buenos Aires: Información urbana* (Buenos Aires, 1945). In 1930 the city issued 22,247 building permits; in 1932 half that number – 11,281 (for the first nine months of the year). *VTCD* (November 10, 1932), p. 4010.

10 MCBA, *Revista de Estadística*, 1940, p. 359.

Carlos Gardel visiting the Villa de Desocupación (Village of the Unemployed)
in the Puerto Nuevo (no date)

To deal with the effects of the crisis, the post-1930 governments made important concessions to foreign governments and investors, notably the British. These concessions involved matters over which the municipal government had sought to exercise some control, especially in the area of public transportation. As the consequences of these concessions became apparent, they served to stimulate a strong public reaction and an emerging economic nationalism, which had its roots in such issues as the struggle over streetcar fares and subway construction in the 1920s. At the same time, the national government sought to protect and promote industrial development as a way to balance the reliance on agricultural exports and to avoid the severe disruption that always accompanied interruption of foreign trade. As a result, industrial growth became marked around 1933 and continued well into the next decade. Much of this expansion occurred in and around the city of Buenos Aires. According to calculations from the 1935 industrial census, the metropolitan area then contained a little better than 41 percent of all the republic's industrial establishments. Moreover, whereas the number of industries in the capital had grown from only 10,275 to 13,440 between 1914 and 1935, it almost doubled between 1935 and 1946.[11]

Another consequence of the depression was a dramatic slowdown in foreign immigration. As had been the case during the World War I period, in the early 1930s more persons left the republic than entered it.[12] Despite this decline, however, the population of the city of Buenos Aires continued to grow at predepression rates. The municipal census of 1936 counted a total of 2,413,829 porteños, an increase of 260,000 from the estimate of 2,153,179 in 1930. The increase came from natural birth rates and internal migration from the provinces. In 1914, 18 percent of the capital's native-born population had been born outside of its boundaries. By 1936 that proportion reached 24 percent. With the onset of rapid industrialization in the latter part of the decade and the early 1940s, hundreds of thousands of additional *provincianos* settled in the city. By the mid-1940s, 44 percent of the capital's inhabitants had been born outside of its limits. Native-born laborers, who had constituted less than half of the work force in 1914, by the 1940s represented about three-quarters of employees in major industrial occupations.[13]

In 1914, the number of Argentines in the capital had barely exceeded the number of foreign-born. By 1936, almost two-thirds of the total population was native-born. In addition, women now slightly outnumbered men in the city, reversing a difference of better than 120,000 in 1914. The effects of public education could also be seen in the fact that the literacy rate in the capital, which in 1914 had already been almost 80 percent, was by 1936 almost 93 percent. Finally, as mentioned, the pattern of growth from the center of the city to the outlying suburbs continued throughout the early twentieth century. Between 1914 and 1936, the population of district 16 (Belgrano) had grown two and one-half times, that of district 1 (Vélez Sársfield) had more than tripled, and that of district 15 (San Bernardo) had almost quadrupled (see Appendix, Table A.1).

11 Walter, "The Socioeconomic Growth of Buenos Aires in the Twentieth Century," pp. 71–99.
12 Di Tella and Zymelman, *Las etapas del desarrollo económico argentino*, pp. 400, 441.
13 Tamarin, *The Argentine Labor Movement*, pp. 40–1.

A few days after the coup that deposed Yrigoyen, the provisional government of Uriburu named José Guerrico to serve as the capital's new
intendente. An auctioneer by profession and a member of an old porteño
family, Guerrico had served on the council off and on for two decades.
Although a staunch conservative, he was respected and well regarded even
by his political opponents for his deep and passionate pride in and concern with the city and its place in the world.[14] Named as secretary of
public works and, provisionally, of finance was Adolfo Mugica, who had
served on the council with Guerrico as a conservative representative in the
1920s.

During his year and a half in office, Guerrico had the luxury of managing the city without the encumbrance of a city council. That body, like
the national Congress, had been dissolved, allowing the local executive,
like the provisional president, to rule by decree. His scope of action,
however, was limited by fiscal constraints imposed by a budget deficit of
several million pesos and the continuing effects of the general economic
crisis. To meet these problems, Guerrico forged an austerity budget for
1931 that was six million pesos less than the previous year's and introduced a scheme that involved withholding a certain proportion of municipal salaries exceeding 300 pesos per month, to be kept in a special
fund until the city's financial status returned to normal. Another savings
was achieved by cutting the number of hours city streets were illumi-
nated.[15]

In addition to reducing expenditures, the intendente also sought to
improve tax collection. A new survey of the city, for example, found over
forty thousand new buildings, which previously had escaped taxation,
with a projected revenue of 2.5 million pesos a year.[16] Guerrico also re-
vamped the city tax collection office, revised and updated the tax rolls,
and claimed to have collected six million pesos in back taxes by the end
of 1931. These increased revenues, Guerrico asserted, enabled him to
retain hundreds of municipal employees he otherwise would have been
forced to fire and to rescind his previous plan to reduce municipal salaries
that were over 300 pesos per month.[17]

Despite the city's financial difficulties, the conservative intendente was
able to oversee the completion of a number of important public works
projects. These included the final stages of channeling and covering the

---

14 Américo Ghioldi, who often exchanged harsh words with Guerrico in council debates, later
   credited the conservative councilman and intendente with a "love and tenderness for the city" and
   for instilling within the members of the council a "pasión municipalista." Di Tella Oral Interview with Américo Ghioldi, p. 8 and personal interview (March 17, 1971).
15 *State Records* (March 22, 1932), 835.00/46.   16 *State Records* (August 27, 1931), 835.00/58.
17 MCBA, *Un año de gobierno edilicio: La Intendencia Municipal da cuenta a la Ciudad de los aspectos más
   salientes de su labor* (Buenos Aires, 1931), pp. 3–4.

Arroyo Maldonado, the inauguration of the municipal slaughterhouse, and the widening of the Avenida Santa Fe from the Plaza San Martín to Calle Callao. After successfully dealing with the purchase and destruction of the 100-year-old church of San Nicolás, one of the last major obstacles to the completion of the Diagonal Norte Roque Sáenz Peña, Guerrico had the satisfaction of seeing through a project that had begun when he was a councilman during the Anchorena administration. Even more satisfying was the grand opening in November 1931 of the impressive new city council building, a pet project of Guerrico's for some time. Topped by a graceful clock tower, the new and spacious council headquarters loomed over the colonial *Cabildo* (city hall) and added another distinctive landmark to the area around the Plaza de Mayo. Finally, Guerrico deserved much of the credit for the completion of the broad Avenida Leandro N. Alem, running north from the Casa Rosada to Retiro station. Divided into special lanes for public and private transportation, the new avenue was bordered by well-tended gardens and attractive street lighting. Some residents suggested that it be named for Guerrico himself, but instead it continued to bear the name of the founder of the Radical party.[18]

The increasing complexity and competition of public transportation in the city plagued Guerrico as it had his successors. Although the streetcar continued to carry many passengers, bus lines, taxis, suburban commuter trains, and especially colectivos continued to grow in popularity and ridership. Responding to consumer demand, larger versions of the colectivo began to appear, with bodies often constructed ad hoc in small workshops to accommodate nine to eleven passengers and then placed on ready-made truck chassis. With a larger capacity, these new colectivos were able to lower their fares to a very competitive twenty centavos a ride. All of these developments, Guerrico argued, produced unnecessary rivalry, with too many vehicles of different types covering the same routes and producing even more congestion. In a March 1931 communication to the national minister of the interior, he stated that this situation cried out for a more comprehensive traffic and transport plan for the city as a way to coordinate more efficiently the various modes of public-service transportation, a point he repeated in a review of his first year in office.[19] At the end of November of the same year, the intendente issued a decree regulating the operation of colectivos, providing, through the bureau of traffic control, stipulations outlining the routes that vehicles could follow; requiring a monthly inspection of the safety, security, and hygiene of each vehicle; establishing rules for where the colectivo could collect and discharge

18 *La Razón* (December 6, 1931), p. 9.
19 *Crítica* (March 28, 1931), p. 8 and MCBA, *Un año de gobierno edilicio*, pp. 30–1.

passengers; and setting fines and penalties for failure to comply with the new provisions.[20]

Guerrico also addressed the pending matter of subway construction. Early in his administration he announced that the Anglo would have to complete the Retiro–Constitutión line within two years or see its concession lapse. At the same time, he assured the Spanish consortium, whose proposal he had voted against as the sole dissenter on the city council, that he would recognize the agreement it had reached with the municipality to construct several new subway lines and that his administration would assist the company to realize its plans "in every way possible."[21] Soon thereafter it was reported that the original consortium had sold its concession to another concern, the Compañía Hispano Argentino de Obras Públicas y Finanzas (CHADOPYF). Although that company struggled to have its construction materials admitted into the country duty free, as the city had agreed to in the original contract, the new national government objected to this clause; the Anglo, meanwhile, continued to delay work on the Retiro–Constitución line pending approval of its request for a fifteen-centavo fare, a request that still had not been granted by the early months of 1932.[22]

Although work on new subways was delayed through the year, the final section of the Lacroze line was opened to the public on December 1, 1931, thereby joining the impressive list of completed public works projects. Another notable inauguration earlier in the year was that of the City Hotel. Located half a block from the southwest corner of the Plaza de Mayo at Bolívar 160, the "City" had cost seven million pesos to build. The capital's largest fine hotel, with 700 rooms, it was modeled after newer hotels in the United States that were done in the "neo-Gothic" and "neo-Tudor" style. *Crítica* lauded its modern features and claimed that the hotel's opening, along with the British Trade Exposition attended by the Prince of Wales, represented the two main events of the year in the capital.[23] Close to the center of governmental power, the City Hotel soon became a favorite gathering spot for politicians. Around the time that the City Hotel opened for business, work began on the Luna Park Stadium, a sports and entertainment facility to the east of Calle Corrientes and Avenida Alem, destined to be the Madison Square Garden of Buenos Aires.[24] In the same year, however, fire destroyed a portion of the Parque

20 *La Razón* (November 30, 1931), p. 11.   21 *State Records* (November 20, 1930), 835.00/38.
22 *State Records* (June 1, 1931), 835.00/51 and (February 12, 1932), 835.00/74.
23 *Crítica* (April 5, 1931), pp. 10–11.
24 Elisea Casella de Calderón, et al., "Calle Corrientes: Su historia en cinco barrios," *Buenos Aires Nos Cuenta*, 7 (Buenos Aires: July 1984), pp. 15–18.

Japonés amusement park and Guerrico decided not to renew its concession.[25]

Considerable irony was involved in the inauguration of the magnificent new building of the Honorable Concejo Deliberante without an elected city council to occupy it. That paradox, however, would soon be resolved. The stunning reversal suffered by the conservatives at the hands of the Radicals in local elections held in the province of Buenos Aires in April 1931 had effectively spelled the end for the Uriburu provisional regime. National elections were scheduled for November to resume constitutional normality, including the reopening of the national Congress. Elections to restore the city council of the capital were slated for January 1932. Certain conditions set on these elections, however, led the Radical party, which still claimed the loyalty of many porteños and Argentines, to abstain from these contests, an abstention that would last until the middle of the decade.[26]

The main focus of the national elections of November 8 was on the presidential contest. The candidate of the conservative coalition, known as the Concordancia, was Agustín P. Justo, leader of the moderate faction that had overthrown Yrigoyen. The Concordancia included the anti-personalista Radicals, with which Justo was nominally affiliated, the Independent Socialists, and the National Democrats (Partido Demócrata Nacional), a party formed with the intention of representing conservative interests nationwide. Opposing Justo were the candidates of an alliance between the Socialists and the Progressive Democrats (Alianza Demócrata–Socialista). Topping that ticket was longtime Progressive Democratic founder and leader Lisandro de la Torre, who selected Socialist Nicolás Repetto for his running mate. Individual parties put forth their own candidates for senator and deputy, with the Socialists and the Independent Socialists the leading contenders for these positions in the federal capital.

The campaign in the city of Buenos Aires was lively and intense. As had been the case from the inception of the Sáenz Peña law, all parties organized speeches and get-out-the-vote efforts in each district, plastered the city with posters extolling the virtues of their candidates (the Independent Socialists even had a poster contest in the Palais de Glace at Alem and Posadas), and concluded their campaign with massive rallies in various downtown plazas. Increasing use was made of the radio and documentary films to spread party messages. Ad hoc groups of women, students, professionals, and workers were formed in support of both coalitions

25 *Crítica* (March 17, 1931), p. 8.
26 These developments are treated in more detail in Walter, *The Province of Buenos Aires and Argentine Politics*, pp. 98–123.

contending for the presidency. At least one less than distinguished tango was composed as a campaign device to promote Justo's prospects as "future President of the Argentine Republic," claiming that the Concordancia candidate was a "true patriot," who would be "the salvation" of the nation.[27]

The Socialists made defense of the Sáenz Peña law and universal suffrage the centerpiece of their campaign. They also advocated nationalization of the nation's petroleum and "its exploitation by the State or by mixed [public–private] enterprises" and sought to take advantage of unpopular taxes imposed by the Uriburu regime with a promise of eliminating imposts that increased prices on consumer goods.[28] The Concordancia's campaign lacked such specifics, but did promise order, stability, and hard work in the face of a serious social and economic crisis. Justo portrayed himself as a stern but fair leader, who would work according to a "nationalist criterion" to protect the Argentine economy, especially the agricultural–export sector, to avoid extremism of the right or left, and to recognize the rights of labor as expressed by legally constituted entities.[29]

The elections themselves showed that, although Argentina's democratic experiment had suffered a grievous blow with the September coup against Yrigoyen, the democratic aspirations of the Argentines still remained high. Despite a steady downpour, which forced voters in a flooded section of La Boca to cast their ballots on a boat, a turnout of 87 percent in the city of Buenos Aires (and 73 percent nationwide) slightly exceeded that of the deputy elections of March 1930.[30] In the presidential contest in the capital, the Alianza Demócrata–Socialista bested the Concordancia by forty thousand votes. In the race for two national Senate seats from Buenos Aires, Socialist candidates Mario Bravo and Alfredo Palacios defeated their Independent rivals by a two-to-one margin (175,169 votes to 88,108) and the party captured twenty-two of thirty-two congressional seats by about the same difference. In the senatorial and congressional races the Socialists swept every district but number 20 and doubled and tripled the votes of their opponents in most working-class areas.[31]

Although turnout in the rest of the country was also high, the results were quite different. In the presidential contest, the Alliance won only in

27 From the "Justo Tango," with words by J. Fernández Blanco and music by Vicente De Cicco. Copy in possession of the author.
28 "Nuestra Plataforma," *La Vanguardia* (October 20, 1931), p. 6.
29 "Con la proclamación de la fórmula presidencial, realizada anoche en Avellaneda, clausuró su campaña electoral el P. Demócrata Nacional," *La Prensa* (November 7, 1931), p. 13.
30 Cantón, *Materiales*, vol. 1, p. 107.
31 "Ley 8871: Elecciones nacionales de 8 de Noviembre de 1931 y complementarias; escrutinios," República Argentina, *Memoria, 1932.*

de la Torre's home province of Santa Fe. Socialist and Alliance candidates did win deputy seats in the provinces of Buenos Aires, Córdoba, and Santa Fe, but overall the Concordancia captured the majority. Contributing to the conservative victory was the generous use of fraud, especially in the provinces of Buenos Aires and Mendoza. This tactic would be used throughout the decade to assure conservative dominance. Elections in the federal capital in these years, however, were generally fair and free from the outright manipulation of results that characterized much of the rest of the country.

For the Socialists, the victory was an especially sweet one. Having lost the advantage they had once held in the capital to the Radicals, and having seen a serious erosion of their strength in the late 1920s, the Socialists felt a clear sense of vindication in their overwhelming triumph in November 1931. They traced the massive outpouring of support they received to a repudiation of the parties associated with the September Revolution and the Uriburu regime, independent voters attracted to "our organization, our doctrine, our political morality," Progressive Democratic allies, the "natural growth of the electorate," and "not a few Radicals who have wanted to express in a positive manner their repudiation of the mistakes of their own governments . . . ."[32] Whether that was the reason for Radical backing of the Socialists cannot be determined, but that the Socialists benefited from Radical abstention and the votes of many of its supporters is abundantly clear. When the Radicals determined to reenter the capital's electoral arena in 1936, the Socialist advantage disappeared as quickly and as dramatically as it had emerged in 1931.

The Socialists' landslide in the 1931 national elections carried over, as expected, to the elections for a new city council held on January 10, 1932. This contest saw a grand total of thirty-three parties compete for a share of the thirty seats to be filled. In addition to the Socialists and Independent Socialists, the National Democrats, whose campaign was directed by former intendente Joaquín de Anchorena, and the anti-personalistas, badly divided at this time, were the major protagonists. Among the many smaller groups participating was the Partido Unión Deportiva which featured appearances by Luis Firpo and other well-known athletes in an effort to have the interests of those associated with sporting activities represented on the city council.[33]

A total of 389,059 voters, including 14,929 foreigners, was declared eligible for this election. Although turnout, at almost 66 percent, was

32 "Las elecciones de la Capital y su significado," *La Vanguardia* (November 19, 1931), p. 1.
33 "Los deportistas se preparan para la lucha comicial," *Jornada* (Buenos Aires: January 3, 1932), p. 13. *Jornada* was the name adopted by *Crítica* for a short period in the early 1930s.

respectable for a local election, it was some twenty points below the national contest. A worker professedly affiliated with the Socialist party, interviewed on election day, traced the relative lack of interest in the contest to a natural letdown following the intense campaign for the presidency and Congress. For his part, he planned to take his family on a picnic in the nearby suburb of Olivos rather than cast his vote, arguing that his main responsibility was to his children and only secondarily to his party.[34] Nonetheless, although interest may not have been at the level sustained for the national election, two of every three eligible voters did take part in the municipal contest, attesting again to porteño faith in the democratic process and providing evidence of one more step toward the restoration of constitutional and governmental normality after the September coup.

When the votes were counted, the Socialists had chalked up another impressive triumph. With 95,111 tallies, they outnumbered their closest competition by a four-to-one margin and gained twelve seats on the council. The Independent Socialists and National Democrats won four seats each, with two anti-personalista Radical groupings winning two apiece. These results produced a standoff between the Socialists and the parties of the Concordancia with twelve seats apiece. The swing votes would be provided by the single votes of the representative of the Progressive Democrats, the Concentración Obrera, and the Partido Popular and the three votes of the Partido Salud Pública (Public Health party).[35] This latter party had been formed in 1917 by Genaro Giacobini, a popular physician from the southern Parque Patricios area. Something of an eccentric, Giacobini believed that all questions ultimately had to be seen within a biological context.[36] A model of persistence, he had participated in each municipal election from 1918 without success until 1932. His vote, along with those of his two allies, would often prove decisive in the next few years of the council.

The new council was sworn in on January 28. For the most part, it was, as one commentator observed, a young and relatively untested group. It included only two members (Germinal Rodríguez of the Independent Socialists and José F. Penelón of the Concentración Obrera) who previously had served as councilmen and among the Socialists were many who had heretofore held only second-line positions within the party apparatus.[37] It did include, however, several who had served, if only briefly, as national deputies (Joaquín Coca of the Socialist party and Felipe Di Tella

---

34 "Hasta mediodía votaron 143,819," *Jornada* (January 10, 132), p. 1.
35 "Ley No. 10,240: Elecciones municipales de 10 de enero de 1932," República Argentina, *Memoria*, 1932. (See also Appendix, Table A.3).
36 "El triunfo de G. Giacobini es un premio a la constancia," *Jornada* (January 15, 1932), p. 1.
37 "El nuevo concejo deliberante y la obra a realizarse," *Jornada* (January 22, 1932), p. 6.

Municipal Intendente Rómulo Naón (1932)

and José Rouco Oliva of the Independent Socialist party). Even before being sworn in, a lottery was held to determine which fifteen would serve a full four-year term and which fifteen would have to seek reelection when new elections were held two years hence, thus reinstating the practice of renovating the council every two years.

To work with the newly reconstituted council, President Justo named Rómulo S. Naón to succeed Guerrico as the capital's intendente. Born in Buenos Aires in 1875, Naón had graduated with a law degree from the University of Buenos Aires in 1896. Active in Radical politics in the 1890s, he joined the anti-personalista faction in the 1920s. A law professor, he had been a national deputy from the federal capital and the province of Buenos Aires, and had served for a while as national minister of education and justice. Moving on to a diplomatic career, he was Argentine ambassador to the United States from 1914 to 1917. His ties with the United States remained strong during the 1920s, when he founded an international bank with North American financial interests and served for several years as the legal representative for the Standard Oil

Company in Argentina. A "definite aristocrat," with the usual Barrio Norte address (in 1939, Juncal 1290), he counted, in addition to membership in the Círculo de Armas and Jockey Club, affiliation with the University Club and Union Club of New York.[38] Although he stayed away from politics in the 1920s, he nonetheless campaigned with fellow antipersonalista Justo in 1931 prior to his appointment as chief executive of the city of Buenos Aires.

Naón clearly fit the mold of most intendentes. He was of the porteño upper classes, had enjoyed a distinguished career, and was close to the president who named him to his post. In other ways, however, Naón was something of an anomaly. For one thing, he was the first intendente of the twentieth century to have clear connections with foreign capitalist interests at a time of growing economic nationalism. For another, although it was standard practice for the intendente to be named by the president, Justo's election was the first since 1916 to smack of the undemocratic practices of the pre-Sáenz Peña era, which made the gap between the appointed executive and the popularly elected council all the more glaring. Moreover, as a result of the open election of January 10, Naón was the first intendente to face a council where initially his own firm base of support rested on the tenuous coalition of the Concordancia and the swing votes of minor parties. All of these anomalies made his life as intendente a difficult one.

That relations between Naón and the council would not be easy quickly became apparent. At its first meeting, the council chose, by a vote of fifteen to thirteen, to select Socialist Andrés Justo, son of the party's founder, as its president. The Socialists then argued that the president of the council, given the de facto nature of the provisional government following the September coup, should assume the executive office as the true representative of the popular will. A resolution to this effect was then approved by a vote of sixteen to twelve. Although Naón and the national government could ignore this particular council action, they must have been troubled by the fact that, whereas the Concordancia coalition had held firm on this vote, the three representatives of Giacobini's Public Health party had sided with eleven Socialists (Justo as council president not voting) and the Progressive Democratic and Concentración Obrera's councilmen on this first major roll call of the new council.[39]

The initial months of the new council saw a steady stream of resolutions calling for a review of actions taken by the city government during the Guerrico regime. Although the bulk of these were initiated by the

38 Biographical information from Bucich Escobar, *Buenos Aires*, p. 209n; William B. Parker, *Argentines of Today* (New York, 1967), vol. 1, pp. 546–9; *Quien es Quien*, 1939, pp. 300–1; and *State Records* (October 14, 1931), 835.101/8.

39 *VTCD* (February 19, 1932), pp. 6–19.

opposition, a number enjoyed unanimous support and a few were introduced by members of the Concordancia coalition itself. Early on, too, the
council addressed the continuing issue of streetcar fares and subway construction. On March 8 the tramway worker's union (Unión Tranviarios)
submitted a report to the council complaining about low salaries (80 to
120 pesos a month), the need to pay 5 percent of what they earned into
their pension fund, and generally poor working conditions in comparison
with other transport workers.[40] The council soon followed up with a critique of Guerrico's relations with the Anglo and a call for an investigation into why the British company had been allowed to forgo 50 percent
of its tax payments to the municipality and to suspend its contribution
to the employees' pension fund. The council also demanded to know what
the present administration was planning with regard to the possible
coordination of all public transportation in the city.[41]

In early April the streetcar workers threatened to strike for higher
wages. The Anglo responded with a message to its employees that its
desperate financial situation barely permitted it to maintain existing salary levels, much less consider an increase. The company provided figures
showing a near 30 percent loss in receipts for 1931, as compared with
1930, and an even greater rate of reduction for the first months of 1932.
On April 5, the company sent a note to Naón describing its financial
woes and called for emergency measures if service was to be maintained.
The intendente responded on April 12 with a suggestion to the council
that the Anglo and the Lacroze be allowed to raise their fares to thirteen
centavos for streetcar rides and fifteen centavos for the subway as a
temporary way to resolve this crisis.[42] One week later, he proposed as a
longer-term solution the establishment of a single corporation to co-
ordinate and manage all forms of public transportation in the capital. The
corporation, as he envisioned it, would contain equal numbers of representatives of both the city and the various private enterprises and profits
would be shared on a fifty–fifty basis between the two, with eventual
municipalization of all services as the ultimate goal. Repeating points
made by others, Naón argued that such a corporation and coordination
would reduce congestion and alleviate the unfair and unnecessary competition between the various forms of transportation that had evolved in
the capital by the early 1930s. None of these suggestions, however, was
sufficient to prevent a twenty-four-hour streetcar worker's strike on April
15.[43]

While the city government wrestled with these matters, the chairman

40 *State Records* (March 11, 1932), 835.00/76 and *VTCD* (March 8, 1932), p. 148.
41 *VTCD* (March 11, 1932), pp. 167–8.   42 *State Records* (April 22, 1932), 835.00/79.
43 *State Records* (May 6, 1932), 835.00/80 and (July 1, 1932), 835.00/84.

of the Anglo's board of directors, the Duke of Atholl, visited Buenos Aires to plead the company's case. Reeling from the effects of the world depression, he argued that the Anglo faced bankruptcy and the loss of its twenty million pounds of investment in Argentina unless actions were taken soon to relieve its difficulties. In speeches before the British Chamber of Commerce and the Rotary Club, he outlined the dim prospects for the company's future in the face of falling receipts and increased competition. He endorsed the idea of a transport corporation under certain conditions and also took a swipe at the colectivos as "pirate" competitors that only served to congest traffic and operated with no sense of "responsibility to the community."[44]

The arguments and action of Atholl and Naón did little to sway the council, which during these months continued to receive petitions from neighborhood associations and others to stand firm against any fare increases. On June 27, Secretary of Public Works Miguel Padilla appeared before the council to discuss progress on the Anglo's project to construct the Retiro–Constitución line. As had been the case for more than a decade, there was little to report other than the fact that the company had until August 22 either to resume serious work on or to complete the line. Socialist Andrés Justo observed that the story was by now a familiar one and repeated his party's refrain that Naón, like his predecessor, seemed more interested in protecting the interests of the Anglo than those of porteño consumers. As he put it, "this company, in its desire to delay as much as possible the initiation of these works so as to obtain a fare increase, has always had the full collaboration of all the executive departments." The proposed transport corporation, he charged, was designed essentially to bail the company out of its financial difficulties, not to benefit all parties concerned. After exhaustive debate on the issue, the council considered a resolution introduced by Socialists, Independent Socialists, and the Progressive Democratic representative declaring that the intendente did not have the authority on his own to formulate plans for transport coordination and that the council remained firmly opposed to any suggested fare increases. The resolution was then approved by a vote of nineteen to one, wherein Socialists of both stripes were joined again by the Progressive Democratic and Concentración Obrera representatives, as well as two councilmen of the Salud Pública party, while National Democrats and anti-personalista Radicals did not vote.[45]

With no immediate relief in sight, the Anglo did little to preserve its chances to finish the much troubled Retiro–Constitución line. On

---

44 As quoted in Winthrop R. Wright, *British-Owned Railways in Argentina: Their Effect on Economic Nationalism, 1854–1948* (Austin, 1974), p. 178. Also, *State Records* (June 3, 1932), 835.00/83; and (July 1, 1932), 835.00/84.
45 *VTCD* (June 27, 1932), pp. 2098–169.

September 1, Naón reported to the council that the concession to the Anglo for construction of the city's third subway had lapsed and that the company had been so notified. On September 10 the press reported that work had begun on the Retiro–Constitución line by the Compañía Hispano–Argentino de Obras Públicas y Finanzas. In late December the council put the finishing touches on the matter by voting unanimously in favor of an ordinance canceling the Anglo's concession and denying the company any further claims to the project.[46]

Transport issues were not the only points of conflict between Naón and the council. In May, when the executive presented his budget for 1933, Socialist spokesman Joaquín Coca made a sharp critique of the growth in municipal salaries as a proportion of the total (from 35 percent in 1910 to 58 percent in 1932) and chastized the administration for not cutting back on the wages of high-level and often superfluous city employees. These and other criticisms aside, the budget was approved in general.[47] In voting on particular articles, however, the Socialists objected to an item that would subsidize the activities of the sisters of charity in municipal hospitals, arguing that this order performed a religious as opposed to a medical function and therefore should not be funded. Gaining support from the Independent Socialists as well as the Progressive Democratic and Concentración Obrera representatives, the Socialists prevailed over the National Democrats, the anti-personalistas, and, on this vote, the three members of Salud Pública by a tally of sixteen to twelve to eliminate the item from the budget.[48]

This vote produced an adverse reaction from the conservative press and from Naón, who praised the work of the sisters of charity and harshly attacked the council members who had voted for the proposal to remove their subsidy from the budget. This attack, in turn, prompted the council, by a vote of sixteen to one, to condemn the intendente's strong statements on the matter as published in *La Nación* as a show of "inconsiderateness" (*desconsideración*) toward the deliberative body.[49] After a long and impassioned debate on the matter several days later, the Independent Socialists reversed themselves and the council voted sixteen to thirteen to overcome Socialist opposition and to restore the previously earmarked funding for the sisters.[50] Similar issues arose in late June when the Independent Socialists voted with the mainline Socialists to disapprove the granting of an official license plate to the archbishop of Buenos Aires and to approve the performance of a controversial anticlerical play in the city.[51] In early September, Naón vetoed both these measures, arguing

46 *VTCD* (December 21, 1932), pp. 4861–70.   47 *VTCD* (May, 3, 1932), pp. 897–966.
48 *VTCD* (May 4, 1932), pp. 1006–32.   49 *VTCD* (May 10, 1932), pp. 1317–18.
50 *VTCD* (May 17, 1932), pp. 1388–444.
51 *VTCD* (June 21, 1932), p. 1988 and (June 24, 1932), p. 2030.

that they not only were offensive to the Catholic Church and its followers, but also encroached on authority that was properly the executive's.[52]

These struggles over religious matters were symbolic of deeper tensions between the intendente and the council. During the confrontation over the sisters of charity budgeting, Naón had sent a message to the federal government complaining that the council was undercutting his authority and asking for assistance.[53] At the same time, a proposal had been introduced into the national Senate to amend the organic municipal law so as to strengthen the hand of the intendente vis-à-vis the council. *La Vanguardia* claimed that this maneuver, along with an allegedly calculated public campaign to defame the council, was a ploy cooked up in collusion with the tramway companies to override the popular will as expressed by the council.[54]

Whatever the motivation for these actions, it was clear by late August that the intendente and the council were headed for – and perhaps were already in – an intractable standoff. In mid-July, the anti-personalista committee of the capital had broken with the mayor over his failure to pay sufficient attention to the party's patronage demands.[55] Nonetheless, within the council Naón could still count on their votes, along with those of the conservative National Democrats. More ominous was the defection of the Independent Socialists, who increasingly sided with their former party colleagues on most issues. The four votes of the Independents, along with the twelve Socialists and a scattering of others, would enable the opposition to come dangerously close to a two-thirds majority to override the intendente's growing resort to the veto.

A clean break between the intendente and the Independent Socialists occurred on September 2. Following a request by Naón and a decree by Justo threatening to revise the governing law of the city, the Independents presented a resolution reaffirming the council's support for the original legislation and lambasting the intendente for attempting to diminish "the dimension of popular sovereignty represented by the Concejo Deliberante." Speaking for his party's proposal, Councilman Gregorio Beschinsky unloaded a devastating attack on the intendente, accusing him of engaging in a deliberate attempt to denigrate and undermine the council and tracing his recent behavior to frustration with the council's actions denying the Anglo's request for a fare increase. He concluded by urging the national Congress to reject any attempts to tamper with municipal autonomy and affirmed that "the principal culprit of the conflicts

52 *VTCD* (September 2, 1932), pp. 2379–80.
53 As described by Minister of the Interior Leopoldo Melo in an interpellation on proposed changes in the law that governed the capital. *Diputados* (September 8, 1932), pp. 603–4.
54 "Un ataque al municipio popular," *La Vanguardia* (June 20, 1932), p. 1.
55 *State Records* (July 15, 1932), 835.00/637.

created is the present Intendente Señor Naón, who has lost our confidence and, repudiated by public opinion, for the good of the city ought to resign . . . ."[56]

Talk that Naón might resign had been rife since mid-July when the anti-personalistas had broken with him. Such reports spread as the intendente's relations with the council, never very good to begin with, continued to deteriorate after September. Although there were many areas of disagreement, the major controversy concerned the alleged favoritism Naón had shown in awarding concessions for gasoline pumps in the capital. He had vetoed legislation that would have awarded them to the state oil company, Yacimientos Petrolíferos Fiscales (YPF), and had given the advantage instead to two private companies, awarding the best locations to the West Indian Oil Company, a subsidiary of Standard Oil of New Jersey. For the former legal representative of Standard Oil to have made such a decision in the midst of an ongoing confrontation with the city council, at a time when economic nationalism was on the rise, and when the intendente's sympathies for the Anglo were abundantly clear, was a political blunder of major proportions.[57]

While Naón, under pressure from the national government, withdrew his veto of the gasoline pump ordinance, the opposition on the council used his actions and the apparent conflict of interest as a major club with which to beat him. For five lengthy sessions in September, the Socialists and the Independent Socialists lacerated the intendente for his actions on the gasoline pump matter. Finally, on September 21, the council approved a resolution of censure and called for him to resign.[58] The real handwriting on the wall for Naón's tenure as intendente came a few days later when the national government, responding to the local executive's request for intervention on his behalf, stated that it was up to the city council, not the federal authorities, to determine the legality of his actions in making the gasoline pump concessions.[59]

The drama, nevertheless, dragged on for two more months. The council continued to attack Naón, criticizing him for delays in reincorporating city employees dismissed during the Guerrico administration and for alleged mismanagement and irregularities in the municipal frigorífico.

56 *VTCD* (September 2, 1932), p. 2458.

57 *State Records* (October 14, 1932), 835.101/8 and (November 17, 1932), 835.00/94. For Naón's role in arguing for Standard Oil's position in a major court case in late 1929, see Carl E. Solberg, *Oil and Nationalism in Argentina: A History* (Stanford, 1979), p. 140.

58 The vote on the resolution was sixteen to eleven, with the Socialists, Independent Socialists, and the representatives of the Progressive Democrats and Concentración Obrera in favor; the National Democrats, anti-personalistas, and representives of Salud Pública opposed. *VTCD* (September 21, 1932), pp. 2945–46.

59 *State Records* (October 14, 1932).

In late October, new charges were raised by the opposition, this time the assertion that Naón had abused his authority by ordering the expropriation of private property for personal gain.[60] A few days later the council voted fourteen to eight to censure the intendente for the "offensive terms" of a note he had sent to the body in response to its question concerning the expropriation issue.[61]

It certainly was clear by now, if it had not been previously, that this standoff could not continue if there was to be any hope for the normal functioning of municipal government in Buenos Aires. The end finally came when Naón again asked Justo to intervene on his behalf and the president informed him that he could no longer offer the beleaguered intendente his support. Accordingly, on November 18 Naón presented his resignation, claiming, after a conversation with Justo, "that I can no longer count, in my work, on the full collaboration of the Executive Power, which, in my opinion, is indispensable in the atmosphere in which public action is carried on in our country, and it led me to conclude that to resign is preferable than to pursue a secondary and fruitless task."[62] He also noted, somewhat ingenuously, given his attempts to limit the powers of the council and his frequent requests for help from the national authorities, that if he had been the official of an "autonomous administration" he would not have been compelled to give up his office.

Crucial to Naón's ultimate fate was his failure to work with the council. Given the delicate political balance of forces, a skilled political hand was necessary. Particularly important was the need to keep the Independent Socialists within the Concordancia coalition, something which Naón was unable to do.[63] Where compromise and conciliation were needed, the intendente used confrontation and inflexibility. As the U.S. embassy reported at the time of his resignation, Naón was considered personally honest and upright, but "in some quarters . . . as not unduly intelligent."[64] Certainly he had shown little in the way of political ability in a situation that while difficult, given the Socialist presence on the council, was not impossible.

In a larger context, the Naón episode was one more chapter in the ongoing story of the struggle between the appointed intendente and the elected city council. In this instance, the council prevailed. The fate of Naón's successor, however, would be quite different. Named to the post on November 21, Mariano de Vedia y Mitre, well-known lawyer, author,

---

60 *VTCD* (October 25, 1932), pp. 3600–47.   61 *VTCD* (October 28, 1932), pp. 3686–712.
62 As quoted in *State Records* (November 25, 1932), 835.101/10.
63 The "Independents" apparently found Naón's antisocialist sentiments and close ties with foreign capital objectionable enough to override their allegiance to the Concordancia. Horacio Sanguinetti, *Los Socialistas Independientes*, pp. 221–2.
64 *State Records* (November 25, 1932).

and historian, promised to work closely with the council and, while expressing his solidarity with the September 1930 Revolution, vowed "to serve the collective interests of the City of Buenos Aires" over any partisan considerations.[65] Avoiding, and perhaps learning from the mistakes of his predecessor, he would prove to be among the capital's most dynamic and successful executives.

65 Ibid.

9

Vedia y Mitre and the council

The administration of Intendente Mariano de Vedia y Mitre was steeped in controversy. Impassioned debate swirled around concessions to foreign capital, expensive construction projects, and the executive's authoritarian style. Often confronted with a hostile council that contained a strong Socialist and later a considerable personalista Radical presence, the mayor often bypassed or ignored the legislative branch and initiated and implemented measures and projects on his own, leaving an impotent and frustrated council to debate and protest the results. His legacy to the capital, however, especially in terms of major public works, was notable and enduring.

Vedia y Mitre conformed to the general profile of most intendentes. Born into an old and well-established porteño family in 1881, he had graduated from the local law school and embarked on a multifaceted career of teaching, journalism, and the writing of history. A professor of law at the University of Buenos Aires, he was appointed to the bench of the Buenos Aires civil court in 1916 and served in that and a number of other juridical positions until the early 1930s. A "definite aristocrat," he belonged to the usual fashionable clubs and boasted a Barrio Norte address.[1] The one discordant note in this picture was his lack of elected office or extensive administrative experience prior to his appointment as intendente. This gap, however, was compensated by the constant support he enjoyed from his close friend, President Justo, for whom he had campaigned in 1931, his own innate intelligence and ability, and the assistance of some particularly able secretaries of finance and public works.[2]

---

1 The 1918 voter registry listed Vedia y Mitre as residing at Puerreydón 834 and in 1939 another source listed his address at Avenida Quintana 483, both in the Barrio Norte. He was also a member of the Círculo de Armas, the Jockey Club, and the Club del Progreso. *Quien es Quien, 1939,* pp. 435–6. Biographical information also from Ulyses Petit de Murat, "Mariano de Vedia y Mitre (1932–1938)," in *Tres Intendentes de Buenos Aires,* pp. 76–102.

2 Accompanying Vedia y Mitre as secretary of finance throughout his six years in office was Atilio Dell'Oro Maini, another lawyer, university professor, and member of the Círculo de Armas. Provisional President Uriburu had appointed Dell'Oro Maini, who was closely associated with the

Having pledged to cooperate with the council upon taking over from the discredited Naón in November of 1932, Vedia y Mitre immediately began to address the city's depression-induced fiscal crisis. In late November, he withdrew his predecessor's proposed budget for 1933 and had his staff work on a revised version, which would reduce expenditures and the deficit for the following year. On December 26, he sent to the council a proposal for a thirty-million-peso bond issue to cover the costs of building expropriations involved in street widening.[3] On December 30, he submitted his slimmed-down budget for 1933. Socialists objected to expenditures for such items as funding for the sisters of charity and protested the submission of the budget at the last possible moment. Defenders pointed out, however, that most of the budget details had been amply debated and finally agreed to after several weeks of committee consideration in which the points of view of all parties were considered. After representatives of all parties were heard from, the council approved the budget proposal with little dissent.[4]

Although Vedia y Mitre's budget for 1933 authorized expenditures of six million pesos less than in 1932, municipal finances overall were still far from secure. As José Penelón had pointed out in the budget debate, the city was running increasing deficits and facing a growing debt burden. With a probable deficit of eight million pesos for 1932, the total deficit for the past two years stood at twenty-four million pesos. The city faced thirty million pesos in obligation for expropriation of property and owed the national government forty-four million pesos for bailing it out of payment on a loan to the Chatham Phoenix Corporation of New York, which fell due soon after the provisional government took office in September 1930, and which the city had been unable to pay. Debt service, which made up 14 percent of all authorized municipal expenses in 1928, had risen to 17 percent by 1933.[5] *La Prensa*, commenting on the report of the secretary of finance to the city council on these matters, was quoted as observing, with perhaps some exaggeration, that "it is difficult to behold a public administration in a more serious state of moral and financial disorder than that which is revealed in the municipality of the city of Buenos Aires . . . ."[6]

Vedia y Mitre alluded to this state of affairs in a March 1933 interview with *Crítica*. Like previous intendentes, he recognized the clear need for

conservative and nationalist Catholic publication *Críterio*, national intervenor in the province of Corrientes prior to his selection by Vedia y Mitre to serve in his administration. Yet another lawyer and university professor, Amílcar Razori, served as secretary of public works for most of Vedia y Mitre's term in office. *Quien es Quien, 1939,* pp. 140–1 and p. 359.

3 *State Records* (January 11, 1933), 835.00/98.   4 *VTCD* (December 30, 1932), pp. 5343–79.
5 *State Records* (January 19, 1934), 835.51/886/62.
6 *State Records* (March 3, 1933), 835.51/893.

improvements in and extension of services to the outlying districts of the city. Although he listed these as a major goal, he observed that "for now we cannot think of expenditures; we do not have the resources to spend." Another factor in the "deplorable financial situation we face," he noted, was the demand by many property owners to be compensated for expropriated properties, making council approval of his thirty-million-peso bond issue a top priority. For his part, he was reviewing each municipal office to determine where economies could be made. In the process, he had recognized that it was vital "to eliminate bad administrative practices, to correct abuses, and to avoid immoralities." Regarding the council, whose collaboration he sought, he claimed to respect the democratic procedures by which it had been chosen and which governed the executive's relations with that body. In that light, he hoped that the council would interpret his vetoes of certain matters, not as obstructionism, but rather as a simple use of the mechanism provided by the city charter for the intendente to express his point of view on matters of common concern. Underlying the interview was the new intendente's clear sense of frustration, anxious as he was to move rapidly in a number of areas, but constrained by the current fiscal crisis, bureaucratic inertia, and a council on which the government's opponents had a substantial say.[7]

The tone of the council opposition's relations with the new intendente during his first full year in office was set, as usual, early on. On February 13, 1933, the executive called the council to extraordinary sessions to consider proposals to reorganize the administration of the Teatro Colón and the thirty-million-peso bond issue for expropriations. The Socialists argued that both these measures were aimed primarily to benefit the upper classes and submitted an agenda of their own, which included stricter implementation of ordinances on children's playgrounds, public housing, and pensions. The council approved the intendente's proposed agenda by sixteen affirmative votes and, in a roll call, defeated the Socialist proposal fifteen to fourteen. Voting with the eleven Socialists were Penelón of the Concentración Obrera, Julio González Iramain of the Progressive Democrats, and Giacobini of Salud Pública. The two other councilmen of Giacobini's party, however, voted with the majority. More significantly, the Independent Socialists clearly had returned to the

---

7 In its introduction to this interview, *Crítica* noted that the intendente of the capital was one of the nation's most important and influential public officials, responsible for a budget equal to that of half of the republic's provinces combined. At this point, *Crítica* had a favorable opinion of Vedia y Mitre, claiming that the new executive had a "clear administrative vision" and an "undoubted understanding" of what needed to be done for the well-being of the capital. "Clearly," it concluded, "Dr. de Vedia y Mitre is the intendente that Buenos Aires and its present progress needs." "Las múltiples necesidades de la ciudad han sido atendidas con preferencia por Vedia y Mitre," *Crítica* (March 3, 1933), p. 11.

Concordancia fold.[8] With their main party leader, Antonio de Tomaso, serving as national minister of agriculture in the Justo administration, they sided with the intendente on most issues. Their renewed alliance with the conservatives and the anti-personalista Radicals meant that the Socialist-led opposition would have a difficult time initiating and passing legislation of their own and, more significantly, almost no hope of overriding Vedia y Mitre's vetoes.

When the regular sessions of the council began in April, it soon became clear that, although the intendente's margin of support was thin, it was usually consistent enough for him to have his way on most issues. The Concordancia coalition, with the support of Salud Pública, beat back opposition attempts to overturn an executive decree limiting the hours of operation of the frigorífico municipal, to override a veto of his power to nominate appointees to regulate municipal playgrounds, and to reverse his decision to eliminate the municipal consignment office.[9] Despite these victories, in September Vedia y Mitre felt frustrated enough by what he considered an uncooperative council to submit his resignation to the national government, the precipitating event apparently being an innocuous council request that he supply information on the progress of work on the Plaza Retiro.[10] Justo reaffirmed his support for the intendente and refused the proffered resignation.

Following the resignation threat, the pattern of the executive's relations with the council remained much as it had been before. For the most part, opposition initiatives were defeated or stymied, while the intendente's position was upheld by slim margins. On a number of items, however, there was broad support. These included earmarking fifty thousand pesos of relief aid to the unemployed in the Puerto Nuevo district, unanimous approval of a fifty-million-peso bond issue for the completion of various public works projects, and, by a vote of twenty-three to two, the granting of a concession to the Compañía Ibero Argentino de Construcciones y Subterráneos to construct a four-line subway system to serve primarily the southern zone of the city.[11] The council also passed an ordinance introduced by Independent Socialist José Rouco Oliva to control and limit excessive street noise in the capital.[12]

8 *VTCD* (February 13, 1933), pp. 8–20.
9 *VTCD* (May 12, 1933), p. 655 and (May 23, 1933), p. 789; (June 28, 1933), p. 1327.
10 *State Records* (October 6, 1933), 835.00/117.
11 *VTCD* (June 10, 1933), pp. 1449–50; (October 23, 1933), pp. 2579–653; and (November 8, 1933), pp. 3086–134. The terms of the subway concession stipulated completion of the first line within three years and a fare of ten centavos for direct trips and fifteen centavos for combinations. As it turned out, the concessionaire could not fulfill his commitments and the project failed.
12 *VTCD* (December 28, 1933), pp. 4557–71.

Although the Socialist-led opposition scored few victories in 1933, it did manage to stake out a popular position on a matter that would dominate the attention of the council and the city for much of the decade, namely, the question of electric rates charged the porteño consumer and the related matter of extending the contracts granted to the two large foreign concerns who provided power to the capital. This issue, which bore many similarities to, and some connections with, the Socialists' struggle against the Anglo, was as complex as it was significant.

Of the two foreign-owned companies that provided electric power to the city of Buenos Aires, one, the Compañía Hispano Americano de Electricidad (CHADE), had been granted a fifty-year concession from the city in 1907. The other, the Compañía Italo Argentino de Electricidad (CIAE), had received a similar concession in 1912. Together, they produced by 1932 almost 60 percent of the nation's electric power, with the CHADE generating between 80 to 85 percent of the total in the capital. Although the official headquarters of the Compañía Hispano were located in Barcelona, it was ultimately controlled, as was the Anglo, by SOFINA of Brussels. Serving on the local board of directors of both the CHADE and the Italo were well-known figures of the Argentine oligarchy, including former intendente Joaquín S. de Anchorena and Carlos Meyer Pellegrini, who had renegotiated the Baring loan for the city in the early 1920s.[13]

Outside of the capital, two United States-owned groups dominated the provision of electricity to the nation's other cities. They, however, were facing increasing competition from a movement to establish municipally operated electric cooperatives, a movement that was especially strong in the province of Buenos Aires.[14] Simultaneously, in the capital, local protest rooted in various neighborhood associations began to grow against the practices of the CHADE and Italo. These companies, it was claimed, were violating the provisions of their concessions by charging higher rates than were allowed and levying fees for the extension of cables. A more or less spontaneous protest movement of various individuals and organizations led in the early 1930s to the formation of the Junta de Sociedades de Fomento y Centros Comerciales e Industriales Pro Rebajas de Tarifas Eléctricas (Junta of Development Societies and Commercial and Industrial Centers for the Lowering of Electric Rates), which petitioned the

13 Pablo Julián Davis, *La cuestión eléctrica en Buenos Aires en la década de 1930: Aspectos económicos y sociales de un escándalo político* (Buenos Aires, 1988), pp. 2–13.

14 Comments on the growth of this movement are provided in a "strictly confidential" dispatch from U.S. embassy Vice Consul Odin G. Loren dated November 21, 1934 and entitled "Cooperative Threat to Foreign Owned Public Service Corporations in Argentina," *State Records* (December 15, 1934), 835.6463/12.

city government for stricter enforcement of the provisions of the concessions and to set maximum rates in line with them.[15]

Within the council, the Socialists, who in the 1920s had called for greater municipal control over the companies and the rates they charged, took up the cause of the protesters. They repeated the complaints of higher rates and unfair charges and requested the municipal executive to call the companies to account. The companies, in turn, denied that the municipality had the authority to interpret the concessions in a way that would force them to change their practices.

The whole matter had been submitted to the council's committee on public service concessions in late December 1932. On October 6, 1933, the chairman of that committee, Independent Socialist Germinal Rodríguez, issued a report which agreed in most respects with the consumer complaints against the CHADE and recommended action to respond to the demands for lower rates. The lack of a quorum, however, prevented a vote on the committee report at this time. Shortly thereafter, according to the results of a later investigation, the Independent Socialist councilmen were summoned to the office of party leader Federico Pinedo, at that time Justo's minister of finance, and ordered not to act against the CHADE, which had just extended the government a seven-million-peso loan.[16]

When the council resumed consideration of the question two weeks later, it was clear that Pinedo's instructions had had an effect. Instead of immediate action, Rodríguez now recommended the naming of a five-man committee to mediate the points of dispute between the city and the company. Included on this "conciliation commission" would be a representative of the municipality, a representative of the companies, and the three deans of the schools of law, sciences, and economics of the University of Buenos Aires. They were to issue their report within thirty days of being organized.

This proposal produced a predictable protest from the Socialist-led opposition. During the several days of lengthy and often impassioned debate that ensued, the opposition charged the intendente and the Concordancia, in terms reminiscent of the debate over streetcar fares, of being more solicitous of the concerns of powerful foreign enterprises than of the well-being of the citizens of the capital. Rodríguez and others rejoined with the argument that the matter of electric rates was an important and highly complex issue, requiring calm and measured consideration

15 Di Tella Oral Interview with Jorge del Río (Buenos Aires: April 27, 1971). Del Río, a young lawyer sympathetic with the Socialist party, was a leading figure in helping to organize this protest movement and in presenting the consumers' case to the press and the local authorities. For more on his interpretation of the development of the whole electric rates issue, see his *Electricidad y liberación nacional: El caso S.E.G.B.A.* (Buenos Aires, 1960).

16 Davis, *La cuestión eléctrica*, pp. 3–4.

by highly qualified experts like those who would serve on the commission. The opposition responded by noting that naming the commission would serve to remove decision-making power from the council and called into question the technical expertise and political credentials of the university deans slated to be named to it.[17] In the end, however, the opposition did not have the votes to defeat this proposal, which was approved unanimously after they abandoned the chamber.[18] When the commission report, generally favorable to the CHADE, was presented to the council at the end of December, the opposition again staged a walkout and the report was also approved unanimously.[19]

Elections to renew the city council were held on March 4, 1934. For the first time, these were held simultaneously with national deputy elections. The decision to combine the two was based on the argument that such an arrangement would save time, money, and effort and do no harm to municipal autonomy. The Socialists objected, claiming that the change was a maneuver to undercut their newfound electoral advantage in the capital.[20] As the results of the contest would show, their concerns were unfounded.

At both the national and the local level, the Socialists made defense of democracy and opposition to higher transportation fares and electric rates cornerstones of their campaign. The program for their national deputy candidates, for example, called for government regulation of electric concessions and rates and encouragement for the development of electric cooperatives.[21] The municipal program called for lower electric rates, revision of the original concession, and the construction of a municipal power plant. Another article claimed opposition both to any increase in transportation fares and to any attempt to allow one company or group of companies to monopolize the capital's public transportation system.[22] In one of the party's final preelection rallies, Councilman Andrés Justo reviewed the Socialists' struggle on these questions within the council and their general efforts on behalf of the working people of the city.[23] *La Vanguardia*'s lead editorial prior to election day pledged the Socialists "to impede the maneuvers of the trusts and the robbery of public services by capitalist enterprises."[24]

17 Jorge del Río later claimed that the deans of law and sciences had links to the companies before and after they served on the conciliation commission. Instituto Torcuato Di Tella Oral Interview, p. 15.
18 *VTCD* (October 25, 1933), pp. 2763–94.   19 *VTCD* (December 27, 1933), pp. 4328–44.
20 *Diputados* (September 20 and 21, 1933), pp. 612–43.
21 *La Vanguardia* (January 31, 1934), p. 9.   22 *La Vanguardia* (February 24, 1934), p. 9.
23 *La Prensa* (February 26, 1934), p. 9.
24 "Hay Que Vencer!," *La Vanguardia* (March 2, 1934), p. 1.

With the Radicals again abstaining, the Socialists faced a variety of disparate and generally divided opponents. The main challenge came from the Concordancia coalition of National Democrats and Independent Socialists. The anti-personalistas who divided themselves into two groups, one of which was headed by ex-intendente Naón, ran separately. At a closing campaign rally for the Concordancia, National Democrat Councilman Carlos Edo pleaded with the voters for a conservative majority on the council that could "impose the passage of ordinances of general interest and not for demagogic ends and that would study issues calmly and profoundly."[25] Beyond this aspiration, the candidates of the Concordancia said little specifically about the pressing issues of the day. The municipal program of the National Democrats, for example, called for street widening, a new property valuation, improvements in public health, and continued support for the work of the sisters of charity in city hospitals, but said nothing about electric or transport rates.[26]

Combining the two elections led to a turnout of 75 percent of the capital's eligible voters, notably higher than had been seen in separately held municipal elections. The outcome, however, was similar to the election two years earlier. In the national deputy election, the Socialists captured twelve of the seventeen seats contested by a margin of three to one over the second-place Concordancia candidates. Their advantage was much the same in the municipal election, in which eighteen parties had taken part. Again, they swept all districts of the capital by convincing margins.[27] They credited their sweep to continuing support from the working class and general popular identification with their "purposes and action."[28] Party leader Nicolás Repetto, however, also traced the party's good showing to the continued abstention of the Radicals and the disarray and fragmentation of other challengers.[29]

A socioeconomic profile of the electorate for whose loyalties the various parties competed in 1934 is provided in Table 9.1. Based on a 10 percent sample of the voter registry for that year, the most notable feature of the profile is how little the class proportions had changed over sixteen years. Although the electorate had grown from 196,385 registered voters in 1918 to 432,867 in 1934, the overall percentages for the working, middle, and upper classes were almost identical in 1934 to what they had been in 1918. White-collar employees, small businessmen, and skilled workers

---

25 *La Prensa*, (February 28, 1934), p. 11.   26 *La Prensa* (February 8, 1934), p. 11.
27 The Socialist's list captured almost 130,000 votes to 36,000 for the second-place Concordancia. *La Prensa* (March 21, 1934), p. 11 (see also Appendix, Table A.3).
28 "Nuestra victoria es el triunfo de la Democracia," *La Vanguardia*, (March 21, 1934), p. 1.
29 "Tres respuestas del líder socialista, acerca de las últimas elecciones, a nuestro redactor E.J. Iglesias," *Caras y Caretas*, 37, 1851 (March 24, 1934).

Table 9.1. Social class composition of the electorate of the city of Buenos Aires, by voting district, 1934[a]

District	Occupational category									Total	Class (%)		
	01 (%)	02 (%)	04 (%)	06 (%)	07 (%)	08 (%)	09 (%)	10 (%)	11		01–04	06–07	08–11
1	590 (12)	440 (9)	1,288 (27)	1,846 (39)	341 (7)	47 (1)	83 (2)	39 (1)	57	4,731	48	46	4
2	169 (9)	168 (9)	585 (32)	642 (37)	129 (7)	28 (2)	41 (2)	15 (1)	16	1,793	50	44	5
3	164 (8)	188 (9)	530 (25)	956 (45)	162 (8)	35 (2)	44 (2)	40 (2)	17	2,136	42	53	6
4	121 (6)	516 (25)	584 (29)	652 (32)	110 (5)	17 (1)	15 (1)	11 (1)	22	2,048	60	38	3
5	68 (3)	124 (5)	413 (17)	1,331 (54)	241 (10)	52 (2)	108 (4)	84 (3)	20	2,441	25	64	9
6	72 (3)	139 (6)	641 (27)	1,080 (46)	200 (9)	46 (2)	85 (4)	54 (2)	22	2,339	36	55	8
7	35 (3)	70 (6)	281 (23)	581 (48)	129 (11)	24 (2)	44 (4)	40 (3)	8	1,212	32	59	9
8	63 (4)	113 (7)	462 (28)	720 (43)	171 (10)	41 (2)	60 (4)	30 (2)	10	1,670	39	53	8
9	48 (3)	64 (4)	329 (23)	689 (48)	171 (12)	45 (3)	36 (3)	37 (3)	11	1,430	30	60	9
10	51 (5)	64 (6)	208 (21)	468 (46)	113 (12)	34 (3)	37 (4)	29 (3)	6	1,010	32	58	10
11	17 (2)	45 (5)	164 (17)	471 (48)	126 (13)	30 (3)	48 (5)	69 (7)	5	975	24	61	15
12	81 (5)	105 (7)	272 (18)	805 (53)	140 (9)	31 (2)	28 (2)	41 (3)	11	1,514	30	62	7
13	63 (4)	77 (5)	194 (12)	894 (54)	203 (12)	50 (3)	53 (3)	86 (5)	16	1,636	21	66	11
14	24 (1)	66 (4)	169 (10)	846 (51)	229 (14)	87 (5)	74 (4)	147 (9)	14	1,656	15	65	18
15	428 (8)	507 (10)	1,603 (31)	1,928 (38)	362 (7)	67 (1)	103 (2)	58 (1)	64	5,120	49	45	4
16	325 (9)	330 (9)	960 (27)	1,463 (41)	282 (8)	42 (1)	71 (2)	70 (2)	57	3,600	45	49	5
17	111 (5)	206 (9)	604 (26)	944 (40)	193 (8)	43 (2)	129 (6)	66 (3)	40	2,336	40	48	11
18	86 (4)	213 (9)	590 (24)	1,042 (45)	228 (9)	52 (2)	84 (3)	90 (4)	33	2,418	37	52	9
19	82 (4)	128 (6)	351 (18)	934 (47)	151 (8)	77 (4)	92 (5)	147 (7)	23	1,985	38	55	16
20	38 (2)	255 (17)	165 (11)	564 (37)	114 (7)	84 (5)	175 (11)	133 (9)	10	1,538	30	44	24
Total	2,636 (6)	3,818 (9)	10,393 (24)	18,856 (43)	3,795 (9)	932 (2)	1,410 (3)	1,286 (3)	462	43,588	39	52	8

[a] Ten percent sample.

[b] For occupational categories, see Table 1.2.

Source: República Argentina, Registro Electoral de la Nación: Distrito Electoral de la Capital Federal: Lista Definitiva de Electores, 1934, 5 vols. (Buenos Aires, 1934).

made up three-quarters of the electorate. There were few changes among the subgroups, although the proportion of unskilled and menial workers doubled from 3 to 6 percent of the total, whereas that of semiskilled and skilled workers declined slightly by a combined 4 percent.

For the most part, despite the dispersion of the population outward, there were also remarkably few changes in the class distribution of the electorate. The southern districts 1 through 4 and western districts 15 and 16 continued to have a substantial proportion of working-class voters, whereas the highest proportion of upper-class voters remained concentrated in the central downtown areas, especially districts 14 and 20. All districts, with the exceptions of 4 and 15, continued to count 40 percent or better of their registered voters as middle class, whereas sections 5 and 9 through 14 had better than 60 percent so classified. Central districts 6 and 7 and western and northern districts 15, 17, and 18 did register some declines in the proportion of working-class voters and some increases in the middle-class component, whereas the opposite occurred to some degree in districts 10 and 11, 13, 16, 19 and 20. Generally, however, these were minor shifts of ten percentage points or less.

With regard to specific occupational groups, as described in Table 9.2, the story was again more of continuity than of change. With some slight variations, the proportions in 1934 were much the same as they had been in 1918. One exception was the day laborers, who in 1918 composed only 1 percent of the electorate and by 1934 represented 5 percent of all eligible voters. Distribution patterns were also much the same. Employees and merchants could be found in substantial numbers throughout the city, as could students, although their largest number was located in the central and downtown areas. Lawyers, physicians, and hacendados–estancieros still were concentrated in the central and near northern districts. Sixty percent of all lawyers were registered in districts 13, 14, 19, and 20, as were 38 percent of all physicians and 57 percent of all hacendados–estancieros. At the other end of the spectrum, 69 percent of all day laborers registered were found in districts 1 through 4, 15, and 16. Seventy-one percent of the city's seamen were inscribed in the rolls of La Boca, although a fairly substantial number could now be found in the New Port area encompassed in district 20.[30]

Even with their smashing victory in the March elections, because of the proportional system used to allocate council positions, the Socialists only

30 This information on the electorate for 1934 comes from República Argentina, *Registro Electoral de la Nación: Distrito de la Capital Federal – Lista Definitiva de Electores: 1934*, 5 volumes (Buenos Aires, 1934). These five volumes were located in the Biblioteca Nacional in Buenos Aires. The registry for 1934 was used because it was the latest set available (after 1918) for the period under consideration.

Table 9.2. Selected occupations of voters enrolled in the 1934 registry of the city of Buenos Aires, by voting district[a]

District	Employees	Students	Merchants	Lawyers	Estancieros/ hacendados	Seamen	Physicians	Financiers	Day laborers	Others	Total
1	1,572	233	313	5	7	2	7	20	511	2,061	4,731
2	588	64	122	2	4	1	6	4	114	908	1,813
3	834	116	152	2	6	1	14	5	135	855	2,120
4	539	57	100	2	2	371	6	6	109	856	2,048
5	1,057	279	202	8	11	9	20	30	52	803	2,471
6	852	211	186	4	2	4	16	12	49	1,003	2,339
7	437	137	120	4	1	1	14	7	27	464	1,212
8	593	122	148	2	3	1	12	13	47	728	1,669
9	520	154	101	7	8	—	10	6	43	581	1,430
10	385	79	108	4	11	3	3	4	45	368	1,010
11	317	150	118	10	6	1	22	7	17	327	975
12	675	118	121	6	13	9	15	15	65	477	1,514
13	765	121	185	25	16	11	19	8	54	429	1,633
14	684	151	212	41	22	3	29	13	19	482	1,656
15	1,600	290	328	1	5	10	15	29	361	2,481	5,120
16	1,185	265	241	10	7	23	8	26	297	1,538	3,600
17	730	199	178	15	8	4	11	9	99	1,083	2,336
18	774	257	201	14	13	4	24	16	78	1,037	2,418
19	664	279	130	37	44	7	39	18	68	719	2,005
20	401	160	98	42	52	45	40	13	24	663	1,538
Total	15,172	3,442	3,364	241	241	510	330	261	2,214	17,863	43,057

[a] Ten percent sample.
Source: See Table 9.1.

netted a gain of one seat. The failure of the Progressive Democrats to elect a representative left the Socialists with only one reliable ally, José Penelón of the Concentración Obrera. Combined, this gave the opposition fourteen seats to six for the Concordancia, six for the anti-personalistas, and two for Salud Pública. Two seats remained vacant. In practice, this meant that on most votes the best the Socialists could hope for was a tie and only with major defections from the intendente's coalition did they have a chance to override his veto.

When the city council's sessions were resumed in May 1934 following the March elections, the electric rates issue was momentarily set aside. For the next two months, the council debated the intendente's actions in the long-discussed coordination of public transportation in the capital, a matter that resulted in one of the most controversial political issues of the "infamous decade."

In January 1933, Vedia y Mitre had appointed a special committee headed by Alvear's former minister of public works and future president of the republic, Roberto M. Ortiz, to study the question of how best to organize public transportation in the capital.[31] The committee issued its report in March 1934 and recommended the establishment of the Buenos Aires Transport Corporation as an entity that would regulate and co-ordinate all means of public transportation in the city. The corporation would be formed by the existing Anglo–Argentine, Lacroze, Southern Electric, Town and Dock Tramways Company, and the Central Terminal Railway as a mixed corporation, in which, as it turned out, the Anglo would have the determining voice. The corporation would also have the power to grant all new concessions, including those for buses and colectivos.

Critics rightly saw the proposal as a scheme to bail out the financially troubled Anglo, which had been consistently frustrated by the city government in its attempts to increase fares. The committee's conclusions were also traced to provisions in the Roca–Runciman treaty signed in May 1933 whereby the Argentine government, in exchange for continued preferences in the sale of its agricultural products, would extend "benevolent treatment" to the British-owned enterprises that provided public services to the republic.[32] When the committee report was issued, *The Review of the River Plate* greeted it with undisguised enthusiasm and observed that "the question, we hope, will be placed in the hands of Congress and the National Government. If that comes to pass, there is a

---

31 Ortiz had also served as a legal advisor to several British-owned railroads and was seen as a supporter of their interests. Wright, *British-Owned Railways*, p. 177n.
32 For more on the Roca–Runciman agreement and the reactions it produced, see Ciria, *Partidos y poder en la Argentina moderna*, pp. 35–51; Ysabel F. Rennie, *The Argentine Republic* (New York, 1945), pp. 230–64; and, Peter H. Smith, *Politics and Beef in Argentina: Patterns of Conflict and Change* (New York, 1969), pp. 142–50.

distinct possibility that the treatment of the inter-urban transport problem may in the near future enter upon a new phase, based on practical
and sane considerations liberated from all the baneful influences and petty
bickerings of municipal politics."[33]

It did not take long for the *Review*'s hope to be realized. Following the
suggestion of the Ortiz committee, which had argued that because the
transport companies' charters were granted by the national government,
therefore the ultimate decision should rest at that level, Vedia y Mitre
submitted the committee's decision to the Justo administration for dis-
position. The national executive, in turn, determined to remove the issue
from municipal jurisdiction and to submit the matter to the Concordancia-
controlled national Congress for consideration.

That decision, however, did not put a stop to what the *Review of the
River Plate* judged to be the "petty bickerings" of the city council. On
June 1, the Socialist delegation on the council charged Vedia y Mitre
with having violated the organic municipal law by submitting to the
national government a proposal "to confer a monopoly on passenger
transports to a foreign financial consortium" without having consulted
the council and with having ignored the will of the majority of the
capital's population by backing a measure that surely would lead to an
unfair and unjustified increase in fares. As a result, the delegation urged
a vote of no confidence in the intendente. Recently elected National
Democratic Councilman Lizardo Molina Carranza presented a minority
report, claiming there were no grounds for such a vote and urging its
rejection.[34]

The ensuing debate on the Socialist initiative took up most of the
month. Secretary of Public Works Amílcar Razori defended the intendente's
actions. In a presentation filled with facts and figures, he underscored the
growing confusion resulting from uncoordinated and competing modes of
transportation and argued that its importance and its involvement with
the capital's surrounding jurisdictions meant that the solution to these
problems could only be resolved at the national level. He also pointed to
the plans resembling those proposed by the Ortiz committee that had
been successfully implemented in certain European and North American
cities and observed that the proposal aimed to lower, not increase, the
costs of public transportation.[35] Socialist spokesmen, of course, disagreed,
arguing that the Ortiz proposal and the intendente's actions would simply turn over the control of all urban transport to the Anglo and inevitably
lead to higher fares. While recognizing the need for a more coherent organization and coordination of existing systems, control of transportation

33 *RRP*, 2205 (March 16, 1934), 7–9.   34 *VTCD* (June 1, 1934), p. 229.
35 *VTCD* (June 5, 1934), pp. 269–92 and (June 6, 1934), pp. 294–307.

in the capital, they claimed, should remain in the hands of the municipality. They persisted in their position that Vedia y Mitre had exceeded his authority and violated the city's trust by passing the matter on to the Justo administration. Speaking for his party, Andrés Justo concluded, "We condemn this attempt [removing the decision from municipal authority] because the wishes of the people have to be heard, and if the popular referendum [the results of the 1934 election] is not accepted by the executive branch or by the companies, the public will make its voice heard all the same."[36]

On July 4, the debate concluded with votes on several resolutions protesting the removal of transport coordination from municipal jurisdiction and calling for an investigation into the financial situation of the Anglo. Drawing support from Salud Pública's Giacobini and two antipersonalista Radicals, the Socialists passed their proposals on these matters by a two-to-one margin over the Concordancia opposition. The Socialist resolution expressing no confidence in the intendente, however, was replaced with a milder, unanimously approved version: "That the council did not authorize nor authorizes the intendente to carry out actions intended to organize by law the collective transport of passengers in the Capital whose solution belongs exclusively to the Concejo Deliberante."[37]

These resolutions were too little and too late. By the time they were passed, the ultimate decision on the transport corporation had already passed to the national Congress. There, despite two years of strong Socialist opposition, frequent strikes by colectivo drivers, an outraged public opinion, and even support for the protests from the United States-based General Motors Company, which provided the colectivo chassis, the measure became law on September 30, 1936.[38] The Anglo, moreover, consistently resisted submitting its financial records for examination despite repeated requests from most parties on the city council to do so. The council did, however, gain some satisfaction in its struggle with the Anglo when, in December 1934, it passed an ordinance declaring that the company's concession to build a subway from the Plaza de Mayo to the Plaza Italia had lapsed.[39] That concession then passed to the CHADOPYF, which initiated construction of its second line in April of 1935.[40]

The other main question of the day involving public services to the city provided by foreign companies, that of electricity rates, still remained within the purview of the municipal government. For the Socialist opposition, however, the consideration of relations between the municipality and the power companies continued to produce a series of frustrations.

36 *VTCD* (June 11, 1934), pp. 365–70.   37 *VTCD* (July 4, 1934), pp. 860–90.
38 For a review of these developments, see Rennie, *The Argentine Republic*, pp. 238–44 and Wright, *British-Owned Railways*, pp. 177–86.
39 *VTCD* (December 18, 1934), pp. 3720–3.   40 *State Records* (April 24, 1935), 835.78/44.

When Vedia y Mitre soon vetoed the ordinance that resulted from the deliberation of the five-man conciliation commission (according to some because the decisions of that "conciliation" were not sufficiently favorable to the CHADE), a new but similar manner of resolving the dispute was devised. Early in 1934, a three-man arbitration panel was named to review the claims of the city and the companies. It was composed of three well-known lawyers, one of whom represented the city, one the company, and one, designated by the Supreme Court of the Nation, to provide the deciding vote.[41] On the council, the Socialists consistently objected to this manner of decision making, arguing that it represented one more instance of authority being removed from the hands of the council and, hence, from the will of the people they represented. Throughout 1934 and 1935 they introduced and passed a long series of resolutions and ordinances that sought to reaffirm the council's primacy in deciding such matters and requested specific information from the intendente and the electric companies concerning the details of the companies' operations. Vedia y Mitre consistently vetoed those initiatives, and his vetoes were sustained by the Concordancia coalition.

After a year of deliberation, the three-man panel issued its decision. Despite Socialist fears, the arbitration board sided with the city on eight of the eleven points of contention. Most importantly, it agreed that the CHADE had imposed charges not covered by the original concession and that maximum rates should be established, thereby opposing the company's assertion that no limits should be set.[42] When the intendente delayed action on the results of these deliberations, the Socialists on the council continued to press the issue with more resolutions calling for immediate action to lower rates for individual consumers. In a discussion of the intendente's reluctance to consider favorably a number of resolutions aiming to lower electric rates, Socialist Héctor Iñigo Carrera blamed the lack of positive action on the "passivity and ineptitude of the executive branch," which consistently has resisted "the most justifiable demands for reasonable electric rates to which the community has full right."[43]

Although these observations had obvious partisan intent, the executive's actions pointed to their accuracy. His consistent rejection of any measures to pressure the companies to lower the rates and to respect the original concessions, which he often couched in legal and technical terms,

41 The lawyer for the city was Agustín N. Matienzo, a professor of law at the local university and a member of the board of directors of several national and foreign-owned companies. The CHADE's representative was Carlos M. Mayer, also on the boards of several companies and, like Matienzo, a member of the Jockey Club and the Círculo de Armas and a resident of the Barrio Norte. The third representative, Alberto Uriburu, was also on the board of numerous companies and was a professor of law at the University of Buenos Aires. *Quien es Quien, 1939*, pp. 278–9 and 427.
42 Davis, *La cuestión eléctrica*, pp. 4–10.   43 VTCD (November 22, 1935), p. 2553.

continued to give the companies breathing space and to postpone resolution of the matter. Like his decision to send the transport corporation matter to the national government, his manner of operation here was consistent with the "benevolent treatment" promised to foreign capital by the Justo administration.[44]

In December 1935 the Socialists tried again to prod the Vedia y Mitre government to act on the electric rate issue. They proposed the creation of an office of "Municipal Electric Service," which would place under city control the production and distribution of electric power in the capital. The Concordancia coalition rejected the proposal by a vote of fourteen to thirteen and a final resolution of the issue remained pending.[45]

By the end of 1935, the question had been before the council and the city for better than three years. It had consumed much of the local government's time and had emerged as a major political issue, rivaling the transportation corporation in capturing public attention. Company resistance and apparent executive foot dragging had postponed a definitive conclusion, which was achieved by the end of the following year, but only after a major realignment of political forces on the council and continued controversy.

Although relations between the conservative intendente and the Socialists on the council were often tense and conflictive, there were, as usual, moments of agreement. The council, for example, unanimously and enthusiastically approved the concession of municipal land for the construction of modern stadiums for the Boca Junior and River Plate soccer teams. Although the Socialists made their usual criticisms of specific items and continued to vote, unsuccessfully, against the subsidy for the sisters of charity in municipal hospitals, they nonetheless gave their general approval to the executive's annual budget. Despite some hesitation from the Socialists, the council unanimously approved an arrangement worked out by the executive branch to repay the sixteen million pesos owed to the national government for its assumption of the city's obligation to the Chatham Phoenix Corporation.[46] A few months later, the council also approved a new bond issue of forty-five million pesos.[47]

By the end of 1935, Vedia y Mitre could point to the agreement on the Chatham Phoenix loan as a major achievement of his administration. Also noteworthy was the broadening of Calle Corrientes and ongoing

44 Further discussion of Vedia y Mitre's role in the electric rates dispute and other matters involving foreign enterprises must await future research. The one admiring biographical sketch of him makes no mention of these issues. Petit de Murat, "Mariano de Vedia y Mitre," *Tres Intendentes*, pp. 102–17.

45 *VTCD* (December 10, 1935), pp. 2918–96.

46 *VTCD* (August 7, 1935), pp. 1414–22.   47 *VTCD* (December 15, 1935), p. 3525.

construction on two new subway lines and the Costanera Norte.[48] Despite his difficulties with the council and the unprecedented number of vetoes issued, the intendente retained the support of the national government throughout and was reappointed to another three-year term in late 1935. With the state of municipal finances improving and the nation showing signs of recovery from the worst consequences of the depression, the local executive began to contemplate major public works projects, projects that would symbolize the renewed growth and vitality of Argentina's capital and help to ensure his own place in the history of the city's physical development. Like his actions concerning the transport corporation and the electric companies, these projects would produce intense controversy and political opposition. In these, as in most matters, however, his position would prevail.

48 Vedia y Mitre heralded his accomplishments in a paid advertisement, "La Labor de la Intendencia Durante Tres Años Fué Muy Intensa," *Crítica* (November 19, 1935), pp. 10–11.

10

Celebrations and controversies

Intendente Vedia y Mitre's second term was eventful and memorable. In 1936, the capital celebrated the four hundredth anniversary of its founding, mourned the death of the nation's most popular entertainer, and enthusiastically welcomed the president of the United States, Franklin D. Roosevelt, who addressed a special inter-American conference at the end of the year. To celebrate the quatercentennial, Vedia y Mitre proposed and carried through to completion several major monumental public works. At the same time, there was a resolution to the electric rates issues, a resolution surrounded by conflict and controversy. In this case, the way in which an agreement was reached would ultimately do long-term damage to the democratic image of the elected city council.

Although it was not clear at the time, the local elections of March 1936 would have a great bearing on the rates dispute. Although they were momentarily overshadowed by the massive outpouring of grief that accompanied the funeral in February of Carlos Gardel following his untimely death in a Colombian airplane crash, preparations for these elections had begun early in the year.[1] The most important feature of these efforts was the Radical party's decision to end its policy of abstention and again to participate. Early in January, the Radicals called on their eighty-five thousand members in the capital to select candidates for the national Chamber of Deputies and the city council by direct vote. In early February these were chosen, with about two-thirds of the membership taking part in the process.[2] The party's municipal program advocated revision and improvement of the retirement and pension plan for municipal employees; intensification of the struggle against tuberculosis, a major public health problem; the establishment of well-defined industrial zones in the city; the diffusion and encouragement of all sporting activities; and abolition of the city tax on professional soccer matches.[3] On the most

1 Gardel's funeral is described in some detail in Simon Collier, *Carlos Gardel*, pp. 238–43.
2 *La Prensa* (February 12, 1936), p. 11. The Radical candidate list for national deputies included former intendentes José Luis Cantilo and Carlos M. Noel as well as Emilio Ravignani, who had served as Noel's secretary of finance.
3 *Crítica* (January 7, 1936), p. 5.

important issues of the day, the Radicals expressed their approval of greater regulation of public transportation, but with lower fares and allowing for free competition between all carriers, and they opposed any monopoly. Although not coming out specifically for lower electric rates, the party did support the "permanent intervention of the Municipality in the [setting of] rates by enterprises which provide public services."[4]

The Radical campaign was ably directed by Julián Sancerni Giménez, a successful party boss from Palermo who had led the movement to end abstention. Under his direction, the Radicals hardly missed a beat despite their five years on the sidelines. Committees and subcommittees were established throughout the capital and candidates and party officials gave numerous stirring speeches to large and enthusiastic gatherings, including a well-attended rally in the new Luna Park stadium. Adhering to the party custom of avoiding specifics, Radical manifestos and spokesmen emphasized past achievements, the accomplishments of party founder Leandro Alem, of Yrigoyen, and now of former president Alvear, who had assumed leadership of the Radicals in the mid-1930s following the death of Yrigoyen in 1933; they contrasted their commitment to "freedom and social justice" with the reactionary policies of the Concordancia regime. They also sharply criticized the Socialists for continuing to participate in the flawed electoral process while they had adopted the more "noble" course of abstention. Overlooking strong Socialist opposition to government concessions to foreign capital, the Radicals charged their rivals with collaborating with the conservatives on legislation that aggravated the nation's "political, economic, and financial problems."[5] By the end of the year the Socialists could easily turn this charge back onto their attackers.

The Socialists approached this election with their usual fine-tuned organization and sense of optimism. For the first time the party created a "registry of sympathizers," which by early February had inscribed 105,232 persons. This total represented 23 percent of the capital's electorate distributed throughout the city, with the highest proportions found in working-class districts.[6] Socialist candidates for the council called for the extension of municipal services and attention to suburban areas, deplored alleged municipal harassment of colectivo drivers, and underscored the party's opposition to the transport corporation and its role in the struggle to lower electric rates.[7] Promoting themselves as the "true defenders"

---

4 *Crítica* (January 9, 1936), p. 6.   5 *La Prensa* (February 28, 1936), p. 12.

6 The list of "sympathizers" comprised 26 to 27 percent of the registered voters in districts 1, 3–4, 8 and 15, but only 13 percent of those in district 20 and 15 percent in district 14. *La Prensa* (February 3, 1936), p. 11 and (March 12, 1936), p. 12.

7 *La Prensa* (February 20, 1936), p. 12; "Problemas municipales," *La Vanguardia* (February 6, 1936), p. 8 and "No cesan las persecuciones contra los colectiveros," *La Vanguardia* (February 26, 1936), p. 4.

of democracy following the coup of September 1930, they observed that whereas the Radicals took refuge in abstention, their representatives in the national Congress oversaw the passage of a lengthy list of social welfare measures, including a federal subsidy of five million pesos to physicians who previously had worked without pay in municipal hospitals. Radical abstention, they concluded, meant "a total abandonment of the interests of the people, which, in turn, have been constantly cared for by the Socialist party."[8]

Both Radicals and Socialists, as was customary, confidently predicted victory. Given the Radical absence for five years, however, and the fluctuating fortunes of the two parties in the capital since 1912, some observers were reluctant to speculate on the outcome. A commentator in the popular magazine *Mundo Argentino* observed that the only certainty was a sound defeat for the conservative forces, whose role in the city had been negligible since the Sáenz Peña law, even with a conservative government in control at the national level.[9] Whatever slim chances the conservatives had to make a respectable showing in this contest were dimmed by the decision of the National Democrats not to participate, leaving the Independent Socialists and the anti-personalista Radicals as the sole representatives of a severely weakened Concordancia coalition.[10]

The election itself, like the preceding one in 1934, produced a substantial turnout of almost 80 percent. By the time the votes were counted in the first district, it was clear that the Radicals were on their way to a dramatic victory. In that predominantly working-class district, the Radicals bested their leading opponents by a two-to-one margin, prompting one of the earliest Socialist concessions of defeat on record. Although the margins in other working-class districts were narrower, the Radicals still easily swept each of the capital's twenty *circunscripciones*, including the Socialist stronghold of La Boca. The Radical total in the national deputy elections of almost 186,000 votes was nearly two and a half times greater than the number of party members (85,000) inscribed to select candidates, suggesting a continuing and significant Radical appeal to independent voters. The Socialist total of a little better than 103,000 votes was almost exactly equal to the number of "sympathizers" (105,000) registered in early February, underscoring that party's failure to reach the uncommitted. The Independent Socialists, with 12,042 tallies, and the

8 "Lección de los hechos:Labor socialista y demagogia radical," *La Vanguardia* (February 28, 1936), p. 1.
9 Saúl Selles, "¿Hacia dónde se inclinará el electorado metropolitano?" *Mundo Argentino* (Buenos Aires: February 12, 1936), p. 16.
10 A dissident group of National Democrats disagreed with the decision of the party leadership and entered its own candidates for both deputies and councilmen, but with little realistic chance of drawing many votes. *La Prensa* (February 16, 1936), pp. 11–12.

anti-personalistas, with 10,787 votes, came in a very distant third and fourth, respectively.[11]

If the election was taken as a referendum on the conservative national government of Agustín P. Justo, the results in the federal capital and in other areas where the Radicals entered candidates represented a dramatic rejection of the Concordancia's management of the country. In addition to their decisive win in the city of Buenos Aires, Radicals swept the deputy elections in the large provinces of Córdoba, Entre Ríos, and Santa Fe and were only denied victories in the provinces of Buenos Aires and Mendoza through the generous use of fraudulent practices. Nationwide, the Radicals took 42 percent of the vote to 21 percent for the National Democrats.[12] The party that had lost so much popular support six years earlier had now recuperated much of its former strength and clearly claimed the backing of most of the country's voters.

Their victories in March 1936 gave the Radicals forty new deputies in the national Congress, eleven from the federal capital. Combined with the twenty-five Socialists and six Progressive Democrats and others, this gave the democratic forces in the lower house a substantial base from which to challenge the Concordancia majority. This potential, however, was dissipated when differences over the seating of deputies from the provinces of Buenos Aires and Mendoza produced a stalemate in the chamber and led to one of the least productive congressional years.[13]

More significant than the Radicals' role in the national Congress was their activity within the Concejo Deliberante of Buenos Aires. Enjoying a victory in the municipal elections of the same dimensions as their congressional triumph (see Appendix, Table A.3), the Radicals placed thirteen men on the city council. Despite their defeat, the Socialists retained a like number, with the balance provided by four representatives of the Concordancia. The new preeminence of the Radicals on the council was reflected in the election on May 1, 1936 of that party's Pedro Villemur as president of the local legislature, with Socialist Vincente Russomanno as first vice-president and Radical Francisco A. Turano as second vice-president. At first glance, the presence of twenty-six members of the opposition on the council would seem to present an insurmountable challenge for conservative Intendente Vedia y Mitre. As events would show, that apparent disadvantage did not prove to be that serious a handicap to the executive.

Signs of a continuing confrontation between the intendente and the council were soon revealed. On May 15, at the first full regular session

11 Results from *La Prensa* (March 12, 1936), p. 12.
12 Cantón, *Materiales*, vol. 1, pp. 115–16.
13 For more on the congressional standoff, see Walter, *The Province of Buenos Aires*, pp. 158–9.

of the council, Vedia y Mitre submitted better than two dozen vetoes of council-initiated resolutions and ordinances passed the year before. These included measures to lower gas rates, regulate gasoline pumps, establish the completo for colectivos, control traffic and parking in the city center, provide for consultation with the council before signing public service contracts, and various ordinances pertaining to the operations of the two electric companies. The council, for its part, ordered the committee on constitutional interpretation to study the possibility that the intendente had exceeded his authority in erecting a major monument to mark the city's four hundred years in the newly named Plaza de la República at the intersection of Corrientes and the Diagonal Norte.[14]

The construction of this monument, the "Obelisco," or Obelisk, turned into one of the most debated actions of Vedia y Mitre's administration and symbolized his often stormy relations, not only with the council but also with porteño public opinion. Acting essentially on his own, although apparently with the blessing of President Justo, the intendente on February 3, 1936 issued a decree, while the council was in recess, to construct the monument. Soon thereafter, following a design by architect Alberto Prebisch modeled generally after a similar monument in the Place de la Concorde in Paris, work on the structure began. Built of reinforced concrete and reaching a height of 67.5 meters, the new monument was inaugurated with much fanfare and a presidential address on May 23. Marking the ceremonies were the release of hundreds of pigeons whose wing tips had been dyed the national colors of blue and white and street dances that lasted into the early hours of the following day.

Public reaction to the new landmark was mixed. As soon as plans for the Obelisco were announced, *La Vanguardia* was quick to denounce the intendente for expenditures on a project that ran counter to earlier council resolutions.[15] For *Crítica*, the new monument, "a naked obelisk in Egyptian style," was neither consonant with the "modern" image of the city nor aesthetically pleasing to the average porteño. The popular daily also criticized Vedia y Mitre for proceeding on the project without first consulting public opinion.[16] Man-on-the-street interviews in another publication found many critics, but also a few supporters, one of whom observed that too many porteños practiced negative criticism almost as though it were a competitive sport.[17] Another commentary observed that

14 *VTCD* (May 15, 1936), pp. 44–156.
15 "Plaza de la República: Transgresiones del departamento ejecutivo para su ejecución," *La Vanguardia* (February 12, 1936), p. 1.
16 "Buenos Aires no quiere el obelisco," *Crítica* (March 22, 1936), p. 6.
17 Facundo Las Heras, "Que piensa la población sobre el Obelisco?," *Mundo Argentino*, 26, 1322 (May 20, 1936), p. 40.

Construction of the Nueve de Julio, with the "Obelisco" in the center (no date)

the new monument and plaza would further complicate downtown traffic flow, a problem that the city's director of urban planning assured would soon be overcome.[18] Although public debate over the merits of the Obelisco began to fade after its completion, its manner of authorization and construction would continue to be a sore point between the council and the intendente even after Vedia y Mitre left office.

The dispute over the Obelisco, however, paled to insignificance when compared with the still pending matter of the electric companies' contracts and the rates they charged. The key to how this matter would fare lay with the newly elected Radical members. Within that party, in June 1935, a group of dissidents had formed the Fuerza de Orientación Radical de la Joven Argentina (FORJA) to protest both the increasingly favorable treatment of foreign capital and the party leadership of former president Alvear, which they considered too passive in the face of encroachments by foreign companies. The bulk of the party and its elected officials, however, continued to follow Alvear's directions.

A sign of how the Radical councilmen might vote on matters related to the electric companies and their concessions came in late July 1936.

18 Facundo Las Heras, "Si no lo resuelve, tampoco agrava el problema del tráfico la Plaza de la República," *Mundo Argentino*, 26, 1327 (June 24, 1936), pp. 18–19.

Following a lengthy interpellation of Secretary of Public Works Razori over Vedia y Mitre's vetoes of previous council resolutions seeking to lower electric rates, Socialist Héctor Iñigo Carrera, on July 28, presented three proposals intended to clarify and reinforce various provisions of the original contracts and concessions that the companies allegedly had ignored. Radical spokesmen argued that, despite days of discussion, the issues involved were too complex for immediate consideration and, joined by the Concordancia representatives, voted to send the proposals to committee for further review. Radical Councilman Enrique Descalzo agreed with Razori that the long-standing dispute would be best resolved by reaching a reasonable agreement with the companies that would avoid "extreme" measures and would most benefit the interests of the larger community, "the defense of which we are firmly disposed to assume."[19]

Although the Radicals had disagreed with the Socialists on this issue, they had voted with their rivals on a motion to protest the removal from local authority of the decision on the transport corporation. Moreover, in early October they joined with the Socialists in a unanimous vote in favor of an ordinance to give the state-owned YPF a monopoly over the sale of gasoline in the capital, an ordinance that the intendente vetoed two weeks later.[20] In December, when the Socialists sponsored a resolution to override the executive's veto on the gasoline ordinance, the Radicals, again claiming that it was a complex issue that required more study and consideration, voted to send it to committee.[21]

The Radical position on the council, then, was a fluctuating and shifting one. Sometimes the Radicals voted with the Socialists and sometimes they defended the intendente. Usually, they tried to couch their arguments, whichever way they voted, in terms of conciliation, searching for solutions that would avoid sterile standoffs and that, in the long run, would bring the greatest benefits to the city. The Socialists, in contrast, were consistent in their dogged opposition to almost all of Vedia y Mitre's actions and to the concessions being granted to foreign enterprises.

As the year neared its end, the matter of electric service reappeared. In early October, apparently responding to a suggestion by Argentine Foreign Minister Carlos Saavedra Lamas, steps were taken to move the concession of the CHADE to the Compañía Argentina de Electricidad, S.A. (CADE), headquartered in Buenos Aires. This move appeared to shift the ownership from the Spanish-based concern to a national one, but in reality ultimate control still rested in SOFINA of Brussels.[22] Shortly thereafter, the CADE introduced a new proposal for the city's consideration.

19 *VTCD* (July 28, 1936), pp. 960–86.
20 *VTCD* (October 6, 1936), pp. 1684–700 and (October 27, 1936), pp. 1920–1.
21 *VTCD* (December 11, 1936), pp. 2886–93.   22 Davis, *La cuestión eléctrica*, p. 16.

This offer promised to set a lid on rates in return for an extension of its concessions.

This new company proposal went to the council's committee on public services. The Socialist majority, adopting a typical Radical tactic, argued that the matter was too complicated and too important for rapid consideration. In fact, they opposed the new proposal, but because they knew the Radicals favored it, they seized on delay as the only possible strategy given the lineup of votes in the council. On November 6, the Radicals, claiming to respond to "the unanimous clamor of public opinion for lower electric rates," moved to break the deadlock. They presented a motion to name a special committee to study the company's proposal and to make a recommendation. The committee would be composed of three Radicals, three Socialists, and one representative of the Concordancia. Realizing that they would be outvoted on this motion, as well as on the committee, the Socialists left the council chamber and the motion was approved. The Radicals then submitted their own lengthy proposed ordinance for regulating electric rates in the capital.[23] On November 10 the new committee was named, again over Socialist opposition.[24]

As the special committee deliberated, it and the council were subjected to an intense and unprecedented lobbying effort by the interested parties on both sides. The various development societies and other organizations that had begun to protest the rate increases of the early 1930s bombarded the council with petitions opposed to extending the existing concessions and placed advertisements in newspapers like *La Prensa* and *La Nación* urging rejection of the new proposals.[25] Radical councilmen in favor of extending the concessions, in turn, had included in the record communications from other neighborhood associations that called for the quick approval of the proposals being considered.[26]

There was intense behind-the-scenes maneuvering as well. Elements within the Radicals' capital committee opposed to the concession extensions pressured the councilmen not to vote on the matter until the party convention at the end of December. Representatives of the CADE, however, were busy applying their own forms of pressure. In mid-December,

---

23 *VTCD* (November 6, 1936), pp. 2055–86.
24 *VTCD* (November 13, 1936), pp. 2090–2108.
25 Some of the details of this campaign are described in the Instituto Torcuato Di Tella Oral Interview with Jorge del Río. According to del Río, the editor of *La Prensa* was particularly sympathetic to the position of his organization whereas *Crítica's* Natalio Botana ridiculed both its journalistic rival, "the newspaper of the lantern," and the leader of the opposition to the concessions, whom he called, "with regard to questions of light, a real bat." Botana may have been influenced by the fact that the CADE and the Italo frequently carried full-page advertisements for their services in his newspaper.
26 *VTCD* (December 11, 1936), p. 2911.

the local director of the CADE met with Alvear, and although the details of the conversation are not known, later investigations revealed significant subsequent contributions from the company to the construction of the new *Casa Radical*, or party headquarters, on Calle Tucumán, and to the Radical presidential campaign. Alvear, in turn, urged his colleagues to allow the councilmen to make their report before the party convention. Furthermore, the same investigations revealed, that, in order to assure that the Radicals on the council retained their enthusiasm for the company proposal, at least a dozen councilmen received bribes from the company in amounts of up to one hundred thousand pesos each.[27] These essential details, however, would not become known and confirmed to the general public until several years after the fact.

Finally, on December 14 the council began to consider the committee report. As recommended by the Radical majority, it called for a fifteen-year extension of the concession of the CADE, due to expire in 1957, and beyond that, the establishment for twenty-five years of a mixed public–private company. The original concession of 1907 had stipulated that in 1957 the company would turn over its facilities free of charge to the city and establish a fund, based on a percentage of its earnings, that also would revert to the municipality. Both of these provisions were canceled and instead the city was obligated, at the end of the new concession, to purchase the company's facilities. In return, the company would set a limit on the rates it charged to industrial, commercial, and individual customers.[28]

The principal Radical spokesmen for the committee, Carlos Rophille and Enrique Descalzo, dominated the first two days of discussion. In their presentations, they underscored the hard work of the committee, which had interviewed company representatives, engineers, and technical experts in order to unravel the many complexities involved in determining electric services and their costs. Arguing that their electoral abstention had removed them from the emotionalism of earlier debates and had allowed them a more dispassionate view of the matter than other parties, they accused the Socialists of deliberately delaying any decision so as to reap political rewards from their opposition. In the meantime, they pointed out, the capital's consumers continued to suffer from high rates.[29]

After some delay, the council reassembled on December 22 for a final vote on the committee report. Secretary of Public Works Razori, speaking for the until then silent executive, gave that branch's stamp of approval for the project, which would produce, through lower charges, "a positive

27 Davis, *La cuestión eléctrica*, p. 18 and Luna, *Alvear*, pp. 196–221.
28 Davis, *La cuestión eléctrica*, p. 17 and del Río, *Electricidad y liberación nacional*, pp. 29–33.
29 VTCD (December 14, 1936), pp. 2973–96 and (December 15, 1936), pp. 3032–99.

benefit . . . for all the consumers of the Federal Capital."[30] Socialists argued that the short-term gains promised by the new contract would prove illusory and that the long-term implications definitely favored the CADE to the detriment of the municipality. They credited the company, under the direction of SOFINA, for cleverly maneuvering the Radicals (although at that time they did not know how cleverly) to a position of support.

To avoid sure defeat for their position, the Socialists proposed that final consideration be postponed. Independent Socialist Felipe Di Tella, however, noting that the discussion had gone on for twelve hours and into the early morning of December 23, introduced a motion to close the debate and to come to a final vote. The Socialists responded that if the motion carried, they would leave the council chamber in protest. The motion was then approved, with the Radicals and Concordancia in favor and the Socialists opposed. As promised, the Socialists withdrew and the remaining council members unanimously supported ordinance number 8028, which sanctioned the new agreement with the CADE, and a companion ordinance, number 8029, which established essentially the same kind of agreement with the Italian power company.[31] After the balloting, according to one account, the brother of one of the councilmen who had voted in favor approached him on the council floor and publicly berated him for having "sold" his vote and dishonored the family name.[32]

Press reaction varied. *Crítica* hailed the new concession and credited the Radicals with bringing about a satisfactory resolution to the conflict with the companies, a resolution that would lead to lower rates for all consumers, accomplishing in seven months what the Socialists had failed to do in fourteen years.[33] The Socialist *La Vanguardia* was predictably critical. Its lead editorial on December 24 labeled the council vote an "assault on the people of the city" and the approval of the new concession as "precipitous and scandalous."[34] The conservative *La Prensa*, which rarely agreed with the Socialists on anything, also found the new concession approved by the council objectionable, albeit stated in more measured terms. In a Christmas day editorial, the powerful daily examined the details of the new agreement carefully and determined that the alleged benefits to the porteños were more apparent than real. At the most, its editors calculated, individual consumers might receive a 10 percent decrease in rates, a savings that could be eliminated with the invoking of provisions allowing further increases down the road. This seemed a

30 *VTCD* (December 22, 1936), p. 3272.   31 Ibid., pp. 3226–401.

32 Rennie, *The Argentine Republic*, p. 261.

33 "La rebaja de las tarifas eléctricas beneficiará enormemente al pueblo," *Crítica* (December 18, 1936), p. 5.

34 "Se consumó el atentado," *La Vanguardia* (December 24, 1936), p. 8.

minor and ephemeral benefit for the consumer in return for the undoubted advantages gained by the companies with the new agreements.
The "general skepticism and disagreement" over the council decision,
they concluded, had ample justification and was solidly based.[35]

Reactions among the Radicals themselves were also varied. At a
boisterous special meeting of the party's capital convention, called especially
to consider the actions of the Radical concejales, a resolution was introduced
to discuss their vote on the new concession. After a lengthy and lively
debate, punctuated by frequent cries of protest from the audience and
what appeared to be the firing of a few pistol shots, a compromise
resolution, crafted by delegate Arturo Frondizi (later elected president of
the republic in 1958) was approved. It called for the appointment of a
nine-member committee to investigate the concessions and the Radical
councilmen's support of them and urged that no new public service
concessions be voted on by the party's representatives "without an ample discussion and without an express pronouncement of the party
convention."[36]

The full dimensions of the scandal surrounding the vote on the electric
concession would not be revealed for several years. The controversy that
it sparked, even in 1936, however, did the general image of the council
little good. Earlier in the year, one critic had described the council as a
"deficient and almost useless organism." Referring to the many vetoes
that the council failed to override, he argued that the national executive,
which named the intendente, and the national Congress were the real
governing bodies of the city. Councilmen, he added, were generally of
poor quality and more concerned with serving their various political
clients than addressing the real needs of the city. Members who had
served without pay in the early 1920s were now receiving excessive
salaries and "fringe benefits" for the few real services rendered. Too much
time was taken up with heated discussion of partisan issues and not
enough with such pressing matters as how to improve city hospitals or
control the eighty thousand unlicensed dogs that roamed the city. This
critic recommended, as in 1915, that the elected council be replaced with
a "junta of vecinos," a commission removed from partisan considerations
and dedicated "to resolving the problems of health, culture, esthetics and
the well-being and progress of the population."[37] This was a proposal that
eventually became fact a few years later when another scandal rocked the
council.

---

35 "El nuevo régimen sobre electricidad," *La Prensa* (December 25, 1936), p. 8.
36 "La convención metropolitana de la Unión Cívica Radical consideró anoche la actitud del grupo
de Concejales de dicho partido," *La Prensa* (December 24, 1936), p. 8.
37 Anibal Colón, "Buenos Aires tiene un gobierno comunal desequilibrado, arbitrario y anacrónico,"
Mundo Argentino, 26, 1335 (August 19, 1936), pp. 18–19.

In the final year of Vedia y Mitre's term as intendente there were only faint echoes of the turmoil that had surrounded the electric power concessions: As this issue gradually faded from the scene, a new one arose to pit the local executive against the council. Beginning in February 1937, the intendente announced a number of decrees, based on national law 8855 passed in 1912, to initiate construction on the long planned for and long delayed north–south avenue, an avenue that eventually would link by a surface boulevard the Retiro–Constitucíon rail stations. Citing the general healthy state of municipal finances as the country and the capital had recovered from the worst effects of the Great Depression, the local executive also quickly and easily floated a thirty-million-peso bond issue to help meet the costs of the project, which were estimated to reach a total of seventy million pesos.[38]

The original proposal had called for an avenue thirty-three meters wide. Claiming that the growth of the city and its vehicular traffic over the past twenty-five years had made those calculations obsolete, the executive argued that to assure sufficient relief of downtown congestion, the new avenue should now be one hundred meters wide, making it, as city fathers boasted, the widest boulevard in the world – and, of course, adding substantially to the cost. Vedia y Mitre did not, however, foresee constructing the entire stretch from Retiro to Constitución, but rather a five-block initial portion with the new Plaza de la República and the Obelisco in the center and bounded by Calle Bartolomé Mitre on the south and Calle Tucumán on the north.

To achieve the desired width of the new avenue, to be named the Nueve de Julio in honor of Argentina's independence day, required the acquisition and demolition of all buildings on the five blocks between Calle Cerrito and Calle Carlos Pellegrini. Issuing decrees to this effect in March and April, the city rapidly and aggressively began the process of acquiring the property and notifying the owners of their obligations to move, often with only a few weeks notice.[39] This procedure, catching most property owners unaware, produced a predictable protest. Most affected were the hundreds of stores and shops in the area, employing perhaps as many as twelve thousand persons. For some fortunate few, the impending demolition meant an opportunity to move to a new and more desirable location. For most, however, it represented a real hardship. To add to the woes of those forced to relocate, property owners in other parts of the commercial center of the city, taking advantage of the desperate

---

38 *Crítica* (February 17, 1937), p. 12 and *State Records* (March 5, 1937), 835.51/1148.

39 The various administrative measures included in this process are described in MCBA, *Avenida 9 de Julio: Leyes, ordenanzas, decretos, estudios, datos, informes, referentes a su construcción* (Buenos Aires, 1938).

circumstances of their less fortunate brethren, significantly increased either the purchase price or rents of their available property.[40]

Soon after the announcement of construction plans, groups of owners petitioned Vedia y Mitre to extend the time for abandoning their properties from twenty days to six months. When the intendente refused that request, they turned to the national executive, who also turned them down. At the same time, a group of writers, actors, and impresarios pleaded with Vedia y Mitre to postpone the destruction of four theaters, which lay in the way of the proposed avenue, also to no avail.[41]

Direct petitions were only one method of protest. Property owners also took the city to court to contest the amount of compensation they were slated to receive and others delayed the abandonment of their buildings beyond the deadline for departure. Nonetheless, the local administration was relentless in its pursuit of this project and actual demolition began on April 10. Secretary of Public Works Razori was a key figure in this process, energetically overseeing the removal of recalcitrant families from their dwellings while simultaneously providing alternative temporary lodgings for them and their property at city expense.[42]

Although the project meant dislocation and inconvenience for those in its way, it also meant employment for several thousands of others involved in its construction. To achieve the goal of completing the new avenue in time for the October 12th celebration, three eight-hour shifts were established to work around the clock. The workers themselves were a diverse group, a mixture of native- and foreign-born, with foreigners predominating, drawn from various parts of the city and from various trades by the relatively high wages that were offered. Most, instead of the usual practice of returning home for lunch, set up makeshift grills on the site itself and prepared multiethnic meals, which ranged from a "*churrasco criollo*" to "*cappelletti a la bolognesa.*" As with any construction project anywhere in the world, work on the new avenue attracted thousands of curious spectators, who at midday were treated to a feast of sights and smells.[43]

The work on the Nueve de Julio had been initiated prior to the city council convening for its regular sessions on May 1. Before discussing the intendente's actions in this regard, however, the council first dealt with what some considered another high-handed maneuver by the executive. During the recess, Vedia y Mitre had proceeded to an agreement with YPF to be the sole supplier of gasoline in the city. This had been the

40 *Crítica* (March 20, 1937), p. 7.
41 *Crítica* (March 14, 1937), p. 4.   42 *Crítica* (October 11, 1937), p. 6.
43 Onofre Contreras, "En las obras de demolición se come en todos los idiomas," *Aquí Está*, 2, 123 (July 22, 1937), pp. 18–20.

Municipal Intendente Mariano Vedia y Mitre (center), in the company of
Secretary of Public Works Amílcar Razori (third from the right with his
hands in his pockets), inspecting construction of the Avenida Nueve
de Julio (July 1937)

intent of an earlier ordinance passed by the council that Vedia y Mitre
had vetoed because he objected to one of its provisions. The Socialists
argued, and the Radicals seemed to agree, that the intendente had bypassed the council on this matter and should be called to account for his
actions. Both Socialists and Radicals voted in favor of a resolution to
nullify the agreement. A motion to censure Vedia y Mitre over his
actions, however, was defeated by a vote of twenty-two to five.[44] A significant feature of this latter vote was the fact that the five votes in favor
came from former Socialist concejales who had split with the main party
to form the Partido Socialista Obrero (PSO). A dissident faction of younger
Socialists who believed the party should adopt a more revolutionary course,
the Obreristas, whose concejales had been read out of the party in late
1936, diluted even more the position of the intendente's main opposition
on the council.[45]

44 *VTCD* (May 21, 1937), pp. 262–93.
45 Instituto Torcuato Di Tella Oral Interview with Ingeniero Emilio Dickmann (Buenos Aires:
   December 18 and 26, 1972), p. 15 and *La Prensa* (December 31, 1936), p. 12.

In the first session after the vote on the YPF concession, Obrerista Juan Unamuno introduced a series of resolutions criticizing the local executive for the way he had proceeded in the construction of the Nueve de Julio. Although not opposed to urban progress, he argued, it should not be done at the cost of an incalculable debt for future generations, as this project seemed to imply. Taking advantage of what he called a momentary "reanimation" of the Argentine economy, Unamuno charged that the intendente was foolishly spending money on a monumental and questionable public works project in the style of Europe's fascist dictators. Adopting more moderate language, the mainline Socialists agreed that the project appealed to the porteño trait of *"farolería,"* or pride in being able to boast about having the widest avenue in the world without considering either its cost or usefulness. They also referred to the human price paid "as a result of the inconvenient, uneconomic, and preemptory compulsive measures against the occupants of buildings affected by the opening of the north–south avenue, with grave harm to the numerous employees and workers who lost their jobs because of the businesses removed from the area."[46]

During the sessions of June 1 and June 8, the council considered a number of resolutions related to these issues. Socialist proposals, usually from both factions, calling for a complete halt in construction, were defeated. The Radical position favored the ongoing work, but objected to the unilateral manner in which the executive had operated and demanded that future construction be based on prior consultation with the council. Accordingly, they voted with the Socialists to demand that the secretaries of public works and finance appear to explain the details of financing and construction and to "suspend all *new work* related to the opening of the Nueve de Julio avenue . . . ."[47] (emphasis mine).

The ensuing conflict between the council and the intendente over the new avenue soon took on familiar dimensions. At the end of June and the beginning of July, Secretary of Public Works Razori and Secretary of Finance Atilio Dell'Oro Maini made lengthy presentations before the council in defense of the executive's actions. The project, they argued, was a needed public improvement, long overdue. They admitted that some individuals had suffered discomfort and inconvenience as a result of removal and demolition and that the undertaking had its share of critics. They also noted, however, that the construction of the Avenida de Mayo and the diagonales had occasioned the same disruptions and outcries, but were now universally perceived as positive benefits to the city at large. Every action the intendente had taken in this matter, Razori argued, had been authorized by the provisions of national law 8855, which had

46 *VTCD* (June 1, 1937), pp. 819–58.   47 *VTCD* (June 8, 1937), pp. 401–18.

originally sanctioned the north–south boulevard as part of an overall plan to open up the crowded downtown area. Once the work began, he observed, it was imperative to complete it as soon as possible in order to avoid the delays and disruptions that had plagued projècts like the diagonales. An expensive and ambitious enterprise, it had so far, he concluded, not yet exceeded budgeted expenditures.[48]

The Socialists argued to the contrary. They questioned the soundness of the financing for the project and argued as usual that the funds spent on the new avenue would be better utilized in improving basic conditions in southside working-class neighborhoods. Various Socialist proposals to halt construction, however, ran into Radical support for continuing it.[49] In the final analysis, while the council debated, the massive public works effort initiated by Vedia y Mitre proceeded without interruption. The story was by now familiar, and so was the result. What the intendente wanted, the intendente got, regardless of council objections.

As the council initiated its discussions on the new north–south avenue, Vedia y Mitre sought to respond to his critics in a lengthy interview in *El Hogar*. The projected Nueve de Julio, he observed, was essential for the modern transformation of the city. Answering those who saw it as only of benefit to the wealthy core of the capital, he claimed that the new avenue, of which "any city in the world would be proud," would not only "modify fundamentally the characteristics of the urban center," but would also "channel an extraordinary current of progress toward the thickly populated southern neighborhoods." The avenues would also bring more light and more beauty to the city, the main aim of all such boulevard constructions based on "the principles of urbanistic science." It would also complement other street expansions, such as that of the Avenida Belgrano running parallel to and several blocks south of the Avenida de Mayo, another recently completed block of the Diagonal Sur, and the greatly expanded Calle Corrientes, the "Great White Way" of Buenos Aires. His administration also oversaw the completion of the third section of the peripheral highway, the Avenida General Paz, construction of which had begun in 1934. At the same time, in the remaining months of his administration he hoped to do even more for the outer districts of the city, which already had benefited from his extension of parks and plazas.[50]

By 1937 the sense of frustration that had marked a similar interview with the intendente four years earlier had been replaced by a buoyant sense of pride in accomplishment. Indeed, whatever the controversy surrounding his terms in office, few intendentes could claim to have so

48 MCBA, *Avenida 9 de Julio*, pp. 79–143.   49 *VTCD* (August 3, 1937), pp. 1153–63.
50 "Contesta a un interrogante de 'El Hogar' el Intendente de Buenos Aires," *El Hogar* (June 4, 1937), pp. 23–4.

changed the face of the city as had Vedia y Mitre. Comparisons were made between his administration and that of Torcuato de Alvear, whose late nineteenth-century regime had done so much to modernize the capital. Although Vedia y Mitre had his critics, the general public seemed to approve of what he had done. One fruit dealer interviewed at the end of the year stated that "Buenos Aires can be proud of its intendente . . . . He has transformed its [the city's] appearance as if by magic."[51]

And of these transformations, none was more magical than the new Avenida Nueve de Julio. Inaugurated on schedule on October 12 after three months of feverish construction, its opening, like that of the Obelisco one year earlier, was marked by a presidential address, the release of thousands of patriotically painted pigeons, and street dances into the early hours of the following day. Although there was still landscaping to be done, the surface was embellished by fountains, recently planted trees and shrubs, and ornamental lighting. Just as impressive as the surface of "the world's widest avenue" was what had been built underground. Under the Obelisk, at the center of the new boulevard, was the intersection and interconnection of three subway lines: the already completed Lacroze line B from Alem to Chacarita; the recently completed CHADOPYF line C from Retiro to Constitución; and the in-progress CHADOPYF line D from the Plaza de Mayo to Plaza Italia, which by the year's end had opened operations from Cathedral station to the law courts at Tribunales. Well-lighted and well-ventilated tunnels connected the three lines to allow for easy transfers. They, in turn, were linked to a pedestrian tunnel, which provided underground passage from one side of the new avenue to another. Along these small underground passageways, stores and food stands were set up to accommodate subway passengers. In addition, a modern underground garage able to hold one thousand automobiles was slated to open on December 1, indicating a clear if not totally adequate response to long-standing complaints about the difficulty of finding parking space downtown.

The new avenue and its attendant facilities represented one of the city's most impressive engineering feats. As mentioned, crews worked around the clock to meet the October 12 deadline, taking off only for, appropriately enough, the traditional independence day celebration of July 9 and national election day, September 5. Special lights were set up so that construction could proceed at night. Work proceeded in several stages, beginning with demolition, followed by excavation and then construction. In the process, 240,000 square meters of earth were removed by a caravan of 100 trucks, with most of the dirt destined for another section of the Costanera Norte, which, by action of the city council at the end

51 *Aquí Está*, 2, 162 (December 6, 1937), p. 36.

Panoramic view of the newly completed Nueve de Julio, "the broadest
avenue in the world" (no date)

of the year was named for nineteenth-century poet Rafael Obligado. Sewers, gas lines, electric cables, and streetcar tracks had to be removed and
then reinstalled. Demolition and excavation had, as on previous projects,
unearthed thousands of rats, which had to be contained and killed. That
all this was done in the space of three months made the new avenue
almost a miracle of efficiency and teamwork. As *Crítica* enthusiastically
commented, "at no time in the city's history has a work of such colossal
magnitude been carried out in such a short time."[52] As time would also
show, however this "colossal" work involved substantial costs.

The Obelisco and the new north–south avenue symbolized a resurgence
of public and private building in the city reminiscent of the heyday of
the prewar period and of the 1920s. Many of the new structures, both
public and private, were much influenced by the rationalist style associated with the Swiss architect and modern city planner Le Corbusier (Charles
Edouard Jenneret), who had given a series of lectures in Buenos Aires in

---

52 *Crítica* (October 11, 1937), p. 6. Another enthusiastic view of the project, with a map and
  photograph, is "The Widest Avenue in the World," *BPAU*, 72 (January 1938), pp. 38–9.

The completed obelisk and the Plaza de la República (1936)

1929.[53] Soon thereafter, a number of buildings in the unadorned and strictly functional form advocated by Le Corbusier and his disciples began to make their appearance in Buenos Aires. One of the first, completed in 1932, was the eighty-five-meter tall Edificio Comega, an office building located at the corner of Corrientes and Alem. The most notable new structure, however, was the Edificio Kavanagh, constructed northeast of the Plaza Hotel on the curve of Calle Florida leading to the Retiro Station. An apartment building of thirty-two floors, it was, for some time, the tallest building in Latin America. Inaugurated in 1935, it was also the first building in Buenos Aires to boast central air conditioning.

A number of other important structures were either completed or initiated during the final years of the Vedia y Mitre administration. In 1937, work began on the new medical school of the University of Buenos Aires, an enormous rationalist building occupying most of a square block on Avenida Córdoba. The new ministry of public works, a major multistory government building, began to take shape at a location south of the Obelisk along the projected extension of the Nueve de Julio. At the same time, the final touches were put on the massive central market located at Corrientes 3200, a building dominated by five monumental vaulted arches.[54] In mid-1937, the city's largest movie theater, the Gran Rex at Corrientes 857, opened for business. With a seating capacity of four thousand, the Gran Rex was seen as the porteños' answer to New York's Radio City Music Hall and was one more symbol of the capital's pride in being able to compare itself with the great metropolis of the north.[55] Another monument of note was a large sculpture of former president Roque Sáenz Peña at the intersection of Calle Florida and the avenue that bore his name.

Although these were the best-known and among the most visible structures and monuments of the period, thousands of other buildings and homes sprouted as well. Many of these followed in the rational style or were much influenced by art deco motifs or combined the two. The vertical growth of the city, which began in earnest in the 1920s, continued apace. Leading this growth upward were multistory apartment buildings, found in greatest numbers in the center and near north side. A typical advertisement for a recently completed five-story, twenty-unit building located at Viamonte 1784 highlighted its "modern" facade and

53 For more on the impact of Le Corbusier on Argentine architects and on Latin America generally, see Hardoy, "Teorías y prácticas urbanisticas," pp. 208–15.

54 For a history of the market, see Sonia Berjman and José V. Fiszelew, *El mercado de abasto de Buenos Aires* (Buenos Aires, 1984).

55 Casella de Calderón, "Calle Corrientes," pp. 59–61 and Adolfo R. Aviles, "Buenos Aires me guardaba la sorpresa del cine Gran Rex: Ya nos estamos acercando a Nueva York," *Aquí Está*, 2, 106 (May 24, 1937), pp. 34–5.

The Kavanagh Building and to its right the Plaza Hotel (no date)

features. The ground floor, as in most such dwellings, was slated for small shops and housing for the portero. The apartments boasted spacious bedrooms, an ample living room cum dining room, a kitchen equipped with a gas stove, and a bathroom complete with "luxurious fixtures and modern comfort." The building itself, constructed, as were most in this period, of reinforced concrete, had central heating, a "safe and silent" Otis elevator, and a "well-designed stairway" with marble steps.[56] Although the details differed from place to place and price to price, this building was fairly typical of the city apartments constructed in these years.

Progress was not without its price. As *Aquí Está* noted, in discussing the demolition to clear the way for the Nueve de Julio, with that destruction "a thousand memories" had vanished as historic landmarks, private homes, and businesses fell to the city's construction crews.[57] By 1937, plans were even afoot to demolish the Casa Rosada to make way for an extension of the Avenida de Mayo to the port area. These plans were eventually abandoned, but they underscored the near frenzy of projects that were being considered and implemented in these years. In the downtown and near north side, some of the city's most elegant

56 "Construcciones Modernas," *Crítica* (March 10, 1936), p. 11.
57 Pancho Nutria, "Otro cacho porteño se nos va...," *Aquí Está*, 86 (March 15, 1937), pp. 2–5.

The statue to Roque Sáenz Peña and the Diagonal Norte toward the "Obelisco"
(no date)

turn-of-the-century mansions were sacrificed to street widening or replaced by modern-style apartments of what some considered to be dubious architectural merit.[58] The last public gas lights in the city also were extinguished and a municipal ordinance prohibited the circulation of horse-drawn carriages for hire in the downtown area.[59] These developments coincided with the deaths of several well-known downtown characters, including the "Negro Petronita," who sang operatic arias for passers-by, and "Il Romano," who dressed in the latest finery and strutted through the center of the city casting snobbish glances in every direction, but lacked any visible means of support. A writer in *El Hogar* speculated that with the new and "tumultuous" life of the growing and changing capital there would no longer be a place for these personalities and the "picturesque" note they added to downtown life.[60]

58 Lucio Morel, "Como los rascacielos reemplazarán en Buenos Aires a los viejos palacios," *Mundo Argentino*, 26, 1320 (May 6, 1936), p. 25.

59 Andrés Vanegas, "Buenos Aires apaga sus últimos faroles a gas," *Aquí Está*, 2, 164 (December 13, 1937) and Oscar Velarco, "La derrota de la Victoria," *Aquí Está*, 2, 161 (December 2, 1937).

60 Josué Quesada, "Se acabaron los 'locos lindos' del viejo Buenos Aires?," *El Hogar*, 1441 (May 28, 1937).

The Diagonal Norte (ca. 1936)

As Vedia y Mitre's term neared its end, national presidential elections were held in September of 1937, scheduled to coincide more or less with the seventh anniversary of the coup against Yrigoyen. The two principal contenders were former president Marcelo T. de Alvear for the Radical party and his former minister of public works, Roberto M. Ortiz, for the Concordancia. Alvear promised to restore the full and open operation of democratic institutions in the country, to end political and electoral fraud, and to respect to the letter the nation's constitution. Ortiz committed himself to continue the economic progress achieved under Justo within a framework of political order and legality and to avoid the "demagoguery" that most conservatives associated with Radicalism. Both candidates concluded their extensive nationwide campaign with large rallies in Luna Park.[61]

On election day, turnout in the capital, as for all elections during the "infamous decade," was high, with 88 percent of the eligible electorate casting their ballots. The Radicals retained the enormous advantage they had displayed in the 1936 congressional elections with Alvear receiving 256,607 votes to 110,225 for Ortiz. The Socialist ticket, led by Nicolás Repetto, came in a far distant third with 26,422 votes.[62] Although the Radical ticket also carried the provinces of Córdoba and Tucumán, it lost by substantial margins in most other major provinces, especially those of Buenos Aires and Santa Fe, primarily because of the continued use of fraud. As a result, Ortiz emerged the victor. Despite the questionable practices by which he himself had been elected, Ortiz would soon set in motion an effort to restore full democracy to Argentina. Ortiz, moreover, was also the first president of the nation who also had served as an elected member of the Concejo Deliberante of the city of Buenos Aires.

At the municipal level, relations between Intendente Vedia y Mitre and the council remained generally confrontational. When the council reassembled for its second period of ordinary sessions on September 21, the executive presented them with fifteen vetoes he had issued during the brief recess that had begun at the end of August. As the sessions began, the mainline Socialists introduced a new issue for consideration, one that echoed previous debates over transportation and electricity. In September, they pressed the executive to roll back price increases instituted by the main supplier of gas to the city, another British-owned monopoly, the Compañía Primitiva de Gas. Soon, Obreristas and Radicals allied with them to urge consideration of a shift of the city's concession for gas provision from the British supplier to the state-owned Yacimientos Petrolíferos Fiscales, which could provide abundant natural gas as opposed

61 *La Prensa* (September 2, 1937), p. 11 and (September 4, 1937), p. 10.
62 Cantón, *Materiales*, vol. 1, p. 119.

to the coal-based fuel of the Primitiva. The executive delayed any action on these measures, causing the opposition to charge him again with favoring the interests of a foreign enterprise over those of the porteño consumer.[63] Finally, during consideration of the budget proposal for 1938, Radical and Socialist councilmen complained of the intendente's "profligate and dangerous" spending on such projects as the Nueve de Julio, which put the municipality in an "uncertain financial condition."[64] The council approved the new budget, but concerns raised over Vedia y Mitre's spending practices would resonate with even greater force and volume in succeeding months.

63 For the debate on this issue, see *VTCD* (September 24, 1937), pp. 2036–44; (December 7, 1937), pp. 3245–51; (December 10, 1937), pp. 3339–53; and (December 23, 1937), pp. 3836–7.
64 *VTCD* (December 23, 1937), pp. 3872–992.

11

Scandal and dissolution

Vedia y Mitre's mark on the city of Buenos Aires was substantial. Beyond the lasting and visible monuments, however, his successors as intendente were forced to confront the enormous deficits and debts that resulted from his lavish spending, which left them little opportunity to develop bold projects of their own. The city council, for its part, sought to highlight what it considered Vedia y Mitre's excesses, while glossing over its own responsibility for the resulting financial chaos. While continuing to debate issues that involved the provision of public services to the city, the council became embroiled in a series of scandals that eventually led to the dissolution of the democratically elected local legislature and a temporary halt to the new form of municipal elections and government begun in 1918.

In early 1938, a major fiscal crisis turned the assumption of the capital's executive office into a not so pleasant prospect. Newly elected President Roberto M. Ortiz, who would assume office on February 20, was rumored in late January to have narrowed his choices for the post to two men, one of whom, prominent conservative politician Rodolfo Moreno, was reported to have made it known he would turn down the offer because of the financial mess he would assume.[1] The other choice, anti-personalista Arturo Goyeneche, did accept the nomination and was sworn in as the new intendente on February 21.

Goyeneche was similar to most intendentes. A friend of Ortiz, with whom he had served as a fellow Radical elected from the capital to the national Chamber of Deputies in the early 1920s, he had also, with the future president, moved away from Yrigoyenismo shortly thereafter. Under Alvear, he had been director general of the national postal and telegraphic services and later had served on the boards of several corporations. He lived at Pueyrredón 1777 in the Barrio Norte and belonged to the Jockey Club, the Club de Gimnasia y Esgrima, and the Buenos Aires Rowing Club.[2]

1 Juan Escucha, "Dos intendentes y un ministerio," *Aquí Está*, 3, 177 (January 27, 1938).
2 *Quien es Quien*, 1939, pp. 206–7.

In an interview one month after taking office, Goyeneche revealed the major priorities of his administration: expansion and modernization of the city's hospital system, major efforts to lower the costs of basic necessities, and renewed attention to the capital's housing situation. According to his calculations, some 150,000 porteños still lived in conventillos, sometimes with as many as seven persons to a room. Public housing provided by either the local or the national government met only a small fraction of these needs. Promising to examine carefully European and North American approaches to resolving these problems, he called on the aid of the people of the city, the various parties represented on the Concejo Deliberante, and the press for assistance and cooperation in these efforts.[3] The greatest obstacle to realizing his goals came not from those sources, which generally supported his administration, but from the fiscal constraints imposed by his predecessor's spending excesses.

As Goyeneche assumed office, all political parties were gearing up for the national and local elections slated for the end of March. Both of the two traditionally strongest rivals faced serious internal difficulties. The Socialists still suffered from the defection of the Obreristas, who submitted their own list of candidates for national deputies and city councilmen. As the Radicals proceeded to select their candidates for congressmen, councilmen, and national senator, they faced an increasingly restive minority of mostly younger elements. With Arturo Frondizi as a prominent spokesman, they continued to criticize the party's apparent accommodations with the Justo administration and the Radical councilmen's decision to vote in favor of the concessions to the electric power companies. When their candidates were badly defeated in the party's internal elections, the dissidents claimed they had been the victims of fraud and determined to submit their own lists under the rubric Unión Cívica Radical, Bloque Opositor (Opposition Bloc of the Radical Party).[4]

The municipal programs of both Socialists and Radicals, albeit to different degrees, sought to respond to their perception of a growing public demand for greater government control over the activities of private enterprises supplying the city with public services. Both called for eventual municipalization of such services, advocated a minimum wage for workers employed by firms that received municipal contracts, and stressed renewed attention to improved housing and health care.[5]

While the Radicals and Socialists struggled with defectors from their ranks, the various parties of the Concordancia seemed to have overcome

3 "Grandes viviendas obreras, nuevos hospitales y abaratamiento de los artículos de primera necesidad, es el plan del nuevo intendente municipal," *Crítica* (March 21, 1938), p. 4.
4 This decision was made after a typically tumultuous meeting of the party's capital convention. *La Prensa* (February 25, 1938), p. 10.
5 *La Vanguardia* (March 9, 1938), p. 6 and *Crítica* (March 12, 1938), p. 3.

many of the internal difficulties that had doomed their chances in previ-
ous elections. For the national elections, the Independent Socialists and
the conservatives, now grouped in an entity called the Frente Nacional
(National Front), along with the anti-personalistas (Unión Cívica Radical,
Junta Reorganizadora), agreed to support a combined candidate list with
Mariano Vedia y Mitre as their choice for the capital's vacant Senate seat.
For the council, the Frente Nacional and the anti-personalistas would
submit separate lists. The Frente's municipal program echoed those of
other parties with regard to health care and housing, but did not mention
municipalizing public services. The conservative program, introduced by
Independent Socialist José Rouco Oliva, emphasized continued growth
for the city, including completion of the Nueve de Julio from Retiro to
Constitución.[6]

Three other parties, running separate lists, promised some significant
competition at the municipal level. The Concentración Obrera, with longtime councilman José Penelón leading its slate, had steadily picked up
support throughout the decade and promised to make a respectable
showing. So, too, did the dissident Partido Socialista Obrero, which entered
capital elections for the first time with a list of relatively well-known
candidates and threatened to draw backing away from the main party.
The first plank of the Obreristas' platform called for a thorough review
of the spending practices of the Vedia y Mitre administration, especially
the costs of the Nueve de Julio, and promised to hold the intendente to
account for any excesses.[7] Finally, the Unión de Contribuyentes Municipales
(Union of Municipal Taxpayers), a professedly nonpartisan group of small
businessmen and property owners, which had seen the number of votes
for their council candidates grow from 3,157 in 1932 to 14,968 in 1936,
represented another force to be reckoned with. Speakers at the closing
campaign rally of the Unión complained of ever more burdensome
municipal taxes, skyrocketing budgets and deficits, and unnecessary spending on massive public works while basic social needs, such as the condition of the city hospitals and poor neighborhoods, were ignored.[8]

When the votes were counted, all three main parties were in for some
surprises. Maintaining the hold on the capital electorate they had established with their reentry into the electoral process two years earlier, the
Radicals easily swept both the national and city council contests. In
addition to capturing eleven of sixteen national deputy slots and six of
fifteen council seats, UCR national senatorial candidate Fernando Saguier,
with 140,302 votes, easily outdistanced the Socialist Mario Bravo, with
84,781 votes, and former Intendente Vedia y Mitre, who gained 82,929

tallies. The Radicals' margin of victory, however, was due more to the diversity of the opposition than their own strength. Their total votes in the national and local elections of 1938 had declined since 1936 by about fifty- to fifty-five thousand. The UCR Bloque Opositor, although far from posing any serious challenge, did drain about seven thousand votes away from the main party. The Concordancia, overwhelmed by Radicals and Socialists in previous elections, managed to capture the five minority national deputy seats, beating the Socialists by more than twenty thousand votes. Although the Concordancia had clearly benefited from the adherence of all its constituent groups for the national election, the Socialists had just as clearly suffered from the defection of the Obreristas, who gained better than twenty-six thousand votes that ordinarily would have gone to the main party. In the city council elections, the Socialists did place second, but again, as in the national election, with about twenty-six thousand fewer votes than in 1936 (see Appendix, Table A.3). If the components of the Concordancia had run together rather than separately for council positions, the Socialists would have placed third in that election as well.[9]

Thanks to their second consecutive decisive victory, the Radicals, with sixteen representatives, now had a clear majority on the council. The once potent Socialists had been reduced to six members, although they could usually count on the support of the two councilmen each of the Obreristas and the Concentración Obrera. The Concordancia had a total of four representatives on the council, two each from the Frente Nacional and the anti-personalista Radicals.

During its first few months, the new council focused primarily on the fiscal crisis inherited from the previous administration. Goyeneche's representatives presented the details of that crisis to the council on July 15 and their story was a grim one. As of the beginning of the year, the city had a total debt of almost 314 million pesos, a floating debt of almost 132 million pesos; debt service now took up about 20 percent of municipal revenues. Revenues, in turn, were inadequate to make up expenses, producing a current deficit of 16 million pesos. The reasons for the situation were clear – the extraordinary expenditures for various public works projects, most notably the Nueve de Julio, which, with its parking garages, had cost the city 91.5 million pesos (21.5 million pesos more than projected). Not only had such expansions been intrinsically expensive; they had also removed, through demolition, thousands of tax-paying properties from the rolls. The cost of expropriations associated with the new avenue, and for other projects, had greatly exceeded expectations. The crisis meant that work had to be halted on current projects and no

9 Cantón, *Materiales*, vol. 1, p. 121 and *La Prensa* (April 12, 1938), p. 11.

new construction could be initiated. Somehow, funds had to be found to meet obligations incurred in the expropriations of property. The implications for the city budget were major cuts in expenses and improved revenue collection.[10]

To resolve the crisis, the municipality determined to petition the federal government for assistance, primarily by allowing the city to negotiate for a foreign loan guaranteed by the national authorities to see it through its present difficulties. Resolutions to this effect were introduced by the council's Radical bloc on August 5 and approved with no recorded dissent or discussion.[11] The national Congress responded quickly, authorizing on August 12 the flotation of a foreign loan not to exceed thirty years in length or thirty million dollars in amount.[12] The contracting of the loan itself took a bit longer and ran into some complications, but by early November National Minister of Finance Pedro Groppo had arranged with New York bankers a loan of twenty-five million dollars to meet the city's needs.[13] The city council, for its part, on October 25, voted twenty-one to three to approve a new bond issue to cover the costs of various expropriations associated with street and park expansion.[14]

Criticism of the Vedia y Mitre administration continued to resound through the council chamber. The following year in June 1939, the council approved by a vote of twenty-three to three (with only the Concordancia's Lizardo Molina Carranza, Reinaldo Elena, and José Rouco Oliva opposed) the demolition of one of the former intendente's proudest monuments, the Obelisco. Radical and Socialist critics argued that it was the unanimous opinion of the porteño public that the obelisk was inappropriate, poorly placed, and "an unpleasant note in the heart of the city which Buenos Aires does not deserve." In the previous year, two substantial sections of the monument had fallen to the ground (see photo). Although no one was injured, opponents took this opportunity to question the obelisk's hasty construction, the costs involved (208,000 pesos), and the fact that Vedia y Mitre had contracted his own architect and proceeded on the project without consulting the council or other proper municipal authorities. Goyeneche's representatives retorted that the defects that had caused the two pieces to fall had been rectified and the monument was now perfectly safe. The intendente himself claimed that the project had been funded primarily by the federal government, which had the principal

10 VTCD (July 15, 1938), pp. 1177–197 and (July 19, 1938), pp. 1274–300.
11 VTCD (August 5, 1938), pp. 1569–70.   12 State Records (August 13, 1938), 835.51/1232.
13 State Records (November 4, 1938), 835.51/1253.
14 Opposed to the bond issue were the two members of the Concentración Obrera and one Socialist Obrerista. The mainline Socialists disclaimed any responsibility for the city's financial crisis, but saw no alternative to supporting this partial solution to it. VTCD (October 25, 1938), pp. 3122–33.

authority over it. Therefore, he refused to implement the council's decision. The furor soon died down and the Obelisco remained as perhaps the city's best-known and most distinctive landmark.[15]

Another major item that was discussed in these years was the question of gas service to the capital. On August 9, 1938, the council's special committee for examining the matter of gas and gasoline provision recommended to the executive a reduction of basic rates charged by the Compañía Primitiva de Gas to go into effect as of October 1, a recommendation approved by all parties on the council.[16] At the following session, Socialist Andrés Justo accused the committee, dominated by a Radical majority, and the executive of unduly delaying action on resolving the question of who would be supplying gas to the city after the Primitiva's concession expired on January 14, 1940.[17] The very next day, Goyeneche submitted to the council a proposal on the subject, the first article of which read: "As of January 14, 1940, the service of the provision of gas to the city of Buenos Aires will be supplied by the Municipality, be it on the base of a mixed society or a consortium in which will participate the general board of YPF."[18]

In his lengthy message accompanying this proposal, Goyeneche laid out in some detail the complexities involved. Beginning with the observation that this had been "one of the most important . . . problems to occupy the executive from his first day in office," he described the various studies into and conclusions about the expenses entailed in making the transition from a private company concession to a municipal enterprise based on gas supplied by YPF. Although the intendente favored such a transition, the costs would be considerable. Most importantly, in addition to the purchase of existing lines from the Primitiva, a new system of subterranean lines would have to be constructed to handle the natural gas from YPF. One commission estimated the price tag for these installations at almost forty-seven million pesos. Moreover, the construction process itself would take time, perhaps more than allowed before the lapse of the concession. Nonetheless, Goyeneche committed himself to this alternative and requested of the council authority to proceed.[19]

Slightly more than two months later, the Radical and Concordancia majority on the special committee on gas questions, to which the intendente's proposal had been sent, reported favorably on it. The Socialist and Concentración Obrera minority dissented and presented a proposal of their own calling for a rapid and complete transition to municipal operation. The Radicals countered that, like the Socialists, they favored

15 VTCD (June 13, 1939), pp. 498–504; (June 30, 1939), pp. 709–19; and (July 11, 1939), pp. 816–23.
16 VTCD (August 9, 1938), pp. 1766–73.   17 VTCD (August 11, 1938), pp. 1863–97.
18 VTCD (August 12, 1938), p. 1944.   19 Ibid., pp. 1939–44.

Repair on two panels fallen from the obelisk (1938)

eventual municipalization of gas service with YPF participation, but that such a result could not be achieved overnight. Therefore, they supported the intendente's more gradual and cautious approach. More important than arguments, of course, were votes. After two days of debate, the Radicals and Concordancia representatives passed the majority report by a vote of sixteen to seven, with the Socialist minority report defeated by the same margin.[20] On November 4, the intendente named three members of the executive branch to work with the council and YPF to plan the transition scheduled for 1940. One year later, however, the special committee reported that little progress had been made on that transition. Over Socialist objections, therefore, the council voted to extend the Primitiva's concession for six more months.[21]

The national and municipal elections of March 1940 in the federal capital took place in a substantially different climate from the one that had prevailed for most of the previous decade. On the world stage, western democracies began to do battle with the rising dictatorships of Europe and Asia. At home, President Ortiz made his most serious effort yet to restore full adherence to the democratic practices of pre-1930 Argentina. At the heart of these efforts was national intervention to assure free and fair elections in the province of Buenos Aires.

Within the capital, as usual, the Socialists and the Radicals were the principal competitors. For both, the campaign featured by-now familiar trademarks. The Socialists chose their candidates in mid-February and produced a municipal program in early March. In their campaign for the council, party spokesmen sought to emphasize what they considered the Socialists' positive contribution to the work of that body. In turn, they attacked the Radicals for lacking a coherent ideology and for still depending on "machine-style" politics for their success, a machine, according to Américo Ghioldi, that was associated with "gambling groups," "the electric gang," and "the gas circle."[22] Most significant in enhancing the party's chances in this contest was the decision by the Obreristas to abandon their separate campaign in this election and to urge their backers to vote for the Socialist candidates as an expression of "democratic solidarity in defense of legality . . . ."[23] The momentary return to the fold of the younger dissidents permitted the Socialists to be optimistic about their chances for reversing the pattern of defeat that had begun in 1936.

In late February, the UCR held internal elections for its candidate lists

20 *VTCD* (October 14, 1938), pp. 2824–42 and (October 19, 1938), pp. 2960–3018.
21 The vote on this decision came on the final day of the 1939 sessions. In favor were the Radicals and conservatives, opposed were the Socialists and their allies. *VTCD* (December 29, 1939), pp. 4208–14.
22 *La Prensa* (March 30, 1940), p. 12.   23 *La Prensa* (March 19, 1940), p. 12.

with 117,000 affiliates inscribed. This figure represented an increase of 32,000 party members since 1938 and although only about one-third of them actually participated in the selection process, the total enrolled suggested that the Radicals were attracting ever-greater numbers of formerly uncommitted voters.[24] If a "Tammany style" machine was running party affairs, as had been charged, at least it was performing with maximum efficiency. As one publication noted, the Radicals had "committees, sub-committees, discussion groups, and libraries operating in all districts. Their posters predominate on the walls of the city, from Constitución to Retiro, and their orators are heard everywhere . . . ." A visit to the headquarters of the capital campaign committee at Lavalle 1556 found "an extraordinary animation" with intense activity by "persons of all social classes: Lawyers, doctors, workers, financiers, shop-keepers, legislators and councilmen . . . ." The man again in charge of these activities, Julián Sancerni Giménez, expressed his optimism in victory because "the Unión Civica Radical is in the heart of the Argentine multitudes, because under Radical governments they obtained the recognition of beneficial rights that, systematically, were denied them by governments of the upper class."[25]

In addition to the Socialists and Radicals, two other competitors of note were entered in this contest. The Frente Nacional again entered the fray, representing the various parties of the Concordancia. In this election, the anti-personalista Radicals (Unión Civica Radical, Junta Renovadora Nacional) joined with the Frente for a combined slate of national deputy and senatorial candidates, but presented their own list for the council positions. The Frente's municipal program, drawn up by Councilman José Rouco Oliva, emphasized major urban renovations and improvements, but said nothing about political reform or city control of public services.[26] The other competitor, the Unión de Contribuyentes, which had seen its total votes grow from a paltry 3,157 in 1932 to a respectable 23,386 in 1938 (see Appendix, Table A.3), promised to keep a tight lid on municipal expenses and to monitor carefully the spending practices of the council and of individual councilmen.[27] The increased strength of the Unión seemed to reflect a growing discontent on the part of a substantial number of porteños with what they considered unfair and even illegal local taxes on the one hand and the enormous expansion of municipal expenditures and deficits on the other.[28]

24 *La Prensa* (February 18, 1940), p. 11 and (February 24, 1940), p. 10.
25 L.S. Labal, "El Radicalismo espera triunfar el 31 en la Capital," *Aquí Está*, 5, 398 (March 11, 1940), pp. 50–1.
26 *La Prensa* (February 13, 1940), p. 13.   27 *La Prensa* (March 26, 1940), p. 13.
28 An expression of these concerns could be found in a series of editorials on these subjects in the pages of *El Hogar*, 1560 (September 8, 1939); 1563 (September 29, 1939); and 1578 (January 12, 1940).

Election day, March 31, produced what had become the customary high turnout of almost 81 percent of all eligible voters. As was also customary, Radical and Socialist spokesmen expressed satisfaction with their respective efforts and confidence in their ultimate triumph or, at the least, in the case of the Socialists, an improvement over past performances. These predictions proved correct. The Radicals again reaffirmed their hold over the capital electorate, sweeping the national elections with an increase of over 30,000 votes (about equal to the increased number of party members) from 1938. Of even greater significance, thanks to Ortiz's intervention, they also recorded victories in the provinces of Buenos Aires, Córdoba, Entre Ríos, and Santa Fe, giving them a near majority in the national Chamber of Deputies. In the capital, the Socialists came in a strong second, besting the Concordancia this time by 50,000 votes, although trailing the Radicals by 45,000 tallies.[29] The results in the municipal contest were about the same, with the Radicals collecting almost 141,000 votes to 107,000 for the Socialists. The anti-personalista Radicals came in third with 45,000 votes, and the Unión de Contribuyentes fourth with 40,445 (see Appendix, Table A.3).

Although of the city's twenty districts the Socialists only managed to recapture their traditional stronghold in La Boca, they showed marked improvements in their performance in other working-class areas, largely due, it would seem, to the support of the Obreristas. The Radicals more than held their own in the south and west and continued to enjoy clear predominance in the middle-class center and northern parts of the city.[30] In a pioneering statistical analysis of the social base of party support in this and other elections of the 1940s, Gino Germani found the same strong correlations between the working class and the Socialists (and the Concentracion Obrera) and between the middle class and the Radicals that had been evident two decades earlier. Among the eight social groups Germani examined, the Concordancia in 1940 showed positive correlations only with public employees and professionals.[31] These findings indicate that, despite the many political crises, fluctuations, and fragmentations of the period, the bases of party loyalty and support changed but little. Although momentary inroads were made on the basic pool of the other parties' backers, workers generally supported the Socialists, white-collar employees backed the Radicals, and the upper class identified with the conservatives. Some significant changes in these alignments would occur, however, with the advent of the Perón regime, shifts that would most profoundly affect the fortunes of the Socialists, who would lose the bulk

---

29 Cantón, *Materiales*, vol. 1, p. 125.   30 Ibid., vol. 2, p. 149.
31 Germani, *Estructura social de la Argentina*, pp. 251–60.

of their traditional working-class backing to the new phenomenon of Peronism.[32]

The results of the 1940 elections produced only minor changes in the composition of the council. The Radicals, although lacking an absolute majority, still held a several-seat edge over the Socialists and their allies. On most votes, they could also count on the backing of the anti-personalistas and the representatives of the Concordancia. For the first time, however, two members of the Unión de Contribuyentes, Emilio Leveratto and José Mazzei, were represented on the council. Their actions would have significant consequences.

In many ways, the council sessions of 1940 and 1941 were a replay of the previous two years. Matters related to the legacy of the Vedia y Mitre administration continued to predominate, as did matters of even longer standing. In April 1940 high winds and torrential rains struck the city, producing some of the worst flooding of the century and forcing 100,000 families from their homes. Again, the low-lying area of the capital along the Riachuelo and the Río de la Plata suffered from this disaster. The city administration responded by finding temporary lodgings, food, and clothing for those affected and in June the council approved a resolution to reduce city taxes for those parts of La Boca and Barracas that had been particularly hard hit by the catastrophe.[33] The fact remained, however, that despite decades of complaints, promises, plans, and rhetoric, neither the national nor the local government had implemented projects to prevent such disasters and to protect many of the city's most disadvantaged from suffering the periodic blows of this natural calamity. This failure added weight to arguments that local and national officials seemed more concerned with showy monuments and broad central avenues than with addressing some of the basic needs of much of the capital's population.

The point was reinforced at the end of the year. In mid-December, the council began to consider two proposals aimed to address the particular needs of La Boca and Barracas. One called for extensive repavement of their streets and the other suggested naming a special committee to study various conditions in these neighborhoods and to suggest improvements. Speaking for the proposals, Radical Francisco Rabanal described a desperate situation in terms that echoed depictions dating from the turn of the century. For example, although the conventillo had gradually disappeared from the rest of the city, a recent survey showed that almost 40 percent

32 For more on the voting patterns that accompanied the rise of Peronism, see Manuel Mora y Araujo and Ignacio Llorente, eds., *El voto peronista: Ensayos de sociología electoral Argentina* (Buenos Aires, 1980).
33 The details of the flooding and attempts to cope with its results are provided in various editions of *Crítica* for April of 1940. The council's response is in *VTCD* (June 14, 1940), pp. 267–75.

of La Boca's population still resided in such dwellings, for which they often paid exorbitant rents. In words that almost exactly paraphrased Socialist Alfredo L. Palacios four decades earlier when, as a deputy representing La Boca, he sought to bring national attention to conditions in conventillos, Rabanal cited the following description from a journalistic investigation of these residences:

> In a conventillo, one does not live, one exists. The main room is the scene of all the activities of daily life. In it, one cooks, one eats, and one sleeps. In some can be found eight or nine persons; men and women, boys and girls of all ages; there are conventillos in which 200 persons live, which, at the hour of personal hygiene, find residents waiting in line to use filthy baths and toilets, utilized by males and females indiscriminately.[34]

The council had tried to respond to these conditions two months earlier with approval of a project for a major public housing project in La Boca. Even with this project, however, it was clear that much remained to be done.[35] Although the upcoming completion of the new Boca Junior's soccer stadium promised a major source of neighborhood pride, the construction had caused severe traffic problems, which, some councilmen claimed, had been worsened by the alleged failure of the new transport corporation to do its part in resolving them. It was estimated, too, that more than 900 blocks of streets in Barracas and La Boca were in need of repaving because of the effects of the recent flooding and at a cost that would take up better than half the city's budget for such expenditures. Finally, the Riachuelo, which served as the southern boundary for these and other working-class districts and whose straightening and channeling was still not complete, was becoming increasingly polluted and a major health hazard. With many industries, especially chemical, metallurgical, and meat-packing plants along its banks discharging their waste into the river as well as being the repository of millions of liters of the city's discharge system, the slow-moving Riachuelo itself was turning into an open sewer.

With only minor differences, all parties on the council backed the two resolutions proposed to improve matters in La Boca and Barracas.[36] What the discussion revealed once again was that, despite the repeated verbal commitment by the city fathers to attend to the needs of the capital's working-class south side, and despite considerable representation on the

---

34 VTCD (December 16, 1940), p. 1694. For Palacios's observation on the conventillo and his role as Argentina's first Socialist congressman, see Walter, *The Socialist Party*, pp. 73–92.

35 When finished, the new project would have 441 apartments, housing at most 3,000 persons, leaving ten to fifteen times that number still in conventillos. Octavio Palazzola, "Monobloque de cemento para reemplazar conventillo de madera," *Aquí Está*, 5, 421 (May 30, 1940), 62–3.

36 VTCD (December 16, 1940), pp. 2684–733.

council sympathetic to the area's plight, little of substance had been accomplished over the course of the past several decades. The debate of December 1940 and the conditions described were variations on a common theme that had been reiterated since the turn of the century. Although the elected council should not be the target of all the blame, given the part played by the local executive and the national government, the failure to provide a more balanced pattern of growth to the capital and the general neglect of the working-class districts must be recorded as one of the major failings of city government in these years. This neglect, in turn, was yet one more ingredient in the formula that would allow Juan Perón to capture the nation's working class and assume the presidency. In the 1946 presidential election, Perón carried La Boca by a two-to-one margin and did exceptionally well in working-class districts 1, 2, and 15.[37]

Along with concerns over the effects of flooding, the ongoing saga of public transportation continued to occupy the council. In February and March of 1940, the newly formed transport corporation began to incorporate individually owned colectivos into its operations, producing occasionally violent protests. While these protests continued, commentators noted the increasingly deplorable state of public transportation in the city despite efforts at coordination. Streetcars, they reported, were antiquated and insufficient in number, leading to long delays in service. The subways, although new, suffered from a lack of cars, producing extremely crowded conditions. The colectivos, although fast and popular, ran with almost no regulation. As one observer put it, for "the drivers [of the colectivos], their principal concern is to go as rapidly as possible and they always seek the middle of the street and, when it is time for the passenger to descend, instead of pulling up to the curb, stop their vehicle in its tracks, regardless of other traffic passing at great speed on the left and the right. This leaves the passenger hesitating, looking to find the least dangerous side to descend." The result was a growing number of passengers being struck by passing vehicles.[38] No matter what the conveyance, only the fortunate few were able to find seats and most were forced to stand, jammed cheek by jowl with their fellow passengers. The number of vehicles had failed to keep up with the growing population and little effort was made to enforce the completo.[39]

The city council, responding to the growing complaints about transportation service, in July asked the executive to report on what the municipality was doing to address these issues. His response was to argue that because of the national law that had created the transport corporation, an essentially autonomous entity, there was little the municipality could

37 Cantón, *Materiales*, vol. 2, p. 157.   38 *La Prensa* (March 22, 1940), p. 8.
39 Octavo Palazzolo, "Viaje como pueda," *Aquí Está*, 5, 470 (November 18, 1940).

do. That response led to a lengthy discussion in the chamber wherein many of the deficiencies of the capital's transport system noted in the press were elaborated in more detail. Socialist Héctor Iñigo Carrera blamed the Anglo for its failure to modernize its rolling stock and to extend its lines, even after its triumph with the creation of the transport corporation. He argued that working-class districts suffered most from the failure to extend service, appending numerous notes from southside neighborhood associations to that effect and including photographs of the crowded and rickety cars still in operation. The colectivos, he agreed, were unregulated, with too few city inspectors to assure that they adhered to existing ordinances with regard to routes, schedules, and the maximum number of passengers carried. "In America," he concluded, "a life is still an appreciable value; in Buenos Aires, however, accidents occur daily that cannot be attributed so much to the lack of pedestrians or drivers following rules as to the general anarchy of the system, the deterioration of rolling stock, and the egoism and desire for excessive profits on the part of small entrepreneurs and large capitalist enterprises that still have sufficient influence on the politics of the country as to impose measures which are harmful to our economy and sovereignty."[40]

The Radicals, as was often the case, agreed with both sides. The city was limited, their spokesman noted, in what it could do because of the national transportation law. On the other hand, more efforts could be made to find the personnel necessary to enforce existing regulations on the colectivo, whose drivers were not only "true artists" in making their way through the capital's traffic, but who also excelled at avoiding the few city inspectors available to monitor their activities. The Radicals then joined the Socialists to pass yet another resolution calling on the national Congress to overturn the national transport coordination law.[41] This resolution, like the preceding ones, had no result. Some of the issues raised in this discussion, ironically by chief Radical spokesman Mario A. Posse, would return to haunt him and the council one year later.

In late November 1940, Goyeneche became the first intendente of the twentieth century to die in office. Goyeneche's death was the second severe blow to hit the anti-personalistas in 1940. Several months earlier, a seriously ill President Ortiz had been forced to turn over the reins of office to his conservative vice-president, Ramón S. Castillo, a development that brought an abrupt halt to the "redemocratization."

Castillo named fellow conservative Carlos Alberto Pueyrredón as Goyeneche's successor. A Buenos Aires-born and educated lawyer, Pueyrredón had been elected a national deputy for the Partido Demócrata

40 *VTCD* (July 19, 1940), pp. 645–6.   41 Ibid., pp. 637–73.

Nacional from the province of Buenos Aires in 1932. At the time of his appointment, he was chairman of the board of two insurance companies and a member of the board of several other banks and businesses. His law office, like that of most attorneys and businessmen, was in the city center. In addition to his legal and commercial interests, he dabbled in history and was a member of the national academy. He was also a member of the Sociedad Rural and belonged to one of the nation's elite land-owning families.[42]

Pueyrredón's relations with the council were brief but stormy. When the local legislature reconvened in May 1941, it was confronted with fifteen vetoes from the new executive, including one of a council-inspired ordinance to provide tax breaks for buildings begun in 1941 and 1942. Pueyrredón argued that the city's financial situation did not allow for such a measure. At the same time, the executive presented his own proposed ordinance, which would prohibit any municipal employee, including concejales, from simultaneously working for or having a primary interest in any private firm that did business with the city.[43] This proposal suggested a growing concern with apparent conflicts of interest between city officials and businesses seeking municipal contracts, a process that involved both the executive and legislative branches.

Later in the month, the council directed a petition to the executive asking why he had prohibited the showing in the capital of Charlie Chaplin's antifascist film, *The Great Dictator*. Because certain important sectors of the administration, the military, and some intellectuals were displaying sympathy for the Axis in the early stages of World War II, this was a question of more than passing interest to the democratically elected and mostly democratic-minded councilmen. In two lengthy sessions in June, Secretary of Public Works Martín Aberg Cobo gave a detailed explanation of the executive's decision regarding the Chaplin film, arguing that its aim was to avoid offending important nations (Germany and Italy) with which Argentina had long and close ties. Most councilmen did not accept this reasoning and approved a Socialist-inspired resolution calling on the executive to permit the showing of *The Great Dictator*.[44]

Pueyrredón, in turn, responded to this resolution with a tartly worded rebuff. The decision not to show the film, he observed, was not his but rather came from the chief executive and his minister of foreign relations, both charged by the constitution with the "maintenance of good relations with foreign powers." By its action, he went on, the council sought to place the intendente in a position of violating the constitution and had

42 *Quien es Quien*, *1939*, p. 351.   43 *VTCD* (May 16, 1941), pp. 51 and 67.
44 *VTCD* (June 10, 1941), pp. 442–9 and (June 13, 1941), pp. 504–88.

exceeded its own authority and functions, which "ought to be limited to matters involved with building construction, street sweeping and cleaning, [and] the security, health, and morality of the city," and which did not include meddling in foreign affairs. For his part, he would not deem to exceed the limits of his own office and authorize "scoffing and insults against the heads of foreign nations . . . with whom our country is at peace . . . ."[45] Whatever the constitutional soundness of Pueyrredón's position, the tone and content of his message indicated that his feelings toward the council were anything but friendly.

On the other side and on another issue, some members of the council, especially the Socialists, accused both the national and local executives of slowing progress on the gas service questions. According to Socialist Councilman Andrés Justo, the council committee had been working well with Goyeneche and his representatives on this question, but Pueyrredón had so far proved less cooperative.[46] After appointing yet another committee to work on a resolution of this issue, the council on August 8 approved conceding to YPF the authority to provide gas to the capital, but also extended the Primitiva concession on a provisionary basis until January 15, 1945, with the stipulation that the intendente could terminate the agreement with six months' notice. This compromise solution, the result of a lengthy process marked by many delays and extensions, enjoyed the support of both Radicals and Socialists.[47]

The most important issue the council considered in 1941 involved, as it had so many times in the past, the matter of public transportation. To nobody's surprise, the conditions described in the council's discussion of this matter the previous year had shown little, if any, improvement. On June 3, therefore, a rare coalition of Socialists and representatives of the Concordancia and the Unión de Contribuyentes presented resolutions calling for the executive to report to the council on various aspects of the deteriorating service, especially with regard to the health and safety of passengers, given the general inadequacy of vehicles and failures to observe the completo regulations. Responding to petitions from some sixty neighborhood associations, they also requested information on plans to extend lines to areas of the city not yet served. For reasons that would soon become clear, Councilman Mario A. Posse, speaking for the Radicals, suggested postponing consideration until his party had had time to prepare fully its position on these matters. Despite Radical objections, a resolution to look into the problems noted above was approved by a vote of twelve to ten.

45 *VTCD* (June 27, 1941), p. 687.   46 *VTCD* (May 26, 1941), pp. 204–39.
47 *VTCD* (August 8, 1941), pp. 1123–83.

Within the larger framework of the overall debate on transportation service, the key item was introduced by José Mazzei of the Unión de Contribuyentes. While carrying out his own investigation of why some colectivos passed the whole day packed with riders in violation of the completo and why others proceeded according to the established regulations, he had been informed that rule evaders had been "accommodated"; that is, they had paid a certain sum to have the traffic inspectors in charge of enforcement look the other way. Accordingly, Mazzei and his Unión colleague, Emilio Leveratto, presented a proposal to name a special multiparty committee to look into the activities of the city's traffic director and his office. While the Socialists and the Concordancia's Rouco Oliva supported this request, the Radicals summoned enough votes to defeat it. Nonetheless, a motion introduced by the Concentración Obrera's José F. Penelón to have the council's own transit and transportation committee, a committee with a Radical majority, carry out this investigation, received unanimous endorsement.[48]

Three weeks later, in an interim report, this committee disclosed that two councilmen, Radicals Posse and Carlos L. Aversa, might have been involved in the bribery of the traffic inspectors and recommended that they be suspended from attending council sessions until their involvement had been clarified.[49] On July 1 the committee reported that Posse had been arrested on the orders of Judge Ernesto J. Ure of the local criminal court, who was carrying out his own investigation of the bribery allegations, and recommended that he be suspended altogether from his functions as councilman, a recommendation the council approved.[50] Three days later Posse resigned from the body to which he had been elected less than two years earlier.

From this point on, events involving the council began to take the shape of a snowball on a steep incline, gathering size and velocity until it was eventually destroyed at the bottom. On July 11, Councilman José Rouco Oliva, president of the prestigious and influential "Los Amigos de la Ciudad" and one of the council's most respected members, asked to be excused from the traffic and transit committee until his own legal position had been clarified. The judge looking into the matter had apparently determined that Rouco Oliva had been associated with an individual implicated in the bribery operation. As Rouco Oliva made his request, which was honored, Socialist spokesmen warned that the council was presently under severe attack from "antidemocratic" forces looking for any excuse to dissolve it. Indeed, just such a proposition had been introduced

48 *VTCD* (June 3, 1941), pp. 312–62.
49 *VTCD* (June 24, 1941), pp. 649–52.   50 *VTCD* (July 1, 1941), p. 721.

into the national Chamber of Deputies by conservative congressman Reynaldo Pastor of the province of San Luis.[51] Therefore, it was especially urgent that the council itself vigorously proceed with its investigation and clean its own house before the entire structure was destroyed from the outside. The council then unanimously approved three projects introduced by Socialist Iñigo Carrera aimed to assure the proper and ethical behavior of all its members.[52] As both the council's and the federal judge's investigations proceeded, the next to fall was conservative Councilman Lizardo Molina Carranza. On July 15, the council committee announced that Molina Carranza had been arrested in connection with the growing investigation and recommended his suspension, which the council also unanimously approved.[53]

Following this action, the council devoted much of its next session to defending itself against proposed dissolution. Spokesmen for all parties underscored the body's ongoing investigation of and action against its own members and noted the irony of a campaign to undermine one of the republic's genuinely democratic institutions stemming from congressmen and others placed into office by undemocratic practices. After these observations, the council unanimously passed a resolution that rejected the proposed dissolution and claimed that it was proceeding rapidly and effectively to put its own house in order.[54]

Help came from other quarters as well. Neighborhood development societies began to mobilize in defense of the council, writing letters to the capital's newspapers and public officials that underscored the importance of the local legislature to their own efforts. One, sent to the national Chamber of Deputies and reprinted in the council records, observed that "for entities like ours, dedicated for many years to the physical and cultural advancement of important neighborhoods in the city, the existence of the council has been of great benefit because through its clearly popular-based origin it has responded to the requests we have formulated, understanding our needs."[55]

On August 11, the transit and traffic committee reported on the results of its investigation. The Unión de Contribuyente's José Mazzei, whose efforts had produced the investigation in the first place, detailed the committee's activities and findings. After meeting forty-four times,

---

51 Pastor based his proposal on "recent developments which have deserved the unanimous repudiation of the press and the enlightened citizens of the federal capital" as well as alleged instances of the council exceeding its authority, especially with taxation and expenditures on "superfluous items and vain extravagances." Following dissolution, he called for a new law that would establish the direct election of the councilmen, who would than receive no salary and who would have clearly defined and restricted duties. *Diputados* (July 17, 1941), pp. 265–6.

52 *VTCD* (July 11, 1941), pp. 820–40.   53 *VTCD* (July 15, 1941), p. 853.

54 *VTCD* (July 18, 1941), pp. 871–94.   55 *VTCD* (July 22, 1941), pp. 905–6.

interviewing 177 persons, and amassing thousands of pages of documentation, the committee had unearthed irrefutable evidence of some councilmen's involvement in the bribery of inspectors to avoid the enforcement of the completo. Several witnesses testified, for example, that former councilman Mario Posse used frequent dinner meetings at the popular El Tropezón restaurant on Calle Callao to arrange for funds to be passed from the owner of a colectivo line to the city inspector. Posse also was reported to have met with the owners of other lines in his home where he had promised to grant them certain routes in exchange for an illegal payment of fifty thousand pesos. For other councilmen, the evidence was more circumstantial, but the investigation raised at the least serious questions about their associates, many of whom were clearly involved in wrongdoing, and about their judgment.

Mazzei pointed out that while the committee gathered its information, it worked in tandem with two other parallel investigations. As soon as the issue had come to light in early June, the intendente had named a special representative to look into the charges and the local judiciary had also sprung into action. The work of the former led to the eventual dismissal of the city's traffic director and several of his key officials, whereas the efforts of the latter led to the arrests already mentioned. The council committee, for its part, discovered that the practice of bribing inspectors had been going on for about eight months, during which time the city traffic office had totally neglected its regulatory duties and had based nearly every one of its decisions on the payment of bribes and other favors. Mentioning only some of the more flagrant abuses from the masses of evidence at his disposal, Mazzei concluded that in the traffic office "unrestrained corruption and immorality" reigned throughout this period.

After his lengthy exposition, Mazzei and the committee recommended that the members implicated in the scandal be expelled from the council. Because Posse already had resigned and been replaced, this meant action against Radical Carlos L. Aversa, who had been closely associated with an individual responsible for carrying bribe money from one person to another, and conservative Lizardo Molina Carranza, who apparently had served as a conduit for influence peddling. The committee had determined that the evidence against José Rouco Oliva was too weak to justify expulsion. When it came time to vote on these expulsions, the Socialists argued that even if the legal cases against the implicated persons were not airtight, councilmen should avoid even the appearances of impropriety. If they did not, they should be expelled. The Radicals, with two of their members deeply involved, took a more cautious stance, urging that expulsion be delayed until the external legal process made a final determination of guilt or innocence. Therefore, they voted against expelling either Aversa or Molina Carranza, forestalling decisive council action on either case.[56]

Although the Radicals' reluctance showed a healthy respect for the rights of individuals under the law, it probably did little to enhance the image of the increasingly besieged council. On the one hand, the council had collected, analyzed, and revealed an enormous amount of material that showed extensive wrongdoing in the city government, wrongdoing in which several councilmen were deeply implicated. On the other hand, when it came time to punish those involved, the response had been weak. This lack of action contrasted sharply with that of the intendente, who had begun a thorough housecleaning of the city traffic office. A few days later, however, the council did vote unanimously to expel Molina Carranza from its ranks when the judge investigating the colectivo bribery scandal had uncovered proof that the conservative councilman had illegally intervened with city officials on behalf of a hotel owner in order to bypass certain municipal regulations.[57]

The expulsion of Molina Carranza was the last major action of this particular democratically elected council. Over the next two months the situation of the local legislature and its supporters rapidly went from bad to worse. Later in August, more arrests were made of persons implicated in the colectivo scandal, including that of former anti-personalista Councilman José Dufour. By this time, then, representatives or past representatives of four of the main parties on the council over the past decade, the Radicals (Posse and Aversa), Independent Socialists (Rouco Oliva), conservatives (Molina Carranza), and anti-personalistas (Dufour), had been found to be involved to one degree or another in wrongdoing. At about the same time, an executive branch investigation of the city's tax assessment and collection office uncovered possible cases of bribery there as well. Although this did not directly involve the council, it did little for the overall public perception of municipal government.[58]

By early October, rumors were thick within the capital that President Castillo would soon dissolve the council. According to some reports, Intendente Pueyrredón was strongly urging such an action.[59] On October 10, Castillo met with his cabinet to discuss the matter. Following several hours of discussion and with total unanimity from his cabinet, the president announced the dissolution of the council. In the official decree accompanying the announcement, several reasons were given for the action. The misdeeds of the council, the chief executive argued, had led to a general loss of "public confidence" in the institution; several members of the

56 *VTCD* (August 11, 1941), pp. 1223–306.   57 *VTCD* (August 14, 1941), pp. 1512–15.
58 *La Vanguardia* (September 9, 1941), p. 3 and (September 12, 1941), p. 3.
59 *Crítica* (October 9, 1941), p. 5.

council had been accused of illegal activities and were now facing trial as a result; the council had failed to exercise "due diligence" in maintaining its own integrity and to take appropriate measures against the wrongdoers among its membership; the council had too often exceeded its authority and, at the same time suffered from "fundamental deficiencies inherent in its system of organization" (without detailing specifically what these were); and, finally, that the national Congress was itself currently considering two proposals to dissolve the council. With this last point, Castillo seemed to imply that he was merely doing what the Congress, then in recess, would sooner or later do on its own, a flimsy argument, given the large Radical presence in that body. In press conferences following the cabinet meeting, Castillo stated that the decision was based on the three well-known issues of the possibility of bribery in the granting of the electric concessions (recently under congressional investigation), delays in converting gas service from the Primitiva to YPF, and the colectivo scandal. Anticipating the response of those who would claim that this was an executive attack on democracy, the president observed that it was up to democratic institutions to behave responsibly and to police themselves and that when they were unable to do so he was fully within his constitutional rights and duties to take the action he had.[60]

There were certain similarities between this dissolution of the council and the previous measure carried out in 1915. Both, coincidentally, were ordered by conservative vice-presidents (De la Plaza and Castillo) who had succeeded more moderate and democratically minded presidents. Both occurred in the early stages of world wars, which were beginning to have an impact on Argentina. More significantly, both followed periods when scandal had stained the council, when that body seemed in disarray, and when the public's perception of the local legislature's probity and effectiveness were at a low ebb. Finally, both actions resulted in the executive's appointment of a "junta de vecinos" to replace the elected council. In 1941, and in 1915, the new list of appointees was peppered with the names of Argentina's aristocratic elite – Alzaga Unzué, Bosch, Lanusse, Paz Anchorena – whose knowledge of and concern with the poorer and more neglected areas of the city were questionable at best.

There were, however, also important differences in the two instances. The council dissolved in 1941 was the product of ever-expanding democratic processes that had been in operation for better than two decades. The council of 1941, therefore, had a much firmer base of popular legitimacy than did that of 1915. De la Plaza, despite his conservatism, had been committed to following through with the reforms of his predecessor Sáenz Peña, whereas Castillo was widely regarded as having reversed Ortiz's attempts to end the fraudulent practices of the "infamous decade" and of being under the influence of reactionary, antidemocratic elements. There was general agreement in the press that the dissolution of the council was at the least an overreaction to recent events. For some, it was part of a larger plan to undermine further the country's democratic institutions. *Crítica* went so far as to see it as part of a Nazi–fascist plot to eliminate democracy in Argentina altogether.[61]

Because the dissolution of 1941 occurred in a substantially different context from that of 1915, the general reaction to it was also substantially different. The previous dissolution had taken place with barely a murmur of protest. In 1941, however, there was a more widespread resistance. The councilmen themselves tried to force their way back into the council building following Castillo's announcement of his decision. When confronted by the police, who had occupied the premises on Calle Perú, they continued their demonstration in the streets outside. Meeting on an ad hoc basis, they issued declarations that rejected the basis of the president's actions and claimed that they remained the legal, constitutional representatives of the city's voters and, as such, should be permitted to resume their normal functions.[62] The Radicals, Socialists, and other parties held rallies to protest the action, underscoring the unfairness of a chief executive with a dubious claim to popular legitimacy himself dissolving a democratically elected institution while leaving in office his own hand-picked and unelected intendente.[63]

The press generally condemned Castillo's decision. Even *The Review of the River Plate*, certainly no great friend of the council, found the executive's decree justifying his decision "a curiously vague and obscure document . . . ." The *Review* also agreed with councilmen who claimed that both the national government and the intendente shared responsibility for the matters that lay at the root of the dissolution and credited the council with bringing such things as the colectivo scandal into the light of day. Although some "cleaning up in the affairs of the City Council was long overdue," their editorial concluded, "public confidence appears to have been far more shaken and disconcerted by the nature of the remedy than it ever was by the discovery of the malady."[64]

Some of the loudest voices of protest came from the many neighborhood

61 *Crítica* (October 10, 1941), p. 1. *Crítica*, it might be recalled, had held a rather cynical view of the council in previous years, but by this time had become one of its staunchest defenders.
62 *La Vanguardia* (October 12, 1941), pp. 1 and 3 and (October 14, 1941), p. 1.
63 *Crítica* (October 12, 1941), p. 12 and (October 13, 1941), p. 5 and *La Vanguardia* (October 15, 1941), p. 1.
64 "The dissolution of the 'concejo,'" *RRP*, 2601 (October 17, 1941), 5.

development societies that had appeared in the interwar period and whose evolution paralleled that of the democratically elected council. Spokesmen for these groups claimed that Castillo's action had "stupefied" them and agreed with many that it was a grievous blow to Argentine democracy. Vicente Galatro, president of the Sociedad de Fomento 1° de Mayo, representing the southeastern part of the city, praised the council as a place where his group had "continuous contact with regard to the multiple and frequent problems of our neighborhood" and where his organization received encouragement, sympathy, and support. He, like many others, questioned whether the members of the new junta would be as sensitive and responsive to the needs of the area he represented, given the fact that they seemed, on the whole, to be in little "accordance with our liberal traditions." "The urban problems to be resolved in this zone of the city," he concluded, "are many, because Buenos Aires, contrary to what a member of the Junta might believe, is not only the area of the great central avenues."[65] Other interviews reflected the widespread frustration and anger felt by these popular organizations because of the removal of an institution that, for all its flaws, had been seen as a main ally in the struggle for local improvements.[66]

A final difference between the two dissolutions was the factor of economic nationalism. Issues related to the municipal concessions granted for public services were absent in the events of 1915, but were prominent in those of 1941. The council had played something of a contradictory role in this regard. On the one hand, certain members, especially the Socialists, but also others, had brought to light the unfair treatment accorded to, and the often shoddy service provided by, foreign monopolies and struggled persistently to keep the costs of such service low. Other councilmen, however, defended the role and position of these companies in municipal life and a few succumbed to illegal payments from them to protect and further their interests. Whatever the part played by the council and individual councilmen in these matters, public awareness of the issues and public concern with the implications of concessions to foreign companies were more pronounced in 1941 than they had been twenty-five years earlier, mostly because of the activities of the local legislature. This growing sense of economic nationalism, it should be noted, was yet another important factor in the later success of Juan Perón, who eventually would nationalize and municipalize urban transportation, gas, and electricity. Castillo, himself sensitive to these issues, shortly after dissolving the council approved the expenditure by the YPF of seventy-two million

65 *Crítica* (October 21, 1941), p. 7.
66 Numerous interviews with representatives of the neighborhood development societies can be found in the pages of *Crítica* (October 19–25, 1941).

pesos toward the construction work involved in establishing a new pipe-line network in preparation for the conversion from the service provided by the Primitiva.[67]

Although the context and reaction to the dissolution of the council in 1915 and 1941 were substantially different, the result was the same. The decision held and the named junta and intendente ran municipal affairs after October. What many perceived as an antidemocratic campaign by Castillo and his allies continued when the president declared a state of siege following the Japanese attack on Pearl Harbor in December, a move intended to limit further the constitutional rights of the Argentines. Despite the restrictions imposed and the general return to fraudulent electoral practices, congressional elections in the federal capital proceeded normally in March 1942, with the Socialists gaining a surprising victory over the Radicals.[68] A little more than a year later, however, a military coup overthrew Castillo and dissolved the Congress, momentarily halting again the democratic experiment that had began in 1912. For the next three years, government was by decree until the election of Juan Perón and the beginning of a new era in the life of the city and the nation.

67 *Crítica* (October 18, 1941), p. 5.   68 Cantón, *Materiales*, vol. 1, p. 127.

12

Buenos Aires in the early 1940s

Buenos Aires at the time of the dissolution of the Concejo Deliberante was in many ways a clearly different city from what it had been in 1910. Despite the change, however, there was also considerable continuity. The population continued to grow, more than doubling, from 1.2 million in 1910 to almost 2.5 million in 1940 and on its way to almost 3 million by the time of the fourth national census of 1947. The pattern of growth outward from the center to the outlying western and southern districts continued much as it had throughout the early twentieth century. Better than half of the city's population growth between 1936 and 1947 occurred in the dynamic districts 1, 15, and 16. Beyond the limits of the capital, the surrounding area of Greater Buenos Aires, to which the city was increasingly linked, also experienced phenomenal growth, from 458,217 persons in 1914 to 1,816,180 in 1947 (see Table 1.1).

The foreign immigration, which had fueled so much of the city's expansion through the 1920s, had slowed dramatically by the 1930s, although it had begun to pick up by the end of that decade.[1] The foreign contribution to population growth, as mentioned, had been replaced by natural birthrates and by the significant inflows of native-born internal migrants. By 1947, of the 2,161,962 Argentines in the capital, 56 percent (1,215,187) had been born within its boundaries and 44 percent (946,775) outside its limits in other parts of the country. Also by that year, a city almost half of whose inhabitants had been foreign-born thirty years earlier now had only about one in four who were not born in Argentina.[2]

Industrial growth continued apace and served to attract many provincial migrants looking for employment opportunities in the capital. From the mid-1930s to the mid-1940s, as noted previously, the number of industries in the capital almost doubled, from 13,440 to 25,156. The

---

1 At the beginning of the 1930s, only a few thousand immigrants settled in Argentina due to the restrictions imposed following the Great Depression. By the second half of the decade, however, the annual balance of foreigners who remained in the republic ranged between 21,160 and 44,108. Rafael García-Mata and Emilio Llorens, *Argentina económica* (Buenos Aires, 1940), p. 22.

2 Walter, "The Socioeconomic Growth of Buenos Aires," pp. 70–2.

number of personnel employed also almost doubled and although small-scale enterprises continued to compose the great majority of the capital's industries, larger-scale operations employing hundreds and thousands of workers began to appear. Industrial establishments could be found in substantial numbers in all parts of the city, although the most notable increases in this period occurred in the areas of greatest population growth, districts 1, 15, and 16. There the numbers of industries tripled during this period, and by the mid-1940s they contained almost 38 percent of all the capital's establishments.[3] The rapid growth of the capital's industries concerned would-be city planners. On the one hand, they believed that the dispersion of such activities into residential and commercial areas produced serious "hygienic" problems, whereas, on the other, they bemoaned industrial concentration in areas like the one southeast of the capital, which was leading to even more severe problems of "health, housing, traffic, and recreation." The solution, they argued, was serious study of the matter and proposals to create clearly defined industrial zones.[4] Such zoning, as Scobie observed, had been mandated by the city council in 1914, but thirty years later was clearly in need of updating and enforcement.[5]

Even with industrial expansion, Buenos Aires remained basically as Scobie had described it at the turn of the century – a "commercial-bureaucratic" city. In the forty years after 1914, the number of commercial establishments in the city of Buenos Aires grew from 27,761 to 92,877 and the number of persons employed in them more than doubled, from 116,813 to 246,918. The capital, of course, also remained the seat of national government, which, in tandem with the municipality, significantly expanded its size and the scope of its activities in these years. The third national census of 1914 listed 49,438 of the capital's citizens as government employees, whereas the fourth national census of 1947 counted 170,005 in roughly the same category.[6]

All of these developments reinforced the capital's historically dominant position within the nation. By 1914 the city of Buenos Aires already contained one in five of all Argentines and the metropolitan area, including the nearby counties (*partidos*) of Greater Buenos Aires, one in four of the nation's inhabitants. By 1947 the city and surrounding area held almost one in three of the country's residents. Moreover, by the mid-1940s the metropolitan area had almost 40 percent of Argentina's industries and almost 60 percent of its industrial personnel. At the same time, the city of Buenos Aires contained better than 30 percent of the nation's

3 Ibid., p. 96.
4 MCBA, *Planeamiento de Buenos Aires: Información urbana* (Buenos Aires, 1945).
5 Scobie, *Buenos Aires*, pp. 198–9.
6 Walter, "The Socioeconomic Growth of Buenos Aires," p. 106.

commercial establishments and almost 37 percent of all personnel employed in commercial activities.[7]

The port of Buenos Aires continued to dominate the flow of goods into and out of the republic. In 1938, for example, it handled 85 percent of the nation's imports, 40 percent of its exports, and 40 percent of its shipping.[8] The main rail lines still converged on the capital as they had at the turn of the century. The capital also boasted, by the late 1930s, 54 percent of the country's telephones and almost 40 percent of all newspapers and magazines published in Argentina.[9] In other words, proponents of the argument that Argentina was Buenos Aires and Buenos Aires was Argentina were even more justified in their claim in 1940 than they were in 1910.

Despite the many complaints and defects, the city was still well served by its public transportation system. In 1910, the dominant means of urban transport had been the streetcar, supplemented by the railroad. Private taxis had just made their entrance at this time. As we have seen, new competitors began to make serious inroads on the streetcar's virtual stranglehold on passenger traffic in the city, beginning with the bus in the early 1920s and the colectivo later in the decade. The railroads in these years added new electrified commuter lines linking the downtown with the growing suburbs. With the completion of the Plaza de Mayo to Plaza Italia underground, the capital by 1940 had four subway lines, with a fifth scheduled for initiation a few years later. By 1940, too, there were about four thousand licensed taxicabs in the city and about 77,000 private automobiles.[10]

Over a thirty-year period, then, the transportation system had become more varied, flexible, extensive, and competitive. As Table 12.1 indicates, even with the decline in quality and service, the increasingly antiquated streetcars still carried almost 30 percent of the capital's passengers in 1940. The impact of competition was also clear because buses and colectivos together carried more. The figures also show that the colectivo, which by now had evolved to the size of a small bus that could accommodate from twenty-five to thirty passengers, provided far wider coverage of the city in terms of trips per kilometer and operated substantially more vehicles than either of its two main competitors. These factors forecast what would be the colectivo's continuing advantage in its struggle with the streetcar

7 Ibid., pp. 68–9, 72–3, 95, and 106.
8 García-Mata and Llorens, *Argentina económica*, p. 182.
9 Ibid., pp. 187 and 216. For a good overview of the federal capital's national predominance, see José Victor D'Angelo, "La conurbación de Buenos Aires," in Francisco de Aparicio and Horacio F. Difrieri, eds., *La Argentina: Suma de geografía* (Buenos Aires: 1963), vol. 9, pp. 92–105.
10 Parapugna, *Historia de los coches de alquiler*, p. 316 and Iñigo Carrera, "El transporte automotor," p. 40.

Table 12.1. *Public transportation in the city of Buenos Aires, 1940*

	Streetcars	Subways	Buses	Colectivos
Extent of lines by kilometer	734.1	52.3	1,905.5	1,653.7
Total kilometers covered per year	115,642,956	14,927,965	109,127,476	265,249,089
Coaches in daily service	2,151	217	1,298	2,955
Existing coaches	2,559	271	1,670	3,039
Employees	11,673	2,022	10,329	NA[a]
Total trips per year	5,369,319	1,139,268	3,956,320	11,346,181
Annual revenue	$33,985,577	$10,586,545	$37,412,348	$52,411,938
Passengers per year	357,945,664	118,804,556	372,615,793	388,473,051

[a] NA, not available.
Source: MCBA, *Revista de Estadística,* 1940, p. 471.

and the bus, until, by the 1960s, it would follow regular routes and carry about three-quarters of the city's passengers.[11]

Over these years, public transportation continued to play a vital role in the dispersion of the population to the city's borders and beyond. Despite this outward expansion, what many called the microcenter of the city remained its vital heart, the most important and valuable six square kilometers in the nation. Delimiting a space bounded on the east by the Río de la Plata, on the west by Calle Pichincha (just west of the Plaza del Congreso), on the north by Santa Fe, and on the south by Belgrano, a 1940 article in *Aquí Está* graphically underscored the predominance of this particular piece of real estate. There, in addition to most of the nation's main governmental buildings – the Casa Rosada, the Congress, the main law courts – could be found the headquarters both of the republic's principal political parties and of the parties representing the province of Buenos Aires. A survey of the country's 154 national deputies in 1939 located 130 as living in this zone as well as twenty-nine of thirty-five senators. The area also included most of the foreign embassies accredited to the nation, the headquarters of all but twenty of the nation's 350 largest and most important commercial enterprises and banks, and the buildings housing Argentina's major social clubs, newspapers, religious, athletic, cultural, and labor organizations.[12] A later study of the Buenos Aires upper class showed that, although many aristocrats had moved to the north and some to the suburbs, the majority by the 1960s still lived in the city center or the nearby Barrio Norte.[13] In sum, the dominance of the centro, with the Plaza de Mayo at its heart, and which Scobie described for 1910, continued to prevail with even greater force up until 1940 and, with some exceptions, to the present day.

The center and its immediate environs also contained most of the city's best-known hotels, restaurants, and theaters. The *South American Handbook* for 1940 listed as "de luxe" and "high class" the Plaza (Florida and Charcas), the Alvear Palace (Avenida Alvear 1891), the City Hotel (Bolívar 160), the Continental (Avenida Roque Sáenz Peña 725), the Jousten (Corrientes 300), and the Nogaro (Avenida Julio Roca 556), with prices ranging from twelve to thirty-five dollars a day including meals. Recommended restaurants included those in these hotels as well as the tearoom at Harrods, La Emiliana at Corrientes 1431, the De l'Odeon at Esmeralda 335, the Conte at Victoria 420, and the London Grill at Reconquista

11 República Argentina, Oficina Regional de Desarrollo Area Metropolitana, *Organización del espacio de la región metropolitana de Buenos Aires: Esquema director año 2000* (Buenos Aires, 1969), p. 55 and Chart 33.

12 Enrique Méndez Puig, "Ese Buenos Aires sólo tiene 6 km² de extensión," *Aquí Está*, 5, 404 (April 1, 1940).

13 José Luis de Imaz, *La clase alta de Buenos Aires* (Buenos Aires, 1965), p. 15.

455.[14] A particular favorite of politicians was the Pedemonte, only a few blocks from the Casa Rosada at Avenida de Mayo 676. The new and expanded Calle Corrientes remained the main axis of the entertainment district. In 1940, census district 14, bisected by the city's "Great White Way," contained 58 of the capital's 212 theaters and movie houses. Productions ranged from ballet, opera, and drama to variety reviews, sainetes, and comedies, with the latter predominating in frequency and popularity.[15]

The entertainment choices for the porteño in 1940 were as abundant and as varied as could be found anywhere in the world. On the first Sunday in April, for example, the Gran Rex on Corrientes was showing *Esposa de Día* (*Daytime Wife*) with Tyrone Power and Linda Darnell; at the Gran Splendid on Santa Fe one could see *La Vuelta de Dick Tracy* (*The Return of Dick Tracy*) at 4 and 9 P.M. and *No Estamos Solo* (*We Are Not Alone*) with Paul Muni at 6 and 11 P.M. *Los Hermanos Marx al Circo* (*The Marx Brothers at the Circus*) was playing at the Gran Cine Florida on the street of the same name. *El Jorobado de Notre Dame* (*The Hunchback of Notre Dame*) with Charles Laughton and Maureen O'Hara was at the Ambassador on Lavalle, *Ninoska* with Greta Garbo played at the Gran Cine Ideal on Suipacha, *Caballero Sin Espada* (*Mr. Smith Goes to Washington*) with James Stewart and Jean Arthur appeared at the Normandie on Lavalle, and dozens more were showing in the centro and throughout the city. Most films were Hollywood productions, but several national and European films were also available. Far removed as they were from the fields of battle in Europe, porteños could view recent newsreel footage of the war flown in from Germany at the Cineac on Corrientes and Florida.

There were many live performances as well. At the beautiful Teatro Cervantes, a revival of the 1906 drama *Facundo*, based on the life of nineteenth-century caudillo Facundo Quiroga, had opened the night before to enthusiastic reviews. There was nothing on at the Colón this particular Sunday, but one could buy tickets for six scheduled upcoming recitals by famed violinist Jascha Heifetz. For two pesos, one could see a review at the popular Maipo at Esmeralda 443, known for its satires. This April evening's shows included *Decimelo Con Música* (*Say It To Me With Music*) and *Tres Cosas Hay en la Vida: Salud, Dinero y Acomodo* (There Are Three Things in Life: Health, Wealth, and Lodgings). Long since retired from the Concejo Deliberante, the ever-popular Florencio Parravicini could be seen at the Buenos Aires on Corrientes and Callao in the comedy *El Viudo Alegre* (*The Happy Widower*) and the equally popular actress and entertainer Libertad Lamarque was performing at the National at Corrientes 960.

14 Howell Davies, ed., *The South American Handbook,* 1940 (London, 1940), pp. 63–5.
15 *Revista Estadística Municipal,* 1940, p. 495.

On any Sunday porteños could choose from a wide range of sporting events. At the Palermo racetrack, where attendance had almost resumed predepression levels, the "Santiago Luro" classic was on tap. There were seven first-division soccer matches scheduled in the capital as well as in nearby Avellaneda and La Plata. The most attractive match of the day found Independiente of Avellaneda at the new massive River Plate stadium in Núñez in the northern part of the city, a match won by Independiente two goals to one. Other activities ranged from auto racing to yachting. The night before, Argentine middleweight Raúl Rodríguez had defeated Panamanian José Martínez after seven rounds in a well-attended fight in Luna Park. A local tennis tournament, which had been rained out the day before, was rescheduled for Sunday. At the amateur level, the Confederación Argentina de Deportes Comité Olímpico Argentino (Argentine Sports Confederation of the Argentine Olympic Committee) had organized an exhibition and competition for young people at the athletic facilities of the Club de Gimnasia y Esgrima in Palermo. Scheduled for this day were competitions in basketball, chess, handball, and rowing.

For the more serious minded, there were celebrations and organizational meetings to attend. On this day the Colegio de Abogados de Buenos Aires (Buenos Aires College of Lawyers) marked the fiftieth anniversary of the founding of the Pan American Union with speeches from lawyers, academics, and diplomats in a public ceremony on the seventh floor of the Palace of Justice. In preparation for celebration of the "Día de las Américas" on April 14, the Asociación Argentina del Sufragio Femenino (Argentine Association of Women's Suffrage), part of the Comité Internacional de la Juventud por la Paz (International Committee of Youth for Peace), had organized a meeting in the halls of the Club Honor y Patria at Juncal 857. The program featured operatic selections as well as discourses on women's political rights and questions related to war and peace. For others, interested in local history or art, more than a dozen public museums were open on Sunday afternoon, including the Museo Nacional de Bellas Artes, which had been inaugurated in 1933 and was located at Avenida Alvear 2273 in the Barrio Norte. Still more culture could be absorbed in the hefty Sunday editions of *La Nación* and *La Prensa*, which featured extensive book reviews, commentaries on art and music, and rotogravure sections with photographic essays on places of national and international historical or cultural interest as well as items of more popular concern, such as fashions and films.

Although Sunday offered the porteños varied entertainment opportunities, it was also traditionally a day spent with family. Large meals provided the principal focus for these gatherings. Many frequented the capital's ubiquitous restaurants and others picnicked in one of the city's many parks or enjoyed a backyard *asado* (barbecue). For those who preferred to stay at home, the radio offered access to various forms of entertainment. On this Sunday, Radio del Estado, Radio Splendid, Radio Belgrano, and Radio Municipal provided religious services, lectures, news reports from around the world, classical music, and dramatic productions. Radio Argentina featured *La Voz de España* at 8:30 P.M. while others carried soap opera serials. Radio Stentor, beginning at 2:30 in the afternoon, broadcast the soccer showdown between River Plate and Independiente while other stations featured dance music throughout the day. In addition to the eleven local stations, those with shortwave receivers could tune in to broadcasts from Europe, Japan, and the United States.[16]

Many of these Sunday activities were not new. Even in the pre-World War I era Buenos Aires had boasted numerous theaters, restaurants, cinemas, and sporting events. What was new was the scope and the setting, as these institutions had grown dramatically in size and variety. Theaters and movie houses whose capacity was limited thirty years earlier, by 1940 could seat thousands of spectators and included the latest projection and sound devices. Soccer matches that had been played before relatively small crowds on little better than open fields in 1910 were by 1940 held in monumental modern stadiums, which could accommodate tens of thousands of spectators. Public transportation to reach stadiums and theaters had been adequate but limited in 1910. By 1940 colectivos, buses, and subways had significantly eased access to cultural, entertainment, and athletic functions. The growing number of private automobiles added to the recreational alternatives available, including extensive Sunday drives into the suburbs or surrounding countryside. People who still preferred a quiet stroll through Palermo Park or a visit to the port area to watch the docking of the latest ocean liner found these opportunities still available, but on a wider and grander scale than thirty years earlier. Palermo Park itself had been expanded and improved and had been joined by dozens of new parks and plazas dotted throughout the city. The new port had been completed in the late 1920s and was complemented on either side by the Costanera Sur and Norte, important promenades that added new areas for walking as well as greater access to the Río de la Plata.

For those who entered the city by way of the port, the Buenos Aires skyline underscored the remarkable changes that had occurred since 1910. Instead of a silhouette of one- and two-story buildings with the cupola

---

16 This review of a "typical" porteño Sunday has been drawn from a random selection of *La Prensa* for April 7, 1940. An insightful view of certain characteristics of daily life in Buenos Aires at about this same time is provided by U.S. Ambassador Alexander Wilbourne Weddell's *Introduction to Argentina* (New York, 1939). See also, Gustavo Sosa-Pujato, "Popular Culture," in Mark Falcoff and Ronald H. Dolkart, eds., *Prologue to Perón*, pp. 136–63.

Map 3. Buenos Aires, 1913 (drawn by Fredy Merico).

of the new national Congress protruding as the proverbial sore thumb, people who arrived by sea in 1940 viewed a phalanx of multistory buildings along the Avenida Alem and clustered in the area between the Casa Rosada and Retiro Park, dominated by the impressive Edificio Kavanagh. For air travelers who flew over the city, the developments of the past thirty years were even more evident. Most clear were the changes along the southern, eastern, and southeastern borders. A map for 1913 (see Map 3) showed a twisting, turning path for the Riachuelo, an as-yet undeveloped new port area, and a virtual straight line running along the Río de la Plata's edge from Retiro station to the city's border with the suburb of Vicente López. The western General Paz highway was only an

Map 4. Buenos Aires, 1938 (drawn by Fredy Merico).

imaginary line at that time. By 1938 (see Map 4), much of the Richuelo had been channeled and straightened, the port area, including the Costanera Sur and the Balneario Municipal, had been fully developed, construction of the Costanera Norte, virtually complete, had extended the city into the estuary, and work on the General Paz was well under way.

A bird's-eye view also showed substantial changes within the capital's borders. In the downtown centro, construction of the diagonales and the Nueve de Julio, along with the widening of Belgrano, Corrientes, and Santa Fe, had done much to break the colonial grid pattern and to open up the city's most congested area. The Avenida Rivadavia, virtually bisecting the city, had been extended to the western border and beyond. Now the porteños could boast not only the broadest avenue in the world (the Nueve de Julio), but also the longest (Rivadavia). The map of 1913 had shówn at least a third of the city as undeveloped open land, especially to the west and south. By 1938, approximately 90 percent of the capital had been filled in with established streets and housing, with the only major open area in the southwest corner between Villa Lugano and Villa Soldati.

The pace and scope of the city's growth continued to fill the porteños with undeniable pride in their collective accomplishment. A January 1940 article in *El Hogar* noted that while European cities prepared for war, with some, like Madrid, already severely damaged by conflict, Buenos Aires in 1939 had seen a major building boom over the past few years, a boom that showed few signs of abating. Such expansion, the author argued, should do much to erase the melancholy many associated with the Argentines, based in part, so it was speculated, on the strong desire of many immigrants to return to their European homeland as well as a certain sense of inferiority when they compared their capital and country with the continent or the United States. "The pride of being a porteño," however, "is something that few porteños can [now] deny. Buenos Aires is one of the cities of the world that has grown so rapidly so as to be on a par with the great European and North American capitals . . . ."[17] The city itself served as an important integrating mechanism for the many porteños who knew other cities well and who could now revel in a sense of identification with their own, which could compare with and in some areas surpass those of greater age and renown.

For many, the rapid growth of the city was not only astonishing, but also a bit bewildering and disorienting. A commentator in *Aquí Está* reflected that in 1940 Buenos Aires ranked seventh in the world in terms of size of population (including its suburbs) and fifth in terms of extent. The rate of growth and change had been so rapid, however, that many porteños felt like tourists in their own home. Forty years ago, he reflected, most residents knew the city in "all its details." Then the western edge had been defined by Calle Boedo (thirty-three blocks west of the Plaza de Mayo), beyond which was "infinite pampa." "Today," he noted, "that 'campo' encloses great neighborhoods, extends its public transport lines to the city's edge by way of paved, tree-lined streets, with modern buildings, with residences for workers and employees, with theaters and movie houses – Flores has more than twenty – with all that even the centro did not have scarcely four decades ago." A city in "constant construction," it seemed to grow almost of its own volition, overlooking certain deficiencies and proceeding without plan, without attention to detail, and without producing a well-defined shape or character.[18]

17 Ernesto Valderama, "Buenos Aires, ciudad portentosa, ha florecido como nunca durante el año 1939," *El Hogar*, 1579 (January 19, 1940).
18 Octavio Palazzolo, "Como fue creciendo Buenos Aires," *Aquí Está*, 5, 400 (March 18, 1940).

These concerns were echoed in a 1942 report commissioned by Intendente Pueyrredón. The study emphasized the need for legislation to provide the city with greater powers to expropriate property and regulate construction in order to assure more controlled and orderly growth. Although such legislation might run afoul of the notoriously individualistic and independent porteño character, the committee predicted that city residents would soon see that measures to limit buildings to uniform height, to establish specified commercial, industrial, and residential zones, and to assure the overall attractiveness of the capital worked to the advantage of all. Legislation to reinforce the city's right to eminent domain was particularly urgent, especially given the too common practice of the courts to grant overly generous compensation to private property owners, thereby severely straining municipal finances and limiting the possibilities of extending public services. Lack of adequate planning still plagued Buenos Aires, the committee observed, and placed the Argentine capital well behind North American cities, particularly New York, in this regard. Such efforts initiated twenty years earlier in the United States, in the judgment of the committee, had been successful in directing urban growth along rational and efficient lines. The adoption of such practices for Buenos Aires, the report concluded, would equally lead to a more rational and efficient use of land and property and serve as a model for cities throughout the republic.[19]

Complaints about the lack of planning for the city of Buenos Aires were hardly new. As was often the case, well-documented reports like this one were primarily useful for identifying and emphasizing the strengths and weaknesses of the capital's growth, but rarely were their recommendations translated into action. Similar studies and reports issued decades later repeated many of the same concerns and pleas for attention. Buenos Aires continued to grow in a more or less haphazard fashion, with little in the way of a coherent or well-conceived plan. The results, however, were not uniformly unsatisfactory. As many foreign visitors observed, the capital's eclectic architectural style and overall beauty possessed undeniable charm and it had a pace and style of life that compared favorably with most major American and European metropolises.

For the city's social classes, the developments of the decades since the centenario were marked as much by continuity as by change. The upper class, which continued to concentrate in the centro and the Barrio Norte, still dominated the capital's social and political life. It was the elite who had season tickets to the Colón, frequented Palermo Park, and who set

19 MCBA, *Dirección del plan regulador de la urbanización y extensión de Buenos Aires* (Comisión de Legislación y Finanzas Asesora del Plan Regulador) (Buenos Aires: November 1942).

the standards of fashion and taste. It was still the aristocracy whose parties, celebrations, marriages, and travels filled the society pages of the capital's newspapers and magazines.[20] Thanks to the coup of September 1930, it was the upper classes and their representatives who had regained control of the direction of national political life, especially at the executive level. National executive control, in turn, meant control of the executive branch of the capital. With the intendente, himself invariably of the upper class, as the dominant actor in local affairs, the growth of the city for this period was, as it had been from the nineteenth century, led and determined by what the local elite had decided it should be. Buenos Aires, in many ways, was "their" city. Nonetheless, part of the process of change that had begun in the mid-1930s in the city and the nation, namely, the influx of thousands of native-born migrants to fill the jobs new industries demanded, would soon help to undermine the preeminent position in national and local affairs that the elite, whose power and influence traditionally had been based on ownership of large estates and agriculture, had enjoyed for so long.

For the middle classes, these were years of expansion and opportunity. The continued growth of commerce, government, services, and the professions offered employment and security. The university reform movement of 1918 opened up the main institutions of higher learning, especially the University of Buenos Aires, the largest in the nation, to the middle classes and, combined with a strong system of primary and secondary education in the capital, provided an important means of mobility and access to improved employment possibilities.[21] The ever-increasing number and range of athletic, cultural, and entertainment activities in the city were aimed largely at the expanding middle-class audience, which took advantage of these in growing numbers.

In some respects, the city's working classes experienced the most marked changes of any of the capital's three main social groups. Its composition saw a dramatic shift, as internal native-born migrants flocked to the city and its suburbs to mix with the foreign-born proletariat and their offspring. A new central labor federation, the Confederación General del Trabajo (CGT), had appeared in the early 1930s and, although not keeping pace with the rapid growth of the industrial working class in these years, showed steady increases in membership and had become the capital and the nation's predominant labor confederation by the early 1940s. A combination of union pressure, largely through strike activity, and political

20 For more on the composition and characteristics of the traditional Buenos Aires elite, see José Luis de Imaz, *Los que mandan* (Buenos Aires, 1964), pp. 106–25.
21 Jorge P. Graciarena, "La universidad y el desarrollo de un estrato profesional urbano en la Argentina" (Buenos Aires: Instituto de Sociología, Facultad de Filosofía y Letras, Universidad de Buenos Aires, 1963).

efforts, led at the local and national level principally by the Socialist party, had produced significant social legislation aimed at improving the living and working conditions of the city's laboring classes. Moreover, although a precise estimate cannot be made, it seems clear that a substantial number of working-class families in the capital saw their sons and daughters ascend into the ranks of the middle classes in these years.

Despite these changes and improvements, there were certain important continuities as well. Living conditions, for example, in working-class districts such as La Boca and Barracas, had remained much the same for four decades. Furthermore, whereas unemployment had ceased to be a major problem by the late 1930s, the average working-class family in the capital still found itself facing an inexorable increase in prices with wages generally insufficient to cover basic necessities. Comparative studies in 1940 showed the purchasing power of the Argentine worker substantially below that of the worker in the United States.[22] In addition, although considerable social legislation had been enacted over the past several decades, a constant refrain of the labor movement was for the authorities to enforce existing laws "effectively."

The status of women in the capital continued to undergo some significant changes. Women made up the majority of the internal migrants into the capital in these years, and many found employment as domestic servants. Women continued to be important members of the city's work force, representing by the early 1940s one in four of all wage-earning porteños. By 1947, they made up almost 28 percent of employees in industry (compared with almost 16 percent in 1914) and predominated in the large clothing and textile industries. By that time they also constituted about one in three of workers in communications, health services, and the liberal professions. Although the 1947 census, unfortunately, does not list individual occupations, the growth of the number of women in these categories implies a significant increase in female lawyers, physicians, and other professions, professions in which they were scarcely represented at all in 1914. By 1947, too, women composed better than 20 percent of government employees in the capital, a small but still significant increase from the 14 percent so employed in 1914.[23] Feminist organizations continued to push for women's suffrage and equal rights for women, and new groups emerged in the 1930s to advocate greater equity in wages and to combat conservative attempts to reverse legal rights already achieved.[24]

22 Felix J. Weil, *Argentine Riddle* (New York, 1944), pp. 57–76. See also, Adriana Marshall, "La composición del consumo de los obreros industriales de Buenos Aires, 1930–1980," *Desarrollo Económico*, 21, 83 (October–December 1981), 352–73 and John H. White, *Argentina: The Life Story of a Nation* (New York, 1942), pp. 298–300.
23 Walter, "The Socioeconomic Growth of Buenos Aires," pp. 99–105.
24 Caro Hollander, "Women: The Forgotten Half of Argentine History," pp. 149–50.

Foreign visitors continued to flock to Buenos Aires in the 1930s and still mixed their observations with praise and criticism. Two of the world's greatest poets, Chile's Pablo Neruda and Spain's Federico García Lorca, spent time in Buenos Aires in the 1930s: Neruda later commented sarcastically on the ostentation of some of the capital's wealthier residents (*Crítica* editor Natalio Botana in particular) whereas García Lorca exulted in the freedom he found in the city.[25] Early in the decade, French social scientist André Siegfried found considerable charm in a city that "seems to be a New York set on top of a Barcelona, and curiously enough by this method they have created a new type of Paris!" He also decried what he discerned as a lack of "local colour" and observed that "if only this city had a little originality it would be a complete success." Nonetheless, countering Keyserling's emphasis on Argentine melancholy and his own observations as well, Siegfried concluded that Buenos Aires "has a certain flavour entirely of its own, the impression it gives of living intensely and joyously."[26]

North American writer Waldo Frank traveled to Buenos Aires often and knew it well. In a 1940 essay on the city, he argued that "no modern city has been more swiftly swollen by alien bloods . . . . Yet so potent is the transforming spirit of the city that it is inhabited exclusively by Porteños." Describing the city in lush and romantic tones, he saw several forces molding the diverse nationalities and physical features into a cohesive whole; the muddy and languid Río de la Plata, the atmosphere of the pampa, and the constant pulse of the tango, each contributing to a rhythm and spirit of urban life that, in contrast to observers who focused on the capital's frenetic pace, produced what Frank called a "mellow coolness" characteristic of the city.[27] In less poetic terms, *The National Geographic Magazine* provided an equally favorable view of the "Queen of the River of Silver." In an article replete with the kinds of photographs for which the *Geographic* was justifiably famous, the author focused on recent developments in the ongoing modernization of the city, including the row upon row of new, multistory apartments on the near north side, the parking garage under the Nueve de Julio, and the opening of the Plaza de Mayo to Plaza Italia subway. Descriptions were provided, as well, of the active porteño interest in sports, the importance of the tango, and the vibrant night life of the city.[28] At about the same time, U.S. Ambassador Alexander Wilbourne Weddell's *Introduction to Argentina* included yet

25 Pereira, *Viajeros del siglo XX*, pp. 59–61.
26 André Siegfried, *Impressions of South America* (translated by H.H. Hemming and Doris Hemming) (New York, 1933), pp. 90–5.
27 Waldo Frank, *America Hispana: South of Us; The Characters of the Countries and the People of Central and South America* (New York, 1940), p. 113.
28 Maynard Owen Williams, "Buenos Aires: Queen of the River of Silver," *The National Geographic Magazine*, 76, 5 (Washington, D.C.: November 1939), 563–95.

another detailed and positive description of the capital and its people. Repeating a frequent observation, Weddell noted that "the new arrival in Buenos Aires will be at once struck by an animation suggestive of New York, and a physical exterior reminiscent of Paris, yet with a kind of Latin grace lending suavity to the deep rhythmic pulse of what one feels to be a great city."[29]

Throughout the 1930s, as in the 1920s, well-known Argentine commentators tended to offer a more critical and ambiguous evaluation of the city and its growth than did foreigners. The debate over the nature and image of Buenos Aires intensified. Early in the decade, Raúl Scalabrini Ortiz had dissected the porteño character in his classic *El hombre que está solo y espera* (*The Man Who Is Alone and Waits*), emphasizing the alienation and passivity characteristic of the urban scene. Roberto Arlt and Manuel Gálvez continued to publish novels set in the city, novels that featured basically frustrated and profoundly unhappy porteños whose search to assuage their fundamental loneliness with meaningless love affairs and bizarre schemes only perpetuated the cycle of their despair. As in their earlier writings, the impersonalism and the materialistic values that seemed to dominate the life of Buenos Aires provided the larger setting for these individual tragedies.

Few writers, however, were harsher in their judgments of Buenos Aires than Ezequiel Martínez Estrada. In his famous analysis of Argentine history, culture, and character, *Radiografía de la pampa* (*X-ray of the Pampa*), published in 1933, Martínez Estrada viewed nearly every facet of city life in the capital as impersonal and alienating. City buses for example, with their uncommunicative, uncomfortable, and crowded passengers, were "the symbol of the individual's isolation . . . ."[30] The Calle Florida, the fashionable downtown pedestrian mall, site of Harrods and other luxury establishments – and favorably described by almost every foreign visitor – was, for Martínez Estrada, "a salon of urbanity and sympathy where no one knows or bothers anyone else."[31]

Like many, Martínez Estrada did realize the significant accomplishment that the rapid construction of a great city on the edge of the pampa represented. He also recognized that Buenos Aires had a certain kind of superficial beauty. He argued, however, that its very rapid growth also condemned it to artificiality. Construction had been haphazard, without plan or aesthetic sense. Architectural styles were hopelessly jumbled and capriciously placed skyscrapers overshadowed other buildings of various shapes and sizes. There was too much improvisation, too much

29 Weddell, *Introduction to Argentina*, p. 53.
30 Ezequiel Martínez Estrada, *X-Ray of the Pampa* (translated by Alain Swietlicki) (Austin, 1971) p. 249.
31 Ibid., p. 235.

impermanence. The whole city, moreover, was too isolated and removed from the rest of Argentina.

Another essayist of note, with a more ambivalent perspective on Buenos Aires, was Eduardo Mallea. In his best-known work, *Historia de una pasión Argentina* (*History of an Argentine Passion*), published in 1936, he recalled his sense of wonder and excitement when, at the age of sixteen, he and his family moved from Bahía Blanca to Buenos Aires. Echoing the words of many foreign visitors, he observed, "What a city! What a civilization! How imposing and vast was all that construction over an area that fifty years before was just flat wasteland. A universe now, a stone cosmos."[32]

With time, however, Mallea also began to see the city as an impersonal force driven by its inhabitants' materialistic concerns and suffocating all idealism and creativity. In the process, men with ideals and dreams, like himself, were driven to frustration and loneliness. As with Gálvez, Arlt, and many others, he saw the capital as dividing the nation into two unequal parts. On the one hand was the "visible" Argentina, the dominant and dominating city of Buenos Aires, the center of attraction for Argentine and foreigner alike; and, on the other hand, the "invisible" Argentina, "silent, obstinate, emotional and hard working in the vast depths of the country, in the rural areas, in the provinces, the towns, the jungles, the territories."[33]

A more positive portrait of the city was provided by Argentine writer Alberto Gerchunoff. Although critical of the lack of a uniform architectural style, the growing and unregulated noisiness, and the ostentatious displays of wealth, he still considered Buenos Aires a magnificent achievement – a great world capital constructed on the empty plain, "our most beautiful work." And, whereas some lamented the lack of tradition, for him the city's newness and openness offered more opportunities for innovation and modernization than older, more traditional European cities. Moreover, he asked, rhetorically, what did European cities have to offer that Buenos Aires, a place of opportunity, social mobility, comfort, and an extraordinarily rich cultural life, did not? Besides, because of its youth, its dynamism, and its flexibility, it could take the best of what the rest of the world had to offer and incorporate it as its own. "We do not concern ourselves with the origin of anything," he observed. "English or French, German or Norwegian, all elements of progress immediately become normal factors, a means assimilated into our lives."[34]

32 Eduardo Mallea, *History of an Argentine Passion* (translated by Myron I. Lichtblau) (Pittsburgh, 1983), pp. 104–5.
33 Ibid., p. 36. For more on Mallea and Martínez Estrada, see Sarlo, *Una modernidad periférica*, pp. 221–46.
34 From a collection of the author's essays and poems about the city published between 1918 and 1942. Alberto Gerchunoff, *Buenos Aires, la metrópoli de mañana* (Buenos Aires, 1960), p. 18.

Whatever the view of Buenos Aires, favorable or critical, foreign or Argentine, all had to admit that in 1940, as in 1910, it was still the leading city in Latin America and one of the world's great capitals. All commented on its similarities with other major metropolises – Paris, London, Barcelona – but all also recognized its own particular character and flavor and its own unique features. As we have seen, the local government of the city had a large part in shaping the Buenos Aires of the early 1940s. The government's role was particularly evident in developing the physical character of the city, extending public services, and seeking to regulate growth and activity within the urban sphere. Both the executive and legislative branches were critical to street improvements, especially the widening of existing thoroughfares and the creation of new avenues. The city government was also a major player in creating the Buenos Aires subway system and in seeking to regulate the operation of other forms of public transportation. Between 1914 and 1940, the local administration oversaw either the creation or expansion of 119 public parks, plazas, and gardens, increasing their overall extent by almost two million square meters.[35] For the same period, the area of paved streets doubled, the amount of garbage collected by the municipality tripled, and the number of city blocks swept and cleaned increased two and a half times.[36] The number of city-sponsored summer camps for children also steadily increased, accommodating at first, in 1919, five hundred children per day and by 1938 some ten thousand per day.[37]

These projects and services, although not without their controversial aspects, were ultimately well received by the general public. Regulation was a different matter. Attempts to control building heights, establish a uniform architectural style, and plan for the coherent growth of the city met with many exceptions and evasions. Measures to regulate traffic usually produced such firm and widespread resistance that they had to be drastically modified or abandoned altogether. Moreover, although the legislative branch of municipal government produced hundreds of ordinances in these years, the executive branch often preferred either to ignore or to weakly enforce many of these. Former Councilman José Rouco Oliva later recalled the failure of the executive to follow through on two of his pet projects of the early 1930s: one was the creation of a city planning office and the other was an ordinance to control urban noise. When he returned to the council later in the decade he encountered an ineffective planning office and a rarely observed noise-abatement ordinance. "Our great weakness in such matters," he concluded, "is our inconsistency. We lack discipline, method, and organization. We also lack a sense of responsibility."[38]

35 *VTCD* (December 20, 1940), pp. 2973–5.   36 Ibid., pp. 3218–19.
37 Ibid., p. 2976.   38 Amigos de la Ciudad, *Cinco Lustros*, p. 104.

Although this harsh assessment was not without foundation, like many criticisms, it obscured certain undeniable accomplishments. A lack of "consistency," among other factors, may have delayed the completion of such projects as the diagonales and the Nueve de Julio, as Rouco Oliva complained, but by 1940 they, along with the Costanera, the Avenida General Paz, and the widening of important downtown streets were either finished or well on their way to ending. Furthermore, whereas many regulatory ordinances were probably ill conceived, ignored, and evaded, many others were undoubtedly reasonable responses to the dynamic and changing conditions of urban life. Most measures were intended to promote and protect the health, safety, and general well-being of all porteños. Even if they were not always strictly observed, they were evidence that the local authorities were constantly seeking responsible solutions to the complex and difficult problems affecting the citizens whose interests they represented.

Measuring precisely the efficacy of the new system of municipal government implemented in 1918, highlighted by the democratically elected city council, is difficult. The city had undergone impressive growth and modernization under various administrations prior to the reforms of 1918. This modernization might well have proceeded apace under the former system, or with an appointed commission, and municipal affairs might have been managed more efficiently without the often divided and contentious elected council. The more broadly elected council showed itself just as susceptible to corruption, especially in the 1930s, as the prereform council, negating the reason for the original support of the 1918 changes. Neglect of the south side of the city and the concentration of attention and resources in the centro and near north side, a major factor that motivated the Socialists and others to advocate the 1918 reforms, continued to afflict Buenos Aires into the 1940s. Public works projects, initiated by the intendente and approved by the council, brought improvements in some areas of city life, but also contributed to the continuing imbalance in the city's pattern of growth, put great strains on municipal finances, and often produced a new set of problems to be resolved.

An answer to the question of whether things might have been different or "better" under the prereform system must remain in the area of speculation. For all its flaws, however, it should be recognized that the city council of Buenos Aires after 1918 played a significant role in the overall development of democratic practices and institutions in the country, practices and institutions that by the 1980s and 1990s seem to have taken some hold. Beginning with the electoral reform of 1918, increasing numbers of the city's citizens participated in selecting the council's members from a wide range of competing parties representing an equally wide range of competing interests. The council was also one of the few important elected bodies in the 1930s not tainted directly by electoral fraud, although, as we know, in the matters of the electric contracts and the colectivo bribery scandal, it was seriously tarnished by other sorts of misdeeds. During these years, too, the council provided significant access to various popular groups, especially local neighborhood associations, and allowed them to express their opinions and to seek to translate these into effective legislative action. Again, although this is difficult to measure, the democratic council probably allowed for more groups and areas of the city to voice their concerns than a more limited and select body would have. The council also served as an important voice for new issues to be considered and aired in public, most significantly matters dealing with the operation of foreign-owned enterprises providing municipal services. Such issues might well not have been brought to public attention and introduced into the political discourse without the elected council. Finally, in the 1930s, as in the 1920s, the council served as a training ground for politicians moving up the career ladder to higher office. Sixteen of the men elected to the national Congress from the capital between 1930 and 1942, for example, had served previously as concejales.[39]

The elected council represented only one branch of local government. The other main players were the chosen intendente and the officials he appointed. After 1918, the council became an aggressive, articulate, and increasingly active body. Throughout these decades, however, there was no doubt as to who provided the main leadership for the growth of the city. Dominant and strong-willed executives – Anchorena, Noel, Vedia y Mitre – set in motion the major plans and projects of the period. The council might raise objections and produce delays, but in the end it was the executive who usually prevailed. The council, overcoming executive opposition, did win the battle of the ten-centavo streetcar and subway fare in the 1920s, but lost the larger war over the transport corporation in the 1930s. Backed by the authority of the national government, the intendente enjoyed a latitude and freedom of action that was denied to the council, which was concerned more than the executive with responding to various popular interests and its own reelection. Some, like Noel, sought to consult and to compromise with the council to assure that his plans and proposals proceeded on sure footing. Others, like Vedia y Mitre, ran roughshod over the council, vetoing as many measures as he approved and going ahead more or less on his own with monumental public works and leaving it up to his successors to pay the final bill. In direct confrontations with the council, the executive almost always emerged triumphant.

39 They included nine Socialistas (Rómulo Bogliolo, Alejandro Castiñeiras, Américo Ghioldi, Alberto Iribarne, Enrique Mouchet, Manuel Palacín, Julio González Iramin, Héctor Iñigo Carreras and Andrés Justo), two Independent Socialists (Manuel González Maseda and Carlos Manacorda), and one conservative (Adolfo Mugica). República Argentina, *El parlamento argentino*.

The resignation of Naón was an exception to this pattern, but there, too, the withdrawal of President Justo's backing was the decisive factor in resolving this conflict, not the actions of the council itself.

Division of municipal government between an appointed intendente and an elected council produced undeniable tensions and inevitable confrontations and deadlocks. The system still prevails to the present day and continues to be a focus of controversy and dispute. Proponents of an elected intendente have historically underscored the anomaly of government by two branches chosen in such dissimilar fashion and have called for the full "democratization" of the capital's administration. Proponents of the existing system have underscored the city's special status as the nation's capital and the need for an executive who enjoys the confidence and support of the national authorities. For the period under consideration, at least, the system seemed to work reasonably well. Despite the many moments of controversy and confrontation, there was enough cooperation and consensus between the council and the intendente to proceed on many projects of common concern. The trajectory was not at all smooth and the results far from perfect. However, when city officials stopped in 1940 to take stock of what they had achieved over the past thirty years, they had reason to feel they had not done badly. They had overseen a continued overall growth and modernization of the capital, a capital known for its beauty, its charm, its culture, and its dynamism. Problems and "inconsistencies" persisted, but the status of Buenos Aires as one of the major cities of the world was an undeniable fact and an achievement in which all of the capital's citizens and those who directed its growth could take pride. It was, as Gerchunoff described it, their "most beautiful work."

Appendix

Table A.1. Population growth in the city of Buenos Aires, by census district: 1909–47

District	1909[a]	1914[b]	1936[c]	1947[d]
1 Vélez Sársfield	47,917	103,358	330,848	444,719
2 San Cristobal Sud	53,466	70,629	88,947	101,620
3 Santa Lucia	94,965	104,188	103,168	118,288
4 San Juan Evangelista	65,370	76,024	73,596	76,088
5 Flores	46,600	79,660	123,339	149,663
6 San Carlos Sud	61,007	77,705	105,808	118,190
7 San Carlos Norte	50,930	67,007	78,311	92,440
8 San Cristóbal Norte	78,246	82,095	72,634	79,921
9 Balvanera Oeste	72,999	83,252	84,639	97,322
10 Balvanera Sud	45,968	42,293	44,226	52,367
11 Balvanera Norte	38,746	43,530	51,783	63,602
12 Concepción	68,236	73,165	74,855	95,819
13 Monserrat	68,178	75,064	81,214	100,312
14 San Nicolás	57,493	62,598	74,807	83,165
15 San Bernardo	48,381	106,716	396,097	497,913
16 Belgrano	52,146	89,866	228,826	306,799
17 Palermo	48,596	76,182	115,514	136,597
18 Las Heras	103,007	111,939	123,002	149,847
19 Pilar	74,990	86,968	99,394	137,123
20 Socorro	45,596	49,748	62,831	76,234
River	8,960	14,828		
Total	1,231,797	1,576,545	2,413,839	2,978,029

Sources:
[a] General Census of the Population, 1909, pp. 3–18.
[b] Tercer censo nacional, vol. 2, pp. 129–49.
[c] Cuarto censo general de la ciudad de Buenos Aires, vol. 2, pp. 12–129.
[d] Cuarto censo general de la nación, vol. 1, p. 47.

Table A.2. *Municipal election results, city of Buenos Aires: 1918–28*

Party	October 6, 1918	(%)	November 21, 1920	(%)	November 26, 1922	(%)	November 16, 1924	(%)	November 21, 1926	(%)	December 2, 1928	(%)
Partido Socialista	47,971	(34)	52,082	(35)	49,581	(31)	57,159	(32)	42,897	(24)	44,680	(17)
Unión Cívica Radical	47,146	(33)	56,760	(38)	61,786	(39)	55,769	(31)	70,548	(39)	88,549	(35)
Comité Comunal del Comercio	20,679	(15)	10,313	(7)								
Partido Constitucional	9,681	(7)										
Confederación Gremial	3,763	(3)										
Partido Socialista Internacional	3,258	(2)	5,601	(4)								
Partido Socialista Argentino	2,912	(2)	2,306	(2)								
Comité del Progreso Comunal	2,576	(2)									773	
Confederación Comercial Popular	1,512	(1)										
Partido Demócrata Progresista			19,936	(13)	8,394	(5)	4,788	(3)				
Concentración Nacional							6,008	(3)				
Unión Cívica Radical												
Principista					9,888	(6)						
Partido Comunista					3,824	(2)	4,628	(3)	6,836	(4)	6,681	(3)
Partido Salud Pública					924	(1)	898	(1)	450			
Unión Cívica Radical Tacuari							35,721	(20)	31,165	(17)	12,600	(5)
Sindicato de Médicos							2,249	(1)	1,359	(1)	3,130	(1)
Gente del Teatro									9,450	(5)		
Partido Nacionalista									5,065	(3)	6,676	(3)
Partido Socialista Independiente											35,237	(13)
Union de Contribuyentes											1,408	(1)
Partido Comunista de la República Argentina					9,893	(6)	8,040	(5)	8,113	(5)	17,606	(7)
Others	2,289	(2)	1,785		14,450	(2)	3,264	(2)	3,409	(2)	39,043	(15)
Voted	141,787		148,783		159,010		178,524		179,292		256,383	
Registered	217,415		247,265		280,026		309,481		336,571		338,552	
Turnout	65.0%		60.0%		57.0%		58.0%		53.0%		70.0%	

Source: República Argentina, *Memoria del Ministerio del Interior, 1918–1928.*

Table A.3. Municipal election results, city of Buenos Aires: 1932–40

Party	January 10, 1932	(%)	March 4, 1934	(%)	March 1, 1936	(%)	March 27, 1938	(%)	March 31, 1940	(%)
Partido Socialista	95,111	(37)	129,422	(39)	92,547	(26)	65,686	(17)	107,033	(24)
Unión Cívica Radical					167,896	(47)	117,033	(31)	140,771	(32)
Partido Socialista Independiente	25,469	(10)	36,068	(11)	10,757	(3)			4,257	(1)
Partido Demócrata Nacional	25,886	(10)	28,688	(9)	4,670	(1)				
UCR (Comité Nacional)	15,015	(6)	5,724	(2)						
Partido Demócrata Progresista	7,607	(3)	29,668	(9)						
UCR (Talcahuano)	12,451	(5)	11,997	(4)						
Partido Salud Pública	20,062	(8)	3,683	(1)	5,911	(2)	5,348	(1)		
UCR Comunal	3,072	(1)	9,086	(3)						
Partido Popular	4,087	(2)	7,696	(2)	3,189	(1)	2,890	(1)	2,154	(-)
Unión de Contribuyentes	3,157	(1)	15,448	(5)	14,968	(4)	23,386	(6)	40,445	(9)
Concentración Obrera	5,768	(2)								
Partido Radical					9,546	(3)	3,868	(1)	4,851	(1)
UCR–Junta Reorganizadora							43,332	(11)	45,019	(10)
Frente Nacional							41,508	(11)	16,571	(4)
Partido Socialista Obrero							21,571	(6)		
UCR Bloque Opositor							5,563	(1)		
Others	38,014	(15)	55,876	(17)	51,161	(14)	52,051	(14)	77,068	(18)
Voted	255,699		333,356		366,645		382,236		438,169	
Registered	389,059		448,282		449,283		491,614		509,468	
Turnout	60.0%		74.0%		80.0%		78.0%		86.0%	

Source: República Argentina; Memoria del Ministerio del Interior, 1932 and La Prensa (1932–40).

Bibliography

Government publications

Intendencia Municipal de la Ciudad de Buenos Aires, Comisión de Estética Edilicia. *Proyecto orgánico para la urbanización del municipio: El plan regulador y de reforma de la capital federal* (Buenos Aires, 1925).

Municipalidad de la Ciudad de Buenos Aires. *Avenida 9 de Julio: Leyes, ordenanzas, decretos, estudios, datos, informes referentes a su construcción* (Buenos Aires, 1938).

Cuarto censo general, 1936 (Buenos Aires, 1939), four volumes.

1880–1930 Cincuentenario de federalización de Buenos Aires: Comprende el proceso de su evolución histórica, política, económica y social (Buenos Aires, 1932).

Dirección del plan regulador de la urbanización y extensión de Buenos Aires (Comisión de Legislación y Finanzas Asesora del Plan Regulador) (Buenos Aires, 1942).

General Census of the Population, Buildings, Trades, and Industries of the City of Buenos Aires (taken on October 16 to 24, 1909) (Buenos Aires, 1910), four volumes.

Ordenanzas y resoluciones de 1932 (Buenos Aires, 1933).

Planeamiento de Buenos Aires: Información urbana (Buenos Aires, 1945).

Reglamento de construcciones: Noviembre 1910 (Buenos Aires, 1911).

Revista de Estadística Municipal, 1940 (Buenos Aires: January–March 1940), 3–495.

Un año de gobierno edilicio: La Intendencia da cuenta a la Ciudad de los aspectos más salientes de su labor (Buenos Aires, 1931).

Versiones taquigráficas de las sesiones del Concejo Deliberante de la Ciudad de Buenos Aires (Buenos Aires: 1910–41).

Municipalidad de la Ciudad de Buenos Aires, Dirección General de Obras Públicas y Urbanismo, Departamento de Urbanización. *Planeamiento de Buenos Aires: Información urbana* (Buenos Aires, 1945).

República Argentina. *Constitución de la Nación Argentina* (Buenos Aires, 1961).

Cuarto censo general de la nación, 1947 (Buenos Aires, 1947), three volumes.

Memoria del Ministerio del Interior (Buenos Aires: 1910–32).

Registro cívico de la nación: Padrón definitivo de electores, distrito electoral de la Capital, 1917–1918 (Buenos Aires, 1918), four volumes.

Registro electoral de la Nación: Distrito de la Capital Federal – Lista definitiva de electores: 1934 (Buenos Aires, 1934), five volumes.

Tercer censo nacional, levantado el 1° junio de 1914 (Buenos Aires, 1916), ten volumes.

República Argentina, Congreso Nacional. *Diario de Sesiones de la Cámara de Senadores* (Buenos Aires: 1915–41).
República Argentina, Cámara de Diputados de la Nación. *Diario de Sesiones* (Buenos Aires: 1910–42).
República Argentina, Cámara de Diputados de la Nación. *El parlamento argentino: 1854–1957* (Buenos Aires, 1948).
República Argentina, Departamento Nacional del Trabajo. *La desocupación en la Argentina, 1931: Informe del Jefe del Censo Nacional de Desocupados, Dr. José Figuerola* (Buenos Aires, 1933).
República Argentina, Ministerio del Interior. *La desocupación obrera en 1915: Minuta del Honorable Senado (junio 10 de 1915); Mensaje del Poder Ejecutivo (agosto 13 de 1915). Antecedentes nacionales* (Buenos Aires, 1915).
República Argentina, Oficina Regional de Desarrollo Area Metropolitana. *Organización del espacio de la región metropolitana de Buenos Aires: Esquema director año 2000* (Buenos Aires, 1969).
United States National Archives. *Department of State Records Related to the Internal Affairs of Argentina* (Washington, D.C.: 1910–39).

Magazines and newspapers

Aquí Está (Buenos Aires: 1936–41).
Bulletin of the Pan American Union (Washington, D.C.: 1910–42).
Caras y Caretas (Buenos Aires: 1910–39).
Crítica (Buenos Aires: 1920–41).
El Hogar (Buenos Aires: 1910–40).
La Nación (Buenos Aires: 1914).
La Prensa (Buenos Aires: 1910–42).
La Razón (Buenos Aires: 1926–31).
La Vanguardia (Buenos Aires: 1910–41).
Lyra (Buenos Aires: 1969).
Mundo Argentino (Buenos Aires: 1936–38).
The Review of the River Plate (Buenos Aires: 1910–41).

Articles, books, dissertations, and pamphlets

Amigos de la Ciudad. *Cinco lustros al servicio de la ciudad: MCMXIV–MCMLXIX* (Buenos Aires, 1951).
Aparicio, Francisco de, and Horacio F. Difrieri, eds. *La Argentina: Suma de geografía* (Buenos Aires, 1963), vol. 9.
Arlt, Roberto. *Los lanzallamas* (Buenos Aires, 1931).
Baily, Samuel L. "The Adjustment of Italian Immigrants into the United States and Argentina: A Comparative Analysis," *The American Historical Review*, 88, 2 (April 1983), 281–305.
Barletta, Leonidas. *Boedo y Florida: Una versión distinta* (Buenos Aires, 1967).
Bergquist, Charles. *Labor in Latin America: Comparative Essays on Chile, Argentina, Venezuela, and Colombia* (Stanford, Calif., 1986).
Berjman, Sonia, and José V. Fiszelew. *El mercado de abasto de Buenos Aires* (Buenos Aires, 1984).

Bilsky, Edgardo J. *La semana trágica* (Buenos Aires, 1984).

Bingham, Hiram. *Across South America* (Boston, 1911).

Blasco Ibáñez, Vicente. *Argentina y sus grandezas* (Madrid, 1910).

Boffi, Luis. *1,259 días concejal de la ciudad de Buenos Aires: Memorias de una época materialista* (Buenos Aires, 1943).

Borges, Jorge Luis. *Selected Poems, 1923–1967* (edited with Introduction and Notes by Norman Thomas Di Giovanni) (New York, 1972).

Brown, Jonathan D. *A Socioeconomic History of Argentina, 1776–1860* (Cambridge, U.K., 1979).

Bryce, James. *South America: Observations and Impressions* (New York, 1913).

Bucich Escobar, Ismael. *Buenos Aires, Ciudad* (Buenos Aires, 1936).

Cantón, Darío. *Materiales para el estudio de la sociología política en la Argentina* (Buenos Aires, 1968), two volumes.

Cárcano, Miguel Angel. Sáenz Peña: *La revolución por los comicios* (Buenos Aires, 1963).

Cárdenas, Isabel Laura. *Ramona y el robot: El servicio doméstico en barrios prestigiosos de Buenos Aires (1895–1985)* (Buenos Aires, 1986).

Caro Hollander, Nancy. "Women: The Forgotten Half of Argentine History," in Ann Pescatello, ed., *Female and Male in Latin America: Essays* (Pittsburgh, 1973), pp. 141–58.

Casadevall, Domingo F. *El carácter porteño* (Buenos Aires, 1970).

El tema de la mala vida en el teatro nacional (Buenos Aires, 1957).

Casal, Horacio N. *Historia del colectivo* (Buenos Aires, 1971).

Casella de Calderón, Elisea, et al. "Calle Corrientes: Su historia en cinco barrios," *Buenos Aires Nos Cuenta*, 7 (Buenos Aires: July 1984).

Cibils, F.R. "La descentralización urbana de la ciudad de Buenos Aires," *Boletín del Departamento Nacional del Trabajo*, no. 15 (Buenos Aires: December 31, 1909), pp. 87–97.

Ciria, Alberto. *Partidos y poder en la Argentina moderna (1930–46)* (Buenos Aires, 1964).

Collier, Simon. *The Life, Music, and Times of Carlos Gardel* (Pittsburgh, 1986).

Cornblit, Oscar. "European Immigrants in Argentine Industry and Politics," in Claudio Véliz, ed., *The Politics of Conformity in Latin America* (London, 1967).

Couselo, Jorge Miguel, et al. *Historia del cine argentino* (Buenos Aires, 1984).

Danero, E.M.S. *El cafishio* (Buenos Aires, 1971).

Davies, Howell, ed. *The South American Handbook, 1940* (London, 1940).

Davis, Pablo Julián. *La cuestión eléctrica en la década de 1930: Aspectos económicos y sociales de un escándalo político* (Buenos Aires, 1988).

Di Tella, Guido, and Manuel Zymelman. *Las etapas del desarrollo económico argentino* (Buenos Aires, 1967).

Dreier, Katherine S. *Five Months in the Argentine from a Woman's Point of View: 1918 to 1919* (New York, 1920).

Falcoff, Mark and Dolkart, Ronald H., eds. *Prologue to Perón: Argentina in Depression and War, 1930–1943* (Berkeley, 1975).

Falcoff, Mark. "Raúl Scalabrini Ortiz: The Making of an Argentine Nationalist," *Hispanic American Historical Review*, 52, 1 (February 1972), pp. 74–101.

Fernández Lalanne, Pedro. *Los Alvear* (Buenos Aires, 1980).

Frank, Gary. *Juan Perón vs. Spruille Braden: The Story Behind the Blue Book* (Boston, 1980).

Frank, Waldo. *America Hispana: South of Us; The Characters of the Countries and the People of Central and South America* (New York, 1940).

Franck, Henry A. "The South American Metropolis," *Century,* 101 (January 1921), pp. 337–45.

Franco, Ramón. *De Palos al Plata* (Madrid, 1926).

Galasso, Norberto. *Vida de Scalabrini Ortiz* (Buenos Aires, 1970).

Gálvez, Manuel. *El mal metafísico* (*Vida romántica*), 2d ed. (Buenos Aires, 1917).

　　　 Historia de arrabal (Buenos Aires, 1956).

　　　 Hombres en soledad (Buenos Aires, 1935).

　　　 Nacha Regules (translated by Leo Ongley) (New York, 1922).

Garasa, Delfín Leocadio. *La otra Buenos Aires: Paseos literarios por barrios y calles de la ciudad* (Buenos Aires, 1987).

García Costa, Víctor O. "Los primeros diez años del movimiento feminista y la primera sufragista sudamericana," *Boletín del Instituto Histórico de la Ciudad de Buenos Aires,* 4, 6 (1982), pp. 65–75.

García Heras, Raúl. *Automotores norteamericanos, caminos y modernización urbana en la Argentina, 1918–1939* (Buenos Aires, 1985).

　　　 "Los transportes porteños en vísperas de la Revolución del '30: El radicalismo, el socialismo y la embajada británica," *Todo es Historia* (September 1982), pp. 48–64.

García-Mata, Rafael, and Emilio Llorens. *Argentina económico* (Buenos Aires, 1940).

Gerchunoff, Alberto. *Buenos Aires, la metropoli de mañana* (Buenos Aires, 1960).

Germani, Gino. *Estructura social de la Argentina: Análisis estadístico* (Buenos Aires, 1955).

　　　 "La clase media en la Ciudad de Buenos Aires," *Desarrollo Económico,* 21, 81 (April–June 1981), pp. 109–27.

Gobello, José, and Eduardo Stilman. *Las letras del tango de Villoldo a Borges* (Buenos Aires, 1966).

Godio, Julio. *Historia del movimiento obrero argentino: Inmigrantes asalariados y lucha de clases; 1880–1910* (Buenos Aires, 1973).

　　　 La semana trágica de enero de 1919 (Buenos Aires, 1972).

González-Rothos y Gil, Mariano. "La emigración española a Iberoamérica," *Revista Internacional de Sociología,* 7, 26–7 (Madrid: April/September 1949), pp. 179–211.

González Tuñon, Raúl. " 'Crítica' y los años 20," *Todo es Historia,* 3, 32 (December 1969), pp. 54–67.

Gostautas, Stasys. "Roberto Arlt: Novelista de la Ciudad" (Ph.D. Diss.: New York University, 1972).

Graciarena, Jorge P. "La universidad y el desarrollo de un estrato profesional urbano en la Argentina" (Buenos Aires, 1963).

Gravil, Roger. *The Anglo–Argentine Connection, 1900–1939* (Boulder, Colo., 1985).

Gutiérrez, Leandro H., and Luis Alberto Romero. "Sociedades barriales, bibliotecas populares y cultura de los sectores populares: Buenos Aires, 1920–45," *Desarrollo Económico,* 29, 113 (April–June 1989), pp. 33–62.

Gutiérrez, Leandro, and Juan Suriano. "Vivienda, política y condiciones de vida de los sectores populares, Buenos Aires 1880–1930," *Primeras jornadas de historia de la ciudad de Buenos Aires: 'La vivienda en Buenos Aires'* (Buenos Aires, 1985).

Guitérrez, Ramón. *Arquitectura y urbanismo en iberoamérica* (Madrid, 1983).

Guy, Donna J. *Sex and Danger in Buenos Aires: Prostitution, Family, and Nation in Argentina* (Lincoln, Neb., 1991).

"White Slavery, Public Health, and the Socialist Position on Legalized Prostitution in Argentina, 1913–1936," *Latin American Research Review*, 23, 3 (1988), pp. 60–80.

"Women, Peonage, and Industrialization: Argentina, 1810–1914," *Latin American Research Review*, 16, 3 (1981), pp. 65–89.

Hardoy, Jorge. "Teorías y prácticas urbanísticas en Europa entre 1850 y 1930: Su traslado a América Latina," *Revista de Indias*, 47, 179 (Madrid, 1987), pp. 187–224.

Horowitz, Joel. *Cooperation and Resistance: Argentine Unions, the State and the Rise of Perón, 1930–1945* (Berkeley, Calif., 1990).

Imaz, José Luis de. *La clase alta de Buenos Aires* (Buenos Aires, 1965).

Los que mandan (Buenos Aires, 1964).

"Información social," *Revista de Ciencias Económicas*, año 17, serie 2, no. 20 (Buenos Aires: January 1929), pp. 75–82.

Iñigo Carrera, Héctor J. "El transporte automotor entre la Ciudad de Buenos Aires y los partidos vecinos (1936–1941). Aproximación a su influencia metropolitana," *Boletin del Instituto Histórico de la Ciudad de Buenos*, 4 (1982), pp. 39–49.

Los años 20 (Buenos Aires, 1971).

Iusem, Miguel. *Diccionario de las calles de Buenos Aires* (Buenos Aires, 1971).

Jauretche, Arturo. *El medio pelo en la sociedad argentina (Apuntes para una sociología nacional)* (Buenos Aires, 1966).

Johnson, Lyman L., ed. *The Problems of Order in Changing Societies: Essays on Crime and Policing in Argentina and Uruguay* (Albuquerque, N. Mex., 1990).

Keyserling, Count Hermann. *South American Meditations: On Hell and Heaven in the Soul of Man* (translated from the German, in collaboration with the author, by Theresa Duerr) (New York, 1932).

Korn, Francis, et al. *Buenos Aires: Los huéspedes del 20*, 2d ed. (Buenos Aires, 1989).

Korzeniewicz, Roberto P. "Labor Unrest in Argentina, 1887–1907," *Latin American Research Review*, 24, 3 (1989), pp. 71–98.

Kraft, Guillermo, ed. *Quien es quien en la Argentina: Biografías contemporáneas, año 1939* (Buenos Aires, 1939).

La ciudad de Buenos Aires a la cabeza del progreso mundial, 1923 (Buenos Aires, 1923).

Larra, Raúl. *Jorge Newberry: El conquistador del espacio* (Buenos Aires, 1960).

Lavrin, Asunción. "Women, Labor, and the Left: Argentina and Chile, 1890–1925," *Journal of Women's History*, 1, 2 (Fall 1989), pp. 88–116.

Lees, Andrew. *Cities Perceived: Urban Society in European and American Thought, 1820–1940* (New York, 1985).

Leland, Christropher Towne. *The Last Happy Men: The Generation of 1922, Fiction and the Argentine Reality* (Syracuse, 1986).

Lichtblau, Myron I. *Manuel Gálvez* (New York, 1972).

Londres, Alberto. *The Road to Buenos Ayres* (London, 1928).

Luna, Félix, et al. *Tres intendentes de Buenos Aires: Joaquín Samuel de Anchorena; José Luis de Cantilo; Mariano de Vedia y Mitre* (Buenos Aires, 1985).

Luna, Félix. *Alvear* (Buenos Aires, 1958).

Yrigoyen (Buenos Aires, 1964).

Macdonald, Austin F. *Government of the Argentine Republic* (New York, 1942).

Mallea, Eduardo. *History of an Argentine Passion* (translated by Myron I. Lichtblau) (Pittsburgh, 1983).

Marshall, Adriana. "La composición del consumo de los obreros industriales de Buenos Aires, 1930–1980," *Desarrollo Económico*, 21, 83 (October–December 1981), pp. 352–73.

Martínez, Albert B. *Baedeker of the Argentine Republic, 1913*, 4th ed. (Barcelona, 1914).

Martínez Estrada, Ezequiel. *X-Ray of the Pampa* (translated by Alain Swietlicki) Austin, Tex., 1971).

Martini, José Xavier, and José María Peña. *La ornamentación en la arquitectura de Buenos Aires* (Buenos Aires, 1967).

Matamoro, Blas. *La casa porteña* (Buenos Aires, 1971).

Matsushita, Hiroshi. *Movimiento obrero argentino, 1930–1945: Sus proyecciones en los orígenes del Peronismo* (Buenos Aires, 1983).

McGann, Thomas F. *Argentina, the United States and the Inter-American System, 1880–1914* (Cambridge, Mass., 1957).

McGee Deutsch, Sandra. *Counter-revolution in Argentina, 1900–1931: The Argentine Patriotic League* (Lincoln, Neb., 1986).

Molinari, Ricardo Luis. *Buenos Aires, 4 siglos* (Buenos Aires, 1980).

Mora y Araujo, Manuel, and Ignacio Llorente, eds. *El voto peronista: Ensayos de sociología electoral argentina* (Buenos Aires, 1980).

Munck, Ronaldo, et al. *Argentina: From Anarchism to Peronism; Workers, Unions and Politics, 1855–1985* (London, 1987).

Navarro, Marysa. "Hidden, Silent, and Anonymous: Women Workers in the Argentine Trade Union Movement," in Norbert C. Solden, ed., *The World of Women's Trade Unionism: Comparative Historical Essays* (Westport, Conn., 1985), pp. 165–98.

Noel, Martín. "Breve historia de la evolución urbana de la ciudad de Buenos Aires," *Boletín de la Academia Nacional de la Histora*, 1 (1924), pp. 103–10.

Oddone, Jacinto. *Gremialismo proletario argentino* (Buenos Aires, 1949).

Ortega y Gasset, José. *Toward a Philosophy of History* (New York, 1941).

Ospital, María Silvia. *Estado e inmigración en la década del 20: La política inmigratoria de los gobiernos radicales* (Buenos Aires, 1988).

Panettieri, José. *Los trabajadores* (Buenos Aires, 1967).

Parapugna, Alberto. *Historia de los coches de alquiler en Buenos Aires* (Buenos Aires, 1980).

Parker, William B. *Argentines of Today* (New York, 1967), two volumes.

"Pequeño calendario contemporáneo," *Todo es Historia*, 2, 20 (Buenos Aires: December 1968), pp. 92–5.

Pereda, Manuel Enrique. *Nuestra querida Villa Pueyrredón: Narraciones de nuestro barrio y la ciudad* (Buenos Aires, 1985).

Pereira, Susana. *Viajeros del siglo xx y la realidad nacional* (Buenos Aires, 1984).

Petit de Murat, Ulyses. *La noche de mi ciudad* (Buenos Aires, 1979).

Pintos, Juan Manuel. *Así fué Buenos Aires: Tipos y costumbres de una época, 1900 – 1950* (Buenos Aires, 1954).

Potash, Robert A. *The Army and Politics in Argentina: 1928–1945; Yrigoyen to Perón* (Stanford, Calif., 1969).

Puccia, Enrique Horacio. *Avenida Santa Fe: Ayer y hoy* (Buenos Aires, 1989).

Puente, J. *El Fútbol* (Buenos Aires, 1971).

Rennie, Ysabel F. *The Argentine Republic* (New York, 1945).

Rio, Jorge del. *Electricidad y liberación nacional: El caso S.E.G.B.A.* (Buenos Aires, 1960).

Rock, David. "Machine Politics in Buenos Aires and the Argentine Radical Party," *Journal of Latin American Studies*, 4, 2 (November 1972), pp. 233–56.

    Politics in Argentina, 1890–1930: The Rise and Fall of Radicalism (Cambridge, 1975).

Romero, José Luis, and Luis Alberto, eds. *Buenos Aires: Historia de cuatro siglos* (Buenos Aires, 1983), two volumes.

Ross, Stanley R., and Thomas F. McGann, eds. *Buenos Aires:400 Years* (Austin, Tex., 1982).

Rowe, Leo. *Problems of City Government* (New York, 1908).

    The Federal System of the Argentine Republic (Washington, D.C., 1921).

Salas, Horacio. *El tango* (Buenos Aires, 1986).

Saldias, José Antonio. *La inolvidable bohemia porteña: Radiografía ciudadana del primer cuarto de siglo* (Buenos Aires, 1968).

Sanguinetti, Horacio. "Breve historia política del Teatro Colón," *Todo es Historia*, 1, 5 (September 1967), pp. 66–77.

    Los Socialistas Independientes (Buenos Aires, 1981).

Sargent, Charles S. *The Spatial Evolution of Greater Buenos Aires, Argentina, 1870 – 1930* (Tempe, Ariz., 1974).

Sarlo, Beatriz. *Una modernidad periférica: Buenos Aires, 1920 y 1930* (Buenos Aires, 1988).

Sarmiento, Domingo F. *Life in the Argentine Republic in the Days of the Tyrants, or, Civilization and Barbarism* (New York, 1961).

Scalabrini Ortiz, Raúl. *El hombre que está solo y espera*, 16th ed. (Buenos Aires, 1983).

Scenna, Miguel Angel. "El tranvía porteño," *Todo es Historia*, 2, 20 (Buenos Aires: December 1968), pp. 64–86.

    "Las cafés: Una institución porteña," *Toda es Historia*, 2, 21 (January 1969), pp. 68–90.

Scobie, James R. *Buenos Aires: Plaza to Suburb, 1870–1910* (New York, 1974).

Sebrelli, Juan José. *Apogeo y ocaso de los Anchorena* (Buenos Aires, 1972).

Shipley, Robert E. "On the Outside Looking In: A Social History of the 'Porteño' Worker During the 'Golden Age' of Argentine Development, 1914–1930" (Ph.D. Diss.: Rutgers University, N.J. 1977).

Siegfried, André. *Impressions of South America* (translated by H.H. Hemming and Doris Hemming) (New York, 1933).

Smith, Peter H. *Argentina and the Failure of Democracy: Conflict Among Political Elites, 1904–1955* (Madison, Wisc., 1974).

Politics and Beef in Argentina: Patterns of Conflict and Change (New York, 1969).

Sofer, Eugene F. *Invisible Walls: Jewish Residential Patterns in Gran Buenos Aires: 1880–1947* (New York, 1977).

Solberg, Carl. *Immigration and Nationalism: Argentina and Chile, 1890–1914* (Austin, Tex., 1970).

Oil and Nationalism in Argentina: A History (Stanford, Calif., 1979).

Spalding, Hobart. *La clase trabajadora argentina (Documentos para su historia – 1890/1912)* (Buenos Aires, 1970).

Szuchman, Mark D., and Eugene F. Sofer. "The State of Occupational Stratification Studies in Argentina," *Latin American Research Review*, 11, 1 (1976), pp. 159–72.

Tamarin, David. *The Argentine Labor Movement, 1930–1945: A Study in the Origins of Peronism* (Albuquerque, N. Mex., 1985).

Van Dyke, Harry Weston. *Through South America* (New York, 1912).

Villamayor, Luis C., and Enrique Ricardo del Valle. *El lenguaje del bajo fondo: Vocabulario lunfardo* (Buenos Aires, 1969).

Waisman, Carlos H. *Reversal of Development in Argentina: Postwar Counterrevolutionary Policies and Their Structural Consequences* (Princeton, N.J., 1987).

Walter, Richard J. "Elections in the city of Buenos Aires during the First Yrigoyen Administration: Social Class and Political Preferences," *Hispanic American Historical Review*, 58, 4 (November 1978), pp. 595–624.

"Municipal Politics and Government in Buenos Aires, 1918–1930," *Journal of Interamerican Studies and World Affairs*, 16, 2 (May 1974), pp. 173–97.

Student Politics in Argentina: The University Reform and Its Effects, 1918–1964 (New York, 1968).

The Province of Buenos Aires and Argentine Politics, 1912–1943 (Cambridge, U.K., 1985).

The Socialist Party of Argentina, 1890–1930 (Austin, Tex., 1977).

Weddell, Alexander Wilbourne. *Introduction to Argentina* (New York, 1939).

Weil, Felix J. *Argentine Riddle* (New York, 1944).

White, John H. *Argentina: The Life Story of a Nation* (New York, 1942).

Williams, Maynard Owen. "Buenos Aires: Queen of the River of Silver," *The National Geographic Magazine*, 76, 5 (November 1939), pp. 563–95.

Wright, Winthrop R. *British-Owned Railways in Argentina: Their Effect on Economic Nationalism, 1854–1948* (Austin, Tex., 1974).

Oral interviews

Oral interviews were conducted by Leandro Gutiérrez and Luis Alberto Romero for the Instituto Torcuato Di Tella, Buenos Aires, from 1970 to 1971 with the following people:

Emilio Dickman, Américo Ghioldi, Roberto Giusti, Carlos Ibarguren, Arturo Jauretche, José Luis Peña, Francisco Pérez Leirós, José Luis Portas, Jorge del Rio, and Julian Sancerni Giménez.

Index

278 *Index*

CAMBRIDGE LATIN AMERICAN STUDIES

CHKOUT 6 8/16/05